U0920910

杭州统计年鉴 2014

HANGZHOU STATISTICAL YEARBOOK

杭州市统计局
国家统计局杭州调查队
杭州市社会经济调查局

中国统计出版社
China Statistics Press

图书在版编目（CIP）数据

杭州统计年鉴. 2014 / 杭州市统计局,国家统计局杭州调查队,杭州市社会经济调查局编.
-- 北京：中国统计出版社,2014.8
ISBN 978-7-5037-7138-5

Ⅰ. ①杭…
Ⅱ. ①杭… ②国…
Ⅲ. ①统计资料-杭州市-2014-年鉴
Ⅳ. ①C832.551-54

中国版本图书馆CIP数据核字(2014)第161957号

杭州统计年鉴 2014

作　　者/ 杭州市统计局　国家统计局杭州调查队　杭州市社会经济调查局
责任编辑/ 陈越月
装帧设计/ 张子杰
出版发行/ 中国统计出版社
地　　址/ 北京市丰台区西三环南路甲6号
邮政编码/ 100073
电　　话/ 邮购（010）63376909　书店（010）68783171
网　　址/ http://csp.stats.gov.cn
印　　刷/ 浙江新中商务印刷有限公司
经　　销/ 新华书店
开　　本/ 890mm×1240mm 1/16
字　　数/ 870千字
印　　张/ 25.25
版　　别/ 2014年8月第1版
版　　次/ 2014年8月第1次印

ISBN 978-7-5037-7138-5
9 787503 771385 >

定价：300.00元

如有印装差错，由本社发行部调换

HANGZHOU
STATISTICAL YEARBOOK

杭州统计年鉴

2014 编委会和编辑人员

HANGZHOU
STATISTICAL YEARBOOK
杭州统计年鉴

Editorial Board and Staff

编者说明

一、《杭州统计年鉴—2014》是一部信息密集的资料性年刊。本书通过大量统计数据，真实地记录了在改革开放中杭州的经济和社会的发展变化。本年鉴在前几年年鉴的基础上作了进一步的调整和改进，充实了数据信息量，并与前几年在版本内容、指标数据等方面基本保持连贯性。

二、与2013年版《杭州统计年鉴》相比较，本年鉴篇章结构和内容上主要做了如下修订：新增了房地产企业财务经营情况、省级产业集聚区发展情况、限额以上批发零售和住宿餐饮业分地区经营情况等表式；调整充实了农村居民家庭耐用消费品拥有状况、邮政业含快递企业的数据内容；对农村收入分配、城乡居民收入分组、就业人员工资分经济类型等数据根据现行实际进行删减。

三、本年鉴内容包括：综合；人口和就业人员；农业；工业、能源；建筑业；交通运输、邮电；固定资产投资；国内贸易；对外经济、旅游；财政、金融、保险；城市建设、环境保护；科技、教育、文化、卫生、体育；人民生活、物价、民政等十三部分。

四、本年鉴辑入的统计数字，以2013年为主，为方便读者使用，主要指标还列入了1978年以来有关年度的统计数字。

五、2001年起，萧山、余杭撤市建区，市区数据为新市区口径。

六、本年鉴表中符号使用说明："-"表示这一栏没有数字；"…"表示该数字极小，不足计量单位；"#"表示其中的主要项；空白栏表示未掌握资料；"*"表示表下有注解。

七、读者在使用统计资料时，凡与本年鉴有出入的，均以本年鉴为准。

八、《杭州统计年鉴》公开出版以来，受到了广大读者的关心和支持，对此我们深表谢意。欢迎广大读者对年鉴内容、编排等方面提出宝贵意见，以利于我们进一步提高年鉴的编辑工作水平，更好地为广大读者服务。

Editorial Note

Ⅰ. *Hangzhou Statistical Yearbook 2014* is an informative annuals that covers comprehensive data series of Hangzhou ′s social and economic development. Through the statistical data, it reflects the changes and development of Hangzhou′s economy and society since China adopted the policy of reform and opening to the outside world. This book is adjusted and progressed on basis of last years′ books. It enriches the data, and keeps the consistency with last years′ book in content and indicators.

Ⅱ. In comparison with Hangzhou Statistical Yearbook 2013, following revisions have been made in this new version in terms of the statistical contents and in editing: Some tables are added as follows: Financial Statistics of Enterprises for Real Estate Development; Development Statistics on Provincial – Level Industry Cluster Districts; The Situation of Wholesale and Retail Trade, Hotels and Catering Services Enterprises above designated Size by Region, etc. The items of durable consummer goods owed in rural households, and the post services industry including express enterprises are justed amplified. The items and data which reduced accroding to actual conditions are as follows: distribution of income in rural areas, income of urban and rural households by groups, wages of employed persons grouped by registration.

Ⅲ. The book contains the following thirteen chapters: 1. General Survey; 2. Population and Employment; 3. Agriculture; 4. Industry and Energy; 5. Construction; 6. Transportation, Post and Telecommunication Services; 7. Investment in Fixed Assets; 8. Domestic Trade; 9. Foreign Economic Cooperation and Tourism; 10. Finance, Banking and Insurance; 11. Urban Construction and Environmental Protection; 12. Science and Technology, Education, Culture, Public Health and Sports; 13. People′s Livelihood, Price Indices and Civil Administration.

Ⅳ. The book mainly reflects statistical data in 2013. And it also contains some selected data series in important years after 1978.

Ⅴ. The administrative of area urban district has been adjusted since 2001, the new administrative area is composed of eight district including Xiaoshan and Yuhang. Data of urban district belong to new administrative area.

Ⅵ. Notations used in this book:"—" indicates that the column has no figure;"…" indicates that the figure is not large enough to be measured with the smallest unit in the table;"blank" indicates that the data not available;"#" indicates the major items of the total;" * " indicates"see footnotes below".

Ⅶ. In any case the data of this book shall be deemed as the authoritative ones.

Ⅷ. Previous editions of Hangzhou Statistical Yearbook have won wide acclaim among the readers. In order to excel, we welcome all candid comments and criticism from our readers.

目　　录
Contents

一、综合
Ⅰ. General Survey

二、人口和就业人员

Ⅱ. Population and Employment

三、农业

Ⅲ. Agriculture

四、工业、能源

Ⅳ. Industry and Energy

五、建筑业
Ⅴ. Construction

六、交通运输、邮电
Ⅵ. Transportation, Post and Telecommunications

七、固定资产投资

Ⅶ. Investment in Fixed Assets

八、国内贸易

Ⅷ. Domestic Trade

九、对外经济、旅游
Ⅸ. Foreign Economic Cooperation and Tourism

十、财政、金融、保险

Ⅹ. Finance, Banking and Insurance

十一、城市建设、环境保护

Ⅺ. Urban Construction and Environmental Protection

十二、科技、教育、文化、卫生、体育

Ⅻ. Science and Technology,Education, Culture,Public Health and Sports

十三、人民生活、物价、民政

XIII. People's Livelihood, Price Indices and Civil Administration

2013 年杭州市国民经济和社会发展统计公报

杭 州 市 统 计 局
国家统计局杭州调查队
杭州市社会经济调查局
(2014 年 2 月)

2013 年是杭州经济社会发展经受挑战的一年。面对复杂多变的外部环境和频发的自然灾害,市委、市政府带领全市人民,深入学习贯彻党的十八大及十八届二中、三中全会精神,以科学发展观为统领,加快转变经济发展方式为主线,扎实推进稳增长、促转型、惠民生各项工作,经济社会呈现和谐共进的发展局面。

一、综 合

(一)经济总量

2013 年,全市实现地区生产总值 8343.52 亿元,比上年增长 8.0%。其中:第一产业增加值 265.42 亿元,第二产业增加值 3661.98 亿元,第三产业增加值 4416.12 亿元,分别增长 1.5%、7.4% 和 9.0%。人均生产总值 94566 元,增长 7.3%。按国家公布的 2013 年平均汇率折算,为 15271 美元。三次产业结构由上年的 3.3:45.8:50.9 调整为 2013 年的 3.2:43.9:52.9。

2009-2013年全市生产总值及其增速

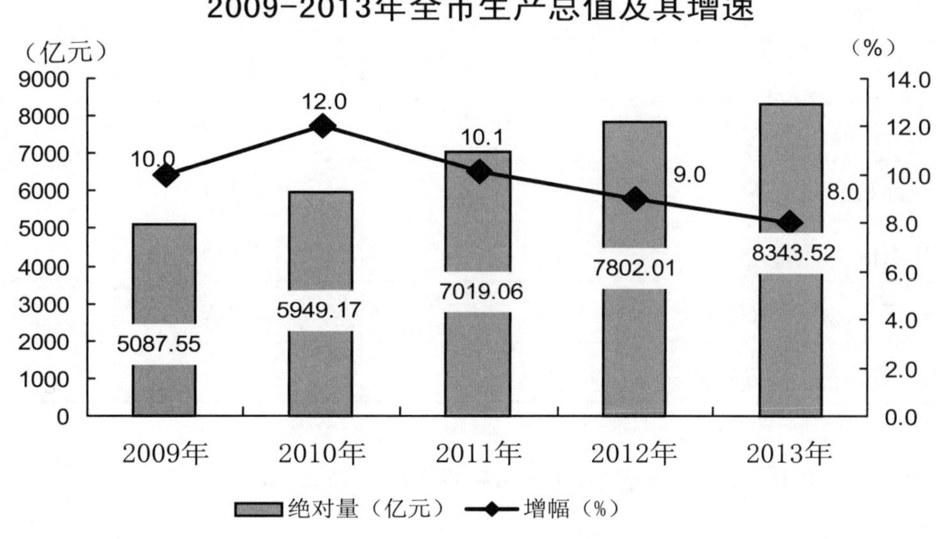

(二)民营经济

全市民营经济实现生产总值 4964.97 亿元,占全市比重的 59.5%,比上年回落 0.2 个百分点。民营商贸企业实现商品销售总额 12713.67 亿元,占全市的 73.4%;规模以上民营工业实现销售产值 6904.60 亿元,占 51.1%;民营经济实现财政收入 736.76 亿元,占 42.5%。年末,全市共有私营企业 22.52 万户,比上年末增长 15.5%,个体工商户 32.80 万户,增长 2.5%,私营企业和个体工商户从业人员分别为 186.76 万人和 66.13 万人。

(三)十大产业

全市文化创意、旅游休闲、金融服务、电子商务、信息软件、先进装备制造业、物联网、生物医药、节能环保、新能源等十大产业实现增加值3908.74亿元,比上年增长12.1%,占全市生产总值的比重由上年的45.0%提高至46.9%。全市十大产业投资项目1916个,比上年增加80个,完成投资848.58亿元,增长18.0%,占全部项目投资的35.2%,提高1.4个百分点。

(四)财政收支

全年完成财政总收入1734.98亿元,比上年增长6.6%,其中地方公共财政预算收入945.20亿元,增长9.9%。全市公共财政预算支出855.74亿元,增长8.8%,其中用于民生支出627.79亿元,增长9.0%,占财政总支出的73.4%,同比提高0.1个百分点,住房保障、教育、科学技术等民生项目支出分别增长18.8%、10.5%和15.1%。

(五)市场价格

市区居民消费价格总水平比上年上涨2.5%,涨幅与上年持平。八大类商品和服务项目价格呈“六升二降”格局(见下表)。

市区居民消费价格指数(上年=100)

项目	2013年	2012年
市区居民消费价格指数	102.5	102.5
1.食品	104.2	105.7
2.烟酒及用品	99.5	101.3
3.衣着	101.3	100.9
4.家庭设备用品及维修服务	103.3	101.7
5.医疗保健和个人用品	101.1	101.7
6.交通和通信	99.5	99.9
7.娱乐教育文化用品及服务	103.9	100.6
8.居住	102.1	101.9

全市工业生产者出厂价格下降1.5%,工业生产者购进价格下降2.7%。

(六)劳动就业

全年新增城镇就业人员23.19万人,安置失业人员再就业13.13万人。年末城镇登记失业率1.85%。

二、人口、人民生活和社会保障

(一)人口

据人口变动抽样调查,2013年末,全市常住人口884.4万人,比上年末增加4.2万人,其中城镇人口662.42万人,占比由上年末的74.3%提高为74.9%;人口出生率为9.09‰,人口自然增长率为4.12‰。公安部门户籍登记人口706.61万人,其中非农业人口393.88万人,占比由上年末的54.8%提高为55.7%;人口出生率为10.07‰,人口自然增长率为4.73‰。

(二)人民生活

全市城镇居民人均可支配收入39310元,比上年增长10.1%,农村居民人均纯收入18923元,增长11.2%,扣除价格因素,实际分别增长7.4%和8.5%。城镇居民人均生活消费性支出24833元,增长10.3%,农村居民人均生活消费性支出14600元,增长8.9%。年末,城镇居民人均住房建筑面积34.68平方米,每百户居民家庭拥有家用汽车42辆、空调196台、家用电脑112台、淋浴热水器94台;农村居民人均居住面积70.4平方米,每百户农村居民家庭拥有家用汽车37辆、空调151台、家用电脑67台、淋浴热水器88台、洗衣机87台、电冰箱100台。

年末城乡居民本外币储蓄存款余额达6408.59亿元,比上年末增长5.2%。

(三)社会保障

年末全市参加社会基本养老保险人数达637.10万人,比上年末增加31.5万人;参加社会基本医疗保险822.28万人,增加17.48万人;参加职工失业、工伤、生育保险人数分别达316.36、394.82、292.01万人,分别比上年末净增16.58、12.61、14.90万人。全市开工建设保障房36334套,竣工39009套,全面完成省下达目标任务。市区新增廉租住房保障家庭833户,公开销售经济适用房4798套,推出公租房2550套。市区农村和城镇低保标准分别由每人每月450元和525元统一提高到588元,五县(市)农村低保标准每人每月平均为345元,城镇平均为485元,分别增长23.5%和9.5%。向10.53万户困难家庭发放"春风行动"慰问金、慰问品1.22亿元;向4047户因急难病险的临时性困难家庭发放临时救助金1025.5万元。

(四)社会福利

建成居家养老服务站2730家、老年食堂951家,建设农村公益金居家养老服务照料中心530家。市第三福利院建成启用。年末全市拥有各类福利院、敬老院284所,比上年增加11所,床位42869张、收养人员17072人,分别增长3.1%和3.6%。全市城镇享受最低生活保障人数11201人,农村享受最低生活保障人员63675人。开展第十三次"春风行动",共募集社会帮扶资金4310万元。

三、城市建设、环境保护和安全生产

(一)城市基础设施建设

全年完成基础设施投资852.47亿元,增长9.5%。铁路东站枢纽投入使用,杭宁、杭甬高铁开通运行。地铁2号线东南段全线贯通,1号线下沙延伸段和4号线首通段(部分)车站主体工程完工。整治建设延安路、同协路、沿江大道等城市主次干道130条,打通断头路13条。德胜高架、彩虹大道(滨江段)等快速路和钱江通道、之江大桥建成使用。杭甬运河(杭州段)全线贯通。萧山机场高速公路西兴互通开工建设,秋石快速路四期工程动工。城西污水处理厂(一期)工程建成,闲林水库大坝主体工程完工。

(二)公用事业

全年杭州电网建设投入31.61亿元。新开工110千伏及以上输电工程19项,容量223.15万千伏安,线路167.69公里。至2013年末,杭州电网拥有110千伏以上公用变电所254座,变电容量4931万千伏安,线路6205.15公里。全市用电量638.55亿千瓦时,比上年增长7.9%,其中城乡居民生活用电89.52亿千瓦时,增长

12.9%。市区自来水日供水能力达到350万立方米。年末市区居民家庭天然气用户91.08万户,比上年末增长11.5%。地铁1号线日均运送乘客达32万人次。新增或优化公交线路49条,建成公交专用道50公里,新增公交车512辆。新增停车泊位59852个,新增免费单车布点261个,累计建成运行公共自行车租赁点3223个,投入公共自行车7.8万辆。

(三)环境保护

新增国家级生态乡镇(街道)13个。建成"三江两岸"沿江生态景观带75公里,完成绿化150万平方米。建成污水管网190.41公里,新增截污量3.14万吨/日。整治黑臭城市河道53.8公里。整治制革、印染、造纸等高污染排放企业379家。淘汰黄标车31170辆。城市污水集中处理率93.9%,比上年提高0.5个百分点;主要水系监测断面水质三类以上比例为83.0%,比上年提高0.9个百分点。市区AQI优良天数217天,优良率60%(PM2.5达标天数245天,达标率67.1%)。至年末,市区人均公园绿地面积达15.13平方米,建成区绿化覆盖率为40.2%。垃圾分类小区占比由上年79.6%提高为94.3%。全年单位GDP综合能耗下降3.5%,规模以上工业单位增加值能耗下降5.1%。

(四)安全生产

全市发生各类安全生产事故次数、死亡人数、受伤人数和直接经济损失分别比上年下降5.3%、2.9%、10.3%和5.2%。亿元GDP安全生产事故死亡人数为0.09人,比上年下降10.1%。全市餐饮服务环节食品评价性抽检合格率由上年的97.7%上升至99.3%,食品生产加工环节抽检合格率由上年的94.9%提高至95.1%,药品评价性抽检合格率由上年的99.5%提高至99.8%。

四、农　　业

全市实现农林牧渔业增加值265.42亿元,增长1.5%。其中,农业增加值156.19亿元、林业增加值32.66亿元、牧业增加值45.89亿元,分别增长2.0%、4.7%和1.5%。渔业增加值27.08亿元,下降5.7%。新增省级现代农业园区18个、市级粮食生产功能区201个、市级"菜篮子"基地66个。全年粮食总产量95.92万吨,下降1.0%;肉类产量34.04万吨,增长1.6%;禽蛋产量15.29万吨、水果81.41万吨,分别下降2.8%和0.6%。全年茶叶、花卉苗木、水产品、节粮型畜禽、蔬菜、竹业等"六大优势产业"和水果、干果、蚕桑、药材、蜂业等"五大特色产业"实现产值276.38亿元,增长3.6%,占农林牧渔业总产值的69.1%。

五、工业和建筑业

(一)工业生产

全市实现工业增加值3246.67亿元,增长7.8%,其中规上工业增加值2664.13亿元,增长8.0%。战略性新兴产业实现增加值636.59亿元,装备制造业实现增加值900.50亿元,高新技术产业实现增加值785.37亿元,分别增长7.1%、8.6%和8.9%。新产品产值率由上年的24.5%提高到28.2%。

(二)工业效益

全市规模以上工业企业实现主营业务收入12424.15亿元,比上年增长7.0%;实现利税1450.55亿元,增长7.5%,其中利润853.60亿元,增长7.9%。工业产品产销衔接良好,全年规模以上工业产品产销率为99.18%。

（三）建筑业

全年实现建筑业增加值415.31亿元，比上年增长3.6%。全市有总承包和专业承包资格的建筑企业1515家，完成施工产值3755.47亿元，增长10.9%；房屋建筑施工面积29537.59万平方米，增长12.0%；房屋建筑竣工面积9613.09万平方米增长14.6%。

六、固定资产投资和房地产业

（一）固定资产投资

全市完成固定资产投资4263.87亿元，比上年增长14.5%。从产业投向看，第一产业投资8.40亿元，增长96.9%；第二产业投资912.53亿元，增长7.0%，其中工业投资910.46亿元，增长6.9%；第三产业投资3342.94亿元，增长16.7%。

（二）房地产业

全市完成房地产开发投资1853.28亿元，比上年增长16.0%。房屋施工面积9327.52万平方米，增长12.6%；竣工面积1172.24万平方米，增长11.1%。全年商品房销售面积1139.13万平方米，增长4.5%，其中住宅销售968.78万平方米，增长5.3%。

七、国内贸易

全市实现社会消费品零售总额3531.17亿元，比上年增长13.0%，扣除价格因素，实际增长11.3%。其中城镇消费品零售额3354.12亿元，增长12.9%；乡村消费品零售额177.05亿元，增长16.1%。分行业看，批发零售贸易业3161.97亿元，增长14.3%；住宿餐饮业369.21亿元，增长3.3%。国家电子商务产品监测中心落户杭州。武林商圈获“中国最具竞争力中央商务区”称号。

八、对外经济

（一）对外贸易

全市完成外贸进出口总额650.71亿美元，比上年增长5.5%。其中进口总额203.05亿美元，下降0.5%；出口总额447.66亿美元，增长8.5%（不含省属出口384.16亿美元，增长10.4%）。出口总额中，机电产品出口170.44亿美元，高新技术产品出口50.24亿美元，分别增长6.9%和6.3%。按贸易方式分，一般贸易出口364.03亿美元，增长9.5%；加工贸易出口74.32亿美元，下降5.9%。出口市场中，对美国、欧盟市场分别增长7.1%和4.2%，对日本出口下降1.8%；新兴及周边市场中，对巴西、东盟、俄罗斯出口增速相对较快，分别增长17.6%、21.8%和10.3%。

（二）对外合作

至2013年末，全市累计设立各类境外投资企业（机构）967个，其中非贸易企业303个。全年境外合同投资27.27亿美元，其中非贸易性投资25.57亿美元。完成对外承包工程和劳务合作营业额8亿美元，增长45.7%。离岸服务外包合同执行额35.64亿美元，增长20.1%。

（三）利用外资

全年批准外商直接投资415项，合同外资91.31亿美元，比上年增长10.5%；实到外资52.76亿美元，增长6.4%。新批总投资3000万美元以上项目131个，总投资125.35亿美元，占新批外商项目总投资的88.3%。引进世界500强投资项目15个，至2013年末，共有102家世界500强企业来杭投资167个项目。

（四）浙商回归

全年共引进内资项目1711个，到位资金860.60亿元，比上年增长10.5%。其中，浙商回归投资480.19亿元，投资5亿元以上项目25个。

（五）开发区建设

杭州经济技术开发区、杭州高新技术产业开发区、萧山经济技术开发区、杭州之江国家旅游度假区、余杭经济技术开发区和富阳经济技术开发区等6个国家级开发区全年实际到资22.33亿美元，占全市42.3%，同比下降0.3个百分点。实现技工贸总收入9560.68亿元，增长14.9%；实现利税889.69亿元，增长12.8%。

九、交通运输、邮电和旅游

（一）交通运输

全社会货物运输总量3.07亿吨，比上年增长2.1%，其中铁路货运283.94万吨，下降11.9%，公路货运23884万吨，增长2.8%，航空货运21.52万吨，增长6.5%；旅客运输量3.64亿人次，增长1.6%，其中铁路客运3717.04万人次，增长19.4%，公路客运30994万人次，下降0.4%，民航客运1150.54万人次，增长16.4%。至年末，萧山国际机场已开通航线185条，其中国际航线22条，港澳台航线7条。境内公路总里程达到15900.31千米，其中高速公路549.53千米。全市社会机动车拥有量达254.30万辆，其中私人汽车167.85万辆，比上年末分别增长12.2%和19.2%。

（二）邮电通讯

全市完成邮政企业和规模以上快递服务企业业务收入70.27亿元，比上年增长31.8%；完成业务总量98.26亿元，增长48.3%。实现电信业务收入175.23亿元，增长9.7%。年末固定电话用户为334.87万户，下降3.3%，移动电话用户为1546.83万户，增长7.5%；计算机宽带用户达到338.63万户，增长22.7%。推进“智慧杭州”建设，实施“三网融合”，加快建设宽带和下一代互联网等信息高速公路。全市近四分之一家庭宽带用户已经升级为光宽带，4M以上宽带用户占60%以上。建成WiFi热点3600余个，AP（无线路由器）28000余个，“无线宽带城市”初步实现。

（三）旅游业

全年旅游总收入达到1603.67亿元，比上年增长15.2%，其中旅游外汇收入21.60亿美元，下降1.9%。接待入境旅游者316.01万人次，下降4.6%；接待国内游客9409.14万人次，增长14.2%。市民出境旅游102.50万人次，增长10.1%。至年末，全市各类旅行社达632家，增长4.3%；星级宾馆达到208家，其中五星级酒店23家，四星级酒店45家；A级景区42个，其中5A级景点3个，4A级景点27个。

十、金融、证券和保险

(一)金融

年末全市金融机构达到342家,其中外资金融机构30家,分别比上年末增长10.3%和7.1%,全市金融机构本外币存款余额22174.71亿元,增长10.1%;贷款余额19350.46亿元,增长7.0%,其中个人消费贷款余额2985.01亿元,增长14.8%。

(二)资本市场

全年新增上市公司4家,募集资金95.40亿元。至年末,全市上市公司累计102家,实现上市融资1067.9亿元。

(三)保险

全市保费收入279.23亿元,比上年增长12.6%,其中,财产险保费收入126.87亿元,增长11.9%,人身险保费收入152.36亿元,增长13.2%。共支付各类保险赔款102.40亿元,增长19.9%,其中财产险77.87亿元,增长25.4%,人身险24.52亿元,增长5.1%。

十一、教育和科技

(一)教育

新建改扩建幼儿园111所、省级示范职业学校4所,启用杭师大仓前校区(一期)。全市共有小学419所,在校学生48.35万人;初中241所,在校学生21.35万人;普通高中70所,在校学生11.39万人。学前三年幼儿入园率为98.6%,初中毕业生升入各类高中比例由上年的99.6%提高到99.7%。优质学前教育覆盖面由上年的72.6%提升到74.5%;优质高中教育覆盖面为84.4%,提高1.7个百分点。普通高等院校38所,在校学生47.18万人,其中在校研究生4.59万人,比上年分别增长2.7%和5.5%。高等教育毛入学率由上年的57.8%提高到59.1%。全市义务教育阶段接纳在读进城务工人员子女23.75万人。

(二)科技

全市专利申请量58279件,专利授权量41518件,分别比上年增长8.4%和2.1%。全年新增国家重点扶持高新技术企业223家,培育认定省级研发中心41家,企业技术中心64家。年内新增12个中国驰名商标,累计121个。新增国家"千人计划"人选13名,省"千人计划"人选15名,新增钱江特聘专家30名,新设博士后科研工作站14家,引进博士后研究人员50名,累计全市已有博士后科研工作站60家、博士后工作省级试点单位29家。全市研究和发展(R&D)经费支出248.73亿元,相当于地区生产总值的比重由上年的2.92%提高为2.98%。

十二、文化、卫生和体育

(一)文化

全市有各类专业艺术表演团体21个、文化馆15个、公共图书馆15个,图书馆藏书1798万册,拥有乡镇街道文化站190个。建设30个乡镇(村)级公共电子阅览室,创建示范性乡镇(街道)综合文化站30个、文化示范村

(社区)146个,社区(村)文化活动室实现全覆盖。全年共举办大型文化活动1754场,成功举办西湖国际博览会、国际动漫节、文化博览会。实施农村数字电影"2131"工程,共放映27633场。送书下乡69.58万册。农村有线电视入户率达95.7%。

(二)卫生

积极推广"智慧医疗",实现医院检查检验结果互认、市民卡诊间结算向市直管民营医疗机构延伸。建成启用市妇女医院、滨江医院和下沙医院,基层医疗机构实现一体化管理率达到96%以上。年末,全市拥有各类医疗卫生机构4139个,其中医院208个,比上年末分别增加1122个和10个。拥有床位5.21万张,其中医院床位4.66万张,分别增长5.2%和5.9%。有各类专业卫生技术人员7.83万人,其中执业(助理)医师2.97万人,注册护士3.10万人,分别增长9.4%、8.5%和9.2%。农村卫生服务继续改善。农村自来水普及率和卫生厕所普及率分别提高到99.9%和99.7%。全市婴儿死亡率及5岁以下儿童死亡率分别由上年的2.60‰、3.51‰下降为2.49‰、3.47‰,每十万孕产妇死亡率为4.55人。

(三)体育

在第十二届全运会上,杭州136名运动员代表浙江省参加了24个大项的比赛,获得27枚金牌、6枚银牌、16枚铜牌。参加浙江省第二届体育大会,以金牌74枚、奖牌总数180枚、总分1969分的成绩获得团体总分、奖牌、金牌三个第一,并被大会评为体育道德风尚奖代表团。成功举办了世界行走(杭州站)健康走活动、安利纽崔莱健康跑活动、钱塘江国际冲浪赛等赛事活动。全市体育锻炼人口占比由上年的35.3%提高至36.0%。

国民经济和社会发展存在的主要困难是:国内外市场尚未明显好转,三大需求持续增长动力不足,部分发展指标增长没有达到预期目标;创新驱动面临压力,经济自主增长动力偏弱;城乡发展还不够平衡,区域发展协调性有待增强;资源环境制约加剧,转型升级步伐亟待提速;民生保障和就业压力较大,城市交通、环境等公共服务与人民群众的要求还有差距。

公报注释:

本公报中增加值为现价,增加值增长速度按可比价格计算。

Statistical Communiqué of Hangzhou on the 2013 National Economic and Social Development

Hangzhou Municipal Bureau of Statistics
Hangzhou survey office of National Bureau of Statistics
Hangzhou Socio – Economic Investigation Bureau
February, 2014

In 2013, Hangzhou's economic and social development withstood severe challenges. Faced with the complicated external situation and frequent occurrence of national disasters, the Hangzhou Municipal Committee of the CPC and the municipal government lead the people of the city to thoroughly implement the spirit of the 18th Party Congress, the second and third plenary sessions, took the scientific development view as its guidance, adhere to the guideline of 'accelerating the transformation of economic development' while maintaining steady growth, promoting economic transformation and people's livelihood. As a result, the economic and social development realized balanced and accelerated development.

I. General Outlook

Economic Aggregate

The gross domestic product (GDP) of the year was 834.352 billion yuan, up by 8.0 percent over the previous year. Of this total, the value added of the primary industry was 26.542 billion yuan, the value added of the secondary industry was 366.198 billion yuan, and the value added of the tertiary industry was 441.612 billion yuan, up by 1.5%, 7.4% and 9.0% respectively. The city's per capita GDP was 94,566 yuan, or 15,271 U.S dollars using the average exchange rate in 2013 which published by the Central Bank, up by 7.3%. The structure of the three industries was adjusted to 3.2:43.9:52.9 in 2013 from 3.3:45.8:50.9 of the previous year.

Figure 1: The city's GDP and its annual growth rate, 2009 – 2013

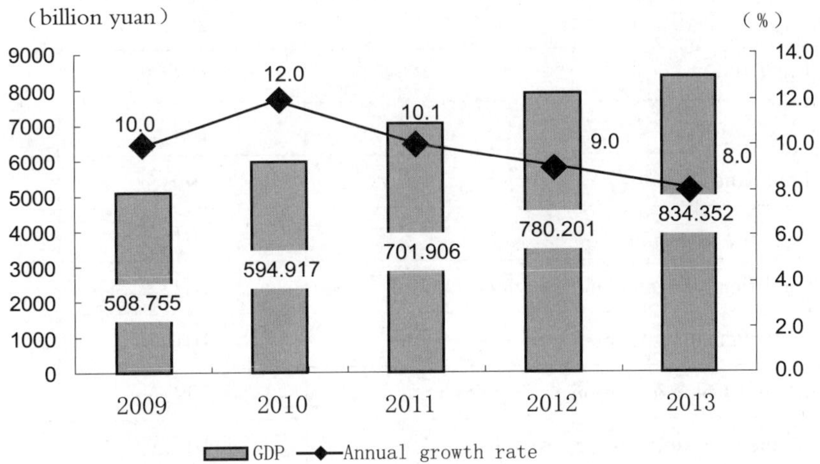

Non – State – Owned Economy

The value added of the non – state – owned economy was 496,4.97 billion yuan, accounting for 59.5% of Hangzhou's GDP, down by 0.2 percent. The total sales value of private business enterprises achieved 1,271.367 billion yuan, accounting for 73.4% of all business enterprises in Hangzhou; The sales value of private industrial enterprises above designated size reached 690.46 billion yuan, accounting for 51.1% of all industrial enterprises above designated size; The fiscal revenue of the private economy reached 73.676 billion yuan, accounting for 42.5% of the total fiscal revenue. At the end of the year, there were 225.2 thousand private enterprises, increasing by 15.5%, with 1867.6 thousand employees, and 328 thousand individual businesses, increasing by 2.5%, with 661.3 thousand employees.

Ten Major Industries

Cultural & creative industry, tourism & leisure industry, financial services industry, e-commerce industry, information & software industry, advanced equipment manufacturing industry, IOT (internet of things) industry, biomedicine industry, energy conservation and environment protection industry, and new energy industry were known as the ten major industries in Hangzhou. The value added of the ten major industries in Hangzhou reached 390.874 billion yuan, up by 12.1% over the previous year, and the proportion of the value added in the city's GDP was raised to 46.9% from 45.0% of the previous year. The investment projects of the ten major industries reached 1,916, adding 80 over the previous year, and completed an investment of 84.858 billion yuan, up by 18.0%, accounting for 35.2% of total investment with an increase of 1.4 percentages.

Fiscal Revenue and Expenditure

The general fiscal revenue of the city reached 173.498 billion yuan, up by 6.6%. Of this total, the general budgetary revenue of the local government was 94.52 billion yuan, up by 9.9%. The fiscal expenditure of the local government was 85.574 billion yuan, up by 8.8%. Of this total, the fiscal expenditure for promoting people's livelihood reached 62.779 billion yuan, up by 9.0%, accounting for 73.4% with an increase of 0.1 percentages, and the fiscal expenditure on housing security, education, and science & technology increased by 18.8%, 10.5% and 15.1% respectively.

Commodity Price

The general level of CPI in urban area rose 2.5% over the previous year, the same rate as the previous year. The price of 8 major kinds of commodity and service items presented the layout of '6 raising and 2 dropping' (see table).

Urban consumer price index (previous year = 100)

Item	2013	2012
The general level of CPI	102.5	102.5
1. Food	104.2	105.7
2. Tobacco, Liquor and Articles	99.5	101.3
3. Clothing	101.3	100.9
4. Household Facilities, Articles and Services	103.3	101.7
5. Health Care and Personal Articles	101.1	101.7
6. Transportation and Communication	99.5	99.9
7. Recreation, Education and Culture Articles	103.9	100.6
8. Residence	102.1	101.9

The producer prices for manufactured goods and the producer purchasing prices fell by 1.5% and 2.7% respectively.

Employment

The newly increased employed people in urban areas numbered 231.9 thousand, and 131.3 thousand unemployed people were re-employed. The urban unemployment rate registered was 1.85% at the year end.

II. Population, Living Conditions and Social Security

Population

By the end of the year, the total number of permanent residents in Hangzhou reached 8.844 millon according to sample survey on population changing, an increase of 42 thousand over that at the end of the previous year. Of this total, urban population reached 6.6242 million, and the proportion increased to 74.9% from 74.3% of that at the end of the previous year; the crude birth rate was 9.09‰, and the natural growth rate of population was 4.12‰. According to the population statistics from the public security department, the population of household registration reached 70.661 million, of which 39.388 million were non – agricultural population, and the proportion increased to 55.7% from 54.8% of that an the end of the previous year; the crude birth rate was 10.07‰, and the natural growth rate of population was 4.73‰.

Living Conditions

The annual per capita disposable income of urban households reached 39,310 yuan, up by 10.1% over the previous year, and the annual per capita net income of rural households reached 18,923 yuan, up by 11.2%, after deducting price factor, the actual increase was 7.4% and 8.5% respectively. The living expense per capita of urban households was 24,833 yuan, up by 10.3%, and the living expense per capita of rural households was 14,600 yuan ,up by 8.9%. By the end of 2013, the per capita floor space of residential building in urban areas reached 34.68 square meters, and every 100 urban households had 42 family cars, 196 air conditioners, 112 home computers, 94 water heaters for shower; the per capita floor space of residential building in rural areas reached 70.4 square meters, and every 100 rural households had 37 family cars, 151 air conditioners, 67 home computers, 88 water heater for shower, 87 washing machines, 100 refrigerators.

At the end of the year, the balance of saving deposit of urban and rural households reached 640.859 billion yuan, up by 5.2%.

Social Security

By the end of the year, a total of 6.371 million people participated in the basic social pension insurance, a year – on – year increase of 0.315 million; a total of 8.2228 million people participated in the basic medical insurance, an increase of 0.1748 million; a total of 3.1636 million people participated in the unemployment insurance, a total of 3.9482 million people participated in the work accident insurance, a total of 2.2901 million people participated in the birth insurance, a year – on – year increase of 0.1658 million, 0.1261million and 0.149 million respectively. A total of 36,334 sets of security housing were newly started to construct, and the security housing projects completed were 39,009 units, fully achieved the aim which was issued by the provincial government. The newly added of low – rent housing security families amounted to 833 households, and a total of 4,798 units of affordable housing and 2,550 units of public rental housing were available. The minimum subsistence guarantee for rural residents and urban residents in urban areas was unified to 588 yuan from 450 yuan and 525 yuan respectively, and the average minimum subsistence guarantee for rural residents and urban residents in county areas was 345 yuan and 458 yuan respectively, up by 23.5% and 9.5% respectively. A total of 0.1035 million vulnerable families received 0.122 billion yuan of consolation and easement; a total of 4,047 temporary vulnerable families received 10.252 million yuan of salvage money.

Social Welfare

By the end of the year, there were 2,730 home – based care service stations, 951 canteens for the aged, and 530 home –

based care service centers for the rural aged. The third welfare house of Hangzhou had been put into use. By the end of the year, there were all together 284 welfare institutions and nursing homes of various types for the aged, an increase of 11 over the previous year, providing 42,869beds and accommodating 17,072 inmates, up by 3.1% and 3.6% respectively. A total of 11,201 urban residents and 63,675 rural residents benefited from the minimum living relief system. A total of 43.1 million yuan of social funds was raised by the 13th 'Spring Action'.

Ⅲ. Urban Construction, Environment Protection and Work Safety

Urban Infrastructure Construction

In 2013, the investment in infrastructure amounted to 85.247 billion yuan, up by 9.5%. The Hangzhou East Railway Station hub, the Hangzhou – Nanjing high – speed railway and Hangzhou – Ningbo high – speed railway had been put into use. The south – east section of Metro Line 2 had run through, the Xiasha section of Metro Line 1 and the first operation section of Line 4 had been completed. 130 primary and secondary urban roads had been renovated, including Yan – an Road, Tongxie Road and Yanjiang Road. 13 broken roads had been repaired. Desheng Elevated Road, Rainbow Road (Binjiang section), Qianjiang Channel and Zhijiang Bridge were put into use. Hangzhou – Ningbo Canal (Hangzhou section) had been opened up. Xixin Interchange of Xiaoshan airport expressway and the 4th project of Qiushi Fast Road were under construction. Chengxi Sewage Treatment Plant (phase 1) and Xianlin Reservior Dam had been completed.

Public Utilities

The annual investment in construction of power grids amounted to 3.161 billion yuan. A total of 19 transmission projects, each of which was above 110 KV, were newly under construction, the transmission capacity and the electrical wiring amounted to 2.2315 million KVA and 167.69 km respectively. By the end of 2013, there were 254 public substations of which each was above 110 KV in Hangzhou, the transmission capacity and the electrical wiring amounted to 49.31 million KVA and 6205.15 km. The electricity consumption of the whole city reached 63.855 billion KWH, up by 7.9%, of this total, the consumption of residents in urban and rural areas was 8.952 billion KWH, up by 12.9%. The daily capacity of water supply in urban areas reached 3.5 million cubic meters. By the end of the year, the number of households using pipeline gas reached 0.9108 million, an annual increase of 11.5%. The dairy passenger volume of Metro Line 1 reached 0.32 million. 49 bus routes were newly added or optimized, 50 km bus – only lanes were put into use, and 512 buses were newly added. 59,852 parking spaces and 261 rental points of free bicycles were newly completed, and the total number of rental points of free bicycles reached 3,223 with 78,000 public bikes.

Environment protection

13 national – level ecological towns (sub – districts) were newly titled. 75 km of the ecological landscape belt around 'banks of 3 rivers' were completed and 1.5 million square meters were converted into green areas. 190.41 km sewage pipe lines were newly put into use, a newly increase of 31,400 tons of dairy treatment capacity of sewage. A total of 53.8 km polluted urban rivers were renovated. 379 polluting manufacture enterprises were improved or shut down, such as leather enterprises, textile printing enterprises, papermaking enterprises. 31,170 heavy polluting vehicles were fallen into disuse. The centralized disposal rate of urban sewage reached 93.9%, an increase of 0.5 percentage over the previous year; the proportion of water quality above the third level in major river system was 83.0%, an annual increase of 0.9 percentages. The number of days which the AQI reached Ⅱ – level or above amounted to 217, the excellent and good rate was 60% (the number of days which reached PM2.5 standard was 245, and rate of reaching the standard was 67.1%). By the end of the year, the per capita green land of parks in urban areas reached 15.13 square meters, and the green coverage rate of built – up areas was 40.2%. The proportion of communities in urban areas that carried out garbage classification reached

to 94.5% from 79.6% of the previous year. The comprehensive energy consumption per 1,000 yuan worth of GDP went down by 3.5% and that of the industrial enterprises above the designated size went down by 5.1%.

Work Safe

The number of accidents, the death doll, the number of injure and the direct economic loss due to various work accidents decreased by 5.3%, 2.9%, 10.3% and 5.2% over the previous year respectively. The death toll from work accidents for every 100 million yuan worth of GDP was 0.09 people, a decline of 10.1% over the previous year. The eligible rate of evaluating supervision in food service area was raised to 99.3% from 97.7% of the previous year, the eligible rate of supervision in food manufacturing and processing area was raised to 95.1% from 94.9% of the previous year, and the eligible rate of evaluating supervision in drug was raised to 99.8% from 99.5% of the previous year.

Ⅳ. Agriculture

The value added of agriculture, forestry, animal husbandry and fishery achieved 26.542 billion yuan, up by 1.5%. Of this total, the value added of agriculture, forestry and animal husbandry was 15.619 billion yuan, 3.266 billion yuan and 4.589 billion yuan respectively, up by 2.0%, 4.7% and 1.5% respectively. The value added of fishery was 2.708 billion yuan, down by 5.7%. In 2013, Hangzhou had newly built 18 provincial level modern agricultural parks, 201 municipal level grain producing areas, 66 municipal vegetable bases. In 2013, the total output of grain was 0.9595 million tons, down by 1.0%; the output of meat was 0.3404 million tons, up by 1.6%; the output of eggs was 0.1529 million tons, that of fruit was 0.8141 million tons, a decease of 2.8% and 0.6% respectively. The '6 competitive industries' of tea, seedling plants, aquatic products, forage-saving livestock & poultry, vegetables, bamboos, and the '5 featured industries' of fresh fruits, dried fruits, sericulture, medicinal materials and apiculture achieved an output value of 27.638 billion yuan, up by 3.6%, accounting for 69.1% of the gross output value of agriculture, forestry, animal husbandry and fishery.

Ⅴ. Industry and Construction

Industry Production

The value added of industry of the industrial sector was 324.667 billion yuan, up by 7.8%. Of this total, the value added of industrial enterprises above the designated size was 266.413 billion yuan, up by 8.0%. The value added of strategic emerging industries, equipment manufacturing industries and high-tech industries reached 63.659 billion yuan, 90.050 billion yuan and 78.537 billion yuan respectively, up by 7.1%, 8.6% and 8.9%. The output value ratio of new products went up to 28.2% from 24.5%.

Industrial Efficiency

The revenue from principal business of the industrial enterprises above designated size amounted to 1242.415 billion yuan, up by 7.0% over the previous year. The profits & taxes of the industrial enterprises above designated size were 145.055 billion, up by 7.5%, of this total, the profits reached 85.360 billion yuan, up by 7.9%. The production and sales linked up well, the sales ratio of industrial enterprises above designated size reached 99.18%.

Construction

The value added of construction enterprises was 41.531 billion yuan, up by 3.6% over the previous year. There were

1,515 construction enterprises with the qualification of general contract and special contract, and the construction output value amounted to 375.547 billion yuan, up by 10.9%; the floor space of buildings under construction was 96.1309 million square meters, up by 14.6%.

Ⅵ. Investment in Fixed Assets and Real Estate

Investment in Fixed Assets

The completed investment in fixed assets was 426.387 billion yuan, up by 14.5% over the previous year. Grouped by sectors, the investment in the primary industry was 0.840 billion yuan, up by 96.9%; the investment in the secondary industry was 91.253 billion yuan, up by 7.0%, of which the industrial investment was 91.046 billion yuan, up by 6.9%; the investment in the tertiary industry was 334.2 billion yuan, up by 16.7%.

Investment in Real Estate

The completed investment in real estate development was 185.328 billion yuan, up by 16.0% over the previous year. The floor space under construction was 93.2752 million square meters, up by 12.6%; the completed floor space was 11.7224 million square meters, up by11.1%. The sold floor space of commercial buildings was 11.3913 million square meters, up by 4.5%, of the total, the sold floor space of commercial residential buildings was 9.6878 million square meters, up by 5.3%.

Ⅶ. Domestic Trade

The total retail sales of consumer goods reached 353.17 billion yuan, a growth of 13.0% over the previous year, or a real growth of 11.3% after deducting price factors. Of this total, the retail sales of consumer goods in urban areas was 335.412 billion yuan, up by 12.9%; and that in rural areas was 17.705 billion yuan, up by 16.1%. Grouped by consumption patterns, the income of wholesale and retail sales of commodities was 316.197 billion yuan, up by 14.3%; and that of hotels and catering services was 36.921 billion yuan, up by 3.3%. Hangzhou was awarded the national monitoring center of e – commercial products'. Wulin business district was awarded the the most competitive CBD in China'.

Ⅷ. Foreign Economic Relations

International Trade

The total value of import and export of goods in 2013 was 65.071 billion US dollars, up by 5.5% over the previous year. Of this total, the value of goods imported was 20.305 billion SU dollars, down by 0.5%; that of exported was 44.766 billion US dollars, up by 8.5% (the value of goods exported excluding the province – owned enterprises was 38.416 US dollars, up by 10.4%). Of the total value of export, the value of electromechanical products exported was 17.044 billion US dollars, and that of high – tech products exported was 5.024 billion US dollars, up by 6.9% and 6.3% respectively. Grouped by trading modes, the general trade of exports was 36.403 billion US dollars, up by 9.5%; the processing trade of exports was 7.432 billion US dollars, down by 5.9%. Grouped by exporting countries, the value of exports to USA and EU increased by 7.1% and 4.2% respectively, that of exports to Japan decreased by 1.8%; of the emerging and neighboring markets, the value of exports to Brazil, ASEAN and Russia grew relatively quickly, up by 17.6%, 21.8% and 10.3% respectively.

International Cooperation

By the end of 2013, the total overseas enterprises (institutions) invested by Hangzhou investors was 967, of which the non - trading enterprises was 303. The contracted overseas investment in 2013 reached 2.727 billion US dollars, of which the non - trading investment was 2.557 US dollars. The accomplished business revenue through contracted overseas engineering projects and labor cooperation was 0.8 billion US dollars, up by 45.7%. The executed value of offshore service outsourcing was 3.564 billion US dollars, up by 20.1%.

Utilization of Foreign Capital

The year 2013 witnessed the authorizing of 415 projects with 9.131 billion US dollars of contracted foreign direct investment, up by 10.5% over the previous year; the total amount of foreign investment actually utilized was 5.276 billion US dollars, up by 6.4%. The investment of 131 newly authorized projects which of each over 30 million US dollars amounted 12.535 billion US dollars, accounting for 88.3% of the total foreign investment of new approved. There were 15 newly introduced investment projects which funded by companies of Fortune Global 500. By the end of 2013, 167 projects had been settled in Hangzhou that invested by 102 companies of Fortune Global 500.

Return of Zhejiang Merchants

In 2013, 1711 projects of domestic investment were introduced with 86.060 billion yuan of actually utilized investment, up by 10.5%. Of this total, the return capital of Zhejiang Merchants reached 48.019 billion yuan, and the number of projects which investment of each over 0.5 billion yuan reached 25.

Construction of Development Zones

There were 6 national - level development zones in Hangzhou including Hangzhou Economic and Technological Development Zone, Hangzhou High - Tech Development Zone, Xiaoshan Economic & Technological Development Zone, Hangzhou Zhijiang National Holiday Resort Zone, Hangzhou Yuhang Economic and Technological Development Zone, and Fuyang Economic and Technological Development zone. The annual actually utilized foreign investment was 2.233 billion U.S. dollars, accounting for 42.3% of the whole city, a decrease of 0.3 percentages. The annual total income of technology, industry and trade was 956.068 billion yuan, an increase of 14.9%, and the profits and taxes reached 88.969 billion yuan, an increase of 12.8%.

Ⅸ. Transportation, Post, Telecommunications and Tourism

Transportation

The annual total freight traffic was 0.307 billion tons, up by 2.1% over the previous year, of this total, the railways traffic was 2.8394 million tons, down by 11.9%, the highways traffic was 238.84 million tons, up by 2.8%, the civil aviation traffic was 0.2152 million tons, up by 6.5%. The total passenger traffic was 0.364 billion persons, up by 1.6%, of this total, the railways traffic was 37.1704 million person - times, up by 19.4%, the highways traffic was 309.94 million person - times, down by 0.4%, the civil aviation 11.5054 million person - times, up by 16.4%. By the end of 2013, 185 routes had been opened, including 22 international routes and 7 routes to Hongkong, Macao and Taiwan. The total length of highways within Hangzhou reached 15900.31 km, including 549.53 km expressways. The total possession of motor vehicles reached 2.543 million of which private - owned cars numbered 1.6785 million, up by 12.2% and 19.2% over the previous year respectively.

Post and Telecommunications

The business income of postal enterprises and express delivery enterprises above designated size totaled 7. 027 billion yuan, an annual increase of 31. 8% ; and the business volume totaled 9. 826 billion yuan, up by 48. 3%. The business income of telecommunication services totaled 17. 523 billion yuan, up by 9. 7%. At the end of 2013, there were 3. 3487 million fixed – line telephone subscribers and 15. 4683 million mobile phone users, down by 3. 3% and up by 7. 5% respectively. The broadband subscribers amounted to3. 3863 million, up by 22. 7%. Hangzhou has been building ' Smart City' , implementing the strategy of ' tri – networks integration ' , and accelerating to improve the information superhighways of broadband and new generation internet. In the city, 1/4 home broadband users have upgraded to the optical broadband, of which 4M broadband users accounted for more than 60%. Hangzhou has built more than 3600 WiFi hotspots, and more than 28000 AP. The ' wireless city' is coming.

Tourism

The annual earnings from tourism reached 160. 367 billion yuan, up by 15. 2% over the previous year, of which the foreign exchange earnings from international tourism was 2. 16 billion US dollars, down by 1. 9%. The number of overseas visitor arrivals was 3. 1601 million person – times, down by 4. 6% ; the number of domestic visitors was 94. 0914 million person – times, up by 14. 2%. The number of outbound visitors of Hangzhou citizens was 1. 0250 million person – times, up by 10. 1%. At the end of 2013, there were 632 travel agencies of various kinds, up by 4. 3% ; 208 star – rated hotels, including 23 5 – star hotels and 45 4 – star hotels; 42 A – rated scenic spots, including 5 – A scenic spots and 27 4 – A scenic spots.

Ⅹ. Financial Intermediation, stock market and Insurance

Financial intermediation

There were 342 financial institutions in Hangzhou at year – end, including 30 foreign financial institutions, up by 10. 3% and 7. 1% respectively. The saving deposits of RMB and foreign exchange from all of the financial institutions in Hangzhou was 2217. 471 billion yuan, up by 10. 1% ; and the loans balance was 1935. 046 billion yuan, up by 7. 0% , of this total, the loan balance of individual consumption was 298. 501 billion yuan, up by 14. 8%.

Capital Market

In 2013, there were 4 newly authorized listed companies in Hangzhou, and raised a total of 9. 540 billion yuan. By the end of 2013, the number of listed companies in Hangzhou accumulated to 102, and funds raised through stock markets amounted to 106. 79 billion yuan.

Insurance

The premiums received by the insurance companies totaled 27. 923 billion yuan, an annual increase of 12. 6% , of this total, the premiums of property insurance was 12. 687 billion yuan, up by 11. 9% , the premiums of life insurance was 15. 236 billion yuan, up by 13. 2%. The payments of insurance indemnity of various kinds totaled 10. 240 billion yuan, up by 19. 9% , of this total, the payments of property insurance was 7. 787 billion yuan, up by 25. 4% , that of life insurance was 2. 452 billion yuan, up by 5. 1%.

Ⅺ. Education, Science & Technology

Education

In 2013, 111 kindergartens and 4 provincial – level demonstrative vocational schools had been newly constructed or reconstructed; Cangqian campus (phrase 1) of Hangzhou Normal University had been put into use. There were 419 primary schools with 483.5 thousand students, 241 junior secondary schools with 213.5 thousand students, and 70 regular senior secondary schools with 113.9 thousand students in Hangzhou. The ratio of enrollment to kindergartens of those who 3 years younger than the school age reached 98.6%, the promotion rate from junior secondary schools to senior schools was rose to 99.7% from 99.6% of the previous year. The coverage ratio of high quality preschool education rose to 74.5% from 72.6% of the previous year, that of high quality senior secondary schools was 84.4%, an increase of 1.7 percentages. There were 38 regular institutions of higher education with 471.8 thousand students, of which 45.9 thousand were graduate students, up by 2.7% and 5.5%. The gross promotion rate to general colleges and universities rose to 59.1% from 57.8% of the previous year. 237.5 thousand children of migrant workers were enrolling in the stage of compulsory education.

Science & Technology

In 2013, 58,279 patent applications were accepted and 41,518 were authorized, up by 8.4% and 2.1% over the previous year respectively. There were 223 newly added national - level supported high - tech enterprises, 41 newly authorized provincial - level R&D centers, and 64 newly authorized enterprises technology centers. 12 China's well - known trademarks were newly authorized, accumulating to 121. In the year, 13 new talents of China's Thousand Talents Program, 15 new talents of Zhejiang's Thousand Talents Program, and 30 new Qianjiang Experts were introduced or hired. 14 new post - doctoral scientific research stations were set up and 50 post - doctors were recruited, reaching a total number of 60 post - doctoral scientific research stations and 29 provincial - level post - doctoral work pilot units. The expenditures on research and development activities (R&D) accounted for 2.98% of GDP, an increase of 0.06 percentages over the previous year.

Ⅻ. Culture, Public Health and sports

Culture

By the end of 2013, there were 21 professional arts performing ensembles of various styles, 15 cultural centers, 190 countryside cultural stations, and 15 public libraries with 17.98 million public books. 30 public e - reading rooms were constructed in villages and towns, 30 demonstrative town - level comprehensive cultural stations and 146 demonstrative cultural villages (communities) were authorized, thus, the coverage rate of cultural activity rooms in communities (villages) reached 100%. In 2013, Hangzhou organized 1,754 large - scale cultural events, and hosted the West Lake International EXPO, the International Animation Festival and the Culture EXPO. Hangzhou is carrying out '2132' project of digital films in rural areas, and showed 27,633 films. 695.8 thousand books were sent to the countryside. The ratio of subscribers to the cable television net reached 95.7% in rural areas.

Public Health

Hangzhou government actively promoted the project of 'Intellectual Medical Treatment', inspection results are mutual recognized by different hospital, and the method of paying in medical clinics through citizen cards were extended to private - operated medical institutions which supervised by Hangzhou municipal government. By the end of 2013, there were 4,139 medical and health institutions of various kinds in Hangzhou, including 208 hospitals, increasing 1122 and 10 over the previous year respectively. The number of beds was 52,100, of which 46,600 were hospital beds, up by 5.2% and 5.9% respectively. There were 78,300 professional medical personnel, of which the licensed (assistant) doctors were 29,700 and registered nurses were 31,000, up by9.4%, 8.5% and 9.2% respectively. The health service in rural areas continued to make progress. The popularity rates of tap water and sanitary toilet in rural areas were 99.9% and 99.7%.

The infant mortality rate and under five – year old child mortality rate declined to 2.49‰ and 3.47‰ from 2.60‰ and 3.51‰ respectively. The mortality per 100,000 pregnant women was 4.55.

Sports

Hangzhou sent 136 athletes as the members of Zhejiang delegation to attend the 12th National Games, and won 27 gold medals, 6 silver medals and 16 bronze medals in 24 sports programs. Hangzhou toped team scores, medals, and gold medals, with 74 gold medals, 180 total medals, and 1969 total scores in the second session of the Zhejiang Sports Assembly, and rated as Sportsmanship Award. The World Walking (Hangzhou Station) Health Walk, Amway Nutrilite Health Run, Qiantang River International Surfing Competition and series of sports activities were carried out successfully in Hangzhou. The proportion of the city's sports population was increased to 36.0% from 35.3% of the previous year.

The major difficulties of economic and social development: The domestic and foreign markets did not take a turn for the better obviously, the sustainable growth of the three demand factors was underpowered, the growth of some development indicators did not reach the expectations; the innovation – driven was faced with pressure, the power of self – improving ability was relatively week; the development of urban and rural areas was not balanced sufficiently, the coordination of regional development should be enhanced; the constraint of resources and environment was increasingly aggravated, the pace of transformation and upgrading should be speed up; more pressure falls on Hangzhou to ensure the people's livelihood and employment, some public services, including urban transport and environmental protection, were still lagging behind the people's demands.

Notes:

Value added as quoted in this Communiqué is calculated at current prices whereas their growth rates are at constant prices.

一、综合

Ⅰ.GENERAL SURVEY

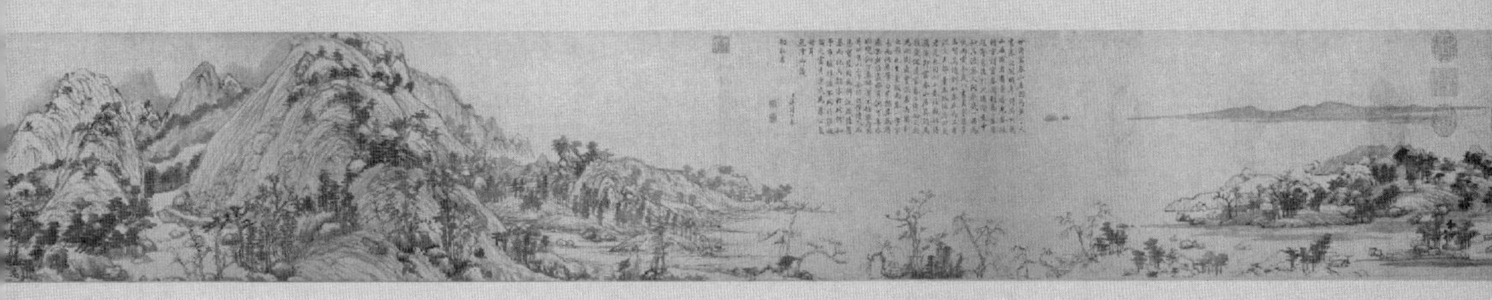

综　合
General Survey

主要统计指标
Major Statistical Indicators

全市生产总值	Gross Domestic Product	8343.52	亿元	(100 million yuan)
为上年	As Compared with the Preceding Year	108.0	%	(%)
第一产业	Primary Industry	265.42	亿元	(100 million yuan)
为上年	As Compared with the Preceding Year	101.5	%	(%)
第二产业	Secondary Industry	3661.98	亿元	(100 million yuan)
为上年	As Compared with the Preceding Year	107.4	%	(%)
# 工业	Industry	3246.67	亿元	(100 million yuan)
为上年	As Compared with the Preceding Year	107.8	%	(%)
第三产业	Tertiary Industry	4416.12	亿元	(100 million yuan)
为上年	As Compared with the Preceding Year	109.0	%	(%)
常住居民人均生产总值	Per Capita GDP (Long-term Residents)	94566	元	(yuan)
为上年	As Compared with the Preceding Year	107.3	%	(%)
生产总值构成	Composition of Gross Domestic Product	100	%	(%)
第一产业	Primary Industry	3.2	%	(%)
第二产业	Secondary Industry	43.9	%	(%)
# 工业	Industry	38.9	%	(%)
第三产业	Tertiary Industry	52.9	%	(%)

1－01 行政区划(2013 年末)

Administrative Division(End of 2013)

单位:个 (unit)

地区	Region	乡镇 Towns and Townships	#镇 Towns	街道 Subdistrict Offices	村、居委会 Villages and Neighborhood Committees	#村 Villages
全市	**Whole City**	**105**	**82**	**85**	**3092**	**2051**
市区	Urban District	27	27	68	1562	648
上城区	Shangcheng	–	–	6	54	–
下城区	Xiacheng	–	–	8	74	–
江干区	Jianggan	4	4	6	174	4
拱墅区	Gongshu	–	–	10	96	–
西湖区	Xihu	2	2	10	199	45
高新(滨江)区	Hi－Tech(Binjiang)	–	–	3	51	–
萧山区	Xiaoshan	15	15	11	580	411
余杭区	Yuhang	6	6	14	334	188
桐庐县	Tonglu	10	6	4	204	183
淳安县	Chun'an	23	11	–	438	425
建德市	Jiande	13	12	3	271	232
富阳市	Fuyang	19	13	5	305	276
临安市	Lin'an	13	13	5	312	287

1－02 土地面积和人口密度(2013 年末)

Land Area and Population Density(End of 2013)

地 区	Region	土地面积(平方公里) Land Area (sq. km)	年末总人口(万人) Population (10000 persons)	人口密度(人/平方公里) Population Density (person/sq. km)
全 市	**Whole City**	**16596**	**884.40**	**533**
市 区	Urban District	3068	635.62	2072
上城区	Shangcheng	18	35.13	19517
下城区	Xiacheng	31	53.14	17142
江干区	Jianggan	210	101.63	4840
拱墅区	Gongshu	88	56.10	6375
西湖区	Xihu	263	83.35	3169
高新(滨江)区	Hi－Tech(Binjiang)	73	32.63	4470
萧山区	Xiaoshan	1163	153.52	1320
余杭区	Yuhang	1222	120.12	983
桐庐县	Tonglu	1780	41.02	230
淳安县	Chun'an	4452	34.14	77
建德市	Jiande	2364	43.69	185
富阳市	Fuyang	1808	72.55	401
临安市	Lin'an	3124	57.38	184

注:年末总人口和人口密度按常住人口计算。

The population and population density were calculated by long－term residents.

1-03 平均每天主要社会经济活动

Selected Indicators on Average Daily Social and Economic Activities

指标 Item	1995	2000	2005	2010	2011	2012	2013
全市生产总值（万元）Gross Domestic Product (10,000 yuan)	20877	37878	80621	162991	192303	213754	228590
工业增加值（万元）Value - Added of Industry (10,000 yuan)	10023	16670	36427	68550	80524	86815	88950
规模以上工业企业利税总额（万元）Total Pre - tax Profits of Industrial Enterprises above Designated Size (10,000 yuan)	1728	4428	12347	33324	36452	36711	39748
农林牧渔业总产值（万元）Gross Output Value of Farming, Forestry, Animal Husbandry and Fishery (10,000 yuan)	2730	4182	6013	8667	9783	10530	10942
固定资产投资（万元）Investment in Fixed Assets (10,000 yuan)	4291	10319	35008	72654	84932	101993	116818
住宅竣工面积（平方米）Floor Space of Residential Buildings Completed (sq. m)	8751	11501	19327	21981	23038	18466	23154
社会消费品零售总额（万元）Total Retail Sales of Consumer Goods (10,000 yuan)	8201	14101	26724	58797	69818	80675	96744
城乡居民储蓄新增额（万元）The Increased Amount of Residents´Savings Deposits (10,000 yuan)	2819	1223	9767	19289	15247	14863	8729
财政总收入（万元）Total Financial Revenue (10,000 yuan)	1510	3914	14268	34121	40792	44600	47534

注：本表按当年价计算。2003年起城乡居民储蓄新增额为本外币合并数据。

a) Figures in value terms in this table are calculated at current prices. The increased amount of residents´savings deposits include both RMB and foreign currencies.

1－04 国民经济

Major Indicators of

指　　标		Item	
年末常住人口	（万人）	Long－term Residents(End of 2013)	(10,000 persons)
年末户籍人口	（万人）	Honsehold Registration Population(End of 2013)	(10,000 persons)
#非农业人口	（万人）	Non－agriculture Population	(10,000 persons)
年末从业人员数	（万人）	Total Number of Employed Persons(End of 2013)	(10,000 persons)
全市生产总值	（亿元）	Gross Domestic Product	(100 million yuan)
第一产业	（亿元）	Primary Industry	(100 million yuan)
第二产业	（亿元）	Secondary Industry	(100 million yuan)
第三产业	（亿元）	Tertiary Industry	(100 million yuan)
人均生产总值(户籍)	（元）	Per Capita GDP(Household)	(yuan)
人均生产总值(常住)	（元）	Per Capita GDP(Long－term)	(yuan)
主要农产品产量		Output of Major Farm Products	
粮食	（万吨）	Grain	(10,000 tons)
棉花	（吨）	Cotton	(ton)
油菜籽	（吨）	Rapeseeds	(ton)
茶叶	（吨）	Tea	(ton)
蚕茧	（吨）	Silk－worm Cocoons	(ton)
猪年末存栏	（万头）	Hogs in Stock at Year End	(10,000 heads)
肉类产量	（万吨）	Output of Meat	(10,000 tons)
淡水产品产量	（吨）	Freshwater Aquatic Products	(ton)
全部工业总产值	（亿元）	The Total Output Value of Industrial Enterprises	(100 million yuan)
规模以上工业总产值	（亿元）	The Output Valne of Industrial Enterprises Above Designated Size	(100 million yuan)
规模以上工业企业利税总额	（亿元）	Total Pre－tax Profits of Industrial Enterprises Above Designated Size	(100 million yuan)
全社会交通运输客运量	（万人次）	Total Passenger Traffic	(10,000 person－times)
全社会交通运输货运量	（万吨）	Total Freight Traffic	(10,000 tons)
固定资产投资	（亿元）	Investment in Fixed Assets	(100 million yuan)
社会消费品零售总额	（亿元）	Total Retail Sales of Consumer Goods	(100 million yuan)

注:1. 交通运输客货运输量1990年以前为交通系统数,1990年起为全社会数。
2. 境外旅游者人数1994年及以前系市区数,1995年开始为全市数。
3. 规模以上工业的计算口径,1997年以前系乡及乡以上数,1998年－2010年为主营业务收入500万元及以上,2011年起为2000万元及以上。

主 要 指 标
National Economy

1980	1985	1990	1995	2000	2005	2010	2011	2012	2013
		583.21		701.7	771.3	870.54	873.80	880.2	884.40
515.53	543.05	574.78	597.96	621.58	660.45	689.12	695.71	700.52	706.61
128.88	153.46	169.00	191.43	226.99	297.54	365.24	376.03	384.09	393.88
293.98	330.37	363.49	422.55	408.11	481.10	626.33	637.77	644.43	650.51
40.65	90.49	189.62	762.01	1382.56	2943.84	5949.17	7019.06	7802.01	8343.52
8.15	15.97	30.94	69.25	103.96	148.21	208.41	236.77	255.11	265.42
25.36	52.08	96.17	410.00	709.32	1494.36	2844.07	3323.79	3572.63	3661.98
7.14	22.44	62.51	282.76	569.28	1301.27	2896.69	3458.5	3974.27	4416.12
791	1675	3310	12797	22342	44871	86691	101370	111758	118589
					38542	69828	80478	88962	94566
151.74	180.00	189.56	174.5	153.08	103.5	100.25	97.81	96.88	95.92
8007	6704	6693	8038	2112	1038	929	828	876	825
46621	51849	60683	61446	80436	70733	76676	79815	76589	79826
18880	22742	26429	19824	24810	25551	30500	31385	32283	28503
6165	7980	11085	13240	9308	16339	15637	16127	15514	14502
190.16	166.10	159.00	147.58	172.16	165.28	192.53	203.23	210.76	219.23
9.53	11.16	14.93	19.21	25.24	30.74	31.79	32.50	33.49	34.04
14080	30400	47588	63294	91626	147800	208945	212277	210527	197992
					6589.51	12810.52	14881.98	15595.28	15211.78
61.79	128.59	292.26	1020.03	1543.57	5441.13	11081.04	12352.92	12959.68	12418.00
13.6	24.81	31.54	63.05	161.61	450.68	1224.48	1330.48	1339.94	1450.55
3905	6724	8119	16620	18607	24124	33772	34778	35819	36409
2070	2488	6522	10347	11459	19909	25915	28831	30089	30734
4.58	14.19	22.92	156.63	376.65	1277.80	2651.88	3100.02	3722.75	4263.87
20.54	47.81	98.17	299.35	514.68	978.43	2146.08	2548.36	2944.63	3531.17

a) Before 1990, the data on passenger traffic and freight traffic was only included transportation system, since 1990, the data was the total number of the whole city.

b) Before 1995, the data on foreign tourists was only included the urban districts, since 1995, the data was the total number of the whole city.

c) The standard for above designated size of industry, before 1997, it was above the sub – district level; 1998 – 2010, it was the annual sales income over 5 million yuan; since 2011, it was the annual sales income over 20 million yuan.

1-04 续表

指　标		Item	
境外旅游者人数	(万人次)	Number of Foreign Tourists	(10,000 person - times)
财政总收入	(亿元)	Total Financial Revenue	(100 million yuan)
公共财政预算支出	(亿元)	Financial Expenditure of Local Government	(100 million yuan)
金融机构存款余额	(亿元)	Deposits of Financial Institutions	(100 million yuan)
金融机构贷款余额	(亿元)	Loans of Financial Institutions	(100 million yuan)
城乡居民储蓄余额	(亿元)	Residents´Savings Deposit	(100 million yuan)
非私营单位就业人员工资总额	(亿元)	Total Wages of Employed Persons in Non - private Units	(100 million yuan)
非私营单位就业人员平均工资	(元)	Average Wage of Employed Persons in Non - private Units	(yuan)
市区居民消费价格指数	(以1978年为100)	Consumer Price Index in Urban District	(Year of 1978 = 100)
市区商品零售价格指数	(以1978年为100)	Retail Price Index in Urban District	(Year of 1978 = 100)
城镇居民年人均可支配收入	(元)	Per Capita Annual Disposable Income in Urban Areas	(yuan)
农村居民年人均纯收入	(元)	Per Capita Annual Net Income in Rural Areas	(yuan)
高等学校在校学生数	(人)	Student Enrollment in Institutions of Higher Education	(person)
中等专业学校在校学生数	(人)	Student Enrollment in Secondary Specialized Schools	(person)
普通中学在校学生数	(人)	Student Enrollment in Secondary Schools	(person)
小学在校学生数	(人)	Student Enrollment in Primary Schools	(person)
卫生机构数	(个)	Number of Health Institutions	(unit)
#医院	(个)	Number of Hospitals	(unit)
卫生技术人员	(人)	Number of Medical Technical Personnel	(person)
#执业(助理)医师	(人)	Number of Certified Doctors(Include Assistant Doctors)	(person)
床位数	(张)	Number of Beds in Health Institutions	(unit)
#医院	(张)	Beds in Hospital	(unit)

continued

1980	1985	1990	1995	2000	2005	2010	2011	2012	2013
12.50	23.84	38.83	44.13	70.71	151.36	275.71	306.31	331.12	316.01
11.85	18.65	25.25	55.13	142.85	520.79	1245.43	1488.92	1627.89	1734.98
2.17	5.77	11.82	24.91	73.43	238.33	616.58	747.50	786.28	855.74
18.10	48.5	133.77	707.97	2088.47	6748.72	17084.35	18396.57	20148.77	22174.71
17.34	58.01	162.27	567.20	1686.64	5545.30	15078.73	16573.74	18090.90	19350.46
4.04	15.96	69.75	342.34	788.56	2191.66	4990.97	5547.48	6089.98	6408.59
6.79	13.01	27.79	89.05	126.75	297.02	933.06	1122.28	1483.90	1758.23
777	1266	2382	7156	14257	31069	48772	54408	56417	63664
109.24	140.21	246.68	503.06	611.07	623.07	701.33	734.99	753.36	772.19
110.28	142.61	256.45	476.99	504.42	470.47	526.76	549.94	560.39	568.80
521	1026	1985	6301	9668	16601	30035	34065	37511	39310
250	624	1171	3012	4894	7655	13186	15245	17017	18923
23545	36996	39866	63124	122386	351918	434811	446721	459181	471820
9453	16527	23564	42784	45238	20344	3999	4100	3909	3656
247734	244399	199940	257071	342533	362257	352997	340634	331353	327346
560244	414839	460514	513988	485679	458942	453897	465289	472613	483489
1381	1582	1738	1712	1599	2196	2819	2958	3017	4139
425	404	440	414	396	127	151	167	198	208
21110	25593	30990	34245	35487	42353	61117	65869	71618	78340
8311	11503	14483	16465	16317	17833	24345	25773	27369	29686
16317	19637	24121	26684	27166	33251	42828	45291	49471	52056
13478	15010	18879	21360	23303	25907	33611	39363	44019	46636

1-05 全市生产总值及发展指数(1978-2013)

Gross Domestic Product and its Indices(1978-2013)

单位:万元 (10000 yuan)

年份 Year	全市生产总值(当年价格) Gross Domestic Product (Current Price)	第一产业 Primary Industry	第二产业 Secondary Industry	第三产业 Tertiary Industry	人均生产总值(元)(按户籍) Per Capita GDP (Household Registered)	人均生产总值(元)(按常住) Per Capita GDP (Long-term Registered)	全市生产总值指数(%) Indices of Gross Domestic product(%) (1978=100)	第一产业 Primary Industry	第二产业 Secondary Industry	第三产业 Tertiary Industry
1978	284046	63372	169344	51330	565	-	100.00	100.00	100.00	100.00
1979	335285	83852	194132	57301	659	-	113.33	114.23	114.00	110.01
1980	406508	81524	253545	71439	791	-	135.65	105.63	151.06	130.71
1981	468206	90955	287632	89619	904	-	154.04	108.74	172.17	162.30
1982	501854	108769	294725	98360	957	-	165.12	129.80	177.73	176.31
1983	558947	101106	334413	123428	1054	-	183.63	115.62	203.10	219.86
1984	694690	126443	405535	162712	1298	-	225.25	140.10	245.38	283.68
1985	904897	159684	520853	224360	1675	-	268.85	139.90	300.80	352.81
1986	1053589	177589	601277	274723	1917	-	299.88	145.01	335.28	409.85
1987	1260162	204366	718892	336904	2276	-	338.38	148.69	382.23	471.62
1988	1525427	256838	855305	413284	2717	-	363.26	145.46	419.82	497.15
1989	1662945	282746	896736	483463	2928	-	352.06	145.10	396.51	508.97
1990	1896216	309404	961673	625139	3310	-	372.37	154.40	422.20	528.01
1991	2279545	334024	1131088	814433	3952	-	439.77	161.12	492.38	669.52
1992	2900690	349033	1487838	1063819	4996	-	540.48	161.61	637.53	814.80
1993	4247094	419364	2264440	1563290	7263	-	703.16	171.15	878.66	1004.65
1994	5855239	575131	3143430	2136678	9924	-	888.09	185.01	1161.59	1225.67
1995	7620055	692510	4100008	2827537	12797	-	1064.82	198.15	1434.56	1445.06
1996	9066133	839985	4776225	3449923	15095	-	1203.25	208.85	1644.01	1621.36
1997	10363299	913611	5415017	4034671	17113	-	1360.88	223.05	1852.80	1861.32
1998	11348899	960558	5879589	4508752	18611	-	1513.30	244.02	2071.43	2060.48
1999	12252795	975821	6307510	4969464	19961	-	1667.66	257.44	2280.64	2287.13
2000	13825616	1039641	7093233	5692742	22342	-	1867.78	272.11	2565.72	2563.87
2001	15680138	1114569	7935809	6629760	25074	-	2095.65	292.25	2891.60	2884.40
2002	17818302	1146388	9018225	7653689	28150	-	2372.28	304.23	3276.18	3308.41
2003	20997744	1265890	10757812	8974042	32819	-	2732.87	322.48	3885.55	3725.27
2004	25431796	1322341	13182254	10927201	39293	-	3142.80	338.93	4534.44	4257.98
2005	29438430	1482145	14943581	13012704	44871	-	3551.36	350.45	5037.76	4956.29
2006	34434972	1548594	17283905	15602473	51908	44128	4059.54	364.71	5672.80	5820.31
2007	41040117	1634719	20458811	18946588	61315	51416	4651.74	372.78	6483.45	6761.14
2008	47889748	1798300	23725807	22365641	70948	58862	5165.17	386.73	7062.80	7705.13
2009	50875529	1905093	23871200	25099237	74761	61533	5680.15	398.74	7521.81	8799.61
2010	59491687	2084144	28440693	28966850	86691	69828	6361.77	408.71	8462.04	9881.96
2011	70190579	2367708	33237887	34584984	101370	80478	7004.31	418.93	9291.32	10968.98
2012	78020058	2551127	35726276	39742655	111758	88962	7634.70	429.40	9978.88	12164.60
2013	83435193	2654154	36619817	44161222	118589	94566	8245.48	435.84	10717.32	13259.41

注:2013年为初步统计数(后同)。

a) All figures of 2013 on this table are preliminary statistics.

1－06 市区生产总值及发展指数(1978－2013)

Gross Domestic Product and its Indices of Urban District (1978－2013)

单位:万元 (10000 yuan)

年份 Year	生产总值(当年价格) Gross Domestic Product (Current Price)	第一产业 Primary Industry	第二产业 Secondary Industry	第三产业 Tertiary Industry	人均生产总值(元)(按户籍) Per Capita GDP (Household Registered)	人均生产总值(元)(按常住) Per Capita GDP (Long－term Registered)	生产总值指数(%) Indices of Gross Domestic product(%) (1978＝100)	第一产业 Primary Industry	第二产业 Secondary Industry	第三产业 Tertiary Industry
1978	141995	5215	106663	30117	1389	－	100.00	100.00	100.00	100.00
1979	167206	6527	126517	34162	1555	－	116.40	109.40	118.10	111.60
1980	208220	5943	159161	43116	1863	－	145.30	94.00	150.90	133.90
1981	229243	6165	171946	51132	2005	－	159.90	90.30	163.90	157.20
1982	248297	7327	183284	57686	2125	－	173.70	107.30	176.00	175.60
1983	282171	5938	200334	75899	2369	－	197.90	83.10	193.80	229.50
1984	353781	8469	244445	100867	2919	－	245.40	114.90	235.50	298.40
1985	448574	11233	293579	143762	3633	－	289.90	120.70	270.10	382.20
1986	513639	12245	324585	176809	4042	－	317.30	122.60	287.70	445.10
1987	605234	15408	370668	219158	4724	－	353.20	137.10	313.80	517.40
1988	708474	19602	425319	263553	5441	－	370.80	136.00	332.70	534.00
1989	772208	23869	435847	312492	5848	－	347.00	146.70	296.70	545.20
1990	896496	23919	470844	401733	6722	－	366.50	147.60	314.60	573.60
1991	1096628	25767	547949	522912	8158	－	426.00	151.40	356.30	691.10
1992	1413278	27611	712697	672969	10420	－	535.30	153.10	447.40	877.80
1993	2086571	36208	1052187	998176	15196	－	687.60	157.70	583.70	1117.40
1994	2788314	48257	1395127	1344931	19945	－	870.90	172.30	779.60	1335.30
1995	3697794	57784	1866784	1773226	25969	－	1041.60	183.50	945.70	1574.30
1996	4727377	110881	2356408	2260088	28552	－	1194.90	194.70	1103.60	1769.50
1997	5414265	130062	2630349	2653853	32227	－	1354.90	214.20	1230.30	2052.60
1998	5905726	134320	2786159	2985247	34620	－	1482.50	230.70	1337.20	2266.10
1999	6317335	145242	2915614	3256479	36394	－	1599.30	254.50	1431.10	2467.80
2000	7111586	145715	3278310	3687561	40127	－	1785.50	255.50	1596.70	2763.90
2001	12260891	582492	6026353	5652046	32607	－	2017.20	275.70	1805.30	3126.00
2002	14042278	605433	6901224	6535621	36640	－	2300.80	290.00	2038.60	3607.40
2003	16647332	665083	8343138	7639111	42675	－	2664.80	302.20	2448.40	4058.30
2004	20362738	664676	10368453	9329609	51241	－	3077.40	313.10	2873.90	4630.50
2005	23495459	732463	11582930	11180067	57934	－	3461.24	318.17	3141.49	5406.57
2006	27483121	755663	13254773	13472684	66731	51073	3955.94	320.48	3493.88	6399.62
2007	32738842	773208	15546960	16418675	78541	58907	4525.33	322.73	3948.39	7455.84
2008	38139834	830741	17926048	19383045	90400	66808	5018.47	324.83	4266.45	8505.21
2009	40698687	874987	18120921	21702778	95342	69753	5539.47	332.99	4563.27	9686.26
2010	47407788	941591	21452228	25013969	109708	78072	6204.21	337.31	5124.56	10867.99
2011	55898574	1054368	24984624	29859582	127745	89330	6824.63	343.72	5601.14	12052.60
2012	62132486	1128362	26735946	34268179	140291	98697	7432.02	350.94	5987.62	13366.33
2013	66398609	1149103	27321500	37928006	148170	104751	8011.72	349.54	6424.72	14489.10

1-07 全市生产总值指数(1978-2013)

Indices of Gross Domestic Product (1978-2013)

(上年=100) (Preceding Year=100)

年 份 Year	生产总值 Gross Domestic Product	第一产业 Primary Industry	第二产业 Secondary Industry	第三产业 Tertiary Industry	人均生产总值(按户籍) Per Capita GDP (Household Registered)	人均生产总值(按常住) Per Capita GDP (Long-term Registered)
1978	120.2	119.1	123.7	111.6	119.0	
1979	113.3	114.2	114.0	110.0	112.1	
1980	119.7	92.5	132.5	118.8	118.4	
1981	113.6	102.9	114.0	124.2	112.6	
1982	107.2	119.4	103.2	108.6	105.9	
1983	111.2	89.1	114.3	124.7	109.9	
1984	122.7	121.2	120.8	129.0	121.6	
1985	119.4	99.9	122.6	124.4	118.2	
1986	111.5	103.7	111.5	116.2	110.3	
1987	112.8	102.5	114.0	115.1	111.3	
1988	107.4	97.8	109.8	105.4	105.8	
1989	96.9	99.8	94.4	102.4	95.8	
1990	105.8	106.4	106.5	103.7	104.9	
1991	118.1	104.4	116.6	126.8	117.3	
1992	122.9	100.3	129.5	121.7	122.1	
1993	130.1	105.9	137.8	123.3	129.1	
1994	126.3	108.1	132.2	122.0	125.2	
1995	119.9	107.1	123.5	117.9	118.8	
1996	113.0	105.4	114.6	112.2	112.0	
1997	113.1	106.8	112.7	114.8	112.1	
1998	111.2	109.4	111.8	110.7	110.5	
1999	110.2	105.5	110.1	111.0	109.4	
2000	112.0	105.7	112.5	112.1	111.1	
2001	112.2	107.4	112.7	112.5	111.1	
2002	113.2	104.1	113.3	114.7	111.8	
2003	115.2	106.0	118.6	112.6	114.0	
2004	115.0	105.1	116.7	114.3	113.7	
2005	113.0	103.4	111.1	116.4	111.5	
2006	114.3	104.1	112.6	117.4	113.0	
2007	114.6	102.2	114.3	116.2	113.6	112.0
2008	111.0	103.7	108.9	114.0	110.1	108.9
2009	110.0	103.1	106.5	114.2	109.1	108.2
2010	112.0	102.5	112.5	112.3	111.1	108.7
2011	110.1	102.5	109.8	111.0	109.1	107.5
2012	109.0	102.5	107.4	110.9	108.1	108.4
2013	108.0	101.5	107.4	109.0	107.1	107.3

注:1.本表按可比价格计算。

a) The indices in this table are calculated at comparable prices.

1－08 市区生产总值指数(1978－2013)

Indices of Gross Domestic Product of Urban District (1978－2013)

(上年＝100) (Preceding Year＝100)

年 份 Year	生产总值 Gross Domestic Product	第一产业 Primary Industry	第二产业 Secondary Industry	第三产业 Tertiary Industry	人均生产总值 (按户籍) Per Capita GDP (Household Registered)	人均生产总值 (按常住) Per Capita GDP (Long－term Registered)
1978	120.1	118.8	122.3	113.6	118.0	
1979	116.4	109.4	118.1	111.6	111.4	
1980	124.8	85.9	127.8	120.0	119.7	
1981	110.1	96.1	108.6	117.4	107.6	
1982	108.6	118.8	107.4	111.7	106.3	
1983	113.9	77.5	110.1	130.7	111.7	
1984	124.0	138.2	121.5	130.0	121.8	
1985	118.2	105.0	114.7	128.1	116.0	
1986	109.4	101.6	106.5	116.7	107.4	
1987	111.3	111.8	109.1	116.0	109.4	
1988	105.0	99.2	106.0	103.2	103.3	
1989	93.6	107.9	89.2	102.1	92.2	
1990	105.6	100.6	106.0	105.2	104.6	
1991	116.2	102.6	113.3	120.5	115.3	
1992	125.7	101.1	125.6	127.3	124.5	
1993	128.5	103.0	130.5	127.3	126.9	
1994	126.6	109.3	133.6	119.5	124.4	
1995	119.6	106.5	121.3	117.9	117.4	
1996	114.7	106.1	116.7	112.4	105.3	
1997	113.4	110.0	111.5	116.0	104.7	
1998	109.4	107.7	108.7	110.4	107.8	
1999	107.9	110.3	107.0	108.9	106.0	
2000	111.6	100.4	111.6	112.0	109.3	
2001	113.0	107.9	113.1	113.1	111.2	
2002	114.1	105.2	112.9	115.4	111.9	
2003	115.8	104.2	120.1	112.5	113.8	
2004	115.5	103.6	117.4	114.1	113.4	
2005	112.5	101.6	109.3	116.8	110.2	
2006	114.3	100.7	111.2	118.4	112.5	
2007	114.4	100.7	113.0	116.5	113.0	110.8
2008	110.9	100.7	108.1	114.1	109.5	108.0
2009	110.4	102.5	107.0	113.9	109.1	108.0
2010	112.0	101.3	112.3	112.2	110.7	107.6
2011	110.0	101.9	109.3	110.9	108.6	106.7
2012	108.9	102.1	106.9	110.9	107.6	108.3
2013	107.8	99.6	107.3	108.4	106.5	107.0

注:1. 本表按可比价格计算。

a) The indices in this table are calculated at comparable prices.

1－09 全市生产

Composition of

单位:万元

行业	Sector	全 Whole 2013	全 Whole 为上年(%) As Compared with the Preceding Year(%)
全市生产总值	Gross Domestic Product	83435193	108.0
第一产业	Primary Industry	2654154	101.5
第二产业	Secondary Industry	36619817	107.4
工业	Industry	32466709	107.8
建筑业	Construction	4153108	103.6
第三产业	Tertiary Industry	44161222	109.0
批发和零售业	Wholesale & Retail Trades	7406295	105.8
交通运输、仓储和邮政业	Transportation, Storage and Post	2226363	105.2
住宿和餐饮业	Hotels and Catering Services	1158114	100.3
信息传输、软件和信息技术服务业	Information Transmission, Software and Information Technology	5997999	123.6
金融业	Financial Intermediation	8793272	110.0
房地产业	Real Estate	5849147	104.3
租赁和商务服务业	Leasing and Busyness Service	1918470	108.8
科学研究、技术服务业	Scientific Research, Technical Service	1886700	111.4
水利环境和公共设施管理业	Management of Water Conservancy, Enviroment and Public Facilities	493649	110.6
居民服务、修理和其他服务业	Services to Households, Repair and other services	753180	108.7
教育	Education	2630810	107.0
卫生和社会工作	Health Care and Social Work	1445370	111.4
文化、体育和娱乐业	Culture, Sports and Entertainment	807782	114.7
公共管理、社会保障和社会组织	Public Management, Social Security and Social Organizations	2794071	105.6

注:1. 本表绝对数按当年价格计算,为上年(%)按可比价格计算。

总值构成(2013 年)

Gross Domestic Product(2013)

(10000 yuan)

市 City		#市 区 Urban District			
比 重 (%) Proportion(%)		2013	为上年(%) As Compared with the Preceding Year(%)	比 重 (%) Proportion(%)	
2013	2012			2013	2012
100	100	66398609	107.8	100	100
3.2	3.3	1149103	99.6	1.7	1.8
43.9	45.8	27321500	107.3	41.1	43.0
38.9	40.6	23991238	107.9	36.1	37.8
5.0	5.2	3330262	102.6	5	5.3
52.9	50.9	37928006	108.4	57.1	55.2
8.9	8.9	6143382	103.9	9.3	9.4
2.7	2.7	1621518	104.9	2.4	2.5
1.4	1.4	936155	97.1	1.4	1.5
7.2	5.9	5583237	122.5	8.4	3
10.5	10.1	7792947	109.9	11.7	11.3
7.0	7.0	4988113	103.0	7.5	7.5
2.3	2.4	1714037	108.7	2.6	2.1
2.3	2.1	1820108	111.5	2.7	2.5
0.6	0.6	422865	111.7	0.6	0.6
0.9	0.9	542690	106.3	0.8	0.9
3.2	3.0	2159386	107.0	3.3	3.1
1.7	1.7	1230924	110.7	1.9	1.8
1.0	0.9	755241	115.7	1.1	1.0
3.3	3.3	2217403	105.5	3.3	3.3

a) Absolute figures in this table are calculated at current prices, while indices are calculated at comparable price.

1－10 地区生产总值(2013 年)

Gross Regional Product and Indices(2013)

单位:万元 (10000 yuan)

地 区	Region	生产总值总计 Gross Domestic Product	第一产业 Primary Industry	第二产业 Secondary Industry	工业 Industry	建筑业 Construction	第三产业 Tertiary Industry	人均生产总值(元)(按户籍) Per Capita GDP (Household Registered)	人均生产总值(元)(按常住) Per Capita GDP (Long－term Registered)
全 市	**Whole City**	**83435193**	**2654154**	**36619817**	**32466709**	**4153108**	**44161222**	**118589**	**94566**
市 区	Urban District	66398609	1149103	27321500	23991238	3330262	37928006	148170	104751
#上城区	Shangcheng	7385886	－	3415947	3230059	185887	3969939	224086	211055
下城区	Xiacheng	6435685	－	516118	256266	259852	5919567	158690	121222
江干区	Jianggan	4221834	6196	1273285	607915	665371	2942353	90812	60511
拱墅区	Gongshu	3723884	－	1113863	944089	169774	2610021	116938	66522
西湖区	Xihu	6968730	43525	1053355	617977	435378	5871850	107112	86990
高新(滨江)区	Hi－Tech(Binjiang)	5986419	17360	2979389	2728950	250438	2989671	341009	184481
萧山区	Xiaoshan	16635270	596503	9658638	8994517	664121	6380129	134182	108582
余杭区	Yuhang	9344138	468624	4354023	3891229	462795	4521491	104188	78086
桐庐县	Tonglu	2780354	208588	1603205	1441376	161828	968562	68642	67855
淳安县	Chun'an	1733057	286566	710164	550959	159205	736327	37964	50808
建德市	Jiande	2716954	273981	1489661	1373020	116641	953312	53373	62265
富阳市	Fuyang	5713954	380104	3241178	3023360	217818	2092672	86931	78851
临安市	Lin'an	4092264	355812	2254109	2086756	167353	1482342	77726	71487

注:1. 本表按当年价格计算。

a) Data in this table are calculated at current prices.

1－11　主要指标占全省比重(2013 年)

Proportion of Main Indicators in Whole Province(2013)

指标 Item		全省 Zhejiang Province	杭州市 Hangzhou City	杭州市占全省(%) Proportion of Hangzhou in Zhejiang(%)
年末常住人口 Long－term Residents(End of 2012)	(万人) (10000 persons)	5498.00	884.40	16.1
年末户籍人口 Household Registration Population(End of 2012)	(万人) (10000 persons)	4826.89	706.61	14.6
#非农业人口 Non－agriculture Population	(万人) (10000 persons)	1545.41	393.88	25.5
年末就业人员数 Total Number of Employed Persons	(万人) (10000 persons)	3708.73	650.51	17.5
生产总值 Gross Domestic Product	(亿元) (100 million yuan)	37568.49	8343.52	22.2
第一产业 Primary Industry	(亿元) (100 million yuan)	1784.62	265.42	14.9
第二产业 Secondary Industry	(亿元) (100 million yuan)	18446.65	3661.98	19.9
第三产业 Tertiary Industry	(亿元) (100 million yuan)	17337.22	4416.12	25.5
常住人均生产总值 Per Capita GDP of Long－term Residents	(元) (yuan)	68462	94566	–
农林牧渔业总产值 Gross Output Value of Farming, Forestry, Animal Husbandry and Fishery	(亿元) (100 million yuan)	2837.39	399.37	14.1
主要农产品产量 Output of Major Farm Products				
#粮食 Grain	(万吨) (10000 tons)	733.95	95.92	13.1
棉花 Cotton	(万吨) (10000 tons)	2.80	0.08	2.9
蚕茧 Silk－worm Cocoons	(万吨) (10000 tons)	5.52	1.45	26.3
生猪年末存栏 Hogs in Stock at Year End	(万头) (10000 heads)	1287.53	219.23	17.0
肉类产量 Output of Meat	(万吨) (10000 tons)	141.58	34.04	24.0
淡水产品总产量 Freshwater Aquatic products	(万吨) (10000 tons)	107.63	19.80	18.3

1-11 续表1 continued 1

指标 Item		全省 Zhejiang Province	杭州市 Hangzhou City	杭州市占全省(%) Proportion of Hangzhou in Zhejiang(%)
规模以上工业企业利税总额 Total Pre-tax Profits of Industrial Enterprises above Designed Size	(亿元) (100 million yuan)	5984.03	1450.55	24.2
主要工业产品产量 Output of Major Industrial Products				
#发电量 Electricity	(亿千瓦时) (100 million kwh)	2883.60	196.11	6.8
氢氧化钠(烧碱)(折100%) Caustic Soda(100% discount)	(万吨) (10000 tons)	144.05	19.31	13.4
碳酸钠(纯碱) Soda Ash	(万吨) (10000 tons)	28.26	28.26	100.0
合成氨 Synthetic Ammonia	(万吨) (10000 tons)	57.87	18.44	31.9
水泥 Cement	(万吨) (10000 tons)	12462.87	2162.35	17.4
钢材 Steels	(万吨) (10000 tons)	3823.44	975.75	25.5
化学纤维 Chemical Fiber	(万吨) (10000 tons)	1839.31	684.70	37.2
纱 Yarn	(万吨) (10000 tons)	239.10	67.00	28.0
自行车 Bicycles	(万辆) (10000 units)	1405.93	426.94	30.4
彩色电视机 Colour TV Sets	(万台) (10000 units)	628.62	68.66	10.9
电冰箱 Household Refrigerator	(万台) (10000 units)	939.61	111.75	11.9
洗衣机 Washing Machine	(万台) (10000 units)	1881.38	354.14	18.8
全社会交通运输客运量 Total Passenger Traffic	(万人次) (10000 person-times)	136790	36409	26.6
全社会交通运输货运量 Total Freight Traffic	(万吨) (10000 tons)	187885	30734	16.4

1－11 续表2 continued 2

指标 Item		全省 Zhejiang Province	杭州市 Hangzhou City	杭州市占全省(%) Proportion of Hangzhou in Zhejiang(%)
固定资产投资 Investment in Fixed Assets	(亿元) (100 million yuan)	20194.07	4263.87	21.1
社会消费品零售总额 Total Retail Sales of Consumer Goods	(亿元) (100 million yuan)	15225.54	3531.17	23.2
出口额 Total Exports	(亿美元) (100 million USD)	2488.04	447.66	18.0
实际利用外资 Foreign Capital Actually Used	(亿美元) (100 million USD)	141.59	52.76	37.3
境外旅游者人数 Number of International Tourists	(万人次) (10000 person－times)	866.28	316.01	36.5
财政总收入 Total Financial Revenue	(亿元) (100 million yuan)	6908.41	1734.98	25.1
#地方公共财政预算收入 Financial Revenue of Local Government	(亿元) (100 million yuan)	3796.92	945.20	24.9
公共财政预算支出 Financial Expenditure	(亿元) (100 million yuan)	4730.78	855.74	18.1
金融机构存款余额(本外币) Deposits of Financial Institutions	(亿元) (100 million yuan)	73732.36	22174.71	30.1
金融机构贷款余额(本外币) Loans of Financial Institutions	(亿元) (100 million yuan)	65338.78	19350.46	29.6
城乡居民储蓄存款余额 Residents´Savings Deposits	(亿元) (100 million yuan)	29360.48	6408.59	21.8
非私营单位就业人员平均工资 Average Wage of Employed Persons of Non－private Units	(元) (yuan)	56571	63664	－
城镇居民人均可支配收入 Per Capita Annual Disposable Income in Urban District	(元) (yuan)	37851	39310	－
农民人均纯收入 Per Capita Annual Net Income in Rural Areas	(元) (yuan)	16106	18923	－
高等学校在校学生数 Number of Institutions of Higher Education	(万人) (10000 persons)	101.74	47.18	46.4
中等职业教育学校在校学生数 Number of Secondary Specialized Schools	(万人) (10000 persons)	54.76	10.05	18.4
普通中学在校学生数 Number of Secondary Schools	(万人) (10000 persons)	232.24	32.73	14.1
小学在校学生数 Number of Primary Schools	(万人) (10000 persons)	349.58	48.35	13.8

1－12 国民经济主要指标人均水平

Major Per Capita Indicators of National Economy

指 标 Item		1995	2000	2005	2010	2011	2012	2013
全市生产总值 Gross Domestic Product	(元) (yuan)	12797	22342	44871	69828	80478	88962	94566
规模以上工业总产值 Gross Industrial Output Value above Designatted Size	(元) (yuan)	17131	24943	82936	130064	141634	147773	106639
农林牧渔业总产值 Gross Output Value of Farming, Forestry, Animal Husbandry and Fishery	(元) (yuan)	1673	2467	3345	3713	4094	4382	4526
社会消费品零售总额 Total Retail Sales of Consumer Goods	(元) (yuan)	5027	8317	14869	25190	29219	33576	40022
财政总收入 Financial Revenue	(元) (yuan)	926	2308	7938	14618	17071	18562	19664
#地方公共财政预算收入 Financial Revenue of Local Government	(元) (yuan)	387	1118	3818	7880	9002	9806	10713
公共财政预算支出 Financial Expenditure	(元) (yuan)	418	1187	3633	7237	8571	8966	9699
城镇居民可支配收入 Annual Disposable Income in Urban District	(元) (yuan)	6301	9668	16601	30035	34065	37511	39310
城镇居民消费性支出 Annual Living Expenditure in Urban District	(元) (yuan)	5559	7790	13438	20219	22642	22800	24833
农民纯收入 Annual Net Income in Rural Area	(元) (yuan)	3012	4894	7655	13186	15245	17017	18923
农民消费性支出 Annual Living Expenditure in Rural Area	(元) (yuan)	2373	3393	6004	10267	12125	13612	14600

注:2010 年后按常住人口平均计算。

a) Since 2010, date in this table based on Long term Residents.

1－13 企业家信心指数(2013 年)
Expectation Indices of Entrepreneurs(2013)

单位:点 (point)

指　标	Item	第一季度 1st. Quarter	第二季度 2nd. Quarter	第三季度 3rd. Quarter	第四季度 4th. Quarter
全市	**Total**	**121.4**	**113.8**	**118.7**	**113.0**
按行业分	**Grouped by Sector**				
工业	Industry	125.4	116.6	120.1	116.4
建筑业	Construction	122.0	117.5	122.5	116.7
交通运输、仓储及邮电通信业	Transportation, Storage and Post	109.0	95.2	93.1	101.4
批发零售贸易业	Wholesale and Retail Trade	109.6	98.1	108.5	108.5
房地产业	Real Estate	98.0	103.0	109.5	97.5
社会服务业	Social Services	136.8	140.5	130.5	109.5
信息传输、计算机服务和软件业	Information Transmission, Computer Service and Software	151.5	138.7	145.3	137.3
住宿和餐饮业	Lodging and Catering	102.9	84.4	114.6	87.3
按经济类型分	**Grouped by Status of Registration**				
国有企业	State－owned	124.8	122.0	117.4	113.2
集体企业	Collective－owned	124.4	108.8	104.7	101.0
有限责任公司	Limited－liability Companies	119.5	111.0	117.8	110.7
股份有限公司	Share Holding Ltd. Companies	127.4	119.6	128.9	121.9
港、澳、台投资企业	Enterprises With Investment from Hong Kong, Macao and Taiwan	126.4	111.9	117.6	120.7
外商投资企业	Enterprises With Foreign Investment	122.5	120.8	120.2	115.5
按企业规模分	**Grouped by Size of Enterprises**				
大型企业	Large	129.4	124.4	127.8	126.4
中型企业	Medium	120.2	112.5	124.7	112.4
小型企业	Small	114.2	104.7	107.0	102.6

1－14　企业景气指数(2013 年)
Expectation Indices of Enterprises(2013)

单位:点　　　(point)

指　标	Item	第一季度 1st. Quarter	第二季度 2nd. Quarter	第三季度 3rd. Quarter	第四季度 4th. Quarter
全市	**Total**	**128.1**	**121.4**	**124.3**	**119.8**
按行业分	**Grouped by Sector**				
工业	Industry	132.4	124.4	125.5	120.8
建筑业	Construction	132.2	130.8	127.9	128.3
交通运输、仓储及邮电通信业	Transportation, Storage and Post	100.7	91.7	85.5	94.5
批发零售贸易业	Wholesale and Retail Trade	123.3	115.3	121.1	117.5
房地产业	Real Estate	123.0	117.5	128.5	124.0
社会服务业	Social Services	132.6	123.7	123.7	111.6
信息传输、计算机服务和软件业	Information Transmission, Computer Service and Software	144.6	141.0	145.3	137.7
住宿和餐饮业	Lodging and Catering	89.8	86.3	111.2	91.7
按经济类型分	**Grouped by Status of Registration**				
国有企业	State－owned	145.0	135.5	137.0	137.5
集体企业	Collective－owned	123.5	114.1	100.1	98.7
有限责任公司	Limited－liability Companies	125.7	118.1	124.6	116.5
股份有限公司	Share Holding Ltd. Companies	139.0	131.8	132.9	136.9
港、澳、台投资企业	Enterprises With Investment from Hong Kong, Macao and Taiwan	126.8	123.6	121.1	121.9
外商投资企业	Enterprises With Foreign Investment	127.0	122.7	121.7	121.9
按企业规模分	**Grouped by Size of Enterprises**				
大型企业	Large	142.3	140.3	140.0	136.7
中型企业	Medium	121.7	113.8	124.2	119.3
小型企业	Small	116.0	107.0	109.3	103.5

1－15　市区分月气象概况(2013 年)

Monthly Meteorological Conditions in Urban District(2013)

月　　份	Month	平均气温(度) Average Temperature(℃)	日照时数(小时) Sunshine Hours(hours)	降雨天数(天) Rainfall Days (day)	降水量(毫米) Precipitation(mm)
全　　年	**Whole Year**	**18.0**	**1665.5**	**146**	**1520.9**
1　月	January	4.5	81.4	8	41.0
2　月	February	7.0	38.7	20	94.0
3　月	March	12.3	130.1	14	109.0
4　月	April	16.9	162.6	12	97.3
5　月	May	23.0	167.6	15	117.7
6　月	June	24.8	79.2	25	337.2
7　月	July	32.3	289.7	8	8.8
8　月	August	31.3	213.2	13	209.8
9　月	September	25.0	127.1	11	49.4
10　月	October	19.3	128.4	8	331.0
11　月	November	13.6	142.1	8	32.6
12　月	December	6.3	105.4	4	93.1

1－16 气　　象
Meteorological

指　　标		Item		市　区 Urban District	#萧山区 Xiaoshan
一、气　温		**The Atmospheric Temperature**			
全年平均气温	（度）	Annual Average Temperature	（℃）	18.0	18.2
极端最高气温	（度）	The Highest Temperature of the Year	（℃）	41.6	42.2
出现日期	（日/月）	Date	（d/m）	9/8	30/7
极端最低气温	（度）	The Lowest Temperature of the Year	（℃）	－4.4	－3.5
出现日期	（日/月）	Date	（d/m）	28/12	28/12
二、降　雨		**Rainfall**			
本年降雨日数	（日）	Total Rainy Days	（day）	146	155
全年降雨总量	（毫米）	Annual Rainfall	（millimeters）	1520.9	1622.5
最长连续降雨日数	（日）	Longest Consecutive Days of Rain	（day）	7	8
最长连续降雨总量	（毫米）	Rainfall	（millimeters）	163.2	43.4
最长连续降雨起止日期	（日/月）	Start/End	（d/m）	24/6－30/6	10/6－17/6
日最大降雨量	（毫米）	Maximum Daily Rainfall	（millimeters）	246.4	261.4
出现日期	（日/月）	Date	（d/m）	7/10	7/10
三、全年日照总时数	**（小时）**	**Total Sunshine Hours**	**（hours）**	**1665.5**	**1926.2**
四、降　霜		**Frost**			
全年降霜日数	（日）	Annual Frost Days	（day）	29	30
初霜日期	（日/月）	Start Date	（d/m）	6/12	27/11
终霜日期	（日/月）	End Date	（d/m）	3/3	15/3
五、降　雪		**Snow**			
全年降雪日数	（日）	Annual Frost Days	（day）	13	11
初雪日期	（日/月）	Start Date	（d/m）	26/12	29/12
终雪日期	（日/月）	End Date	（d/m）	2/3	2/3

概　　况(2013 年)

Conditions by Region(2013)

桐庐县 Tonglu	淳安县 Chun'an	建德市 Jiande	富阳市 Fuyang	临安市 Lin'an
17.6	17.9	17.4	17.8	16.8
41.9	40.9	42.2	42.8	41.8
8/8	7/8	9/8	10/8	11/8
-5.6	-3.8	-5.0	-5.1	-7.3
28/12	9/2	28/12	28/12	28/12
162	148	166	147	138
1559.5	1352.3	1522.5	1486.8	1469.5
8	7	10	7	8
225.2	230.5	250.4	218.1	245.2
25/11 - 14/12	24/6 - 30/6	22/6 - 1/7	24/6 - 30/6	23/6 - 30/6
144.8	146.3	125.7	189.4	179.1
7/10	27/6	27/6	7/10	7/10
1714.4	**2034.9**	**1828.5**	**1948.4**	**1927.1**
29	24	36	28	40
6/12	27/11	4/12	4/12	27/11
4/3	4/3	6/3	3/3	4/3
12	11	12	11	14
29/12	11/12	10/12	26/12	26/12
1/3	2/3	19/2	2/3	2/3

主要统计指标解释

生产总值(GDP)　指一个国家(或地区)所有常住单位在一定时期内生产活动的最终成果。生产总值有三种表现形态,即价值形态、收入形态和产品形态。从价值形态看,它是所有常住单位在一定时期内生产的全部货物和服务价值超过同期中间投入的全部非固定资产货物和服务价值的差额,即所有常住单位的增加值之和;从收入形态看,它是所有常住单位在一定时期内创造并分配给常住单位和非常住单位的初次收入分配之和;从产品形态看,它是所有常住单位在一定时期内最终使用的货物和服务价值与货物和服务净出口价值之和。在实际核算中,生产总值有三种计算方法,即生产法、收入法和支出法。三种方法分别从不同的方面反映生产总值及其构成。

三次产业　是根据社会生产活动历史发展的顺序对产业结构的划分,产品直接取自自然界的部门称为第一产业,对初级产品进行再加工的部门称为第二产业,为生产和消费提供各种服务的部门称为第三产业。它是世界上较为通用的产业结构分类,但各国的划分不尽一致。我国的三次产业划分是:

第一产业:农业(包括种植业、林业、牧业、渔业和农林牧渔服务业)。

第二产业:工业(包括采矿业,制造业,电力、燃气及水的生产和供应业)和建筑业。

第三产业:除第一、第二产业以外的其他各业。由于第三产业包括的行业多、范围广,根据我国的实际情况,第三产业可分为两大部分:一是流通部门,二是服务部门。具体又分为四个层次:

第一层次:流通部门,包括交通运输、仓储及邮电通信业,批发和零售贸易、餐饮业。

第二层次:为生产和生活服务的部门,包括金融、保险业,地质勘查业、水利管理业,房地产业,社会服务业,农、林、牧、渔服务业,交通运输辅助业,综合技术服务业等。

第三层次:为提高科学文化水平和居民素质服务的部门,包括教育、文化艺术及广播电影电视业,卫生、体育和社会福利业,科学研究等。

第四层次:为社会公共需要服务的部门,包括国家机关、政党机关和社会团体以及军队、警察等。

降水量　从天空降落到地面的液态或固态(经融化后)降水,未经蒸发、渗透、流失而在水平面上积聚的深度。降水量以毫米为单位。

空气的温度(简称气温)　表示空气冷热程度的物理量。

日照时数　太阳在一地实际照射地面的时数。

Explanatory Notes on Main Statistical Indicators

Gross Domestic Product (GDP) refers to the final products of all resident units in a country (or a region) during a certain period of time. Gross domestic product is expressed in three different forms, i. e. value, income, and products respectively. The form of value refers to the total value of all products and services produced by all resident units during a certain period of time minus total value of intermediate input of materials and services of the nature of non – fixed assets or the summation of the value – added of all resident units; the form of income includes all the income created by all resident units and distributed primarily to all resident and non – resident units; the form of products refers to the value of all final goods and services for final use by all resident units plus the value of net exports of goods and services during a given period of time. In the practice of national accounting, gross domestic product is calculated with three approaches, i. e. production approach, income approach, and expenditure approach, which reflect gross domestic product and its composition from different aspects.

Three Industries Industry structure has been classified according to the historical sequence of development. Primary industry refers to extraction of natural resources; secondary industry involves processing of primary products; and tertiary industry provides services of various kinds for production and consumption. The above classification is universal although it varies to someextent from country to country. Industry in China comprises:

Primary industry: agriculture (including farming, forestry, animal husbandry and fishery and services for agriculture sector)

Secondary industry: industry (including mining and quarrying, manufacturing, production and supply of electricity, water and gas) and construction.

Tertiary industry: all other industries not included in primary of secondary industry.

Due to the fact that tertiary industry involves in a large variety of industries in China, it is divided into two sectors: circulation sector and service sector and further into four levels:

The first level: circulation sector, including transportation, storage, postal and telecommunications, wholesale and retail trade and catering trade.

The second level: service sector providing services for production and consumption, including banking, insurance, geological survey, water conservancy management, real estates, service for residents, service for agriculture, forestry, animal husbandry, fishery, subsidiary services for transportation and communications, comprehensive technical services, etc.

The third level: service sector for upgrading scientific, educational and cultural level of the people, including education, culture and arts, broadcasting, movies, television, public health, sports, social welfare and scientific research, etc.

The fourth level: sector providing services for public needs, including government agencies, political parties, social organizations, military and police service.

Precipitation refers to the depth of rainfall onto the ground (as well as liquefied from solid forms) from above the air prior to its vaporization, seepage, running off.

It is calculated in the unit of millimeter (mm).

Air Temperature refers to the physical quantity reflecting the extent of coldness and hotness of the air.

Duration of sunshine refers to the real time for the ground to receive sunshine at a certain place.

二、人口和就业人员

Ⅱ.POPULATION AND EMPLOYMENT

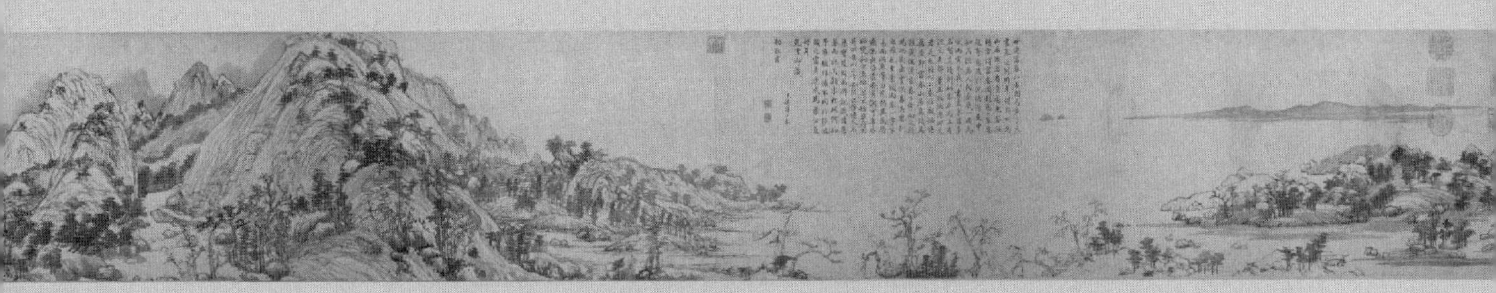

人口和就业人员
Population and Employment

主要统计指标
Major Statistical Indicators

年末常住人口	Long-term Residents	884.40	万人	(10, 000 persons)
为上年	As Compared with the Preceding Year	100.5	%	(%)
年末户籍登记户数	Total Registration Households(year-end)	220.66	万户	(10, 000 Subscribers)
为上年	As Compared with the Preceding Year	100.8	%	(%)
年末户籍登记人口	Total Registration Population(year-end)	706.61	万人	(10, 000 persons)
为上年	As Compared with the Preceding Year	100.9	%	(%)
#男性	Male	353.32	万人	(10, 000 persons)
为上年	As Compared with the Preceding Year	100.7	%	(%)
#非农业人口	Non-agriculture Population	393.88	万人	(10, 000 persons)
为上年	As Compared with the Preceding Year	102.5	%	(%)
人口自然增长率	Natural Growth Rate	4.73	‰	(‰)
年末就业人员	Number of Employed Persons(year-end)	650.51	万人	(10, 000 persons)
为上年	As Compared with the Preceding Year	100.9	%	(%)

2-01 历次普查常住人口情况

Long-term Residents in the Past Population Census

单位:万人 (10000 person)

地　区 Region		第一次人口普查 1953.7.1 the First Population Census (1953.7.1)	第二次人口普查 1964.7.1 the Second Population Census (1964.7.1)	第三次人口普查 1982.7.1 the Third Population Census (1982.7.1)	第四次人口普查 1990.7.1 the Fourth Population Census (1991.7.1)	第五次人口普查 2000.11.1 the Fifth Population Census (2000.11.1)	第六次人口普查 2010.11.1 the Sixth Population Census (2010.11.1)
杭州市	**Hangzhou**	**301.13**	**421.90**	**526.05**	**583.21**	**687.87**	**870.04**
杭州市区	Urban District	172.26	243.65	305.77	346.76	450.23	624.20
上城区	Shangcheng				21.10	33.51	34.46
下城区	Xiacheng				25.66	41.24	52.61
江干区	Jianggan				36.12	56.54	99.88
拱墅区	Gongshu				29.34	42.93	55.19
西湖区	Xihu				35.40	59.33	82.00
高新(滨江)区	Hi-Tech(Binjiang)					11.59	31.90
萧山区	Xiaoshan	56.32	82.34	106.11	113.06	123.33	151.13
余杭区	Yuhang	52.28	64.96	80.50	86.08	81.77	117.03
桐庐县	Tonglu	19.73	26.20	34.83	37.66	37.81	40.64
淳安县	Chun'an	27.49	38.66	42.03	43.55	38.23	33.68
建德市	Jiande	26.42	38.15	43.64	47.63	47.31	43.08
富阳市	Fuyang	29.22	39.66	54.13	58.07	62.86	71.77
临安市	Lin'an	26.01	35.57	45.65	49.55	51.42	56.67

2-02 全市户籍人口和总户数(1978-2013)
Registered Population and Households(1978-2013)

年 份 Year	总户数(万户) Total Households (10000 households)	总人口数(万人) Total Population (10000 persons)	#非农业人口(万人) Non-agriculture Population (10000 persons)	按性别分 By Sex 男(万人) Male (10000 persons)	女(万人) Female (10000 persons)
1978	117.89	505.55	116.06	260.74	244.81
1979	116.61	511.83	124.60	263.97	247.86
1980	119.11	515.53	128.88	266.02	249.51
1981	125.96	520.73	134.56	268.69	252.04
1982	131.53	528.06	139.94	272.72	255.34
1983	135.55	533.06	143.34	275.64	257.41
1984	139.24	537.49	147.46	278.04	259.45
1985	145.23	543.05	153.46	281.11	261.94
1986	151.59	549.53	157.19	284.57	264.96
1987	157.66	557.63	161.12	288.70	268.93
1988	164.41	565.04	164.87	292.21	272.83
1989	169.09	570.98	167.28	295.15	275.83
1990	171.94	574.78	169.00	297.02	277.76
1991	174.78	578.73	171.25	298.85	279.88
1992	177.68	582.40	174.03	300.63	281.77
1993	179.17	587.10	179.11	303.03	284.07
1994	180.65	592.93	186.50	306.00	286.93
1995	182.55	597.96	191.43	308.25	289.71
1996	184.33	603.22	196.68	310.76	292.46
1997	186.28	607.96	204.39	313.02	294.94
1998	187.80	611.64	210.52	314.69	296.95
1999	191.60	616.05	219.05	316.63	299.42
2000	193.48	621.58	227.00	319.09	302.49
2001	195.56	629.14	237.77	322.78	306.36
2002	198.27	636.81	252.02	326.62	310.19
2003	201.12	642.78	263.67	329.04	313.74
2004	204.52	651.68	282.58	332.62	319.06
2005	207.42	660.45	297.54	336.12	324.33
2006	209.91	666.31	309.78	338.23	328.08
2007	211.99	672.35	323.75	340.50	331.85
2008	213.74	677.64	340.76	342.45	335.19
2009	215.28	683.38	354.48	344.51	338.87
2010	216.51	689.12	365.24	346.56	342.56
2011	218.26	695.71	376.03	349.09	346.62
2012	218.95	700.52	384.09	350.90	349.62
2013	220.66	706.61	393.88	353.32	353.29

注:按公安户籍人口统计。

a) Figures in this table are based on the household registered statistics which published by Public Security Bureau.

2-03 市区户籍人口和总户数(1978-2013)

Registered Population and Households of Urban District(1978-2013)

年份 Year	总户数 (万户) Total Households (10000 households)	总人口数 (万人) Total Population (10000 persons)	#非农业人口(万人) Non-agriculture Population (10000 persons)	按性别分 By Sex 男(万人) Male (10000 persons)	女(万人) Female (10000 persons)
1978	25.52	104.53	78.73	53.95	50.58
1979	26.23	110.50	85.05	57.09	53.41
1980	27.23	113.08	87.93	58.56	54.52
1981	29.88	115.59	90.53	59.96	55.63
1982	31.24	118.05	92.72	61.28	56.77
1983	32.69	120.13	94.94	62.43	57.70
1984	34.07	122.29	97.34	63.63	58.66
1985	35.36	124.67	100.01	64.96	59.71
1986	37.02	127.07	102.59	66.29	60.78
1987	38.70	129.16	104.09	67.38	61.78
1988	40.05	131.26	107.30	68.46	62.80
1989	41.19	132.84	108.88	69.28	63.56
1990	42.26	133.89	109.97	69.75	64.14
1991	42.98	134.97	111.20	70.33	64.64
1992	43.63	136.30	112.70	71.08	65.22
1993	44.55	138.33	115.13	72.22	66.11
1994	45.04	141.27	118.48	73.82	67.45
1995	46.06	143.52	121.38	74.91	68.61
1996	52.39	166.73	128.76	87.15	79.58
1997	53.14	169.29	131.76	88.53	80.76
1998	53.92	171.89	134.62	89.86	82.03
1999	54.64	175.27	139.29	91.65	83.62
2000	55.34	179.18	143.69	93.64	85.54
2001	115.81	379.49	193.26	194.59	184.90
2002	117.11	387.01	205.98	198.47	188.54
2003	119.01	393.19	216.13	201.14	192.05
2004	120.56	401.59	233.08	204.43	197.16
2005	122.02	409.52	245.56	207.70	201.82
2006	123.31	414.18	256.42	209.45	204.73
2007	124.40	419.50	269.30	211.59	207.91
2008	125.56	424.30	285.11	213.54	210.76
2009	126.92	429.44	297.83	215.56	213.88
2010	128.43	434.82	307.52	217.65	217.16
2011	130.14	440.34	317.63	219.86	220.48
2012	131.48	445.43	325.50	221.99	223.43
2013	133.27	450.82	334.38	224.24	226.58

注:从2001年起市区数据包括萧山区和余杭区。

a) Figures in this table include Xiaoshan and Yuhang district since 2001.

2 - 04 分地区户籍人口和总户数(2013 年末)
Registered Population and Households by Region(End of 2013)

地　区 Region	总户数 (户) Total Households (household)	总人口数 (人) Total Population (person)	#非农业人口(人) Non - agriculture Population (person)	按性别分 By Sex 男(人) Male (person)	按性别分 By Sex 女(人) Female (person)
全　市 Whole City	**2206634**	**7066098**	**3938760**	**3533238**	**3532860**
市　区 Urban District	1332727	4508151	3343788	2242394	2265757
上城区 Shangcheng	114723	330021	330012	165580	164441
下城区 Xiacheng	128522	405966	405963	204468	201498
江干区 Jianggan	131924	469974	458585	234324	235650
拱墅区 Gongshu	109790	320458	320432	161386	159072
西湖区 Xihu	175421	653900	595772	332197	321703
高新(滨江)区 Hi - Tech(Binjiang)	49128	180685	169696	92397	88288
萧山区 Xiaoshan	375340	1243798	545929	610078	633720
余杭区 Yuhang	247879	903349	517399	441964	461385
桐庐县 Tonglu	147339	405869	127977	203335	202534
淳安县 Chun'an	147467	457503	81625	232894	224609
建德市 Jiande	169420	508942	130076	259643	249299
富阳市 Fuyang	221117	658609	144198	332107	326502
临安市 Lin'an	188564	527024	111096	262865	264159

2-05 分地区户籍人口年龄构成(2013年末)

Age Structure of Household Registered Population by Region(End of 2013)

地 区 Region	18岁以下 under 18 years old		18-35岁 18~35 years old		35-60岁 35~60 years old		60岁以上 over 60 years old	
	人数(人) Number of people (person)	占总人口% of the total population	人数(人) Number of people (person)	占总人口% of the total population	人数(人) Number of people (person)	占总人口% of the total population	人数(人) Number of people (person)	占总人口% of the total population
全 市 Whole City	**1070115**	**15.1**	**1731896**	**24.5**	**2897711**	**41.0**	**1366376**	**19.3**
市 区 Urban District	687888	15.3	1144921	25.4	1790044	39.7	885298	19.6
上城区 Shangcheng	34657	10.5	79695	24.1	129061	39.1	86608	26.2
下城区 Xiacheng	48744	12.0	115067	28.3	150580	37.1	91575	22.6
江干区 Jianggan	76072	16.2	138256	29.4	173029	36.8	82617	17.6
拱墅区 Gongshu	42505	13.3	77648	24.2	127667	39.8	72638	22.7
西湖区 Xihu	103083	15.8	209795	32.1	237786	36.4	103236	15.8
高新(滨江)区 Hi-Tech(Binjiang)	34572	19.1	58522	32.4	63791	35.3	23800	13.2
萧山区 Xiaoshan	203243	16.3	264925	21.3	522612	42.0	253018	20.3
余杭区 Yuhang	145012	16.1	201013	22.3	385518	42.7	171806	19.0
桐庐县 Tonglu	60566	14.9	93450	23.0	172939	42.6	78914	19.4
淳安县 Chun'an	69893	15.3	101474	22.2	202981	44.4	83155	18.2
建德市 Jiande	72863	14.3	119532	23.5	216367	42.5	100180	19.7
富阳市 Fuyang	105960	16.1	151825	23.1	283001	43.0	117823	17.9
临安市 Lin'an	72945	13.8	120694	22.9	232379	44.1	101006	19.2

2-06 全市户籍人口自然变动情况(1978-2013)
Natural Changes of Registered Population(1978-2013)

年份 Year	出生 Birth		死亡 Death		自然增长 Natural Growth	
	人数(人) Birth Population (person)	出生率(‰) Birth Rate(‰)	人数(人) Death Population (person)	死亡率(‰) Death Rate(‰)	人数(人) Natural Growth Population (person)	自然增长率(‰) Natural Growth Rate(‰)
1978	73550	14.63	29928	2.95	43622	8.68
1979	71442	14.04	29500	5.80	41942	8.24
1980	52145	10.15	30727	5.98	21418	4.17
1981	73015	14.09	31352	6.05	41663	8.04
1982	82910	15.81	30805	5.87	52105	9.94
1983	69940	13.18	33598	6.33	36342	6.85
1984	60091	11.23	33070	6.18	27021	5.05
1985	66757	12.36	33715	6.24	33042	6.12
1986	84702	15.50	33576	6.15	51126	9.35
1987	94127	17.00	33238	6.00	60889	11.00
1988	85472	15.23	35356	6.30	50116	8.93
1989	81048	14.27	34031	5.99	47017	8.28
1990	76579	13.37	34977	6.11	41602	7.26
1991	66144	11.47	33534	5.81	32610	5.66
1992	61708	10.63	34681	5.97	27027	4.66
1993	62465	10.68	34127	5.84	28338	4.84
1994	63580	10.78	35099	5.95	28481	4.83
1995	62586	10.51	36186	6.08	26400	4.43
1996	63680	10.60	25417	5.90	28263	4.70
1997	58471	9.65	34663	5.72	23808	3.93
1998	53951	8.85	38302	6.28	15649	2.57
1999	59085	9.63	36866	6.01	22219	3.62
2000	62300	10.07	40218	6.50	22082	3.57
2001	52088	8.33	33827	5.41	18261	2.92
2002	53064	8.38	35867	5.67	17197	2.72
2003	51420	8.04	36662	5.73	14758	2.31
2004	59940	9.26	34078	5.27	25862	3.99
2005	57233	8.72	35417	5.39	21816	3.33
2006	57790	8.71	38892	5.86	18898	2.85
2007	60296	9.01	37833	5.65	22463	3.36
2008	61332	9.09	42648	6.32	18684	2.77
2009	62441	9.18	39159	5.76	23282	3.42
2010	69606	10.14	46193	6.73	23413	3.41
2011	70337	10.16	38225	5.52	32112	4.64
2012	77349	11.08	49789	7.13	27560	3.95
2013	70850	10.07	37544	5.34	33306	4.73

注:本表按公安部门统计。

a) Figures in this table are based on the Public Security Bureau.

2-07 市区户籍人口自然变动情况(1978-2013)

Natural Changes of Registered Population of Urban District(1978-2013)

年份 Year	出生 Birth		死亡 Death		自然增长 Natural Growth	
	人数(人) Birth Population (person)	出生率(‰) Birth Rate(‰)	人数(人) Death Population (person)	死亡率(‰) Death Rate(‰)	人数(人) Natural Growth Population (person)	自然增长率(‰) Natural Growth Rate(‰)
1978	11923	11.56	6449	6.25	5474	5.31
1979	13184	12.26	5808	5.40	7376	6.86
1980	9708	8.68	6511	5.82	3197	2.86
1981	14938	13.06	6599	5.77	8339	7.29
1982	18092	15.49	6494	5.56	11598	9.93
1983	17107	14.36	6949	5.84	10158	8.52
1984	16257	13.41	6892	5.69	9365	7.72
1985	15824	12.81	7403	6.84	8421	6.82
1986	17120	13.60	6865	5.45	10255	8.15
1987	18701	14.60	7070	5.52	11631	9.08
1988	18503	14.21	7503	5.76	11000	8.45
1989	15868	12.02	6985	5.29	8883	6.73
1990	14085	10.56	7490	5.62	6595	4.94
1991	10195	7.58	7025	5.22	3170	2.36
1992	9994	7.37	7259	5.35	2735	2.02
1993	10099	7.35	7196	5.24	2903	2.11
1994	9918	7.09	7082	5.06	2836	2.03
1995	9806	6.89	7367	5.17	2439	1.72
1996	12098	7.80	8221	5.30	3877	2.50
1997	12304	7.32	8630	5.13	3674	2.19
1998	11714	6.87	9060	5.31	2654	1.56
1999	13694	7.89	8148	4.69	5546	3.20
2000	15058	8.50	10996	6.20	4062	2.30
2001	30902	8.22	19439	5.17	11463	3.05
2002	33156	8.65	19922	5.20	13234	3.45
2003	29019	7.44	21176	5.43	7843	2.01
2004	34858	8.77	19445	4.89	15413	3.88
2005	34056	8.39	21310	5.25	12746	3.14
2006	33260	8.08	21156	5.14	12104	2.94
2007	37029	8.88	20051	4.81	16978	4.07
2008	38703	9.17	21428	5.08	17275	4.09
2009	40293	9.44	22178	5.20	18115	4.24
2010	47052	10.89	25404	5.88	21648	5.01
2011	47256	10.80	22140	5.06	25116	5.74
2012	51892	11.72	27271	6.16	24621	5.56
2013	48107	10.74	21332	4.76	26775	5.97

注:从2001年起市区数据包括萧山区和余杭区。

a) Figures in this table include Xiaoshan and Yuhang district since 2001.

2-08 分地区户籍人口自然变动情况(2013年)

Natural Changes of Registered Population by Region(2013)

地区 Region	出生 Birth		死亡 Death		自然增长 Natural Growth	
	人数(人) Birth Population (person)	出生率(‰) Birth Rate(‰)	人数(人) Death Population (person)	死亡率(‰) Death Rate(‰)	人数(人) Natural Growth Population (person)	自然增长率(‰) Natural Growth Rate(‰)
全市 Whole City	**70850**	**10.07**	**37544**	**5.34**	**33306**	**4.73**
市区 Urban District	48107	10.74	21332	4.76	26775	5.97
上城区 Shangcheng	2956	8.97	1677	5.09	1279	3.88
下城区 Xiacheng	3951	9.73	1684	4.15	2267	5.58
江干区 Jianggan	5899	12.69	1681	3.62	4218	9.07
拱墅区 Gongshu	3493	10.97	1310	4.11	2183	6.86
西湖区 Xihu	7323	11.26	2183	3.36	2140	7.9
高新(滨江)区 Hi-Tech(Binjiang)	2934	16.71	587	3.34	2347	13.37
萧山区 Xiaoshan	11513	9.29	6905	5.57	4608	3.72
余杭区 Yuhang	10038	11.11	5305	5.87	4733	5.24
桐庐县 Tonglu	3914	9.64	2583	6.36	1331	3.28
淳安县 Chun'an	4064	8.88	2587	5.65	1477	3.23
建德市 Jiande	4230	8.31	3859	7.58	371	0.73
富阳市 Fuyang	5860	8.90	3722	5.65	2138	3.25
临安市 Lin'an	4675	8.88	3461	6.57	1214	2.31

2-09 分地区户籍人口机械变动情况(2013年)

Mechanical Changes of Registered Population by Region(2013)

单位:人 (person)

地 区 Region	本年迁入人数 Number of the Persons Moved in(person)		本年迁出人数 Number of the Persons Moved Out(person)		本年净迁入人数 Net Persons Moved in
	省 内 From Zhejiang Province	省 外 From Other Provinces	省 内 To Zhejiang Province	省 外 To Other Provinces	
全 市 Whole City	**31447**	**45251**	**24119**	**23543**	**29036**
市 区 Urban District	27216	37836	17249	19955	27848
上城区 Shangcheng	1855	2340	547	926	2722
下城区 Xiacheng	2757	3568	2053	2095	2177
江干区 Jianggan	5438	6778	4579	5458	2179
拱墅区 Gongshu	2251	1774	1317	651	2057
西湖区 Xihu	6520	9343	5657	6929	3277
高新(滨江)区 Hi-Tech(Binjiang)	2400	2597	1187	1065	2745
萧山区 Xiaoshan	2182	4163	858	1586	3901
余杭区 Yuhang	3813	7273	1051	1245	8790
桐庐县 Tonglu	821	1263	1017	610	457
淳安县 Chun'an	825	1403	1296	363	569
建德市 Jiande	730	1389	1762	920	-563
富阳市 Fuyang	1001	1759	1124	837	799
临安市 Lin'an	854	1601	1671	858	-74

2-10 计划生育情况(2013年)

Situations of Birth Control(2013)

单位:%　　(%)

地　区 Region		综合避孕率 Contraception Rate	计划生育率 Rate of Birth Under Control	独生子女领证率 The Only - child Certification Rate
全　市	**Whole City**	**86.26**	**96.94**	**39.38**
市　区	Urban District	84.72	97.73	43.94
上城区	Shangcheng	81.33	97.44	54.88
下城区	Xiacheng	81.71	97.33	43.18
江干区	Jianggan	87.11	97.84	50.77
拱墅区	Gongshu	83.54	97.11	47.39
西湖区	Xihu	86.42	97.02	32.94
高新(滨江)区	Hi - Tech(Binjiang)	83.38	98.12	32.60
萧山区	Xiaoshan	84.00	97.79	40.37
余杭区	Yuhang	86.49	98.39	51.43
桐庐县	Tonglu	88.22	96.06	32.01
淳安县	Chun'an	91.96	95.06	31.35
建德市	Jiande	88.04	94.41	28.18
富阳市	Fuyang	89.31	95.63	33.86
临安市	Lin'an	86.31	95.84	33.59

2－11 婚姻登记情况
Marriage Registration Situations

地　区 Region	2013			2012		
	准予登记结婚对数 Marriages Legally Registered(couples)	#再婚人数 Re－married (person)	离婚对数 Divorces (couples)	准予登记结婚对数 Marriages Legally Registered(couples)	#再婚人数 Re－married (person)	离婚对数 Divorces (couples)
全　市 Whole City	**72160**	**26393**	**18523**	**73566**	**18576**	**16247**
市　区 Urban District	48822	17632	12304	50634	9995	10496
#萧山区 Xiaoshan	10092	3025	2110	10470	2787	1971
余杭区 Yuhang	8299	3284	2119	8267	2904	1879
桐庐县 Tonglu	3815	1571	1149	3491	1438	1017
淳安县 Chun'an	4125	1584	977	4688	1517	898
建德市 Jiande	4774	1745	1220	4590	1546	1132
富阳市 Fuyang	5775	2261	1534	5467	2266	1442
临安市 Lin'an	4849	2146	1339	4696	1814	1262

2-12 全市含规上私营单位

Number of Employed Persons Including

单位:人

地区、行业	Region, Sector	就业人员年末人数 Number of Employed Persons (year-end)	#非私营单位 Non-private
全市	**Total**	**4392574**	**2825625**
市区	Urban District	3747313	2493729
#上城区	Shangcheng District	256607	205906
下城区	Xiacheng District	271090	230404
江干区	Jianggan District	369137	193891
拱墅区	Gongshu District	381648	197381
西湖区	Xihu District	585742	479026
高新(滨江)区	Hi-Tech(Binjiang) District	276987	213683
萧山区	Xiaoshan District	945231	534155
余杭区	Yuhang District	432833	231947
桐庐县	Tonglu County	98246	44525
淳安县	Chun'an County	60658	37634
建德市	Jiande City	82067	48030
富阳市	Fuyang City	246605	111408
临安市	Lin'an City	157685	90299
按国民经济行业分组	**Grouped by Sector**		
农、林、牧、渔业	Farming, Forestry, Animal Husbandry & Fishery	1748	1698
采矿业	Mining	3243	1466
制造业	Manufacturing	1205583	726790
电力、热力、燃气及水生产和供应业	Production & Supply of Electricity, Heat, Gas & Water	22038	21016
建筑业	Construction	1592099	784670
批发和零售业	Wholesale & Retail Trades	252016	180494
交通运输、仓储和邮政业	Transportation, Storage and Posts	129239	111338
住宿和餐饮业	Hotels and Catering Services	107882	71643
信息传输、软件和信息技术服务业	Information Transmission, Software and Information Technology	126928	98208
金融业	Financial Intermediation	92510	91449
房地产业	Real Estate	112784	85876
租赁和商务服务业	Leasing and Business Services	132020	99759
科学研究、技术服务业	Scientific Research, Technical Services	111526	86237
水利、环境和公共设施管理业	Management of Water Conservancy, Environment and Public Facilities	47414	34162
居民服务、修理和其他服务业	Service to Households, Repair and Other Services	19725	8601
教育	Education	174554	169145
卫生和社会工业	Health Care and Social Work	101842	96994
文化、体育和娱乐业	Culture, Sports and Entertainment	27228	23884
公共管理、社会保障和社会组织	Public Management, Social Security and Social Organizations	132195	132195

注:2012 年开始在岗职工口径包含劳务派遣人员。

就业人员数(2013 年)
Units Above Designated Size(2013)

(person)

女性 Female	#非私营单位 Non - private	在岗职工年末人数 Staff and Workers at Year - end	#非私营单位 Non - private	其他就业人员年末人数 Other Employed Persons at Year - end	#非私营单位 Non - private
1330684	**904314**	**4110984**	**2661330**	**281590**	**164295**
1108795	781985	3503013	2344353	244300	149376
101366	86202	231079	182161	25528	23745
108925	92382	256111	218054	14979	12350
78851	50734	313689	185248	55448	8643
80777	49874	355008	178033	26640	19348
154557	125723	535343	440870	50399	38156
83000	66517	267326	205895	9661	7788
268376	149137	917274	518747	27957	15408
154417	87788	417551	223687	15282	8260
35221	18830	91532	41608	6714	2917
24525	13418	55034	35526	5624	2108
30787	17694	75822	44786	6245	3244
78270	42313	232413	107813	14192	3595
53086	30074	153170	87244	4515	3055
505	490	1666	1617	82	81
550	217	3208	1439	35	27
504337	285148	1189068	716831	16515	9959
5306	5058	21544	20522	494	494
129089	44879	1422846	715881	169253	68789
130163	93540	242645	172739	9371	7755
32762	27897	126162	108588	3077	2750
60147	40025	96478	61185	11404	10458
46817	37703	125378	97112	1550	1096
49854	49311	85373	84371	7137	7078
42434	31887	107432	82123	5352	3753
47612	32374	124995	94188	7025	5571
34159	26599	101686	78267	9840	7970
18148	13861	42857	30385	4557	3777
10195	3642	18780	8202	945	399
101779	99448	162288	157057	12266	12088
66817	63819	91338	86781	10504	10213
13422	11828	24127	20929	3101	2955
36588	36588	123113	123113	9082	9082

a) Since 2012, the number of fully employed staff included the labor dispatch personnel.

2－13 全市含规上私营单位

Everage Number of Employed Persons

单位：人

地区、行业	Region, Sector	就业人员年平均人数 Annual Average Number of Staff and Workers (year－end)	#非私营单位 Non－private
全市	**Total**	**4282081**	**2761756**
市区	Urban District	3651755	2436141
#上城区	Shangcheng District	260322	208351
下城区	Xiacheng District	267551	224787
江干区	Jianggan District	354479	195710
拱墅区	Gongshu District	360141	178448
西湖区	Xihu District	569200	465413
高新(滨江)区	Hi－Tech(Binjiang) District	273027	210700
萧山区	Xiaoshan District	904684	507926
余杭区	Yuhang District	427893	231376
桐庐县	Tonglu County	96651	44516
淳安县	Chun'an County	59009	36868
建德市	Jiande City	80893	47704
富阳市	Fuyang City	237815	107055
临安市	Lin'an City	155958	89472
按国民经济行业分组	**Grouped by Sector**		
农、林、牧、渔业	Farming, Forestry, Animal Husbandry & Fishery	1746	1695
采矿业	Mining	3246	1456
制造业	Manufacturing	1212260	731359
电力、热力、燃气及水生产和供应业	Production & Supply of Electricity, Heat, Gas & Water	21530	20503
建筑业	Construction	1488342	725088
批发和零售业	Wholesale & Retail Trades	246761	176169
交通运输、仓储和邮政业	Transportation, Storage and Posts	127722	110333
住宿和餐饮业	Hotels and Catering Services	109946	73305
信息传输、软件和信息技术服务业	Information Transmission, Software and Information Technology	124626	96569
金融业	Financial Intermediation	91450	90330
房地产业	Real Estate	113363	86683
租赁和商务服务业	Leasing and Business Services	131941	100844
科学研究、技术服务业	Scientific Research, Technical Services	108852	84425
水利、环境和公共设施管理业	Management of Water Conservancy, Environment and Public Facilities	47757	34329
居民服务、修理和其他服务业	Service to Households, Repair and Other Services	19245	8695
教育	Education	175867	170566
卫生和社会工作	Health Care and Social Work	98790	94124
文化、体育和娱乐业	Culture, Sports and Entertainment	27268	23914
公共管理、社会保障和社会组织	Public Management, Social Security and Social Organizations	131369	131369

注：2012 年开始在岗职工口径包含劳务派遣人员。

平均人员数(2013 年)

Including Units Above Designated Size(2013)

(person)

在岗职工年平均人数 Staff and Workers	#非私营单位 Non - private	其他就业人员平均人数 Average Number of Other Employed Persons	#非私营单位 Non - private
3997158	**2586232**	**284923**	**175524**
3402222	2274819	249533	161322
232720	182507	27602	25844
252284	212152	15267	12635
302833	184721	51646	10989
333744	159438	26397	19010
519308	428363	49892	37050
261955	201489	11072	9211
877312	491908	27372	16018
412570	223053	15323	8323
89907	41553	6744	2963
54345	35098	4664	1770
74824	44445	6069	3259
224169	103737	13646	3318
151691	86580	4267	2892
1667	1617	79	78
3182	1421	64	35
1195461	720911	16799	10448
21061	20034	469	469
1317074	646833	171268	78255
237796	168815	8965	7354
124999	107910	2723	2423
98655	62928	11291	10377
123395	95793	1231	776
84045	83065	7405	7265
108054	83066	5309	3617
125016	95259	6925	5585
100015	77351	8837	7074
43258	30551	4499	3778
18362	8298	883	397
160058	154905	15809	15661
88456	84063	10334	1061
24294	21102	2974	2812
122310	122310	9059	9059

a) Since 2012, the number of fully employed staff included the labor dispatch personnel.

2－14　三次产业就业人员人数

Number of Employed Persons by Three Industries

单位:万人　　(10000 persons)

指标名称	Item	2013 年末 (End of 2013)	2012 年末 (End of 2012)
全市总计	**Total**	**650.51**	**644.43**
第一产业	Primary Industry	70.07	70.39
第二产业	Secondary Industry	291.51	290.01
第三产业	Tertiary Industry	288.93	284.03
市　　区	**Urban District**	**478.53**	**474.06**
第一产业	Primary Industry	23.14	23.85
第二产业	Secondary Industry	226.64	225.34
第三产业	Tertiary Industry	228.75	224.87

主要统计指标解释

人口数 指一定时点、一定地区范围内的有生命的个人的总和。

年度统计的年末人口数是指每年 12 月 31 日 24 时的人口数。

出生率(又称粗出生率) 指一定时期内(通常为一年)平均每千人所出生的人数的比率,一般用千分率表示。计算公式:

$$出生率=\frac{年出生人数}{年平均人数}\times 1000‰$$

出生人数是指活产婴儿,即胎儿脱离母体时(不管怀孕月数),有过呼吸或其他生命现象。

年平均人数是年初、年底人口数的平均数,也可用年中人口数代替。

死亡率(又称粗死亡率) 指一定时期内(通常为一年)一定地区的死亡人数与同期平均人数(或期中人数)之比,一般用千分率表示。计算公式:

$$死亡率=\frac{年死亡人数}{年平均人数}\times 1000‰$$

人口自然增长率 指一定时期内(通常为一年)人口自然增加数(出生人数减死亡人数)与该时期内平均人数(或期中人数)之比,一般用千分率表示。计算公式:

$$人口自然增长率=\frac{本年出生人数-本年死亡人数}{年平均人数}\times 1000‰$$

人口自然增长率 = 人口出生率 - 人口死亡率

就业人员 指从事一定社会劳动并取得劳动报酬或经营收入人员,包括各级机关企事业单位就业人员、个体户主、个体就业人员、农村就业人员及其他未包括的就业人员(包括宗教职业者、现役军人等)。

单位就业人员 是指在各级国家机关、政党机关、社会团体及企业、事业单位中工作,并取得劳动报酬的全部人员。包括在岗职工、再就业的离退休人员、民办教师、在各单位中工作的外方人员和港、澳、台方人员以及聘用的外单位下岗职工、兼职人员、从事第二职业人员、使用的劳务派遣人员和服务外包人员。各单位的就业人员反映了实际参加生产或工作的全部劳动力。

在岗职工 指在本单位工作并由单位支付劳动报酬的人员,以及在本单位有工作岗位,但由于学习、病伤产假等原因暂未工作,仍由单位支付劳动报酬的人,包括本单位临时性用工并支付劳动报酬的人员。2012 年开始在岗职工包含劳务派遣人员。

非私营单位 包括独立核算的机关、事业单位和国有、集体、股份制、港澳台投资及外商投资企业等。

含规上私营单位 包括独立核算的非私营单位、规模以上私营工业企业、限额以上私营批发零售住宿餐饮企业、私营房地产开发经营企业、具有资质的私营建筑企业、规模以上私营服务企业、100 人及以上的规模以下私营企业。

Explanatory Notes on Main Statistical Indicators

Total Population refers to the total number of people alive at a certain point of time within a given area. The annual statistics on total population is taken at midnight, the 31st of December .

Birth Rate (or Crude Birth Rate) refers to the ratio of the number of births to the average population during a certain period of time (usually a year) ,which is often expressed in ‰. The following formula is used:

$$\text{Birth Rate} = \frac{\text{Number of Births}}{\text{Average Number of Population}} \times 1000‰$$

Number of births refers to live births, i. e. the births when babies had showed any vital phenomena regardless of the length of pregnancy.

Annual Average Number of Population is the average of the number of population at the beginning of the year and that at the end of the year. Sometimes it is substituted for with the mid – year population.

Death Rate (or Crude Death Rate) refers to the ratio of the number of deaths to the average population (or mid – year population) during a certain period of time (usually a year) ,which is often expressed in ‰. The following formula is used:

$$\text{Death Rate} = \frac{\text{Number of Deaths}}{\text{Annual Average Number of Population}} \times 1000‰$$

Natural Growth Rate of Population refers to the ratio of natural increase in population (number of births minus number of deaths) in a certain period of time (usually a year) to the average population(or mid – year population) of the same period, which is often expressed in ‰. The following formulas are applied:

$$\text{Natural Growth Rate of Population} = \frac{\text{Number of Births} - \text{Number of Deaths}}{\text{Average Number of Population}} \times 1000‰$$

Natural Growth Rate of Population = Birth Rate – Death Rate

Employed Persons refer to persons who are engaged in social labour and receive remuneration payment or earn business income, including all employees of government, enterprises and institutions, self – employed workers, employed persons in the rural areas and other employed workers(including religious professionals, servicemen, etc.).

Persons Employed in Various Units refer to all the persons who are working in government agencies of various levels, political and party organizations, social organizations, enterprises, institutions, and receiving wages or other forms of payment. Including fully employed staff and works, re – employed retirees, teachers in schools run by the local people, foreigners and Chinese compatriots from Hong Kong, Macao, and Taiwan working in various units, part – time employees, employees of other units working temporarily, employees holding the second job, dispatch personnels and outsourcing staff. Persons Employed in various units reflect the actual total labor force which are engaged in the production or work.

Fully Employed Staff and Workers refer to persons who work in, and receive wages from their working units, as well as persons who have their work posts, but are temporarily absent from work for reasons of study or on sick, injury or maternal leave and still receive wages from their working units. including persons who are engaged in temporary employment and receive remuneration payment. Since 2012, the number of fully employed staff included the labor dispatch personnel.

Non – private Units include independent accounting units of government organizations and institutions, state – owned enterprises, collective – owned enterprises, and enterprises with funds from Hongkong, Macao and Taiwan.

Including Units above Designated Size include independent accounting units of non – private, private industrial enterprises above designated size, private enterprises above designated size of wholesale & retail trades, hotels, catering serrices, private enterprises for real estate development, private construction enterprises with qualification grade, private enterprises of service industry above designated size, private enterprises below designated size with at least 100 employed persons.

三、农业

Ⅲ.AGRICULTURE

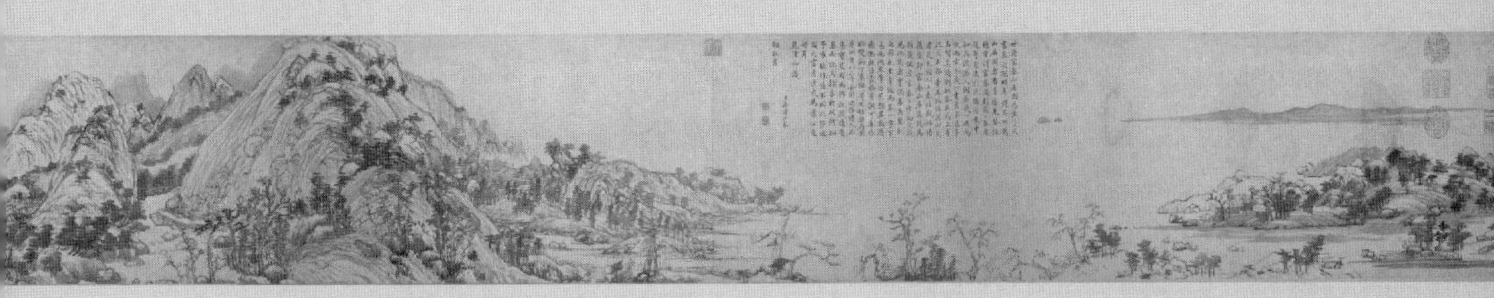

3

农　业
Agriculture

主要统计指标
Major Statistical Indicators

农村机械总动力	Total Power of Agricultural Machinery	348.42	万千瓦	(10, 000 kw)
为上年	As Compared with the Preceding Year	101.6	%	(%)
农村就业人员数	Total Employed Persons in Rural Areas	279.91	万人	(10, 000 persons)
为上年	As Compared with the Preceding Year	108.8	%	(%)
农林牧渔业总产值	Gross Output Value of Farming,Forestry,Animal Husbandry and Fishery	399.37	亿元	(100 million yuan)
为上年	As Compared with the Preceding Year	103.9	%	(%)
粮食总产量	Total Output of Grain Crops	95.92	万吨	(10, 000 tons)
为上年	As Compared with the Preceding Year	99.0	%	(%)
肉类产量	Total Output of Meat	34.04	万吨	(10, 000 tons)
为上年	As Compared with the Preceding Year	101.6	%	(%)

3-01 农村基本情况
Basic Situations of Rural Areas

指　　标		Item		1995	2000	2005	2010	2011	2012	2013
农村基层组织		**Rural Grassroots Units**								
乡镇政府	(个)	Number of Township & Town Governments	(unit)	230	234	149	128	109	109	105
#镇政府	(个)	Number of Town Governments	(unit)	134	140	110	97	86	86	82
农村街道办事处	(个)	Subdistrict Offices in Rural Areas	(unit)	–	–	–	38	49	48	47
农村居民委员会	(个)	Neighborhood Committees in Rural Areas	(unit)	–	–	–	22	22	24	21
农村社区居委会	(个)	Community Residents Committees in Rural Areas	(unit)	–	–	–	335	329	213	216
村民委员会	(个)	Number of Villagers´Committees	(unit)	4681	4616	3681	2098	2081	2078	2058
村民小组	(万个)	Villager Group	(10000 units)	3.61	3.53	3.43	3.26	3.27	3.21	3.19
农村就业人员		**Total Employed Persons in Rural Areas**								
农村就业人员合计	(万人)	Labor Force in Rural Areas	(10000 persons)	257.70	247.11	267.05	261.77	262.10	257.30	279.91
#外出就业人员	(万人)	Labor Force Working Outside	(10000 persons)	–	–	–	48.01	51.46	51.03	51.95
按性别分		Grouped by Sex								
男性	(万人)	Male	(10000 persons)	137.57	130.37	141.43	138.18	137.33	134.85	145.70
女性	(万人)	Female	(10000 persons)	120.13	116.74	125.62	123.59	124.77	122.45	134.21
按行业分		Grouped by Sector								
农林牧渔业	(万人)	Farming, Forestry, Animal Husbandry & Fishery	(10000 persons)	136.65	116.05	88.82	73.24	69.39	66.99	66.10
工　　业	(万人)	Industry	(10000 persons)	63.40	59.27	85.50	93.70	97.00	96.41	108.26
建　筑　业	(万人)	Construction	(10000 persons)	12.04	13.02	16.51	18.68	19.55	19.88	20.84
交通运输、仓储业及邮电通讯业	(万人)	Transportation, Storage, Post & Telecommunications	(10000 persons)	8.67	9.29	11.22	11.48	–	–	–
批发、零售贸易、餐饮业	(万人)	Wholesale, Retail Trade & Catering Services	(10000 persons)	7.28	10.62	18.03	20.76	–	–	–
其它行业	(万人)	Other Trades	(10000 persons)	29.66	38.86	46.97	43.91	76.16	74.02	84.71

注:2002 年起农村住户数、农村人口包括农村居委会户数、人口和农村外来户户数、人口。
注:2013 年起农村就业人员统计范围由原来的常住一年改为常住半年以上。
a) From 2002, rural households and population in rural areas includes the natives and from the outside.
b) From 2013, the statistical coverage of labor force in rural area is changed to those who live in a place for half a year from one year.

3－02 分地区

Basic Situations of

指　　标		Item		全　市 Whole City	市　区 Urban District	#江干区 Jianggan	#西湖区 Xihu
农村基层组织		**Rural Grassroots Units**					
乡镇政府	（个）	Number of Township & Town Governments	(unit)	105	27	4	2
#镇政府	（个）	Number of Town Governments	(unit)	82	27	4	2
农村街道办事处	（个）	Sub－district office in Rural Areas	(unit)	47	30	－	2
农村居民委员会	（个）	Neighborhood Committees in Rural Areas	(unit)	21	－	－	－
农村社区居委会	（个）	Community Residents Committees in Rural Areas	(unit)	216	202	17	47
村民委员会	（个）	Number of Villagers′Committees	(unit)	2058	652	4	40
村民小组	（万个）	Villagers′Group	(10000 unit)	3.19	1.16	0.01	0.07
农村就业人员		**Total Employed Persons in Rural Areas**					
农村就业人员合计	（万人）	Labor Force in Rural Areas	(10000 persons)	279.91	148.97	3.49	8.79
#外出就业人员	（万人）	Labor Force Working Outside	(10000 persons)	51.95	18.02	1.27	1.67
农林牧渔业	（万人）	Farming, Forestry, Animal Husbandry & Fishery	(10000 persons)	66.10	22.45	0.48	2.02
工　　业	（万人）	Industry	(10000 persons)	108.26	68.80	1.10	2.00
建　筑　业	（万人）	Construction	(10000 persons)	20.84	11.99	0.18	0.87
其它行业	（万人）	Other Trades	(10000 persons)	84.71	45.73	1.73	3.90
农村基础设施水平		**Public Facilities in Rural Areas**					
自来水受益村数	（个）	Number of Villages with Access to Tap Water	(unit)	2058	652	4	40
通汽车村数	（个）	Number of Villages with Highways	(unit)	2058	652	4	40
通电话村数	（个）	Number of Villages with Telephone Communication	(unit)	2058	652	4	40

农村基本情况(2013 年)
Rural Areas by Region(2013)

#高新(滨江)区 Hi-Tech(Binjiang)	#萧山区 Xiaoshan	#余杭区 Yuhang	桐庐县 Tonglu	淳安县 Chun'an	建德市 Jiande	富阳市 Fuyan	临安市 Lin'an
–	15	6	10	23	13	19	13
–	15	6	6	11	12	13	13
3	11	13	4	–	3	5	5
–	–	–	–	–	10	–	11
19	70	49	–	–	10	4	–
–	411	188	183	425	232	279	287
–	0.71	0.36	0.26	0.39	0.46	0.46	0.46
5.78	71.01	59.58	20.87	23.63	23.85	33.96	28.63
0.76	7.52	6.80	5.24	8.54	8.50	6.18	5.47
0.26	11.59	7.94	5.42	11.20	9.37	10.24	7.42
2.43	35.63	27.64	8.51	1.61	6.11	12.49	10.74
0.58	7.24	3.12	1.58	1.17	2.17	2.40	1.53
2.51	16.55	20.88	5.36	9.65	6.20	8.83	8.94
–	411	188	183	425	232	279	287
–	411	188	183	425	232	279	287
–	411	188	183	425	232	279	287

3-03 农林牧渔业总产值(1978-2013)

Gross Output Value of Agriculture, Forestry, Animal Husbandry and Fishery(1978-2013)

单位:万元 (10000 yuan)

年 份 Year	农林牧渔业总产值 Gross Output Value	#农业产值 Farming	#种植业产值 Planting	林业产值 Forestry	牧业产值 Animal Husbandry	渔业产值 Fishery
1978	85922	67365	64378	3430	14474	653
1979	115649	84727	81989	4629	25216	1077
1980	112377	79006	76059	7262	25015	1094
1981	120792	87354	81659	8309	23799	1330
1982	150606	107566	103346	8912	31801	2327
1983	148878	103685	96272	9800	32693	2700
1984	177029	122567	115286	14769	35922	3771
1985	212961	136893	126026	19095	50110	6863
1986	238285	150803	138254	19990	58197	9295
1987	281326	173080	155960	26427	70129	11690
1988	358500	208838	187648	31434	101013	17215
1989	386805	225969	201389	27857	113952	19027
1990	421045	260031	233055	26962	113424	20628
1991	463578	284275	254834	37763	117458	24082
1992	497915	300828	256833	35589	133867	27631
1993	600760	365124	300736	47476	154766	33394
1994	812473	496392	415366	58627	217217	40237
1995	996440	620057	526328	81321	244054	51008
1996	1173294	740202	617573	95740	271652	65700
1997	1287650	797812	665172	114510	294153	81175
1998	1367578	845106	701850	121197	289085	112190
1999	1414737	876685	737406	126000	293495	118557
2000	1526530	903322	754311	136848	331563	154797
2001	1649978	965005	816884	149264	362303	173406
2002	1685036	932995	886285	162227	391844	197970
2003	1890129	991556	949138	182595	417798	232599
2004	1982683	1010947	972594	206787	457619	234080
2005	2194799	1136559	1103981	233039	495900	270810
2006	2253822	1224822	1191816	267748	490448	206082
2007	2471427	1308047	1279758	294707	585536	222601
2008	2737605	1408124	1374083	320212	636633	309270
2009	2897371	1497362	1462791	362317	642892	325626
2010	3163392	1698775	1673470	329278	705596	349011
2011	3570744	1907895	1882876	348535	836532	389985
2012	3843403	2077191	2041481	381802	868504	420006
2013	3993712	2161055	2120540	408170	911324	407292

注:本表按当年价格计算;从2003年起农林牧渔总产值包括农林牧渔业服务业产值(下同)。

a) Data in this table are calculated at current prices. From 2003, Gross Output Value includes the value of service for the Agriculture, forestry, animal husbandry and fishery sector.

3-04 农林牧渔业总产值构成(1978-2013)

Composition of Gross Output Value of Agriculture, Forestry, Animal Husbandry and Fishery(1978-2013)

单位:% (%)

年份 Year	农林牧渔业总产值 Gross Output Value	#农业产值 Farming	#种植业产值 Planting	林业产值 Forestry	牧业产值 Animal Husbandry	渔业产值 Fishery
1978	100.0	78.4	74.9	4.0	16.8	0.8
1979	100.0	73.3	70.9	4.0	21.8	0.9
1980	100.0	70.3	67.7	6.5	22.2	1.0
1981	100.0	72.3	67.6	6.9	19.7	1.1
1982	100.0	71.4	68.6	5.9	21.1	1.6
1983	100.0	69.6	64.7	6.6	22.0	1.8
1984	100.0	69.2	65.1	8.3	20.3	2.2
1985	100.0	64.3	59.2	9.0	23.5	3.2
1986	100.0	63.3	58.0	8.4	24.4	3.9
1987	100.0	61.5	55.4	9.4	24.9	4.2
1988	100.0	58.2	52.3	8.8	28.2	4.8
1989	100.0	58.4	52.1	7.2	29.5	4.9
1990	100.0	61.8	55.4	6.4	26.9	4.9
1991	100.0	61.3	55.0	8.2	25.3	5.2
1992	100.0	60.4	51.6	7.2	26.9	5.5
1993	100.0	60.8	50.1	7.9	25.8	5.5
1994	100.0	61.1	51.1	7.2	26.7	5.0
1995	100.0	62.2	52.8	8.2	24.5	5.1
1996	100.0	63.1	52.6	8.2	23.1	5.6
1997	100.0	62.0	51.7	8.9	22.8	6.3
1998	100.0	61.8	51.3	8.9	21.1	8.2
1999	100.0	62.0	52.1	8.9	20.7	8.4
2000	100.0	59.2	49.4	9.0	21.7	10.1
2001	100.0	58.5	52.2	9.0	22.0	10.5
2002	100.0	55.4	52.6	9.6	23.3	11.7
2003	100.0	52.5	50.2	9.7	22.1	12.3
2004	100.0	51.0	49.1	10.4	23.1	11.8
2005	100.0	51.8	50.3	10.6	22.6	12.3
2006	100.0	54.3	52.9	11.9	21.8	9.1
2007	100.0	52.9	51.8	11.9	23.7	9.0
2008	100.0	51.4	50.2	11.7	23.3	11.3
2009	100.0	51.7	50.5	12.5	22.2	11.2
2010	100.0	53.7	52.9	10.4	22.3	11.0
2011	100.0	53.4	52.7	9.8	23.4	10.9
2012	100.0	54.0	53.1	9.9	22.6	10.9
2013	100.0	54.1	53.1	10.2	22.8	10.2

注:本表按当年价格计算。

a) Figures in value terms in this table are calculated at current prices.

3－05 主要年份农林牧渔业分项产值

Gross Output Value of Agriculture, Forestry, Animal Husbandry and Fishery by Branch in Main Years

单位:万元 (10000 yuan)

指 标	Item	1995	2000	2005	2010	2011	2012	2013
农林牧渔业总产值(现价)	**Gross Output Value (Current Price)**	**996440**	**1526530**	**2194799**	**3163392**	**3570744**	**3843403**	**3993712**
#一、农业产值	**Farming**	**620057**	**903322**	**1136559**	**1698775**	**1907895**	**2077191**	**2161055**
1. 种植业产值	Planting	526328	754311	1103981	1673470	1882876	2041481	2120540
粮食	Grain	262321	208546	178981	215990	230246	241471	248550
油料	Oil－bearing Crops	19675	19583	21608	31137	35245	35482	37649
棉花	Cotton	11829	2205	1146	1255	1155	1424	1571
麻类	Fiber Crops	3863	384	176	42	21	16	25
甘蔗	Sugarcane	14274	23815	19075	18756	20067	18417	18496
烟叶	Tobacco	1	5	7	1	2	2	1
药材类	Crude Drugs	1725	6005	15800	42927	50530	60454	67623
蔬菜	Vegetables	151614	303583	357734	535623	607469	664937	665429
茶、桑、果、坚果	Tea, Mulberry & Fruits	48599	106727	254379	484261	565641	605200	630899
其他	Others	12427	83458	255075	343478	372500	414078	450297
2. 其他农业产值	Other Farming	93729	149011	32578	25305	25019	35710	40515
二、林业产值	**Forestry**	**81321**	**136848**	**233039**	**329278**	**348535**	**381802**	**408170**
人造林木生长	Artificial Forestry	11286	18226	23140	27964	23828	32802	33734
林产品	Forest Products	45123	89914	168348	184740	197815	214198	227962
竹木采伐	Lumbering	24912	28708	41551	82063	90806	93552	103425
采集野生植物	Wild Plant collected				34511	36086	41250	43049
三、牧业产值	**Animal Husbandry**	**244054**	**331563**	**495900**	**705596**	**836532**	**868504**	**911324**
牲畜	Livestock Raising	143879	175732	292025	430193	534840	556742	589952
家禽饲养	Poultry Raising	35302	65548	68631	70201	69653	82132	77869
活的畜禽产品	Livestock Products	37197	44098	68143	109625	124024	125886	132151
捕猎野兽野禽	Hunting Wild Beast and Wild Fowl	491	2102	2856	4455	4698	5454	5126
其他动物饲养	Other Animals Raising	27185	44083	64245	91122	103317	98290	106226
四、渔业产值	**Fishery**	**51008**	**154797**	**270810**	**349011**	**389985**	**420006**	**407292**

3－06 主要年份农林牧渔业分项产值构成

Composition of Gross Output Value of Agriculture, Forestry, Animal Husbandry and Fishery by Branch in Main Years

单位:% (%)

指　标	Item	1995	2000	2005	2010	2011	2012	2013
农林牧渔业总产值(现价)	**Gross Output Value (Current Price)**	**100**	**100**	**100**	**100**	**100**	**100**	**100**
#一、农业产值	**Farming**	**62.2**	**59.2**	**51.8**	**53.7**	**53.4**	**54.0**	**54.1**
1. 种植业产值	Planting	52.8	49.4	50.3	52.9	52.7	53.1	53.1
粮食	Grain	26.3	13.7	8.2	6.8	6.4	6.3	6.2
油料	Oil Plants	2.0	1.3	1.0	1.0	1.0	0.9	0.9
棉花	Cotton	1.2	0.1	0.1	–	–	–	–
麻类	Fiber Crops	0.4	–	–	–	–	–	–
甘蔗	Sugarcane	1.4	1.6	0.9	0.6	0.6	0.6	0.5
烟叶	Tobacco	–	–	–	–	–	–	–
药材类	Crude Drugs	0.2	0.4	0.7	1.4	1.4	1.6	1.7
蔬菜	Vegetables	15.2	19.9	16.3	16.9	17.0	17.3	16.7
茶、桑、果、坚果	Tea, Mulberry & Fruits	4.9	7.0	11.6	15.3	15.8	15.7	15.8
其他	Others	1.2	5.4	11.5	10.9	10.5	10.7	11.3
2. 其他农业产值	Other Farming	9.4	9.8	1.5	0.8	0.7	0.9	1.0
二、林业产值	**Forestry**	**8.2**	**9.0**	**10.6**	**10.4**	**9.8**	**9.9**	**10.2**
人造林木生长	Artificial Forestry	1.2	1.2	1.1	0.9	0.7	0.8	0.8
林产品	Forest Products	4.5	5.9	7.6	5.8	5.5	5.6	5.7
竹木采伐	Lumbering	2.5	1.9	1.9	2.6	2.5	2.4	2.6
采集野生植物	Wild Plant collected				1.1	1.1	1.1	1.1
三、牧业产值	**Animal Husbandry**	**24.5**	**21.7**	**22.6**	**22.3**	**23.4**	**22.6**	**22.8**
牲畜	Livestock Raising	14.4	11.5	13.3	13.6	15.0	14.5	14.8
家禽饲养	Poultry Raising	3.6	4.3	3.1	2.2	2.0	2.1	1.9
活的畜禽产品	Livestock Products	3.7	2.9	3.2	3.5	3.5	3.3	3.3
捕猎野兽野禽	Hunting Wild Beast and Wild Fowl	–	0.1	0.1	0.1	0.1	0.1	0.1
其他动物饲养	Other Animals Raising	2.8	2.9	2.9	2.9	2.8	2.6	2.7
四、渔业产值	**Fishery**	**5.1**	**10.1**	**12.3**	**11.0**	**10.9**	**10.9**	**10.2**

3－07 分地区农林牧

Gross Output Value of Agriculture, Forestry,

单位:万元

指　　标	Item	全　市 Whole City	市　区 Urban District	#江干区 Jianggan	#西湖区 Xihu
合　　计	**Gross Output Value**	**3993712**	**1802900**	**10340**	**64479**
#一、农业产值	**Farming**	**2161055**	**946139**	**8868**	**23757**
(一)种植业产值	Planting	2120540	944124	8868	23536
#副产品产值	By－products	13392	6634	－	182
1. 粮食作物	Grain	248550	122915	－	3379
谷　　物	Cereal	175855	91733	－	2506
豆　　类	Beans	36075	18503	－	413
薯　　类	Tubers	36620	12679	－	460
2. 油　　料	Oil Plants	37649	9804	－	79
3. 棉　　花	Cotton	1571	1039	－	－
4. 麻　　类	Fiber Crops	25	13	－	－
5. 甘　　蔗	Sugarcane	18496	13401	－	176
6. 烟　　叶	Tobacco	1	－	－	－
7. 药 材 类	Crude Drugs	67623	699	－	39
8. 蔬　　菜	Vegetables	665429	345590	7952	9652
9. 茶、桑、果、坚果	Tea, Mulberry & Fruits	630899	139700	180	4430
10. 其　　他	Others	450297	310963	736	5781
(二)其他农业产值	Other Farming	40515	2015	－	221
二、林业产值	**Forestry**	**408170**	**78874**	**17**	**641**
1. 人造林木生长	Artificial Forestry	33734	12769	17	577
2. 林产品	Forest Products	227962	41190	－	49
3. 村及村以下竹木采伐	Lumbering	103425	22349	－	15
4. 采集野生植物	Wild Plant collected	43049	2566	－	－
三、牧业产值	**Animal Husbandry**	**911324**	**405707**	**1065**	**3702**
1. 牲畜	Livestock	589952	327463	1065	2946
2. 家禽饲养	Poultry Raising	77869	41950	－	448
3. 活的畜禽产品	Livestock Products	132151	24471	－	212
4. 捕猎野兽野禽	Hunting Wild Beast and Wild Fowl	5126	644	－	－
5. 其他动物饲养	Other Animals Raising	106226	11179	－	96
四、渔业产值	**Fishery**	**407292**	**299658**	**315**	**35477**

注:本表按当年价格计算。

渔业总产值(2013 年)

Animal Husbandry and Fishery by Region(2013)

(10000 yuan)

#高新(滨江)区 Hi-Tech(Binjiang)	#萧山区 Xiaoshan	#余杭区 Yuhang	桐庐县 Tonglu	淳安县 Chun'an	建德市 Jiande	富阳市 Fuyang	临安市 Lin'an
26681	**956805**	**719592**	**306317**	**403910**	**432228**	**534970**	**513387**
20501	**505215**	**374856**	**184848**	**268845**	**229620**	**295989**	**235614**
20501	505144	373133	179317	267975	215610	283371	230143
15	3005	3421	1010	1384	1172	1666	1526
391	46640	72234	31509	18523	21626	29098	24879
370	34462	54124	19141	10969	15910	22063	16039
18	10526	7546	6411	2243	2721	3643	2554
3	1652	10564	5957	5311	2995	3392	6286
–	5974	3751	8398	4735	5324	5892	3496
–	415	624	2	157	371	–	2
–	12	1	–	12	–	–	–
66	11095	2064	1762	1230	965	1085	53
–	–	–	–	1	–	–	–
–	54	606	2695	32928	17349	6853	7099
7049	204147	113820	48433	71995	59600	98064	41747
784	27427	97178	67323	121987	99966	82702	119221
12211	209380	82855	19195	16407	10409	59677	33646
–	71	1723	5531	870	14010	12618	5471
25	**11738**	**66380**	**26717**	**41906**	**22115**	**79243**	**159315**
16	1153	10933	402	8984	1711	5794	4074
9	8336	32796	16936	13164	9554	48745	98373
–	2102	20232	3752	9857	8371	11591	47505
–	147	2419	5627	9901	2479	13113	9363
2401	**295684**	**95544**	**65750**	**66719**	**146689**	**124850**	**101609**
2369	263801	56297	28461	33259	46340	82656	71773
32	16837	24612	3521	1143	10947	15541	4767
–	5618	12336	4750	3912	83726	8005	7287
–	313	331	1112	131	384	2254	601
–	9115	1968	27906	28274	5292	16394	17181
3754	**111123**	**144312**	**22894**	**21137**	**23409**	**31011**	**9183**

a) Data in this table are calculated at current prices.

3-08 主要农作物播种面积及产量

Sown Areas and Yield of Major Farm Crops

指 标	Item	2013			2012		
		播种面积（千公顷）Sown Area（1000 hectares）	总产量（吨）Total Output（ton）	公顷产量（公斤）Yield per Hectare（kg/hectare）	播种面积（千公顷）Sown Area（1000 hectares）	总产量（吨）Total Output（ton）	公顷产量（公斤）Yield per Hectare（kg/hectare）
农作物总计	**Total Farm Crops**	**365.68**	–	–	**370.12**	–	–
一、粮食作物合计	**Grain Crops**	**163.92**	**959224**	**5852**	**165.44**	**968847**	**5856**
#春粮	#Spring Grain	24.7	93813	3798	25.12	92612	3687
秋粮	Autumn Grain	137	851831	6218	138.47	864980	6246
(一)谷 物	Cereals	107.67	730519	6785	108.97	738452	6777
1.稻谷	Rice	70.61	559791	7928	71.99	569233	7907
①早稻及早中稻	Early Rice & Semi-late Rice	2.22	13580	6120	1.85	11255	6074
②晚稻及迟中稻	Late Rice & Semi-late Rice	68.39	546211	7986	70.14	557978	7956
#单季稻	#Single-crop Rice	66.64	533346	8004	68.28	544027	7968
2.小麦	Wheat	14.73	59143	4016	15.05	58850	3908
3.大麦	Barley	0.42	1703	4045	0.45	1774	3916
4.玉米	Corn	20.49	103578	5056	20.03	102059	5096
5.其他谷物	Other Cereals	1.42	6304	4421	1.45	6536	4523
(二)豆 类	Beans	33.36	105980	3177	33.44	105116	3143
1.大豆	Soybeans	24.52	79808	3254	24.7	79421	3215
2.蚕(豌)豆	Broad Beans	4.55	12528	2752	4.53	12205	2691
3.杂豆	Other Beans	4.29	13644	3184	4.21	13490	3208
(三)薯 类	Tubers	22.89	122725	5362	23.03	125279	5440

3－08 续表 continued

指 标	Item	2013 播种面积（千公顷）Sown Area (1000 hectares)	2013 总产量（吨）Total Output (ton)	2013 公顷产量（公斤）Yield per Hectare (kg/hectare)	2012 播种面积（千公顷）Sown Area (1000 hectares)	2012 总产量（吨）Total Output (ton)	2012 公顷产量（公斤）Yield per Hectare (kg/hectare)
二、油料合计	**Oil Plants**	**41.09**	**90151**	**2194**	**41.41**	**86601**	**2091**
1. 油菜籽	Rapeseeds	37.2	79826	2146	37.55	76589	2040
2. 花生	Peanuts	2.64	8376	3168	2.61	8049	3080
3. 芝麻	Sesame	1.25	1949	1559	1.25	1963	1565
三、棉花（皮棉）	**Cotton**	**0.56**	**825**	**1484**	**0.62**	**876**	**1413**
四、麻类合计	**Fiber Cropers**	**0.02**	**75**	**5000**	**0.01**	**33**	**3667**
五、甘蔗	**Sugar Crops**	**2.05**	**120139**	**58748**	**2.11**	**125148**	**59200**
六、烟叶	**Tobacco**	**–**	**1**	**–**	**–**	**2**	**2000**
七、药材类	**Crude Drugs**	**4.33**	**25823**	**5969**	**4.21**	**23266**	**5528**
八、蔬菜	**Vegetables**	**94.96**	**3053390**	**32156**	**97.24**	**3220538**	**33121**
九、果用瓜	**Melon as Fruit**	**11.37**	**404258**	**35555**	**11.92**	**421006**	**35328**
#西瓜	Watermelon	8.64	331299	38354	9.23	348790	37805
草莓	Strawberry	0.91	28427	31136	0.88	27383	31152
十、花卉园艺	**Flower Gardening**	**34.95**	**–**	**–**	**34.55**	**–**	**–**
十一、其他作物	**Others**	**12.43**	**–**	**–**	**12.61**	**–**	**–**
#绿肥	Green Manure	1.81	–	–	2.09	–	–

3 - 09 分地区粮食

Sown Areas and Yield of

指 标		Item		全市 Whole City	市区 Urban District	#江干区 Jianggan	#西湖区 Xihu	#高新(滨江)区 Hi - Tech (Binjiang)
一、粮食播种面积总计	**(公顷)**	**Sown Area of Grain Crops**	**(hectare)**	**163917**	**71526**	**-**	**2520**	**311**
春粮	(公顷)	Spring Grain	(hectare)	24698	12972	-	220	53
早稻	(公顷)	Early Rice	(hectare)	2219	1404	-	-	119
晚稻	(公顷)	Late Rice	(hectare)	68387	34164	-	1315	100
薯类	(公顷)	Tubers	(hectare)	22888	3681	-	247	2
玉米	(公顷)	Corn	(hectare)	20485	5510	-	263	14
大豆	(公顷)	Soybeans	(hectare)	24525	13260	-	292	4
杂豆	(公顷)	Other Beans	(hectare)	4285	1283	-	154	19
其他谷物	(公顷)	Other Cereals	(hectare)	1426	397	-	92	-
二、粮食总产量	**(吨)**	**Yield of Grain Crops**	**(ton)**	**959224**	**444901**	**1**	**17346**	**1626**
春粮	(吨)	Spring Grain	(ton)	93813	55393	-	730	147
早稻	(吨)	Early Rice	(ton)	13580	8873	-	-	629
晚稻	(吨)	Late Rice	(ton)	546211	278775	-	11332	679
薯类	(吨)	Tubers	(ton)	122725	23853	-	2118	36
玉米	(吨)	Corn	(ton)	103578	30981	1	1618	79
大豆	(吨)	Soybeans	(ton)	79808	45453	-	836	10
杂豆	(吨)	Other Beans	(ton)	13644	4515	-	402	46
其他谷物	(吨)	Other Cereals	(ton)	6304	2097	-	599	-
三、粮食平均每公顷产量	**(公斤)**	**Yield of Grain Crops per Hectare**	**(kg)**	**5852**	**6220**	**-**	**6883**	**5228**
春粮	(公斤)	Spring Grain	(kg)	3798	4270	-	3308	2774
早稻	(公斤)	Early Rice	(kg)	6120	6320	-	-	5286
晚稻	(公斤)	Late Rice	(kg)	7986	8160	-	8617	6790
薯类	(公斤)	Tubers	(kg)	5362	6480	-	8575	18000
玉米	(公斤)	Corn	(kg)	5056	5623	-	6152	5643
大豆	(公斤)	Soybeans	(kg)	3254	3428	-	2863	2500

播种面积及产量（2013 年）
Grain Crops by Region（2013）

#萧山区 Xiaoshan	#余杭区 Yuhang	桐庐县 Tonglu	淳安县 Chun'an	建德市 Jiande	富阳市 Fuyang	临安市 Lin'an
42108	**26307**	**15508**	**22094**	**16824**	**22816**	**15149**
9358	3241	1999	1912	2325	3068	2422
408	830	47	–	698	70	–
16883	15733	6239	3573	7599	10757	6055
1230	2202	2997	6685	2721	3703	3101
3417	1816	1952	6240	1624	2865	2294
10558	2406	2217	3839	1891	1952	1366
339	771	524	526	397	910	645
213	92	230	181	170	302	146
240129	**184548**	**91715**	**91856**	**96989**	**145259**	**88504**
42741	11400	5717	5491	7592	11415	8205
2573	5495	280	–	4008	419	–
132951	133113	49132	25417	59450	85373	48064
8184	13515	17848	28258	12986	21685	18095
19121	10162	10015	26819	8417	16905	10441
33451	11156	8261	7849	5745	7865	4635
1292	2775	1691	956	816	3621	2045
1132	366	999	406	629	1580	593
5703	**7015**	**5914**	**4157**	**5764**	**6367**	**5843**
4567	3518	2859	2871	3265	3721	3390
6306	6620	5957	–	5743	5986	–
7875	8461	7875	7114	7823	7937	7938
6654	6137	5955	4226	4773	5856	5835
5596	5595	5131	4298	5182	5901	4551
3168	4636	3728	2045	3037	4029	3393

3－10 油、菜、茶、

Statistics on Rapeseeds, Vegetables, Tea,

指标		Item		全市 Whole City	市区 Urban District	#江干区 Jianggan	#西湖区 Xihu	#高新(滨江)区 Hi－Tech (Binjiang)
一、油菜籽		**Rapeseeds**						
播种面积	(公顷)	Sown Area	(hectare)	37203	8298	－	181	－
每公顷产量	(公斤)	Yield per Hectare	(kg)	2146	2255	－	1851	－
总产量	(吨)	Total Output	(ton)	79826	18715	－	335	－
二、蔬菜		**Vegetables**						
播种面积	(公顷)	Sown Area	(hectare)	94955	55840	1586	2286	765
总产量	(吨)	Total Output	(ton)	3053390	1666154	39760	42245	30649
三、茶叶		**Tea**						
(一)茶园面积	(公顷)	Tea Garden Area	(hectare)	33448	6124	28	908	49
(二)总产量	(吨)	Output of Tea	(ton)	28503	8291	9	438	10
春　茶	(吨)	Spring Tea	(ton)	19541	5294	9	216	10
夏　茶	(吨)	Summer Tea	(ton)	5214	1403	－	48	－
秋　茶	(吨)	Autumn Tea	(ton)	3748	1594	－	174	－
四、桑蚕		**Silkworm Cocoons & Mulberry**						
(一)桑园总面积	(公顷)	Mulberry Garden Area	(hectare)	14363	1230	－	－	－
(二)蚕茧总产量	(吨)	Output of Silkworm Cocoons	(ton)	14502	263	－	－	－
春　茧	(吨)	Spring Silkworm Cocoons	(ton)	6862	168	－	－	－
夏　茧	(吨)	Summer Silkworm Cocoons	(ton)	1048	15	－	－	－
秋　茧	(吨)	Autumn Silkworm Cocoons	(ton)	6592	80	－	－	－

蚕、果生产情况(2013 年)
Silkworm Cocoons and Fruits Production(2013)

#萧山区 Xiaoshan	#余杭区 Yuhang	桐庐县 Tonglu	淳安县 Chun'an	建德市 Jiande	富阳市 Fuyang	临安市 Lin'an
4845	3272	6000	7076	5658	7329	2842
2391	2076	2009	1880	1818	2569	2335
11586	6794	12055	13303	10286	18831	6636
27979	22451	6156	8780	7407	10279	6493
1017575	517365	201805	329570	208979	485322	161560
1279	3517	3673	12913	3603	3688	3447
876	6830	1753	6525	2852	6610	2472
752	4214	1354	5004	1808	4134	1947
43	1301	235	816	844	1516	400
81	1315	164	705	200	960	125
102	1128	1946	6887	1373	1015	1912
6	257	3673	5182	951	2023	2410
6	162	1872	2174	406	935	1307
–	15	56	636	46	273	22
–	80	1745	2372	499	815	1081

3－10 续表

指标	Item	全市 Whole City	市区 Urban District	#江干区 Jianggan	#西湖区 Xihu	#高新(滨江)区 Hi－Tech (Binjiang)
五、水果生产	**Fruits**					
(一)果园面积合计 (公顷)	Area of Orchards (hectare)	28411	5723	－	81	87
柑桔园 (公顷)	Citrus (hectare)	9475	100	－	12	4
梨 园 (公顷)	Pears (hectare)	3921	1207	－	12	30
桃 园 (公顷)	Peaches (hectare)	3416	623	－	7	0
杨梅园 (公顷)	Red Bayberry (hectare)	2940	954	－	7	43
枇杷园 (公顷)	Loquat (hectare)	2420	882	－	－	－
柿子园 (公顷)	Persimmons (hectare)	899	110	－	3	－
葡萄园 (公顷)	Grapes (hectare)	963	349	－	38	3
其他果园 (公顷)	Others (hectare)	4377	1498	－	2	7
(二)水果总产量 (吨)	Yield of Fruits (ton)	814075	211688	－	2708	1867
柑 桔 (吨)	Citrus (ton)	178341	986	－	177	1
梨 头 (吨)	Pears (ton)	66179	15890	－	411	551
桃 子 (吨)	Peaches (ton)	72019	10467	－	125	0
杨 梅 (吨)	Red Bayberry (ton)	13583	2889	－	16	18
枇 杷 (吨)	Loquat (ton)	13396	6150	－	－	－
柿 子 (吨)	Persimmons (ton)	10709	1766	－	45	－
葡 萄 (吨)	Grapes (ton)	18054	5767	－	893	13
果用瓜 (吨)	Melon as Fruit (ton)	404258	163848	－	1005	1284
其他水果 (吨)	Others (ton)	37536	3925	－	36	－

continued

#萧山区 Xiaoshan	#余杭区 Yuhang	桐庐县 Tonglu	淳安县 Chun'an	建德市 Jiande	富阳市 Fuyang	临安市 Lin'an
2509	3046	2947	8879	6484	2682	1696
31	53	377	4665	3946	269	118
236	929	1004	550	308	564	288
199	417	476	874	337	766	340
691	213	476	404	550	354	202
1	881	125	832	498	72	11
82	25	45	444	170	102	28
160	148	124	69	32	253	136
1109	380	320	1041	643	302	573
115649	90124	86400	126431	175375	163617	50564
356	452	6294	66507	98763	5171	620
2168	12760	17238	4576	6232	17871	4372
1698	8644	7380	7135	4087	36904	6046
1805	1050	1890	1269	1215	4837	1483
21	6129	344	4093	1939	745	125
1209	512	556	3265	1119	3848	155
3213	1648	965	643	236	9223	1220
103448	56771	49435	26595	55698	80865	27817
1731	2158	2298	12348	6086	4153	8726

3-11 分地区畜牧业

Statistics on Animal

指　标		Item		全市 Whole City	市区 Urban District	#江干区 Jianggan	#西湖区 Xihu
一、生猪饲养		**Hogs**					
生猪年末存栏	（万头）	Being Raised at Year-end	(10000 heads)	219.23	121.04	-	1.17
#能繁殖的母猪	（万头）	#Reproducible	(10000 heads)	19.39	12.76	-	0.03
年内肥猪出栏	（万头）	Slaughtered Hogs of the Year	(10000 heads)	368.67	196.34	0.02	2.01
全年饲养量	（万头）	Number of Hogs Raised in the year	(10000 heads)	587.90	317.38	0.02	3.18
二、牛		**Cattle & Buffaloes**					
牛年末存栏	（头）	Being Raised at Year-end	(head)	19031	6449	-	7
#良种及改良种乳牛	（头）	#Improved Milk Cows	(head)	9559	5874	-	-
牛年内出栏	（头）	Slaughtered Cattle & Buffaloes of the Year	(head)	11455	1539	-	3
三、羊		**Sheep & Goats**					
羊年末存栏	（万只）	Being Raised at Year-end	(10000 heads)	20.75	12.39	3.69	0.04
羊年内出栏	（万只）	Slaughtered Sheep & Goats of the Year	(10000 heads)	25.61	12.13	2.31	0.05
四、家禽		**Poultry**					
家禽年末存栏	（万只）	Being Raised at Year-end	(10000 heads)	2010.95	543.31	-	14.17
家禽年内出栏	（万只）	Slaughtered Poultry of the Year	(10000 heads)	4080.34	2242.49	-	30.75
五、兔		**Rabbits**					
兔年末存栏	（万只）	Being Raised at Year-end	(10000 heads)	26.66	7.13	-	-
兔年内出栏	（万只）	Slaughtered Rabbits of the Year	(10000 heads)	93.62	9.47	-	-
六、年末养蜂箱数	**（箱）**	**Beehives**	(case)	**162252**	**19001**	**-**	**-**
七、畜禽产品产量		**Output of Livestock Products**					
1. 肉类产量	（吨）	Output of Meat	(ton)	340380	179324	750	1929
#猪　肉	（吨）	Pork	(ton)	270332	142487	13	1510

渔业生产(2013 年)
Husbanday and Fishery by Region(2013)

#高新(滨江)区 Hi - Tech(Binjiang)	#萧山区 Xiaoshan	#余杭区 Yuhang	桐庐县 Tonglu	淳安县 Chun'an	建德市 Jiande	富阳市 Fuyang	临安市 Lin'an
0.28	110.30	8.76	13.06	17.78	21.81	24.14	21.40
0.05	11.55	1.09	0.78	0.77	1.98	1.45	1.65
0.94	165.33	27.39	22.51	23.69	26.35	57.22	42.56
1.22	275.63	36.15	35.57	41.47	48.16	81.36	63.96
–	2296	376	2333	1858	1643	3403	3345
–	2104	–	–	–	301	1452	1932
–	114	672	1579	807	990	4126	2414
–	4.16	4.47	1.30	0.23	1.61	3.00	2.22
–	4.74	5.01	1.85	0.23	0.92	8.22	2.26
0.80	366.47	160.59	86.43	47.26	1005.11	239.29	89.55
1.75	1035.22	1173.57	135.66	54.20	716.98	777.03	153.98
–	1.21	5.92	3.61	0.33	1.70	3.00	10.89
–	2.32	7.15	7.51	0.64	4.63	15.93	55.44
–	**16878**	**2123**	**64505**	**25414**	**11937**	**28663**	**12732**
854	133625	41553	19633	19242	29697	55835	36649
830	117135	22548	16729	18234	18461	42071	32350

指 标	Item	全市 Whole City	市区 Urban District	#江干区 Jianggan	#西湖区 Xihu	#高新(滨江)区 Hi－Tech (Binjiang)
牛 肉 (吨)	Beef (ton)	1811	270	－	1	－
羊 肉 (吨)	Mutton (ton)	5054	2824	737	8	－
兔 肉 (吨)	Rabbit Meat (ton)	1537	189	－	－	－
禽 肉 (吨)	Poultry Meat (ton)	61247	33554	－	410	24
2. 禽蛋产量 (吨)	Poultry Eggs (ton)	152883	24126	－	424	－
3. 蜂蜜产量 (吨)	Honey (ton)	22588	1989	－	－	－
4. 蜂皇浆产量 (公斤)	Honey Tonic (kg)	542556	102569	－	－	－
5. 牛奶产量 (吨)	Milk (ton)	40519	24890	－	－	－
6. 兔毛产量 (吨)	Rabbit Wool (ton)	28	14	－	－	－
八、渔业生产	**Fishery**					
(一)淡水产品产量总计(吨)	Total Output of Freshwater Aquatic Products (ton)	197992	149121	415	25687	2185
其中:养殖产量 (吨)	Artificially Cultured (ton)	183683	141823	335	21455	1380
1. 鱼 类 (吨)	Fish (ton)	107800	73699	273	15335	570
#鲫 鱼 (吨)	#Crucians (ton)	12968	6244	60	2978	265
鳊 鱼 (吨)	Breams (ton)	6542	2573	15	964	15
黑 鱼 (吨)	Snake Heads (ton)	17860	17790	－	1175	－
2. 虾蟹类 (吨)	Shrimps, Prawns & Crabs (ton)	38303	37212	－	889	810
3. 贝 类 (吨)	Shellfish (ton)	1110	99		99	－
4. 其 他 (吨)	Others (ton)	36470	30813	62	5132	－
#甲 鱼 (吨)	#Turtles (ton)	33795	29790	－	4809	－
(二)淡水养殖面积合计 (公顷)	Freshwater Aquiculture Area (hectare)	60220	11499	95	2077	170

continued

#萧山区 Xiaoshan	#余杭区 Yuhang	桐庐县 Tonglu	淳安县 Chun'an	建德市 Jiande	富阳市 Fuyang	临安市 Lin'an
22	105	296	119	158	610	358
900	1177	315	35	185	1229	466
35	154	150	13	69	240	876
15533	17569	2060	841	10798	11664	2330
3294	20360	6152	4549	104581	7205	6270
1646	343	7622	2536	508	8924	1009
102502	67	287616	34675	14687	57336	45673
8661	150	–	–	750	8620	6259
2	12	–	–	–	–	14
57804	61057	7586	13100	12028	11248	4909
57019	59714	7227	10486	9227	10588	4332
18409	38752	3066	10301	8189	8659	3886
185	2705	691	1412	1243	2503	875
0	1568	61	1238	1458	855	357
6415	10196	–	–	–	60	10
32466	1487	123	–	94	839	35
–	–	–	–	758	253	0
6144	19475	4038	185	186	837	411
5725	19253	3040	185	65	420	295
3895	4658	1440	41054	2002	1530	2695

3－12　分地区林业
Statistics on Forestry

指　标	Item	全市 Whole City	市区 Urban District
一、营林情况	**Afforestation**		
1. 当年造林面积　（公顷）	Afforested Areas　(hectare)	5600	492
#用材林　（公顷）	#Timber Forest　(hectare)	583	－
经济林　（公顷）	Economic Forest　(hectare)	1585	68
2. 迹地更新面积　（公顷）	Area of Forest Updating　(hectare)	2606	18
3. 封山育林面积　（公顷）	Area of Afforestation in Enclosed Mountain　(hectare)	88440	14734
4. 零星（四旁）植树　（万株）	Planting Trees　(10000 plant)	506	207
5. 未成林抚育作业面积（公顷）	Area of Seedling Cultivated　(hectare)	133	－
6. 中、幼龄林抚育面积（公顷）	Area of Grown Forest Cultivated　(hectare)	34793	2114
二、林产品产量	**Output of Forest Products**		
1. 油茶籽　（吨）	Tea－oil Seeds　(ton)	9407	－
2. 竹笋干　（吨）	Dried Bamboo Shoots　(ton)	43744	10477
3. 核　桃　（吨）	Walnuts　(ton)	15913	66
4. 板　栗　（吨）	Chestnuts　(ton)	11458	608
三、竹木采伐量	**Lumbering**		
1. 木　材　（万立方米）	Timber Cut　(10000 cu. m)	483210	9733
2. 竹　材　（万支）	Bamboo Cut　(10000 pieces)	2594	977

生产(2013 年)
by Region(2013)

#萧山区 Xiaoshan	#余杭区 Yuhang	桐庐县 Tonglu	淳安县 Chun'an	建德市 Jiande	富阳市 Fuyang	临安市 Lin'an
374	12	667	1741	587	867	1246
–	–	95	255	–	–	233
–	–	72	1145	–	67	233
5	13	527	1135	533	60	333
13339	–	40159	6041	2506	22000	3000
30	177	45	73	20	55	106
–	–	–	–	–	133	–
1000	697	5516	11530	6000	3333	6300
–	–	1480	6527	1300	–	100
1650	8827	1897	4630	1560	1680	23500
–	66	760	5064	50	114	9859
328	280	2290	4040	2600	1067	853
1814	7498	54929	166445	66198	36903	149002
141	836	107	515	186	349	460

3－13 分地区主要农

Possession of Major Agricultural

指 标		Item		全市 Whole City	市区 Urban District
一、农业机械总动力	**（千瓦）**	**Total Power of Agricultural Machinery**	**（kw）**	**3484175**	**1685215**
耕作机械动力	（千瓦）	Cultivation Machinery	（kw）	217918	102509
收获机械动力	（千瓦）	Harvest Machinery	（kw）	38548	18127
植保机械动力	（千瓦）	Plant Protection Machinery	（kw）	49291	7673
排灌机械动力	（千瓦）	Drainage & Irrigation Machinery	（kw）	428633	201663
农副产品加工机械动力	（千瓦）	Processing Machinery of Agricultural Products	（kw）	180366	53786
运输机械动力	（千瓦）	Transport Machinery	（kw）	895821	392435
渔业机械动力	（千瓦）	Fishery Machinery	（kw）	124348	106157
其他机械动力	（千瓦）	Other Machinery	（kw）	1549250	802865
二、主要农机具		**Agricultural Machinery and Machinery For Processing Farm Products**			
大中型拖拉机	（台）	Large & Medium Tractors	（unit）	1019	802
机引农具	（台）	Mechanized Farm Implement	（unit）	2247	2040
农用小型拖拉机	（台）	Mini－tractors	（unit）	14010	5181
联合收获机	（台）	Combine Harvesters	（unit）	935	556
机动割晒机	（台）	Motorized Harvesters	（unit）	8	4
机动脱粒机	（台）	Motorized Thresher	（unit）	149286	70923
谷物烘干机	（台）	Cereal Dryer	（unit）	299	167
机动喷雾（粉）器	（架）	Motorized Sprayer	（unit）	29973	5470
农用水泵	（台）	Water Pump for Agricultural Use	（unit）	151622	43970
节水喷灌机械	（套）	Saving Water and Sprinkling Machinery	（set）	4142	581
粮食加工机械	（台）	Grain Processing Machinery	（unit）	20615	2812
棉花加工机械	（台）	Cotton Processing Machinery	（unit）	256	77
油料加工机械	（台）	Oil Processing Machinery	（unit）	1644	221
农用运输机械	（台）	Vehicles for Agricultural Use	（unit）	38432	16363

机具年末拥有量(2013 年)
Machinery at the Year – end by Region(2013)

#萧山区 Xiaoshan	#余杭区 Yuhang	桐庐县 Tonglu	淳安县 Chun'an	建德市 Jiande	富阳市 Fuyang	临安市 Lin'an
800544	**521787**	**263787**	**301957**	**297300**	**461209**	**474707**
56725	43050	17219	13143	23234	31484	30329
10136	6721	3915	656	4155	10400	1295
4317	3048	1427	2808	4388	3485	29510
87377	88467	36379	22220	48583	57048	62740
31669	16174	11861	49103	23026	13072	29518
259708	122115	98475	54610	74836	127967	147498
80924	12735	1189	12654	2157	2048	143
269688	229477	93322	146763	116921	215705	173674
582	219	28	5	20	149	15
1607	432	27	4	41	111	24
1871	3044	1607	1332	2267	2469	1154
418	116	56	15	55	223	30
0	4	0	1	0	2	1
20339	50360	25081	3146	12539	30371	7226
96	71	28	14	39	36	15
3026	1734	685	1676	1799	1619	18724
17292	22113	16085	5089	24558	17598	44322
193	364	39	539	2928	9	46
1554	1136	1371	7249	2076	1147	5960
65	12	31	61	16	61	10
155	45	244	619	312	85	163
10380	5352	4191	2102	3239	7136	5401

3－14 农业机械作业和
Agricultural Mechanization and

指　　标		Item		全市 Whole City	市区 Urban District
一、农业机械作业		**Agricultural Mechanization**			
当年机械收割面积	（千公顷）	Harvest Area by Tractors	(1000 hectares)	85.33	45.99
二、农村用电量	**（万千瓦时）**	**Electricity Consumed in Rural Area**	**(10000 kwh)**	**1088959**	**535929**
三、农业化肥用量		**Consumption of Chemical Fertilizer**			
（一）按实物量计算	（吨）	Physical Quantity Consumption	(ton)	522760	283724
1. 氮　肥	（吨）	Nitrogenous Fertilizer	(ton)	237004	133029
2. 磷　肥	（吨）	Phosphate Fertilizer	(ton)	71951	40190
3. 钾　肥	（吨）	Potash Fertilizer	(ton)	41162	18372
4. 复合肥	（吨）	Compound Fertilizer	(ton)	172643	92133
（二）按折纯法计算	（吨）	Pure Consumption	(ton)	103300	44050
1. 氮　肥	（吨）	Nitrogenous Fertilizer	(ton)	50353	21670
2. 磷　肥	（吨）	Phosphate Fertilizer	(ton)	11024	4395
3. 钾　肥	（吨）	Potash Fertilizer	(ton)	7949	2898
4. 复合肥	（吨）	Compound Fertilizer	(ton)	33974	15087
四、农用塑料薄膜使用量	**（吨）**	**Use of Plastic Film**	**(ton)**	**10614**	**2964**
五、农用柴油使用量	**（吨）**	**Consumption of Diesel Oil**	**(ton)**	**27138**	**10641**
六、农药使用量	**（吨）**	**Consumption of Pesticide**	**(ton)**	**7761**	**3126**

物资消耗情况(2013 年)
Material Consumption(2013)

#萧山区 Xiaoshan	#余杭区 Yuhang	桐庐县 Tonglu	淳安县 Chun'an	建德市 Jiande	富阳市 Fuyang	临安市 Lin'an
25.67	17.8	7.73	1.47	10.27	14	5.87
227026	**230399**	**60063**	**12380**	**21457**	**346527**	**112603**
213767	60555	38565	60921	51011	21854	66685
99557	29475	18041	32429	23075	11585	18845
30521	8463	8339	7195	7251	2490	6486
12604	5128	4264	6683	4433	487	6923
71085	17489	7921	14614	16252	7292	34431
25688	15052	8041	7626	17295	9214	17074
14117	6189	3696	3132	9691	4866	7298
2747	1269	1435	829	2119	896	1350
1574	1127	1003	418	1609	244	1777
7250	6467	1907	3247	3876	3208	6649
2220	**430**	**794**	**4180**	**1782**	**212**	**682**
8295	**2058**	**4959**	**1743**	**3440**	**301**	**6054**
1843	**1109**	**761**	**705**	**1177**	**838**	**1154**

3－15 乡(镇)

Statistics on Towns

乡镇名称 Town		居民委员会 Number of Neighborhood Offices	村民委员会(个) Number of Villagers´ Committees (unit)	乡镇常住户数(户) Resident Households in Towns (household)	乡镇常住人口数(人) Resident Population in Towns (person)
江干区	**Jianggan District**				
丁桥镇	Dingqiao	17	2	9154	34827
笕桥镇	Jianqiao	20	–	13149	52807
彭埠镇	Pengbu	14	–	12077	50326
九堡镇	Jiubao	21	2	12811	46692
西湖区	**Xihu District**				
留下街道	Liuxia Subdistrict	11	1	7239	74703
转塘街道	Zhuantang Subdistrict	30	12	17523	77663
双浦镇	Shuangpu	7	23	14670	58480
三墩镇	Sandun	27	4	49982	166439
高新(滨江)区	**Hi－Tech(Bingjiang) District**				
浦沿街道	Puyan Subdistrict	18	–	74089	174607
长河街道	Changhe Subdistrict	20	–	27807	106759
西兴街道	Xixing Subdistrict	8	–	12275	82011
西湖风景名胜区	**The West Lake Scenic Zone**				
西湖街道	West Lake Subdistrict	6	9	3834	7486
萧山区	**Xiaoshan District**				
楼塔镇	Louta	1	12	9443	35369
河上镇	Heshang	1	15	8831	27139
戴村镇	Daicun	1	22	10860	37708
浦阳镇	Puyang	–	18	13207	46402
进化镇	Jinhua	1	25	15986	53579
临浦镇	Linpu	5	20	24337	101894

基本情况(2013 年)
and Townships(2013)

乡镇就业人员数(人) Employed Persons in Towns (person)	乡镇常用耕地面积(亩) Commonly used cultivated area of township (mu)	粮食总产量(吨) Yield of Grain Crops (ton)	公共财政总收入(万元) Public Finance Income (10000 yuan)	公共财政支出(万元) Public Finance Expenditure (10000 yuan)
13767	285	–	43688	8409
38181	3931	–	10324	11059
30073	2640	–	50230	10965
17177	4349	–	56937	60399
27901	326	–	7383	7784
32838	17340	1360	143069	77425
31216	23145	10465	6809	6870
79485	15801	5522	86693	89328
20267	3270	188	40965	12882
24640	2595	150	11400	11400
36515	3150	1437	19990	19738
4408	–	–	8011	8539
14542	12571	4099	15200	15138
16621	13050	5330	15829	13880
24148	18180	7004	13500	27300
24968	17443	9088	22000	17550
30890	18225	9130	12108	16355
51427	17055	5769	72130	37601

3－15 续表1

乡镇名称 Town		居民委员会 Number of Neighborhood Offices	村民委员会(个) Number of Villagers´ Committees (unit)	乡镇常住户数(户) Resident Households in Towns (household)	乡镇常住人口数(人) Resident Population in Towns (person)
义桥镇	Yiqiao	2	21	13384	45140
所前镇	Suoqian	1	19	12717	45628
衙前镇	Yaqian	2	11	7035	27843
闻堰镇	Wenyan	4	6	8963	28544
宁围镇	Ningwei	2	15	19090	63165
新街镇	Xinjie	4	15	17067	57748
瓜沥镇	Guali	11	63	53746	191253
益农镇	Yinong	1	19	14349	44915
靖江街道	Jingjiang Subdistrict	3	10	12550	46405
南阳街道	Nanyang Subdistrict	2	13	10872	38981
义蓬街道	Yipeng Subdistrict	3	22	27639	94533
河庄街道	Hezhuang Subdistrict	1	20	13387	49347
党湾镇	Dangwan	1	17	13667	43533
新湾街道	Xinwan Subdistrict	1	12	11704	33486
城厢街道	Chengxiang Subdistrict	22	0	45022	148093
北干街道	Beigan Subdistrict	16	6	34823	83576
蜀山街道	Shushan Subdistrict	2	8	15734	63404
新塘街道	Xintang Subdistrict	5	17	22404	80907
前进街道	Qianjin Subdistrict	–	3	4140	22452
临江街道	Linjiang Subdistrict	1	2	2884	12213
余杭区	**Yuhang District**				
运河街道	Yunhe Subdistrict	5	14	10302	52130
乔司街道	Qiaosi Subdistrict	3	11	20733	84903
塘栖镇	Tangqi	8	27	27315	120987

continued 1

乡镇就业人员数（人）Employed Persons in Towns (person)	乡镇常用耕地面积（亩）Commonly used cultivated area of township (mu)	粮食总产量（吨）Yield of Grain Crops (ton)	公共财政总收入（万元）Public Finance Income (10000 yuan)	公共财政支出（万元）Public Finance Expenditure (10000 yuan)
28874	21210	9938	45251	12458
20782	14727	7503	25530	25467
14734	8235	1841	72321	72319
28040	4485	243	11000	10200
54666	25710	2010	536744	248041
33256	30345	3590	79075	25338
105775	95355	41109	202963	104038
28123	42810	18531	25836	19033
26604	21375	10642	15103	12537
24462	19935	11370	30206	7778
58621	49515	23429	44603	44462
30512	38088	22493	28066	18968
32462	34500	20405	27480	14395
15957	19905	12500	12096	12096
81128	1695	383	120890	120487
22612	2889	–	129717	129717
36221	13485	193	21941	21941
42884	10815	474	13941	13941
16718	8985	4789	3703	3703
9661	6341	4702	3900	3900
31948	11415	4612	13222	12172
51221	13875	2181	10509	10646
80855	31725	16854	67166	54462

3－15 续表2

乡镇名称 Town		居民委员会 Number of Neighborhood Offices	村民委员会(个) Number of Villagers´ Committees (unit)	乡镇常住户数(户) Resident Households in Towns (household)	乡镇常住人口数(人) Resident Population in Towns (person)
仁和街道	Renhe Subdistrict	1	18	17814	68984
崇贤街道	Chongxian Subdistrict	2	11	15095	65251
余杭街道	Yuhang Subdistrict	7	14	26527	95400
闲林街道	Xianlin Subdistrict	5	8	25793	77378
仓前街道	Cangqian Subdistrict	1	9	9675	48486
中泰街道	Zhongtai Subdistrict	2	10	9246	38247
良渚街道	Liangzhu Subdistrict	12	23	32673	213582
瓶窑镇	Pingyao	5	13	19970	68857
径山镇	Jingshan	2	13	11815	37144
黄湖镇	Huanghu	1	5	4389	15154
鸬鸟镇	Luniao	1	6	3722	12264
百丈镇	Baizhang	1	6	3310	10734
临平街道	Linping Subdistrict	20	0	23363	83081
南苑街道	Nanyuan Subdistrict	21	0	26628	92773
星桥街道	Xingqiao Subdistrict	15	0	9515	40587
五常街道	Wuchang Subdistrict	9	0	6689	57027
桐庐县	**Tonglu County**				
桐君街道	Tongjun Subdistrict	8	6	29852	62208
旧县街道	Jiuxian Subdistrict	–	5	3172	8259
富春江镇	Fuchunjiang	2	15	10320	26230
江南镇	Jiangnan	1	20	16138	45547
凤川街道	Fengchuan Subdistrict	–	8	6021	17978
新合乡	Xinghe	–	5	1632	4951
横村镇	Hengcun	–	24	14604	43384
莪山畲族乡	Eshan	–	7	2985	8692
钟山乡	Zhongshan	–	11	6152	15676
分水镇	Fenshui	2	26	26949	70068

continued 2

乡镇就业人员数（人）Employed Persons in Towns (person)	乡镇常用耕地面积（亩）Commonly used cultivated area of township (mu)	粮食总产量（吨）Yield of Grain Crops (ton)	公共财政总收入（万元）Public Finance Income (10000 yuan)	公共财政支出（万元）Public Finance Expenditure (10000 yuan)
42625	37245	19353	20370	12888
41876	16665	6445	20457	9481
51049	49335	27404	54161	22689
35551	10458	5107	45460	12473
35822	26142	19569	37422	14321
24687	19280	7020	18085	8972
136693	43343	17989	112797	109996
41787	41370	18871	23513	13995
21628	47775	18817	20378	20754
8800	14348	5246	2781	5418
7671	19050	5747	851	2666
7169	2318	2595	2860	2778
60491	2610	518	21563	8484
74849	9675	1980	34039	7348
26519	4830	406	14222	5594
40557	3375	249	45202	14957
41590	5181	2809	10731	927
5476	7373	3291	624	603
14179	14318	8420	11303	11603
28925	25763	9911	12800	1872
10713	9255	4840	2998	868
3284	4134	1263	349	560
25676	41130	13917	7343	2313
5343	6707	3203	998	1629
11654	17733	6198	997	993
43147	29790	12003	19600	8765

3－15　续表3

乡 镇 名 称 Town		居民委员会 Number of Neighborhood Offices	村民委员会(个) Number of Villagers' Committees (unit)	乡镇常住户数(户) Resident Households in Towns (household)	乡镇常住人口数(人) Resident Population in Towns (person)
瑶琳镇	Yaolin	–	16	10622	31532
百江镇	Baijiang	–	15	5406	17477
合村乡	Hecun	–	6	2822	8755
城南街道	Chengnan Subdistrict	4	19	32739	96635
淳安县	**Chun'an County**				
千岛湖镇	Qiandaohu	9	22	27354	81027
文昌镇	Wenchang	–	16	4080	12597
石林镇	Shilin	–	8	1394	4599
临岐镇	Linqi	–	17	5850	19541
威坪镇	Weiping	1	44	16142	48628
姜家镇	Jiangjia	1	28	8046	24920
梓桐镇	Zitong	–	19	6010	18408
汾口镇	Fenkou	1	51	16656	53453
中洲镇	Zhongzhou	–	19	5688	18512
大墅镇	Dashu	–	17	4337	13768
枫树岭镇	Fengshuling	–	28	5819	17650
里商乡	Lishang	–	16	3166	10294
金峰乡	Jinfeng	–	11	1638	4977
富文乡	Fuwen	–	10	2029	6298
左口乡	Zuokou	–	11	3239	10614
屏门乡	Pingmen	–	15	3853	11510
瑶山乡	Yaoshan	–	11	2807	9364
王阜乡	Wangfu	–	18	6034	17636
宋村乡	Songcun	–	8	2106	5750
鸠坑乡	Jiukeng	–	9	2495	7358
浪川乡	Langchuan	–	19	6077	18087

continued 3

乡镇就业人员数（人）Employed Persons in Towns (person)	乡镇常用耕地面积(亩) Commonly used cultivated area of township (mu)	粮食总产量（吨）Yield of Grain Crops (ton)	公共财政总收入（万元）Public Finance Income (10000 yuan)	公共财政支出（万元）Public Finance Expenditure (10000 yuan)
20699	26979	9788	1868	1353
10788	13875	4877	1236	992
5857	8205	4340	349	560
42751	11940	6857	18299	1501
63242	8012	2664	5890	7349
8473	6497	3525	321	4042
2987	2599	1148	62	3316
12931	13028	4325	234	1708
39094	20144	7601	378	3188
16349	12449	7346	142	3309
12259	10965	7422	100	1886
39810	26312	14028	1691	1155
12126	8970	4387	61	1353
9305	9426	3617	172	1704
11483	13796	4563	161	2192
6927	3810	2419	50	3114
3308	3885	2129	39	4599
4283	4353	1903	48	1912
6887	4875	2831	46	7635
7808	5310	3442	49	1644
6073	3975	2468	65	2508
11175	4215	2790	49	10015
3889	1860	662	26	5044
4930	1673	1172	30	3295
11855	11394	5571	84	1816

3－15　续表4

乡镇名称 Town		居民委员会 Number of Neighborhood Offices	村民委员会(个) Number of Villagers′ Committees (unit)	乡镇常住户数(户) Resident Households in Towns (household)	乡镇常住人口数(人) Resident Population in Towns (person)
界首乡	Jieshou	－	13	2728	8326
安阳乡	Anyang	－	15	3410	11089
建德市	**Jiande City**				
新安江街道	Xin′anjiang Subdistrict	11	4	36648	97215
洋溪街道	Yangxi Subdistrict	1	5	4909	16071
更楼街道	Genglou Subdistrict	2	14	7438	25639
莲花镇	Lianhua	1	6	3082	10869
乾潭镇	Qiantan	1	24	13665	45095
钦堂乡	Qintang	1	7	2674	8341
梅城镇	Meicheng	5	13	16983	52151
杨村桥镇	Yangcunqiao	1	13	5843	19540
下涯镇	Xiaya	1	11	7846	26236
大洋镇	Dayang	3	19	9988	33378
三都镇	Sandu	1	19	8975	27685
寿昌镇	Shouchang	1	23	15223	51144
航头镇	Hangtou	1	18	9594	30551
大慈岩镇	Daciyan	1	12	6451	19398
大同镇	Datong	3	34	17438	54562
李家镇	Lijia	1	10	5862	19667

continued 4

乡镇就业人员数（人） Employed Persons in Towns (person)	乡镇常用耕地面积（亩） Commonly used cultivated area of township (mu)	粮食总产量（吨） Yield of Grain Crops (ton)	公共财政总收入（万元） Public Finance Income (10000 yuan)	公共财政支出（万元） Public Finance Expenditure (10000 yuan)
5459	4800	1997	43	2665
7072	7725	3697	219	3405
51871	3017	946	63232	7554
9447	2486	845	20166	1848
13350	10331	5248	2418	1111
6647	4665	834	1160	1406
35397	22100	9575	16750	3410
5425	7128	3715	4325	4284
28890	16715	5720	17457	5339
12138	13877	4804	1208	1207
15431	15674	4882	4100	3767
19639	20546	7490	2222	2742
14016	17846	4172	3393	2342
22313	19418	10581	3047	2909
19598	23004	10005	3319	6496
11672	15176	6721	1298	1248
35740	33327	15829	2779	4815
11959	10772	5622	1975	1975

3－15 续表5

乡镇名称 Town		居民委员会 Number of Neighborhood Offices	村民委员会(个) Number of Villagers' Committees (unit)	乡镇常住户数(户) Resident Households in Towns (household)	乡镇常住人口数(人) Resident Population in Towns (person)
富阳市	**Fuyang City**				
万市镇	Wanshi	1	15	7376	22917
洞桥镇	Dongqiao	–	11	5854	18539
胥口镇	Xukou	–	13	5672	17989
永昌镇	Yongchang	–	5	3625	10852
渌渚镇	Luzhu	–	13	5213	15906
新登镇	Xindeng	4	28	36496	101825
上官乡	Shangguan	–	5	2876	8617
常绿镇	Changlu	–	8	4462	13624
大源镇	Dayuan	–	15	11713	37091
灵桥镇	Lingqiao	–	13	9134	28050
里山镇	Lishan	–	5	3250	10200
渔山乡	Yushan	–	4	3859	13102
场口镇	Changkou	1	24	13124	40262
龙门镇	Longmen	–	4	2472	7205
环山乡	Huanshan	–	7	3756	12167
常安镇	Chang'an	–	16	7509	25227
湖源乡	Huyuan	–	10	3272	11063
春建乡	Chunjian	–	6	2907	8816
新桐乡	Xintong	–	7	3705	11872
鹿山街道	Lushan Subdistrict	–	9	7286	20841

continued 5

乡镇就业人员数（人）Employed Persons in Towns (person)	乡镇常用耕地面积（亩）Commonly used cultivated area of township (mu)	粮食总产量（吨）Yield of Grain Crops (ton)	公共财政总收入（万元）Public Finance Income (10000 yuan)	公共财政支出（万元）Public Finance Expenditure (10000 yuan)
13966	20741	10847	5740	5738
11301	16661	6867	4155	4143
10048	16680	6308	3757	3804
6387	8460	4123	6078	5962
10494	11247	6740	11669	11853
62498	35790	15273	24958	24958
5078	2388	1576	2367	2367
9041	3160	2195	2825	2806
25662	9015	3837	9348	9498
15965	7564	3324	15281	5380
6206	3825	2580	4445	2290
8784	4806	3396	2542	2538
25086	23385	11070	8232	8152
4383	4355	2388	1718	1726
7477	6026	3050	2424	3375
15453	15447	6245	2245	4218
8486	8640	2970	8794	7201
5845	7515	3660	1726	4612
7714	8970	4935	2366	2368
13386	11409	5727	13186	4141

3－15 续表6

乡镇名称 Town	居民委员会 Number of Neighborhood Offices	村民委员会(个) Number of Villagers´ Committees (unit)	乡镇常住户数(户) Resident Households in Towns (household)	乡镇常住人口数(人) Resident Population in Towns (person)
富春街道 Fuchun Subdistrict	22	12	89739	275419
春江街道 Chunjiang Subdistrict	–	9	8483	29186
东洲街道 Dongzhou Subdistrict	–	15	12298	43357
银湖街道 Yinghu Subdistrict	–	22	14684	47706
临安市 Lin'an City				
玲珑街道 Linlong Subdistrict	–	16	9388	26325
锦南街道 Jinnan Subdistrict	–	9	7298	23152
锦城街道 Jincheng Subdistrict	17	5	50676	131169
锦北街道 Jinbei Subdistrict	3	12	11934	48515
青山湖街道 Qingshanghu Subdistrict	1	19	13784	51218
高虹镇 Gaohong	–	9	6896	23912
太湖源镇 Taihuyuan	–	20	11671	32350
於潜镇 Yuqian	1	30	19939	55751
太阳镇 Taiyang	–	18	8951	24049
潜川镇 Qianchuan	–	16	8554	21007
昌化镇 Changhua	1	14	8520	27005
河桥镇 Heqiao	–	11	5061	14563
湍口镇 Tuankou	–	13	3781	12118
清凉峰镇 Qingliangfeng	–	17	9713	28093
岛石镇 Daoshi	–	16	9034	26050
板桥镇 Banqiao	–	15	8725	27598
天目山镇 Tianmushan	–	23	11610	33624
龙岗镇 Longgang	–	24	6802	22605

continued 6

乡镇就业人员数（人）Employed Persons in Towns (person)	乡镇常用耕地面积（亩）Commonly used cultivated area of township (mu)	粮食总产量（吨）Yield of Grain Crops (ton)	公共财政总收入（万元）Public Finance Income (10000 yuan)	公共财政支出（万元）Public Finance Expenditure (10000 yuan)
84557	17325	9177	92294	22860
18188	6705	3964	5790	5780
27034	19875	10288	6366	6368
34926	24864	14719	5344	5344
15372	9345	4094	14804	3429
8050	5084	1684	8117	1977
82753	5797	2133	7249	7438
23745	6090	3045	13358	4010
21882	13215	5963	51871	27605
18602	8865	4295	8363	2994
20579	27945	6238	7095	3729
32487	30465	5952	15391	15270
16749	17672	5863	3410	2235
15228	9774	2496	2932	3535
11360	12728	4527	2890	2520
11177	13155	4711	3071	2235
9179	7142	2983	800	1602
19197	16004	6928	1127	2375
16743	8967	4645	340	1721
15411	13469	6414	8939	4718
20654	27555	8150	3692	4443
14970	16565	8383	1734	2388

主要统计指标解释

农林牧渔业总产值　是以货币表现的农、林、牧、渔业全部产品的总量和对农林牧渔生产活动进行的各种支持性服务活动的价值。他反映一定时期内的农林牧渔业生产的总规模和总成果。

农林牧渔业的统计范围是：

(1)农业　包括农作物种植业和其他农业。

农作物种植业　包括谷类、豆类、薯类、棉花、麻类、烟叶、蔬菜、药材、瓜类和其他农作物的种植以及茶园、桑园、果园的生产经营。

其他农业　包括采集野生植物的果实、纤维、树脂、油料以及柴草、野生药材、菌类等。

(2)林业　包括林木的栽培(不包括茶园、桑园和果园的栽培、管理和收获等活动)、林产品的采集和村及村以下合作经济组织和农户的竹木砍伐。

(3)牧业　包括除渔业养殖以外的一切动物饲养和放牧以及野生动物的捕猎和饲养。

(4)渔业　包括水生动物和海藻类植物的养殖和捕捞。

(5)农林牧渔服务业　包括对农林牧渔生产活动进行的各种支持性服务活动。

粮食产量　指全社会的产量，包括国营农场等全民所有制经营、集体统一经营的和农民家庭经营的产量，还包括工矿企业家属办的农场和其他生产单位的产量。粮食除包括稻谷、小麦、大麦、玉米、高粱、谷子及其他杂粮外，还包括薯类和豆类。其产量计算方法，豆类按去豆荚后的干豆计算，薯类按5公斤鲜薯折1公斤粮食计算，其他粮食一律按脱粒后的原粮计算。

猪、牛、羊肉产量　指当年出栏并已屠宰的猪、牛、羊的肉产量，即屠宰后除去头蹄下水后带骨的(即胴体重)重量。

水产品产量　指人工养殖的水产品和天然生长的水产品的捕捞量。包括海水的鱼类、虾蟹类、贝类和藻类以及内陆水域的鱼类、虾蟹类和贝类，不包括淡水生植物。

有效灌溉面积　指具有一定的水源，地块比较平整、灌溉工程或设备已经配套，在一般年景下当年能够进行正常灌溉的耕地面积。

农业机械总动力　指主要用于农、林、牧、渔业的各种动力机械的动力总和。包括耕作机械、排灌机械、收获机械、农用运输机械、植物保护机械、牧业机械、林业机械和其他农业机械[内燃机按引擎马力折成瓦(特)计算，电动机按功率折成瓦(特)计算]。不包括专门用于乡、镇、村、组办工业、基本建设、非农业运输、科学试验和教学等非农业方面的动力机械与作业机械。

农村用电量　指本年度内扣除在农村中的全民所有制工业、交通、基建单位的用电量以后的农村生产上和生活上的全年用电总度数(全年累计数)，包括国家电网的供电量，也包括农村自办电站的供电量。

农用化肥施用量　指本年内实际用于农业生产的化肥数量。包括氮肥、磷肥、钾肥及复合肥。化肥施用量要求按折纯量计算数量。折纯量是指氮肥、磷肥、钾肥分别按含氮、含五氧化二磷、含氧化钾的百分之一百成份进行折算后的数量。复合肥按其所含主要成份折算。

Explanatory Notes on Main Statistical Indicators

Gross Output Value of Farming, Forestry, Animal Husbandry and Fishery refers to the total volume of products of farming, forestry, animal husbandry and fishery in value terms and output value of all kinds of service activities that support farming, forestry, animal husbandry and fishery production. It reflects the total scale and total result of agricultural production during a given period of time.

The statistical scopes for Farming, Forestry, Animal Husbandry and Fishery are:

(1) **Farming** include crop cultivation and other farming crop cultivation, include planting of grain, beans, tubers, cotton, oil – bearing crops, sugar crops, fiber crops, tobacco, vegetables, medicinal materials, melons and others, as well as tea, mulberry and fruit plantation.

Other farming include gathering of wild plant fruits, fiber, gum, oil, firewood, wild medicinal materials, fungi and commodity industry run by rural household.

(2) **Forestry** include planting of trees (not including planting, management & harvest of tea, mulberry and fruit plantation), collection of forest products, cutting and felling of bamboo and trees by villages and other cooperative organizations under villages.

(3) **Animal Husbandry** include raising and grazing of any kind of animal and hunting and raising of wild animal, excluding fish breeding.

(4) **Fishery** include cultivation and catches of aquatic animals and seaweed.

(5) **Service Industry for Farming, Forestry, Animal Husbandry and Fishery** refers to all kinds of service activities that support farming, forestry, animal husbandry and fishery production.

Grain Yield refers to the total yield including grains produced by state farms, collective units, industrial enterprises and mines. Grain includes rice, wheat, corn, sorghum, millet and other miscellaneous grains as well as tubers and beans. Output of beans refers to dry beans without pods. The output of tubers was converted into that of grain at the ratio 5:1. Output of all other grains refers to husked grain.

Output of Pork, Beef, and Mutton refers to the meat of slaughtered hogs, cattle, sheep and goats with head, feet and offal taken away.

Output of Aquatic Products refers to catches of both artificially cultured and naturally grown aquatic products, including fish, shrimps, crabs and shellfish in sea and inland water as well as seaweed. Freshwater plants are not included.

Irrigated Area refers to areas that are effectively irrigated, i. e. level land which has water source and complete sets of irrigation facilities to lift and move adequate water for irrigation purpose under normal conditions.

Total Power of Farm Machinery refers to total mechanical power of machinery used in farming, forestry, animal husbandry, and fishery, including ploughing, irrigation and drainage, harvesting, transport, plant protection, stock breeding, forestry and fishery. The power of internal combustion engines is required to convert horsepower into watts and the power of electric motors is required to be converted into watts. Machinery employed for non – agricultural purposes, such as the machines used in township – run and village – run industry, construction, non – agricultural transport, scientific experiments and teaching, is excluded.

Electricity Consumption in Rural Areas refers to the total degree of electricity consumption in rural production and living (annual aggregate) after discounting the ownership by the whole people in the rural areas of industrial, transport and infrastructure unit of electricity consumption, including the national grid power supply, and also including the power supply in rural areas on their own power station.

Consumption of Chemical Fertilizers in Agriculture refers to the quantity of chemical fertilizers applied in agriculture in the year, including nitrogenous fertilizer, phosphate fertilizer, potash fertilizer, and compound fertilizer. The consumption of chemical fertilizers is required in calculation to convert the gross weight into weight into weight containing 100% effective component (e. g. 100% nitrogen content in nitrogenous fertilizer, 100% phosphorous pentoxide contents in phosphate fertilizer, 100% potassium oxide contents in potash fertilizer). Compound fertilizer is converted with its major component.

四、工业、能源

Ⅳ.INDUSTRY AND ENERGY

工 业 、 能 源
Industry and Energy

主要统计指标
Major Statistical Indicators

规模以上工业企业单位数	Number of Industrial Enterprises above Designated Size	6284	个	(unit)
为上年	As Compared with the Preceding Year	106.0	%	(%)
规模以上工业增加值	Value-added of Industrial Enterprises above Designated Size	2664.13	亿元	(100 million yuan)
为上年	As Compared with the Preceding Year	108.0	%	(%)
规模以上工业总产值	Gross Output Value of Industrial Enterprises above Designated Size	12418.00	亿元	(100 million yuan)
为上年	As Compared with the Preceding Year	104.6	%	(%)
轻工业	Light Industry	4866.38	亿元	(100 million yuan)
为上年	As Compared with the Preceding Year	103.3	%	(%)
重工业	Heavy Industry	7551.63	亿元	(100 million yuan)
为上年	As Compared with the Preceding Year	105.5	%	(%)

4-01 主要年份工业企业单位数

Number of Industrial Enterprises in Main Years

单位:个 (unit)

年份 Year	合计 Total	国有经济 State-owned Enterprises	集体经济 Collective-owned Enterprises	其他各种经济类型 Enterprises of Other Types of Ownership
全市 Whole City				
1978	2868	680	2188	-
1980	3519	691	-	-
1985	5800	823	-	-
1990	6183	921	4966	11
1991	6234	933	5219	82
1992	6235	941	5162	132
1995	6744	1086	4722	936
1996	6148	1011	4268	869
1997	4980	760	3250	970
1998	2559	464	815	1280
1999	2474	396	689	1389
2000	2715	282	598	1835
2001	3580	237	252	3091
2002	4015	172	232	3611
2003	4689	144	219	4326
2004	7738	185	192	7361
2005	7359	124	169	7066
2006	7826	110	162	7554
2007	8674	71	131	8472
2008	9907	73	101	9733
2009	10032	71	84	9877
2010	10370	74	68	10228
2011	5868	52	25	5791
2012	5927	56	20	5851
2013	6284	25	11	6248
市区 Urban District				
1978	787	313	414	-
1980	894	315	579	-
1985	1250	345	859	7
1990	1360	361	971	28
1991	1411	382	990	39
1992	1490	395	1024	71
1995	1998	440	1102	456
1996	2043	458	1109	476
1997	1733	372	951	410
1998	1019	315	315	389
1999	959	255	284	420
2000	1005	182	253	570
2001	2645	195	200	2250
2002	2838	140	178	2520
2003	3230	115	158	2957
2004	5527	156	122	5249
2005	4995	98	104	4793
2006	5195	85	91	5019
2007	5726	54	77	5595
2008	6530	55	64	6411
2009	6477	52	49	6376
2010	6478	51	37	6390
2011	3867	36	10	3821
2012	3862	37	7	3818
2013	4145	18	5	4122

注:1997 年及以前为乡及以上工业;1998－2010 年为主营业务收入 500 万及以上;2011 年为主营业务收入 2000 万及以上(后同)。

a) Data in 2011 refer to all the industrial enterprises with annual Sales income of over 20 million yuan, data in 1998－2010 refer to all the industrial enterprises with annual sales income of over 5 million yuan, data in 1997and before refer to enterprises at township and above level.

4－02 主要年份
Gross Industrial

单位:万元

年　份 Year	规模以上工业 Industry above Designated Size	# 轻 工 业 Light Industry
全市　Whole City		
1978	429624	–
1980	617910	–
1985	1285888	793766
1990	2922600	1848911
1991	3524900	2201757
1992	4527400	2735168
1995	10200259	5600664
1996	8831167	4606720
1997	9114651	4871887
1998	11099357	5726407
1999	12000796	6129963
2000	15435682	7623300
2001	19195133	9957027
2002	24002972	12435498
2003	32025226	15652463
2004	44865779	19761946
2005	54411271	24059690
2006	69754590	29093450
2007	83514029	35878400
2008	93795792	38735329
2009	93907334	40115956
2010	110810397	45764739
2011	123529249	48660810
2012	129596777	51377588
2013	124180035	48663751
市区　Urban District		
1978	304242	–
1980	433623	–
1985	812246	512767
1990	1533000	1026764
1991	1814600	1140394
1992	2291300	1379154
1995	4760900	2507752
1996	4599778	2460319
1997	4997257	2889406
1998	6110192	3068600
1999	6280838	3178286
2000	7804302	3635578
2001	16156245	8377563
2002	20252484	10431428
2003	26945006	13080771
2004	37564968	16361706
2005	44775260	19601053
2006	57255453	23722868
2007	67565456	29452269
2008	74564803	31236743
2009	74059755	32178951
2010	86653885	36440816
2011	97800625	39467105
2012	101396009	41428864
2013	94197123	38407906

工业总产值
Output Value in Main Years

(10000 yuan)

重工业 Heavy Industry	国有经济 State – owned	集体经济 Collective – owned	其他经济 Other Types of Ownership
–	334799	94825	–
–	451349	166561	–
492122	726172	546642	13074
1073689	1532900	1300900	88800
1323143	1779400	1601400	144200
1792232	2141000	2084000	302400
4599595	3585284	3999638	2615337
4224447	2905614	3320757	2604796
4242764	3185886	2971634	2957131
5372950	3422316	2824793	4852248
5870833	3164602	2543981	6292213
7812382	1860336	2698406	10876940
9238106	1788783	1911315	15495035
11567474	2147066	2151485	19704421
16372763	2484171	2444002	27097053
25103833	3419970	558890	40886919
30351581	6054280	603438	47753553
40661140	6776754	667615	62310221
47635629	7688908	517878	75307243
55060463	7440679	386111	85969002
53791378	7576482	354714	85976138
65045658	9050510	300262	101459625
74868439	10220511	171901	113136837
78219189	11507163	167343	117922271
75516284	7140899	39776	116999360
–	248534	55708	–
–	335789	97834	–
301998	536498	267613	8135
599899	1067400	416500	49100
674072	1237600	496800	80200
917085	1497400	601200	192700
2753196	2252300	908900	1599700
2139459	2018768	951432	1629578
2609217	2537740	819984	1639533
3041592	2989467	1123013	1997712
3102552	2668519	979070	2633249
4168724	1498595	968509	5337198
7778681	1695132	1792228	12668885
9821056	2036097	2045450	16170937
13864235	2390424	2305431	22249151
21203262	3097656	419720	34047592
25174207	5592419	390555	38792286
33532585	6305071	347788	50602594
38113187	7123810	323842	60117804
43328060	6812616	219140	67533047
41880805	6880470	148937	67030348
50213069	8155395	156026	78342464
58333520	9253445	70299	88476881
59967145	10452692	72743	90870574
55789218	6332681	22398	87842044

4－03 分县(市)工业

Number of Industrial Enterprises

单位:个

项　目	Item	全　市 Whole City	市区 Urban District	#萧山区 Xiaoshan
规模以上工业合计	**Industrial above Designated Size**	**6284**	**4145**	**1907**
一、按轻重工业分	**Grouped by Light & Heavy Industry**			
轻工业	Light Industry	3120	2079	1111
重工业	Heavy Industry	3164	2066	796
二、按所有制分	**Grouped by Ownership**			
国有企业	State－owned Enterprises	25	18	2
集体企业	Collective－owned Enterprises	11	5	2
股份合作企业	Cooperative Enterprises	12	10	2
联营企业	Joint Ownership Enterprises	1	1	－
股份制企业	Share－holding Corporations	4824	3070	1429
外商及港澳台投资企业	Enterprises with Investment from Foreign、Hong Kong、Macao and Taiwan	1198	953	413
其他企业	Other Enterprises	213	88	59
合计中:国有控股企业	Of the Total:Controlling Share Hold Enterprises	203	146	33
三、按企业规模分	**Grouped by Size of Enterprises**			
大型企业	Large	127	108	39
中型企业	Medium－sized	745	579	281
小微企业	Small	5412	3458	1587

企业单位数(2013 年末)
by Region(End of 2013)

(unit)

#余杭区 Yuhang	桐庐县 Tonglu	淳安县 Chun'an	建德市 Jiande	富阳市 Fuyang	临安市 Lin'an
1228	**357**	**128**	**364**	**713**	**577**
604	216	77	172	310	266
624	141	51	192	403	311
2	1	2	2	1	1
1	1	1	2	–	2
6	–	–	–	2	–
–	–	–		–	–
1011	257	109	325	572	491
191	71	10	14	107	34
17	27	6	21	31	49
32	7	6	10	16	18
14	4	–	2	7	6
141	19	14	17	64	52
1073	334	114	347	642	519

4－04 分县(市)工业
Gross Industrial

单位:万元

项　目	Item	全　市 Whole City	市　区 Urban District	#萧山区 Xiaoshan
规模以上工业合计	**Industrial above Designated Size**	**124180035**	**94197123**	**41510626**
一、按轻重工业分	**Grouped by Light & Heavy Industry**			
轻工业	Light Industry	48663751	38407906	20890077
重工业	Heavy Industry	75516284	55789218	20620549
二、按所有制分	**Grouped by Ownership**			
国有企业	State－owned Enterprises	7140899	6332681	1137508
集体企业	Collective－owned Enterprises	39776	22398	8057
股份合作企业	Cooperative Enterprises	56837	42673	16204
联营企业	Joint Ownership Enterprises	4006	4006	－
股份制企业	Share－holding Corporations	78253872	53646098	28730887
外商及港澳台投资企业	Enterprises with Investment from Foreign、Hong Kong、Macao and Taiwan	37625731	33643198	11248473
其他企业	Other Enterprises	1058914	506070	369498
合计中:国有控股企业	Of the Total: Controlling Share Hold Enterprises	20981609	17638852	2847253
三、按企业规模分	**Grouped by Size of Enterprises**			
大型企业	Large	35758939	32544642	9155804
中型企业	Medium－sized	39013892	28373517	15310917
小微企业	Small	49407204	33278964	17043906

总产值(2013 年)

Output Value by Region(2013)

(10000 yuan)

#余杭区 Yuhang	桐庐县 Tonglu	淳安县 Chun'an	建德市 Jiande	富阳市 Fuyang	临安市 Lin'an
14554528	**4261552**	**2410591**	**4045718**	**12686059**	**6578993**
5231294	1745810	1730894	1222040	3404145	2152956
9323233	2515742	679697	2823678	9281914	4426036
458384	88180	64175	126368	346978	182518
6070	2011	5091	5358	–	4917
19787	–	–	–	14164	–
–	–	–	–	–	–
10922596	2938486	2109603	3602159	10223748	5733779
3066560	1092584	190300	247101	1942362	396537
81131	140291	41422	64732	158807	261242
1148147	197305	86214	418547	1915921	724770
2471896	288135	–	744300	715185	1466678
4433633	1198205	886452	1058195	5541856	1955666
7648999	2775213	1524138	2243223	6429017	3156649

4－05 分县(市)工业
Gross Industrial

单位:万元

项 目	Item	全 市 Whole City	市 区 Urban District	#萧山区 Xiaoshan
规模以上工业合计	**Industrial above Designated Size**	**123159221**	**93653843**	**40826963**
一、按轻重工业分	**Grouped by Light & Heavy Industry**			
轻工业	Light Industry	48177656	38092367	20452706
重工业	Heavy Industry	74981565	55561476	20374257
二、按所有制分	**Grouped by Ownership**			
国有企业	State－owned Enterprises	7115371	6307196	1131933
集体企业	Collective－owned Enterprises	39492	22195	8057
股份合作企业	Cooperative Enterprises	55414	41920	15884
联营企业	Joint Ownership Enterprises	4006	4006	－
股份制企业	Share－holding Corporations	77047275	52856550	28257072
外商及港澳台投资企业	Enterprises with Investment from Foreign、Hong Kong、Macao and Taiwan	37851676	33921532	11049999
其他企业	Other Enterprises	1045987	500445	364019
合计中:国有控股企业	Of the Total:Controlling Share Hold Enterprises	21357841	18074419	2857175
三、按企业规模分	**Grouped by Size of Enterprises**			
大型企业	Large	36196206	33017438	9063001
中型企业	Medium－sized	38480654	27975141	15072123
小微企业	Small	48482361	32661264	16691839

销售产值(2013 年)

Products Sales by Region(2013)

(10000 yuan)

#余杭区 Yuhang	桐庐县 Tonglu	淳安县 Chun'an	建德市 Jiande	富阳市 Fuyang	临安市 Lin'an
14277767	**4212615**	**2380390**	**3984000**	**12440512**	**6487862**
5155300	1724223	1714270	1207407	3316882	2122507
9122467	2488392	666120	2776593	9123630	4365355
459642	88014	64298	126368	346978	182518
6033	2038	5091	5256	–	4913
19360	–	–	–	13494	–
–	–	–	–	–	–
10697613	2903312	2079856	3536377	10011781	5659399
3015004	1082074	190064	251877	1909302	388728
80116	137177	41081	64121	158958	252304
1131110	195788	87314	420695	1869188	710437
2478536	283469	–	731804	689274	1474221
4292289	1205711	865831	1041642	5464314	1928014
7506943	2723435	1514560	2210553	6286923	3085626

4-06 全市规模以上工业

Main Economic Indicators of Industrial

单位:万元

项 目	Item	企业单位数(个) Number of Enterprises (unit)	#亏损企业(个) Loss Making Enterprises (unit)	工业总产值(当年价格) Gross Industrial Output Value (current price)	#新产品产值 Output of New Products
总 计	**Total**	**6284**	**936**	**124180035**	**34961410**
按隶属关系分	**Grouped by Subordination**				
中 央 属	Central	37	7	6189380	920029
省 属	Provincial	53	3	8551725	483584
市 属	Municipal	87	21	6885691	2219657
县(市)属	County and below	61	11	2676378	1230002
按所有制分	**Grouped by Ownership**				
国有企业	State - owned Enterprises	25	2	7140899	167812
集体企业	Collective - owned Enterprises	11	1	39776	689
股份合作企业	Cooperative Enterprises	12	-	56837	3383
联营企业	Joint Ownership Enterprises	1	-	4006	
股份制企业	Share - holding Corporations	4824	652	78253872	22167594
外商及港澳台投资企业	Enterprises with Investment from Foreign、Hong Kong、Macao and Taiwan	1198	263	37625731	12527322
其他企业	Other Enterprises	213	18	1058914	94610
按企业规模分	**Grouped by Size of Enterprises**				
大型企业	Large	127	11	35758939	11957071
中型企业	Medium - sized	745	90	39013892	13571748
小微企业	Small	5412	835	49407204	9432591
按轻重工业分	**Grouped by Light & Heavy Industry**				
轻工业	Light Industry	3120	449	48663751	11038700
重工业	Heavy Industry	3164	487	75516284	23922710

企业主要经济指标(2013 年)(一)
Enterprises Above Designated Size(2013)(Ⅰ)

(10000 yuan)

工业销售产值 Value of Industrial Products Sales	出口交货值 Export delivery value	实收资本 Total Capital Hold	国家资本 State Capital	个人资本 Personal Capital	港澳台资本 Hongkong, Macau and TaiWan Capital	外商资本 Foreign Capital	就业人员年平均人数(人) Annual Average Number of Staff and Workers (person)
123159221	**17046090**	**23634335**	**1567312**	**6553399**	**2750725**	**4164835**	**1196983**
6185624	7848	887252	126034	5184	137500	16077	11633
8501154	193072	902239	470860	18526	110783	168600	31416
7331590	1246852	1265930	324538	111057	48651	147467	53526
2639090	154552	558624	119293	21903	48796	22607	19781
7115371	21011	253875	248453	–	–	–	18618
39492	4972	1934	–	272	–	–	652
55414	–	52370	–	7240	–	–	1399
4006	–	100	–	–	–		62
77047275	8348006	13854102	1020437	6035896	53441	46146	772038
37851676	8541618	9396892	297786	455477	2697284	4118689	388569
1045987	130483	75063	635	54514	–	–	15645
36196206	5011043	5482243	713673	1029830	769614	1350877	264581
38480654	5522306	6951921	312945	1560649	926940	970192	384699
48482361	6512741	11200171	540694	3962920	1054171	1843765	547703
48177656	8728247	8817074	418337	2615613	1203694	1762871	591544
74981565	8317843	14817261	1148975	3937787	1547031	2401964	605439

项 目	Item	企业单位数(个) Number of Enterprises (unit)	#亏损企业(个) Loss Making Enterprises (unit)	工业总产值(当年价格) Gross Industrial Output Value (current price)	#新产品产值 Output of New Products
按市、县分	**Grouped by County**				
市 区	Urban District	4145	645	94197123	26147363
#萧山区	Xiaoshan	1907	220	41510626	11232404
余杭区	Yuhang	1228	246	14554528	4276758
桐庐县	Tonglu	357	25	4261552	1195336
淳安县	Chun'an	128	9	2410591	542564
建德市	Jiande	364	31	4045718	1084741
富阳市	Fuyang	713	112	12686059	3757470
临安市	Lin'an	577	114	6578993	2233938
按国民经济行业分	**Grouped by Economic Sector**				
采掘业	Mining and Quarrying	37	7	224168	11533
黑色金属矿采选业	Ferrous Metals Mining and Dressing	1	-	3428	-
有色金属矿采选业	Nonferrous Metals Mining and Dressing	6	1	64309	5630
非金属矿采选业	Nonmetal Minerals Mining and Dressing	30	6	156431	5903
制造业	Manufacturing Industry	6172	916	115086196	34829870
农副食品加工业	Agricultural Products Processing	122	15	1235439	176459
食品制造业	Food Manufacturing	103	12	1905235	316363
酒、饮料和精制茶制造业	Wine, Beverage and Tea Manufacturing	60	6	2478928	404538
烟草制品业	Tobacco Processing	2	-	2513692	10293
纺织业	Textile Industry	831	106	10158350	2052600
纺织服装、服饰业	Textile Products and Costune Indnstry	368	74	2998171	356978
皮革、毛皮、羽毛及其制品和制鞋业	Leather. Furs. Downand Related and Shoes Products	165	25	1736672	190750
木材加工和木、竹、藤、棕、草制品业	Timber Processing, Bamboo, Cane, Palm Fiber and Straw Products	41	4	262945	62804
家具制造业	Furniture Manufacturing	102	15	1415568	474996

continued 1 (10000 yuan)

工业销售产值 Value of Industrial Products Sales	出口交货值 Export delivery value	实收资本 Total Capital Hold	国家资本 State Capital	个人资本 Personal Capital	港澳台资本 Hongkong, Macau and TaiWan Capital	外商资本 Foreign Capital	就业人员年平均人数(人) Annual Average Number of Staff and Workers (person)
93653843	12944644	18526155	1237759	4619347	2469656	3856818	911952
40826963	5136850	7861001	232862	2091826	1156495	1210436	390645
14277767	2437688	2741929	53746	1043796	368587	346885	206636
4212615	1302265	796209	43890	313730	73198	58338	43476
2380390	145927	240199	13236	83654	17563	8889	18399
3984000	795964	631927	121274	257957	1797	37935	39667
12440512	639027	2201110	101503	888674	87701	143150	101643
6487862	1218264	1238735	49651	390037	100810	59706	81846
227195	2873	67807	4400	24524	-	15	3079
3551	-	500	500	-	-	-	96
68879	-	12148	-	11648	-	-	774
154765	2873	55159	3900	12876	-	15	2209
114102715	17042999	22300027	884555	6501857	2662868	4099319	1173982
1242306	99689	166445	-	75789	6885	6992	11380
1888014	95784	481952	22525	93530	76234	198199	22452
2438168	41054	469473	18769	33641	68720	191311	17844
2535060	2104	69040	-	3630	1400	-	224
9919358	2035089	1771679	7951	806061	226069	209201	146267
2961728	1594705	702898	3541	126346	345766	91638	83185
1723451	1037241	214562	-	60181	38399	24811	32238
260016	33545	44713	-	24162	1768	1214	4519
1390220	542727	331319	-	56010	42199	130996	29334

项 目	Item	企业单位数（个）Number of Enterprises (unit)	#亏损企业(个) Loss Making Enterprises (unit)	工业总产值（当年价格）Gross Industrial Output Value (current price)	#新产品产值 Output of New Products
造纸和纸制品业	Paper Making and Paper Products	324	41	3940688	738201
印刷和记录媒介复制业	Printing and Record Media	85	19	656198	101868
文教、工美、体育和娱乐用品制造业	Cultural, Educational. Industrial Arts. Sports and Entertainment Goods	150	19	1857225	621943
石油加工、炼焦和核燃料加工业	Petroleum Processing, Coking and Nuclear Fuel Processing	10	3	243156	51699
化学原料和化学制品制造业	Raw Chemical Materials and Chemical Products	370	30	12591858	3623018
医药制造业	Medical and Pharmaceutical Products	86	7	2429514	728088
化学纤维制造业	Chemical Fiber	123	12	6620350	2043405
橡胶和塑料制品业	Rubber and Plastic Products	309	48	6300647	1519318
非金属矿物制品业	Nonmetal Minerals Products	352	61	4938750	922057
黑色金属冶炼和压延加工业	Smelting and Processing of Ferrous Metals	134	27	4431056	1027193
有色金属冶炼和压延加工业	Smelting and Processing of Nonferrous Metals	79	14	4468021	1197090
金属制品业	Metals Products	353	46	4237360	1065004
通用设备制造业	Ordinary Machinery	517	58	9485511	3964672
专用设备制造业	For Special Purpose Equipment Manufacturing	233	46	2174606	645845
汽车制造业	Automobile Manufacturing	197	39	3790006	1646586
铁路、船舶、航空航天和其他运输设备制造业	Railway. watercraft. Avigation spaceflight and other Equipment Manufacturing	72	11	449056	111280
电气机械和器材制造业	Electric Equipment and Machinery	527	107	9784631	3641320
计算机、通信和其他电子设备制造业	Computers. Telecommunications and Other Electronic Equipment Manufacturing	283	47	8875175	5627190
仪器仪表制造业	Instruments and Meters Manufacturing	135	22	1968668	1058325
其他制造业	Other Manufacturing	21	2	212260	99693
废弃资源综合利用业	Multiple Utilization of Waste Resouces	16	–	917329	347462
金属制品、机械和设备修理业	Metal Products, Machinery and Equipment Repair	2	–	9134	2832
电力、热力生产和供应业	Production and Supply of Electric Power and Hot Water	45	6	6869578	83356
燃气生产和供应业	Production and Supply of Gas	12	–	1691073	26045
水的生产和供应业	Production and Supply of Tap Water	18	6	309021	10607

continued 2　　(10000 yuan)

工业销售产值 Value of Industrial Products Sales	出口交货值 Export delivery value	实收资本 Total Capital Hold	国家资本 State Capital	个人资本 Personal Capital	港澳台资本 Hongkong, Macau and TaiWan Capital	外商资本 Foreign Capital	就业人员年平均人数(人) Annual Average Number of Staff and Workers (person)
3859021	172716	712888	12704	364737	65843	47568	44839
646116	17898	213774	12712	74397	37431	2838	10622
1823695	501914	274076	485	65209	34922	88818	23301
242742	1010	108158	–	6458	334	–	1297
12399559	1091691	1706995	30877	415928	70800	302041	59039
2646375	302613	657034	85923	65623	47169	235925	30928
6457928	431666	864538	–	274072	101213	90466	29795
6755009	905673	883634	56019	223274	65379	205171	57415
4914308	208427	1019612	55738	316441	127565	143213	49738
4351000	81354	479490	126391	177831	22912	13172	25865
4363110	180124	363408	1500	93169	5541	24518	8919
4161723	572733	774639	42585	324137	153246	51974	48429
9313425	1393413	2128181	59840	679079	174423	363867	100389
2134275	414598	646796	22910	210184	78244	192449	33719
3759489	467754	1583255	4577	326530	271366	269585	44194
443398	172758	89683	20	40570	332	10476	9163
9664662	1658793	2361651	58366	647701	212911	480123	105863
8692432	2622461	2661177	256215	714677	377799	612690	107785
1937860	353002	448170	2812	165286	2434	101721	29873
224104	10465	22701	2093	9876	5565	4138	3509
945141	–	46487	–	27330	–	3907	1698
9023	–	1600	–	–	–	300	159
6847045	217	598237	190981	16350	50000	12919	13774
1685400	–	348011	248467	2669	31357	52582	1267
296866	–	320253	238909	8000	6500	–	4881

4－07 全市规模以上工业

Main Economic Indicators of Industrial

单位:万元

项目	Item	资产总计 Total Assets	流动资产合计 Total Circulating Funds	应收账款 Receivables	存货 Stock
总计	**Total**	**126802813**	**76095149**	**19436062**	**16627607**
按隶属关系分	**Grouped by Subordination**				
中央属	Central	5489949	2751249	404032	1328223
省属	Provincial	6792328	2514583	215248	476578
市属	Municipal	8123217	4389173	1039267	1258876
县(市)属	County and below	3136793	1780397	262267	390594
按所有制分	**Grouped by Ownership**				
国有企业	State－owned Enterprises	5008305	1616008	26049	248719
集体企业	Collective－owned Enterprises	34493	23739	11550	1457
股份合作企业	Cooperative Enterprises	3025982	367276	12087	8907
联营企业	Joint Ownership Enterprises	1606	1541	1080	344
股份制企业	Share－holding Corporations	79155659	47523797	12385949	11117140
外商及港澳台投资企业	Enterprises with Investment from Foreign、Hong Kong、Macao and Taiwan	38905707	26096584	6826854	5164171
其他企业	Other Enterprises	671062	466204	172493	86869
按企业规模分	**Grouped by Size of Enterprises**				
大型企业	Large	35415553	20564496	4569450	4945736
中型企业	Medium－sized	38665343	23443794	5687410	5170970
小微企业	Small	52721917	32086859	9179202	6510900
按轻重工业分	**Grouped by Light & Heavy Industry**				
轻工业	Light Industry	49844712	31129332	6574241	7466620
重工业	Heavy Industry	76958101	44965816	12861821	9160987

企业主要经济指标(2013 年)(二)
Enterprises Above Designated Size(2013)(Ⅱ)

(10000 yuan)

产成品 Finished Products	固定资产合计 Fixed Assets	累计折旧 Accumulated Depreciation	本年折旧 Depreciation of the year	负债合计 Total Liabilities	流动负债合计 Total Current Liabilities	非流动负债合计 Total Non-current Liabilities	所有者权益合计 Creditors' Equity
6356447	**30316878**	**19402995**	**3050857**	**73666008**	**63841570**	**8383578**	**53001577**
137717	1620039	1129777	140338	2879006	2102184	776822	2610942
150389	4499788	3229752	392409	4078315	2782010	1292941	2714012
480639	2349138	1163692	210505	4779432	3553884	1211224	3318673
152842	942542	649505	80039	1738897	1449840	240846	1395395
32997	4001616	2976475	344683	3229326	2144499	1084826	1778945
882	6662	12203	1100	18586	18571	-	15906
3944	18600	12495	1747	2136273	1618588	517685	889709
106	65	126	17	1268	1268	-	338
4231206	18026818	10794496	1819615	46897635	40874548	5091756	32201171
2049794	8101976	5503246	863916	20906462	18738633	1684789	17928757
37518	161140	103955	19779	476458	445464	4523	186751
1462200	9623999	6450732	901670	19093608	15356696	3654127	16321943
2005206	9154818	5974709	959065	22451702	19636420	2403280	16169937
2889041	11538061	6977553	1190121	32120698	28848454	2326171	20509696
2792023	11119837	7824275	1181359	28121820	25475665	2035364	21606309
3564424	19197042	11578719	1869498	45544188	38365906	6348214	31395268

单位:万元　　4－07　续表1

项　目	Item	资产总计 Total Assets	流动资产合　计 Total Circulating Funds	应收账款 Receivables	存　货 Stock
按市、县分	**Grouped by County**				
市　区	Urban District	99213457	59505585	14580260	13337196
#萧山区	Xiaoshan	44903922	25475768	5200264	5544090
余杭区	Yuhang	14790403	9353793	2645043	2001585
桐庐县	Tonglu	3404893	1961446	558479	529681
淳安县	Chun′an	1197114	615667	186325	138990
建德市	Jiande	3593323	1790841	444362	333104
富阳市	Fuyang	13111804	8273871	2192977	1503935
临安市	Lin′an	6282221	3947739	1473659	784700
按国民经济行业分	**Grouped by Economic Sector**				
采掘业	Mining and Quarrying	324236	156345	27539	14552
黑色金属矿采选业	Ferrous Metals Mining and Dressing	1636	1415	457	－
有色金属矿采选业	Nonferrous Metals Mining and Dressing	79340	34466	3778	6824
非金属矿采选业	Nonmetal Minerals Mining and Dressing	243260	120465	23304	7728
制造业	Manufacturing Industry	118706242	74267390	19220107	16538797
农副食品加工业	Agricultural Products Processing	855980	552962	149059	148802
食品制造业	Food Manufacturing	2140169	1381463	574500	209885
酒、饮料和精制茶制造业	Wine, Beverage and Tea Manufacturing	2024585	1041497	189926	199638
烟草制品业	Tobacco Processing	2261046	1582412	111274	1124950
纺织业	Textile Industry	9961894	6268216	1165224	1354091
纺织服装、服饰业	Textile Products and Costune Indnstry	3157965	2127010	394026	494781
皮革、毛皮、羽毛及其制品和制鞋业	Leather. Furs. Downand Related and Shoes Products	1543735	1168046	291407	300769
木材加工和木、竹、藤、棕、草制品业	Timber Processing, Bamboo, Cane, Palm Fiber and Straw Products	216975	150414	44057	35257
家具制造业	Furniture Manufacturing	1321544	932836	175514	188597

continued 1 (10000 yuan)

产成品 Finished Products	固定资产合计 Fixed Assets	累计折旧 Accumulated Depreciation	本年折旧 Depreciation of the year	负债合计 Total Liabilities	流动负债合计 Total Current Liabilities	非流动负债合计 Total Non－current Liabilities	所有者权益合计 Creditors´Equity
5003956	23604876	15817323	2400239	56941543	49135357	6793460	42163636
2309888	9875621	6423431	1052629	27887917	24103741	3112708	16920566
882738	3608816	1993987	352001	9029094	8280864	588191	5766452
148024	932394	508333	91381	2027195	1700792	253130	1377238
69517	375530	254276	51576	570345	483733	56517	623936
140194	1075757	623005	100963	1956071	1726766	205761	1636626
670733	3013031	1417460	273903	8676916	7559127	873981	4410900
324023	1315290	782598	132794	3493938	3235795	200728	2789242
8670	71134	47500	8212	215628	200651	13090	108140
–	221	301	104	29	29	–	1607
4486	12995	11481	1019	27981	27601	380	50891
4184	57918	35719	7089	187618	173021	12710	55642
6334919	23677418	15243471	2529253	68651281	61172952	6086000	49921019
71866	204184	90732	18411	523181	490813	26803	335547
93056	460958	279066	38753	907464	887563	10017	1232009
61148	700037	549687	78119	911722	849889	59186	1086507
46990	320079	302008	45814	402005	401855	150	1859041
637535	2373445	1917672	294638	6395161	5870204	313863	3552758
199464	702636	396142	58720	1876278	1720776	98070	1273961
70565	180227	100490	17233	1167904	1155768	9201	376197
14248	42907	32037	4968	160150	154980	4364	55820
58433	243985	130717	22053	765569	734311	12609	553172

项 目	Item	资产总计 Total Assets	流动资产合 计 Total Circulating Funds	应收账款 Receivables	存 货 Stock
造纸和纸制品业	Paper Making and Paper Products	4841813	3209230	912349	470819
印刷和记录媒介复制业	Printing and Record Media	877377	496137	141139	94660
文教、工美、体育和娱乐用品制造业	Cultural, Educational. Industrial Arts. Sports and Entertainment Goods	1016460	626345	117874	216741
石油加工、炼焦和核燃料加工业	Petroleum Processing, Coking and Nuclear Fuel Processing	95395	64268	32151	17926
化学原料和化学制品制造业	Raw Chemical Materials and Chemical Products	9783106	5667829	1165428	1063319
医药制造业	Medical and Pharmaceutical Products	3343084	1851339	519519	520837
化学纤维制造业	Chemical Fiber	6435853	3511885	337180	748943
橡胶和塑料制品业	Rubber and Plastic Products	5593192	3294520	791337	709135
非金属矿物制品业	Nonmetal Minerals Products	6074590	4005319	1437421	548782
黑色金属冶炼和压延加工业	Smelting and Processing of Ferrous Metals	4720284	3097154	263594	641632
有色金属冶炼和压延加工业	Smelting and Processing of Nonferrous Metals	2459720	1731712	206674	420190
金属制品业	Metals Products	3945387	2776865	791844	767076
通用设备制造业	Ordinary Machinery	11049883	7177584	2170108	1666039
专用设备制造业	For Special Purpose Equipment Manufacturing	2604104	1762144	624300	453406
汽车制造业	Automobile Manufacturing	8572282	3156388	926140	611919
铁路、船舶、航空航天和其他运输设备制造业	Railway. watercraft. Avigation spaceflight and other Equipment Manufacturing	475664	311441	83938	70743
电气机械和器材制造业	Electric Equipment and Machinery	10377138	6867370	2568629	1402021
计算机、通信和其他电子设备制造业	Computers. Telecommunications and Other Electronic Equipment Manufacturing	10081411	7297829	2218589	1554520
仪器仪表制造业	Instruments and Meters Manufacturing	2226820	1647406	700151	343716
其他制造业	Other Manufacturing	146877	111345	16927	45717
废弃资源综合利用业	Multiple Utilization of Waste Resouces	493764	391135	95577	112411
金属制品、机械和设备修理业	Metal Products, Machinery and Equipment Repair	8148	7291	4251	1477
电力、热力生产和供应业	Production and Supply of Electric Power and Hot Water	4662140	764382	128426	35070
燃气生产和供应业	Production and Supply of Gas	1103491	203346	41037	9000
水的生产和供应业	Production and Supply of Tap Water	2006704	703686	18953	30188

continued 2　　　　(10000 yuan)

产成品 Finished Products	固定资产合计 Fixed Assets	累计折旧 Accumulated Depreciation	本年折旧 Depreciation of the year	负债合计 Total Liabilities	流动负债合计 Total Current Liabilities	非流动负债合计 Total Non－current Liabilities	所有者权益合计 Creditors´Equity
230709	1028214	664124	115137	3229845	2952866	123136	1580240
44012	305335	246918	34012	518963	467480	41209	357747
76424	284067	187837	29877	560020	485434	57166	454220
2751	26086	71582	5025	152611	152611	－	－57216
496339	2703422	1379664	258927	5777196	4773454	920118	4003413
212192	984569	340548	59471	1788204	1426517	350871	1538066
421652	1048449	951426	135520	3882167	3605838	216682	2538341
371867	1510308	907975	181786	3312357	2845761	388640	2289387
301311	1372056	992839	154031	4022527	3680722	263900	2049943
207145	791884	929628	95410	3013808	2776780	215140	1704867
141969	401427	123636	31854	1757144	1649201	30799	686637
242566	776703	426752	80921	2606189	2480615	103554	1346488
621832	1715825	894139	168425	5969030	5520052	316837	5077050
138037	610246	321861	55493	1350658	1222578	112083	1253181
258097	1393098	627816	130089	5674388	4177137	1486358	2897760
25955	120310	61132	10425	319690	295066	11608	155065
640148	1787295	1106900	188471	5811087	5253720	518379	4560471
487919	1172953	953270	169954	4341584	3886734	288632	5737474
99375	303986	208822	34159	1028786	948641	40042	1198481
13077	25144	19781	2691	45371	45111	260	102707
48101	87093	27957	8779	374764	255032	66307	119000
138	492	316	90	5461	5444	18	2686
2645	4869659	3232512	406091	3116868	1624149	1460590	1544455
5338	671608	166623	31970	620604	329319	291285	482887
4874	1027059	712889	75330	1061628	514500	532614	945076

4－08 全市规模以上工业

Main Economic Indicators of Industrial

单位：万元

项　目	Item	主营业务收　入 Revenues in Main Business	主营业务成　本 Costs in Main Business	主营业务税金及附加 Sales Taxes and Extra Charges in Main Business
总　计	**Total**	**124241505**	**102930657**	**2151920**
按隶属关系分	**Grouped by Subordination**			
中央属	Central	6182611	3883316	1605451
省　属	Provincial	8607791	7951060	28588
市　属	Municipal	7153670	5691898	43501
县(市)属	County and Below	2726256	2454692	7618
按所有制分	**Grouped by Ownership**			
国有企业	State－owned Enterprises	7147829	6837797	21853
集体企业	Collective－owned Enterprises	39425	35510	453
股份合作企业	Cooperative Enterprises	54997	43699	327
联营企业	Joint Ownership Enterprises	3962	3807	9
股份制企业	Share－holding Corporations	77595905	65246558	1878253
外商及港澳台投资企业	Enterprises with Investment from Foreign、Hong Kong、Macao and Taiwan	38367156	29862666	244336
其他企业	Other Enterprises	1032232	900622	6690
按企业规模分	**Grouped by Size of Enterprises**			
大型企业	Large	36555832	28279782	1747441
中型企业	Medium－sized	38972974	32862943	183879
小微企业	Small	48712700	41787932	220600
按轻重工业分	**Grouped by Light & Heavy Industry**			
轻工业	Light Industry	48661352	38321668	1784509
重工业	Heavy Industry	75580153	64608989	367411

企业主要经济指标(2013)(三)
Enterprises Above Designated Size(2013)(Ⅲ)

(10000 yuan)

销售费用 Sales Expenses	管理费用 Management Expenses	财务费用 Financial Expenses	利息支出 Interest Expenditure	营业利润 Business Profits	利润总额 Total Profits	利税总额 Total Pre - tax Profits	本年应交增值税 Value Added Tax Payable
4676207	**6152034**	**1726667**	**2214244**	**8182963**	**8536012**	**14505471**	**3808840**
152084	245054	29522	57329	306069	331202	2340785	402849
51752	249037	40547	97019	568723	325638	549869	194781
594680	376816	61448	77238	483597	497335	753254	211689
41262	108643	40805	50747	131539	145997	211613	57377
4542	132456	25489	76162	425690	170747	348081	154260
846	1338	258	259	1035	1392	3746	1902
1445	25708	-11020	111806	52212	51949	54016	1740
24	92	-	-	30	27	111	75
1923097	3663639	1353878	1514254	4244784	4576409	8743512	2283297
2729926	2292887	340869	494588	3405110	3681187	5267079	1339642
16328	35915	17195	17176	54103	54302	88926	27924
1917133	1729362	204137	379097	3268800	3163525	6206253	1294093
1457492	1953526	590625	707832	2294718	2599322	3996220	1210596
1301583	2469145	931906	1127316	2619445	2773166	4302998	1304152
2689189	2329970	762480	916011	3348187	3460151	7075697	1826956
1987018	3822064	964188	1298233	4834776	5075861	7429774	1981885

项 目	Item	主营业务收入 Revenues in Main Business	主营业务成本 Costs in Main Business	主营业务税金及附加 Sales Taxes and Extra Charges in Main Business
按市、县分	**Grouped by County**			
市 区	Urban District	95059806	77710091	2025827
#萧山区	Xiaoshan	41407987	36732836	211132
余杭区	Yuhang	14202096	11939604	68849
桐庐县	Tonglu	4090510	3509987	22440
淳安县	Chun'an	2328473	1974566	14377
建德市	Jiande	3938136	3300545	20381
富阳市	Fuyang	12399945	10985452	41940
临安市	Lin'an	6424635	5450017	26955
按国民经济行业分	**Grouped by Economic Sector**			
采掘业	Mining and Quarrying	224668	164292	3725
黑色金属矿采选业	Ferrous Metals Mining and Dressing	3551	2325	13
有色金属矿采选业	Nonferrous Metals Mining and Dressing	66679	50738	728
非金属矿采选业	Nonmetal Minerals Mining and Dressing	154438	111230	2985
制造业	Manufacturing Industry	115136836	94467741	2122788
农副食品加工业	Agricultural Products Processing	1258421	1095974	3857
食品制造业	Food Manufacturing	2237645	1710324	9899
酒、饮料和精制茶制造业	Wine, Beverage and Tea Manufacturing	2375133	1653220	37146
烟草制品业	Tobacco Processing	2458997	469253	1539117
纺织业	Textile Industry	9967798	8834160	45272
纺织服装、服饰业	Textile Products and Costune Indnstry	2991765	2543010	17817
皮革、毛皮、羽毛及其制品和制鞋业	Leather. Furs. Downand Related and Shoes Products	1707099	1514412	7906
木材加工和木、竹、藤、棕、草制品业	Timber Processing, Bamboo, Cane, Palm Fiber and Straw Products	260531	225867	2223
家具制造业	Furniture Manufacturing	1397378	1110892	8121

continued 1 (10000 yuan)

销售费用 Sales Expenses	管理费用 Management Expenses	财务费用 Financial Expenses	利息支出 Interest Expenditure	营业利润 Business Profits	利润总额 Total Profits	利税总额 Total Pre - tax Profits	本年应交增值税 Value Added Tax Payable
3979658	4922043	1174254	1620663	6592942	6815164	11876509	3029697
608299	1541450	760985	1023005	2137520	2241024	3463832	1009629
620086	845652	219609	247498	578741	628026	1127051	429807
78274	158743	50659	50309	308775	316379	478993	139511
117231	65401	22689	21621	145565	152091	227207	60545
111020	175433	54066	55959	328242	341661	470273	107419
180955	432876	340503	377055	513044	593683	908409	272344
209069	397538	84495	88638	294395	317034	544081	199324
8955	18131	7826	7598	22159	22440	40508	14343
270	575	–	–	368	368	491	110
903	7016	1230	1232	6106	6067	10935	4140
7783	10539	6596	6366	15686	16005	29082	10093
4640957	5987656	1630877	2099742	7568615	8144319	13867555	3593654
38888	40197	21684	21223	60226	64603	99084	30575
255720	95457	-2704	13374	218564	227734	332231	94598
434415	57892	7672	12850	246164	254825	399973	108002
76426	111096	-3520	859	288071	275262	2128942	314410
125279	332689	232695	256307	440006	437566	723264	239996
97569	200521	53647	55906	97187	109707	237218	109241
36814	55799	41917	39416	53863	54645	111570	48960
7406	12768	5365	5489	6788	8345	18814	8080
78907	70337	22136	22884	104441	105021	158396	45254

项　目	Item	主营业务收入 Revenues in Main Business	主营业务成本 Costs in Main Business	主营业务税金及附加 Sales Taxes and Extra Charges in Main Business
造纸和纸制品业	Paper Making and Paper Products	3790083	3245693	19765
印刷和记录媒介复制业	Printing and Record Media	655854	558146	2875
文教、工美、体育和娱乐用品制造业	Cultural,Educational. Industrial Arts. Sports and Entertainment Goods	1821723	1660094	7107
石油加工、炼焦和核燃料加工业	Petroleum Processing, Coking and Nuclear Fuel Processing	245904	222550	17283
化学原料和化学制品制造业	Raw Chemical Materials and Chemical Products	12501249	10400162	30901
医药制造业	Medical and Pharmaceutical Products	2627685	1283598	24191
化学纤维制造业	Chemical Fiber	6559844	6052285	17531
橡胶和塑料制品业	Rubber and Plastic Products	6482088	5564291	31023
非金属矿物制品业	Nonmetal Minerals Products	4937537	4152289	23812
黑色金属冶炼和压延加工业	Smelting and Processing of Ferrous Metals	4407441	4101121	15023
有色金属冶炼和压延加工业	Smelting and Processing of Nonferrous Metals	4275797	4059659	6221
金属制品业	Metals Products	4329973	3841876	20267
通用设备制造业	Ordinary Machinery	9567528	7831786	43942
专用设备制造业	For Special Purpose Equipment Manufacturing	2154157	1706340	12610
汽车制造业	Automobile Manufacturing	3909920	3295244	57079
铁路、船舶、航空航天和其他运输设备制造业	Railway. watercraft. Avigation spaceflight and other Equipment Manufacturing	456054	380657	2083
电气机械和器材制造业	Electric Equipment and Machinery	9749330	8094329	37469
计算机、通信和其他电子设备制造业	Computers. Telecommunications and Other Electronic Equipment Manufacturing	8969371	6470362	60498
仪器仪表制造业	Instruments and Meters Manufacturing	1843976	1303559	12448
其他制造业	Other Manufacturing	293082	260513	1505
废弃资源综合利用业	Multiple Utilization of Waste Resouces	894453	819397	7720
金属制品、机械和设备修理业	Metal Products, Machinery and Equipment Repair	9022	6680	78
电力、热力生产和供应业	Production and Supply of Electric Power and Hot Water	6863940	6461688	19005
燃气生产和供应业	Production and Supply of Gas	1686986	1548678	4471
水的生产和供应业	Production and Supply of Tap Water	329076	288258	1930

continued 2 (10000 yuan)

销售费用 Sales Expenses	管理费用 Management Expenses	财务费用 Financial Expenses	利息支出 Interest Expenditure	营业利润 Business Profits	利润总额 Total Profits	利税总额 Total Pre - tax Profits	本年应交增值税 Value Added Tax Payable
65616	161178	148656	166217	184334	195996	326524	110156
14621	39691	13579	14664	35292	36418	61536	21846
27144	58732	22367	22032	51176	51053	90568	32269
3200	18333	5928	5964	-21389	-22045	9002	13763
519415	635594	168170	196974	1012600	1047589	1418005	338619
720067	304511	8235	23676	360266	377529	618896	217072
23903	117920	103355	143709	312953	322538	435790	95720
235243	209424	85512	91246	510465	514704	699949	154072
228302	187480	110309	134609	260136	285670	473223	163657
26075	124078	72431	131015	102614	112047	208674	81525
13014	44614	45729	65930	116474	170533	225551	48764
69855	199726	73497	85270	141620	153914	262962	88525
269838	650114	95211	113103	786792	812092	1178965	322003
82463	202490	29628	30133	144413	154711	228912	61406
155402	329735	43814	183255	139462	183728	377821	136772
12389	34164	12128	11953	17830	18347	29918	9465
455562	617403	161164	165442	442362	470101	744536	236317
444455	840816	33360	63764	1208367	1436008	1812225	315075
115699	212349	12530	14494	181424	216609	316238	87141
3826	11504	1165	1642	14773	16094	27837	10214
2865	9531	5140	6269	51224	52685	109951	49546
583	1513	77	76	120	289	981	614
1174	89074	61614	64180	504910	272516	456303	163527
11604	20803	13847	13700	99031	98481	130601	27649
13517	36370	12503	29023	-11752	-1744	10504	9668

4-09 市区规模以上工业
Main Economic Indicators of Industrial Enterprises

单位:万元

项 目	Item	企业单位数(个) Number of Enterprises (unit)	#亏损企业(个) Loss Making Enterprises (unit)	工业总产值(当年价格) Gross Industrial Output Value (current price)	#新产品产值 Output of New Products
总 计	**Total**	**4145**	**645**	**94197123**	**26147363**
按隶属关系分	**Grouped by Subordination**				
中 央 属	Central	27	7	4812779	542586
省 属	Provincial	44	3	7775943	481740
市 属	Municipal	72	19	5669980	1615796
按所有制分	**Grouped by Ownership**				
国有企业	State - owned Enterprises	18	1	6332681	167812
集体企业	Collective - owned Enterprises	5	-	22398	-
股份合作企业	Cooperative Enterprises	10	-	42673	3383
联营企业	Joint Ownership Enterprises	1	-	4006	-
股份制企业	Share - holding Corporations	3070	414	53646098	14578234
外商及港澳台投资企业	Enterprises with Investment from Foreign、Hong Kong、Macao and Taiwan	953	222	33643198	11342768
其他企业	Other Enterprises	88	8	506070	55166
按企业规模分	**Grouped by Size of Enterprises**				
大型企业	Large	108	10	32544642	10618776
中型企业	Medium - sized	579	78	28373517	9700665
小微企业	Small	3458	557	33278964	5827922
按轻重工业分	**Grouped by Light & Heavy Industry**				
轻工业	Light Industry	2079	319	38407906	8583100
重工业	Heavy Industry	2066	326	55789218	17564262

企业主要经济指标(2013 年)(一)

Above Designated Size in Urban District(2013)(Ⅰ)

(10000 yuan)

工业销售产值 Value of Industrial Products Sales	出口交货值 Export delivery value	实收资本 Total Capital Hold	国家资本 State Capital	个人资本 Personal Capital	港澳台资本 Hongkong, Macau and TaiWan Capital	外商资本 Foreign Capital	就业人员年平均人数(人) Annual Average Number of Staff and Workers (person)
93653843	**12944644**	**18526155**	**1237759**	**4619347**	**2469656**	**3856818**	**911952**
4838070	7848	801965	67476	2184	137500	14495	9420
7726120	193072	872225	445181	17935	110783	168600	27946
6105129	1057073	1046603	302035	79647	48401	142218	47296
6307196	21011	238290	234599	–	–	–	14792
22195	4972	1410	–	210	–	–	423
41920	–	46832	–	1829	–	–	1064
4006	–	100	–	–	–	–	62
52856550	5638657	9744083	716236	4214834	14193	42692	544863
33921532	7248611	8450805	286924	366759	2455463	3814126	341807
500445	31393	44636	–	35715	–	–	8941
33017438	4440213	4785326	597421	796525	768614	1308945	234554
27975141	4405529	5505938	191527	1185802	796120	899780	304122
32661264	4098902	8234892	448811	2637021	904922	1648093	373276
38092367	6358353	7067124	285187	1869946	1070881	1628726	452122
55561476	6586291	11459031	952572	2749401	1398775	2228092	459830

单位:万元　　4-09　续表1

项　目	Item	企业单位数（个）Number of Enterprises (unit)	#亏损企业(个) Loss Making Enterprises (unit)	工业总产值（当年价格）Gross Industrial Output Value (current price)	#新产品产值 Output of New Products
按国民经济行业分	**Grouped by Economic Sector**				
采掘业	Mining and Quarrying	4	-	18979	-
非金属矿采选业	Nonmetal Minerals Mining and Dressing	4	-	18979	-
制造业	Manufacturing Industry	4099	639	86546591	26110711
农副食品加工业	Agricultural Products Processing	67	12	835662	109247
食品制造业	Food Manufacturing	70	8	1618814	215986
酒、饮料和精制茶制造业	Wine, Beverage and Tea Manufacturing	32	3	1742074	205686
烟草制品业	Tobacco Processing	2	-	2513692	10293
纺织业	Textile Industry	649	89	8394352	1635027
纺织服装、服饰业	Textile Products and Costume Industry	267	62	2268418	269013
皮革、毛皮、羽毛及其制品和制鞋业	Leather. Furs. Downand Related and Shoes Products	111	18	1304737	116375
木材加工和木、竹、藤、棕、草制品业	Timber Processing, Bamboo, Cane, Palm Fiber and Straw Products	20	1	151426	37883
家具制造业	Furniture Manufacturing	73	12	1153955	420471
造纸和纸制品业	Paper Making and Paper Products	86	10	1028631	204573
印刷和记录媒介复制业	Printing and Record Media	74	18	613770	101868
文教、工美、体育和娱乐用品制造业	Cultural, Educational. Industrial Arts. Sports and Entertainment Goods	96	17	1576516	516674
石油加工、炼焦和核燃料加工业	Petroleum Processing, Coking and Nuclear Fuel Processing	7	3	225536	43716

continued 1

(10000 yuan)

工业销售产值 Value of Industrial Products Sales	出口交货值 Export delivery value	实收资本 Total Capital Hold	国家资本 State Capital	个人资本 Personal Capital	港澳台资本 Hongkong, Macau and TaiWan Capital	外商资本 Foreign Capital	就业人员年平均人数(人) Annual Average Number of Staff and Workers (person)
18473	–	4124	–	3015	–	–	475
18473	–	4124	–	3015	–	–	475
86037459	12944426	17562395	683816	4595533	2386926	3797775	899223
846187	79692	133213	–	53760	6016	6960	8590
1612598	45359	420406	22525	63405	63108	197186	18858
1712113	12762	334084	369	4996	67890	184298	13215
2535060	2104	69040	–	3630	1400	–	224
8179894	1640413	1610648	1700	717158	211302	194944	125628
2244871	1088341	626683	3541	94181	339602	86768	71029
1291949	726562	178061	–	48642	37082	22329	22435
150180	14181	25943	–	15879	1231	–	2733
1130988	368024	255771	–	43756	25135	104318	24151
1005870	28825	188002	12704	57169	25281	35728	12169
604135	14999	203624	12712	64748	37431	2838	9712
1547191	366003	230420	485	49953	22850	88327	18426
225567	–	104546	–	4258	–	–	1117

项　目	Item	企业单位数（个）Number of Enterprises (unit)	#亏损企业(个) Loss Making Enterprises (unit)	工业总产值（当年价格）Gross Industrial Output Value (current price)	#新产品产值 Output of New Products
化学原料和化学制品制造业	Raw Chemical Materials and Chemical Products	228	13	10210371	2775747
医药制造业	Medical and Pharmaceutical Products	60	4	2020427	480536
化学纤维制造业	Chemical Fiber	115	12	6480290	2014724
橡胶和塑料制品业	Rubber and Plastic Products	213	31	4957558	1175312
非金属矿物制品业	Nonmetal Mineral Products	205	37	3405064	690559
黑色金属冶炼和压延加工业	Smelting and Processing of Ferrous Metals	107	22	3853435	864311
有色金属冶炼和压延加工业	Smelting and Processing of Nonferrous Metals	28	8	791068	217595
金属制品业	Metal Products	215	24	2854652	603863
通用设备制造业	Ordinary Machinery	370	42	7112582	2812806
专用设备制造业	For Special Purpose Equipment Manufacturing	180	36	1792592	532011
汽车制造业	Automobile Manufacturing	166	37	3423951	1485495
铁路、船舶、航空航天和其他运输设备制造业	Railway. watercraft. Avigation spaceflight and other Equipment Manufacturing	44	7	326033	80068
电气机械和器材制造业	Electric Equipment and Machinery	268	54	6254261	2471864
计算机、通信和其他电子设备制造业	Computers. Telecommunications and Other Electronic Equipment Manufacturing	204	37	7546290	4897799
仪器仪表制造业	Instruments and Meters Manufacturing	120	20	1876965	1028132
其他制造业	Other Manufacturing	18	2	196998	92512
废弃资源综合利用业	Multiple Utilization of Waste Resouces	3	-	12056	-
电力、热力生产和供应业	Production and Supply of Electric Power and Hot Water	24	2	5719208	-
燃气生产和供应业	Production and Supply of Gas	9	1	1663117	26045
水的生产和供应业	Production and Supply of Tap Water	9	3	249227	10607

continued 2 (10000 yuan)

工业销售产值 Value of Industrial Products Sales	出口交货值 Export delivery value	实收资本 Total Capital Hold	国家资本 State Capital	个人资本 Personal Capital	港澳台资本 Hongkong, Macau and TaiWan Capital	外商资本 Foreign Capital	就业人员年平均人数(人) Annual Average Number of Staff and Workers (person)
10049707	583492	1260962	21089	230389	55371	225981	43109
2266410	217308	456702	5923	29917	46146	195445	23220
6319566	396444	848130	–	273850	100022	86372	28572
5431035	833742	671314	24928	137719	48858	203026	42438
3386042	183518	649166	21623	236693	62539	135928	34415
3780230	77129	431417	126391	145414	22912	12572	22940
750133	173024	124646	–	14363	5541	6450	3444
2830742	398627	550603	36585	206619	129492	49836	34419
6971667	1020009	1532617	54338	436762	166375	342409	78390
1764565	383736	540996	15910	158509	70109	189706	27213
3404290	390972	1521968	4577	302429	268464	266747	38887
319710	159604	72985	–	32245	332	9926	6156
6191390	1000237	1624363	57296	424889	190675	436505	67379
7406369	2379745	2455693	256215	591148	373766	603110	88624
1853531	352437	413285	2812	143728	2434	101721	28233
209161	7138	21651	2093	8826	5565	4138	3215
12004	–	4457	–	500	–	3907	198
5702527	217	369039	99549	13550	50000	12919	7486
1656909	–	331468	242009	2249	28730	46124	1042
238474	–	259129	212385	5000	4000	–	3726

4－10 市区规模以上工业

Main Economic Indicators of Industrial

单位:万元

项目	Item	资产总计 Total Assets	流动资产合计 Total Circulating Funds	应收账款 Receivables	存货 Stock
总计	**Total**	**99213457**	**59505585**	**14580260**	**13337196**
按隶属关系分	**Grouped by Subordination**				
中央属	Central	4981273	2401073	357894	1283448
省属	Provincial	6340298	2469847	203816	468632
市属	Municipal	6853858	3632859	785033	1092186
按所有制分	**Grouped by Ownership**				
国有企业	State－owned Enterprises	4556782	1580967	25378	246448
集体企业	Collective－owned Enterprises	21912	13351	4941	1079
股份合作企业	Cooperative Enterprises	3000931	345015	8785	6731
联营企业	Joint Ownership Enterprises	1606	1541	1080	344
股份制企业	Share－holding Corporations	56445146	34044117	8538555	8418307
外商及港澳台投资企业	Enterprises with Investment from Foreign、Hong Kong、Macao and Taiwan	34816305	23278092	5918148	4618415
其他企业	Other Enterprises	370776	242502	83374	45873
按企业规模分	**Grouped by Size of Enterprises**				
大型企业	Large	31496616	18647313	3991775	4489742
中型企业	Medium－sized	29567412	18074979	4306353	4144760
小微企业	Small	38149429	22783293	6282133	4702694
按轻重工业分	**Grouped by Light & Heavy Industry**				
轻工业	Light Industry	39334652	24774453	4804329	6307407
重工业	Heavy Industry	59878805	34731132	9775931	7029789

企业主要经济指标(2013 年)(二)

Enterprises Above Designated Size in Urban District(2013)(Ⅱ)

(10000 yuan)

产成品 Finished Products	固定资产合计 Fixed Assets	累计折旧 Accumulated Depreciation	本年折旧 Depreciation of the year	负债合计 Total Liabilities	流动负债合计 Total Current Liabilities	非流动负债合计 Total Non-current Liabilities	所有者权益合计 Creditors´Equity
5003956	**23604876**	**15817323**	**2400239**	**56941543**	**49135357**	**6793460**	**42163636**
120942	1488602	937636	121932	2446273	1699482	746791	2534999
146016	4124481	2962200	357433	3860620	2611206	1246112	2479678
414559	2168830	1078244	194590	4120172	2993730	1122079	2708574
31717	3613731	2682325	307705	3044684	1991458	1053226	1512064
646	4698	10156	672	10969	10969	-	10943
2391	16268	9560	1479	2120469	1602845	517625	880462
106	65	126	17	1268	1268	-	338
3104894	12633455	8115861	1310567	33149897	28914484	3656377	23243360
1844839	7230127	4933057	767862	18348277	16355006	1563778	16410409
19363	106532	66239	11938	265977	259327	2455	106061
1310878	8652720	6135388	839536	17033209	13780684	3191324	14463406
1610563	6770254	4483668	702562	17126493	14826566	1955389	12397314
2082516	8181852	5198267	858141	22781840	20528107	1646747	15302916
2277619	8519279	6535772	934697	21561830	19811648	1301629	17668985
2726337	15085597	9281551	1465543	35379713	29323710	5491831	24494651

单位:万元 4-10 续表1

项 目	Item	资产总计 Total Assets	流动资产合计 Total Circulating Funds	应收账款 Receivables	存货 Stock
按国民经济行业分	**Grouped by Economic Sector**				
采掘业	Mining and Quarrying	21515	13004	5258	726
非金属矿采选业	Nonmetal Minerals Mining and Dressing	21515	13004	5258	726
制造业	Manufacturing Industry	93068640	58280900	14438029	13279483
农副食品加工业	Agricultural Products Processing	664189	430896	109389	115817
食品制造业	Food Manufacturing	1915621	1249435	546613	167261
酒、饮料和精制茶制造业	Wine, Beverage and Tea Manufacturing	1438019	819524	135244	129298
烟草制品业	Tobacco Processing	2261046	1582412	111274	1124950
纺织业	Textile Industry	8837171	5565500	1027682	1201468
纺织服装、服饰业	Textile Products and Costume Industry	2757240	1900079	321090	442857
皮革、毛皮、羽毛及其制品和制鞋业	Leather. Furs. Downand Related and Shoes Products	1316021	1035218	240922	259497
木材加工和木、竹、藤、棕、草制品业	Timber Processing, Bamboo, Cane, Palm Fiber and Straw Products	135346	93404	23693	17200
家具制造业	Furniture Manufacturing	1089792	770098	129362	155257
造纸和纸制品业	Paper Making and Paper Products	872966	568230	191122	105393
印刷和记录媒介复制业	Printing and Record Media	814286	455884	134850	88554
文教、工美、体育和娱乐用品制造业	Cultural, Educational. Industrial Arts. Sports and Entertainment Goods	839918	507698	85711	189664
石油加工、炼焦和核燃料加工业	Petroleum Processing, Coking and Nuclear Fuel Processing	82246	54395	28447	13887

continued 1 (10000 yuan)

产成品 Finished Products	固定资产合计 Fixed Assets	累计折旧 Accumulated Depreciation	本年折旧 Depreciation of the year	负债合计 Total Liabilities	流动负债合计 Total Current Liabilities	非流动负债合计 Total Non - current Liabilities	所有者权益合计 Creditors´Equity
326	4872	10253	1052	10011	10011	–	11505
326	4872	10253	1052	10011	10011	–	11505
4998160	18018016	12464904	1976342	53024673	47224176	4796533	39936505
57653	154699	69931	14178	413880	384009	25337	253057
77040	398966	254872	34006	799465	785716	4095	1115460
35448	450028	416463	44486	584620	559008	23879	827815
46990	320079	302008	45814	402005	401855	150	1859041
574227	2159727	1745758	262495	5710730	5279957	229772	3119739
183310	583439	339816	47950	1619818	1469264	96155	1129739
59347	134254	74018	12531	1020759	1012766	5882	295886
6514	27279	21667	3422	98751	97175	1129	36596
50784	193118	108375	16861	633203	604009	11890	453890
35074	215066	190358	26607	480529	437171	12796	362583
40877	287994	228910	31565	477058	436958	31738	336561
66015	244869	160813	25556	452534	382299	55818	386287
1458	23275	69556	4689	147769	147769	–	-65523

项　目	Item	资产总计 Total Assets	流动资产合　计 Total Circulating Funds	应收账款 Receivables	存　货 Stock
化学原料和化学制品制造业	Raw Chemical Materials and Chemical Products	7143155	4140992	786984	845386
医药制造业	Medical and Pharmaceutical Products	2422348	1545160	433913	446558
化学纤维制造业	Chemical Fiber	6358084	3465901	329858	729117
橡胶和塑料制品业	Rubber and Plastic Products	4661354	2728313	600673	623089
非金属矿物制品业	Nonmetal Mineral Products	4283589	3023374	1095782	427978
黑色金属冶炼和压延加工业	Smelting and Processing of Ferrous Metals	4434677	2902872	206940	594006
有色金属冶炼和压延加工业	Smelting and Processing of Nonferrous Metals	821765	450959	75537	96648
金属制品业	Metal Products	2879785	2026250	583080	593148
通用设备制造业	Ordinary Machinery	8384207	5604079	1656531	1218232
专用设备制造业	For Special Purpose Equipment Manufacturing	2236251	1504819	545229	377729
汽车制造业	Automobile Manufacturing	8097552	2860632	854076	540992
铁路、船舶、航空航天和其他运输设备制造业	Railway. watercraft. Avigation spaceflight and other Equipment Manufacturing	377584	245326	57014	54903
电气机械和器材制造业	Electric Equipment and Machinery	6652398	4472070	1461052	943491
计算机、通信和其他电子设备制造业	Computers. Telecommunications and Other Electronic Equipment Manufacturing	9020593	6603174	1982844	1401895
仪器仪表制造业	Instruments and Meters Manufacturing	2112541	1551894	664254	327723
其他制造业	Other Manufacturing	134675	103916	14477	44618
废弃资源综合利用业	Multiple Utilization of Waste Resouces	20822	15399	2283	2429
电力、热力生产和供应业	Production and Supply of Electric Power and Hot Water	3458822	502599	85281	26471
燃气生产和供应业	Production and Supply of Gas	1071179	191142	39187	8331
水的生产和供应业	Production and Supply of Tap Water	1593301	517940	12506	22185

continued 2 (10000 yuan)

产成品 Finished Products	固定资产合计 Fixed Assets	累计折旧 Accumulated Depreciation	本年折旧 Depreciation of the year	负债合计 Total Liabilities	流动负债合计 Total Current Liabilities	非流动负债合计 Total Non－current Liabilities	所有者权益合计 Creditors´Equity
399093	2101410	1092461	206100	4303837	3482055	778735	2836823
184523	521177	274366	45858	1233661	1166267	60700	1172279
413367	1032689	937300	133388	3827468	3551240	216630	2515321
327467	1304053	812168	158724	2739187	2324616	354073	1929276
246553	794906	632313	98642	2896675	2666722	161837	1384319
187933	712254	892335	83034	2813446	2587275	211235	1619647
39478	222184	59594	14160	605201	552390	12256	216535
161717	566808	316738	57668	1893837	1783156	94298	990672
491055	1266131	716645	128588	4570447	4222196	225854	3809961
110296	529085	282275	48573	1161084	1037344	109387	1074563
240561	1289537	588645	118617	5395660	3925226	1460081	2701758
21601	98536	47506	8038	249046	239703	9344	128537
413278	1138817	771762	127073	3793976	3485336	283735	2856134
421088	931129	833350	142187	3679425	3261857	279807	5337794
90638	291129	199955	32519	966009	886974	39192	1146251
12606	20611	18946	2417	37820	37560	260	98056
2031	4656	5952	586	14323	13853	470	6499
–	4087562	2565748	331444	2490695	1179666	1302268	967310
5067	657773	160755	31118	610836	323052	287784	460344
403	836653	615663	60284	805329	398453	406876	787973

4－11 市区规模以上工业

Main Economic Indicators of Industrial

单位:万元

项 目	Item	主营业务收入 Revenues in Main Business	主营业务成本 Costs in Main Business	主营业务税金及附加 Sales Taxes and Extra Charges in Main Business
总　　计	**Total**	**95059806**	**77710091**	**2025827**
按隶属关系分	**Grouped by Subordination**			
中　央　属	Central	4856358	2619419	1602068
省　　属	Provincial	7831655	7251553	25115
市　　属	Municipal	5942287	4642509	40398
按所有制分	**Grouped by Ownership**			
国有企业	State－owned Enterprises	6337969	6092764	18724
集体企业	Collective－owned Enterprises	22125	19926	267
股份合作企业	Cooperative Enterprises	41004	33040	263
联营企业	Joint Ownership Enterprises	3962	3807	9
股份制企业	Share－holding Corporations	53683773	44587372	1778740
外商及港澳台投资企业	Enterprises with Investment from Foreign、Hong Kong、Macao and Taiwan	34477916	26534830	224869
其他企业	Other Enterprises	493059	438353	2956
按企业规模分	**Grouped by Size of Enterprises**			
大型企业	Large	33436562	25587848	1739586
中型企业	Medium－sized	28554071	23763685	140637
小微企业	Small	33069173	28358559	145605
按轻重工业分	**Grouped by Light & Heavy Industry**			
轻工业	Light Industry	38729497	29872014	1731401
重工业	Heavy Industry	56330309	47838077	294426

企业主要经济指标(2013 年)(三)

Enterprises Above Designated Size in Urban District(2013)(Ⅲ)

(10000 yuan)

销售费用 Sales Expenses	管理费用 Management Expenses	财务费用 Financial Expenses	利息支出 Interest Expenditure	营业利润 Business Profits	利润总额 Total Profits	利税总额 Total Pre - tax Profits	本年应交增值税 Value Added Tax Payable
3979658	**4922043**	**1174254**	**1620663**	**6592942**	**6815164**	**11876509**	**3029697**
144504	237280	24196	41692	266856	290399	2278596	384872
48324	195748	29473	85821	557361	313015	503700	164939
568145	302571	58182	72195	406219	416256	646724	189548
3900	83908	16161	66693	415816	159497	301878	122698
312	938	139	138	574	878	1814	670
720	24450	- 11711	111506	51610	51146	52562	1154
24	92	-	-	30	27	111	75
1353333	2677378	916904	1042991	2920596	3129087	6582305	1671041
2616229	2117088	243715	390057	3187211	3457457	4905266	1221525
5140	18189	9046	9278	17105	17074	32574	12535
1845097	1556633	179055	353120	3052651	2940130	5913575	1232826
1165185	1569802	428614	512827	1761428	1972469	3034625	919499
969376	1795607	566585	754716	1778863	1902566	2928310	877373
2358932	1903264	528815	663976	2844193	2930340	6193717	1529196
1620726	3018779	645440	956687	3748749	3884824	5682791	1500501

单位:万元 4－11 续表1

项　目	Item	主营业务收　入 Revenues in Main Business	主营业务成　本 Costs in Main Business	主营业务税金及附加 Sales Taxes and Extra Charges in Main Business
按国民经济行业分	**Grouped by Economic Sector**			
采掘业	Mining and Quarrying	18546	16040	627
非金属矿采选业	Nonmetal Minerals Mining and Dressing	18546	16040	627
制造业	Manufacturing Industry	87440065	70529698	2005933
农副食品加工业	Agricultural Products Processing	864046	743647	2368
食品制造业	Food Manufacturing	1954833	1469840	8717
酒、饮料和精制茶制造业	Wine, Beverage and Tea Manufacturing	1693156	1172656	27774
烟草制品业	Tobacco Processing	2458997	469253	1539117
纺织业	Textile Industry	8238630	7284087	38700
纺织服装、服饰业	Textile Products and Costume Industry	2280119	1913406	13865
皮革、毛皮、羽毛及其制品和制鞋业	Leather. Furs. Downand Related and Shoes Products	1279173	1145771	5789
木材加工和木、竹、藤、棕、草制品业	Timber Processing, Bamboo, Cane, Palm Fiber and Straw Products	154139	133516	1487
家具制造业	Furniture Manufacturing	1142793	896050	6982
造纸和纸制品业	Paper Making and Paper Products	1013138	873432	4885
印刷和记录媒介复制业	Printing and Record Media	614908	523637	2659
文教、工美、体育和娱乐用品制造业	Cultural, Educational. Industrial Arts. Sports and Entertainment Goods	1548217	1428061	5453
石油加工、炼焦和核燃料加工业	Petroleum Processing, Coking and Nuclear Fuel Processing	228747	209974	17093

continued 1 (10000 yuan)

销售费用 Sales Expenses	管理费用 Management Expenses	财务费用 Financial Expenses	利息支出 Interest Expenditure	营业利润 Business Profits	利润总额 Total Profits	利税总额 Total Pre - tax Profits	本年应交增值税 Value Added Tax Payable
26	1059	251	290	943	1133	2896	1136
26	1059	251	290	943	1133	2896	1136
3957652	4847078	1113950	1545423	6050302	6504854	11392462	2877267
33264	30842	16585	16107	39363	42749	66673	21508
247707	83283	-7168	9295	200711	208650	305272	87905
314085	38578	2946	6846	192726	195872	300088	76442
76426	111096	-3520	859	288071	275262	2128942	314410
105268	288754	207046	228960	349226	346043	591265	206239
88634	176429	44401	47519	60026	73085	171857	84536
24732	40079	37560	36073	28185	27860	68259	34585
5684	8076	2796	3122	2319	3284	9134	4360
67715	59386	16381	17683	93754	94295	136271	34995
26927	42561	18198	19767	53784	57261	91934	29701
13554	36854	12410	13482	34065	35074	58363	20233
19533	47048	18133	18129	32795	32423	62863	24940
1873	16568	5727	5777	-22487	-23246	6901	13054

单位:万元　　4－11　续表2

项　目	Item	主营业务收　入 Revenues in Main Business	主营业务成　本 Costs in Main Business	主营业务税金及附加 Sales Taxes and Extra Charges in Main Business
化学原料和化学制品制造业	Raw Chemical Materials and Chemical Products	10199893	8478418	22051
医药制造业	Medical and Pharmaceutical Products	2260365	1041244	21737
化学纤维制造业	Chemical Fiber	6430499	5938120	17023
橡胶和塑料制品业	Rubber and Plastic Products	5167038	4415799	26817
非金属矿物制品业	Nonmetal Mineral Products	3387008	2918365	15249
黑色金属冶炼和压延加工业	Smelting and Processing of Ferrous Metals	3838780	3583783	13316
有色金属冶炼和压延加工业	Smelting and Processing of Nonferrous Metals	695309	617364	1664
金属制品业	Metal Products	2993476	2666296	15443
通用设备制造业	Ordinary Machinery	7238719	5865566	34434
专用设备制造业	For Special Purpose Equipment Manufacturing	1791046	1421953	10348
汽车制造业	Automobile Manufacturing	3557600	3009190	55849
铁路、船舶、航空航天和其他运输设备制造业	Railway. watercraft. Avigation spaceflight and other Equipment Manufacturing	334387	280332	1472
电气机械和器材制造业	Electric Equipment and Machinery	6282868	5077136	26474
计算机、通信和其他电子设备制造业	Computers. Telecommunications and Other Electronic Equipment Manufacturing	7741303	5458125	56240
仪器仪表制造业	Instruments and Meters Manufacturing	1756428	1234524	11333
其他制造业	Other Manufacturing	278139	248005	1451
废弃资源综合利用业	Multiple Utilization of Waste Resouces	12004	9218	111
电力、热力生产和供应业	Production and Supply of Electric Power and Hot Water	5704388	5431380	13590
燃气生产和供应业	Production and Supply of Gas	1656187	1523765	4097
水的生产和供应业	Production and Supply of Tap Water	240620	209208	1580

continued 2 (10000 yuan)

销售费用 Sales Expenses	管理费用 Management Expenses	财务费用 Financial Expenses	利息支出 Interest Expenditure	营业利润 Business Profits	利润总额 Total Profits	利税总额 Total Pre - tax Profits	本年应交增值税 Value Added Tax Payable
457549	506164	127933	156608	784070	812550	1123519	288211
678095	246882	2964	15786	338633	355891	574338	196703
20991	113471	100654	140328	308088	317378	426578	92175
211836	154206	69631	75384	444581	447410	603881	129600
166481	129279	71633	91618	102891	119194	239699	105221
21931	114474	61823	119739	77193	86873	170445	70177
6303	18019	9385	12575	50751	49224	64564	13659
45480	144094	45034	58131	89715	96817	180923	68442
210036	494380	69797	86697	642846	660605	955727	260294
68282	172245	22680	23585	114180	123143	181889	48213
144655	304707	35036	173363	119670	162220	338485	120184
8742	24524	9505	9513	12222	13169	21341	6678
363250	458767	91628	98327	308701	326640	501431	147982
412990	768388	12925	45616	1112078	1336711	1674967	281380
111622	205165	10500	12720	177315	212097	307804	84334
3443	10920	821	1301	13703	15022	26481	9984
6	1132	432	436	1107	1112	2108	885
167	25779	36876	37313	457609	219456	349463	115444
10042	19223	13939	13690	96449	95897	127135	27141
11771	28905	9238	23946	-12360	-6176	4553	8710

4－12 全市规模以上工业企业

Main Economic Indicators of Industrial Enterprises

单位：万元

项 目	Item	企业单位数（个）Number of Enterprises (unit)	#亏损企业（个）Loss Making Enterprises (unit)	工业总产值（当年价格）Gross Industrial Output Value (current price)	#新产品产值 Output of New Products
按登记注册类型分组	**Grouped by Status of Registration**				
内资企业	Domestic－funded Enterprises	5086	673	86554304	22434088
国有企业	State－owned Enterprises	25	2	7140899	167812
集体企业	Collective－owned Enterprises	11	1	39776	689
股份合作企业	Cooperative Enterprises	12	－	56837	3383
联营企业	Joint Ownership Enterprises	1	－	4006	－
国有联营企业	State Joint Ownership Enterprises	－	－	－	－
集体联营企业	Collective Joint Ownership Enterprises	1	－	4006	－
国有与集体联营企业	Joint State－collective Enterprises	－	－	－	－
其他联营企业	Other Joint Ownership Enterprises	－	－	－	－
有限责任公司	Limited Liability Corporations	964	148	27911842	7470548
国有独资公司	State－funded Corporations	29	2	3403602	201200
其他有限责任公司	Other Limited Liability Corporations	935	146	24508240	7269348
股份有限公司	Share－holding Corporations Ltd.	148	12	10298613	5070942
私营企业	Private Enterprises	3925	510	41102331	9720714
私营独资企业	Private－funded Enterprises	189	15	944174	90272
私营合伙企业	Private Partnership Enterprises	24	3	114739	4338
私营有限责任公司	Private Limited Liability Corporations	3661	479	38332532	9019528
私营股份有限公司	Private Share－holding Corporations Ltd.	51	13	1710885	606576
港、澳、台商投资	Enterprises with Investment from Hong Kong, Macao and Taiwan	532	104	14499275	5996481
内地与港澳台合资经营企业	Joint－venture Enterprises with funds from Hong Kong, Macao and Taiwan	334	48	9187781	3430994
内地与港澳台合作经营企业	Cooperative Enterprises with funds from Hong Kong, Macao and Taiwan	3	－	52624	26884
港澳台商独资经营企业	Enterprises with Sole Investment from Hong Kong, Macao and Taiwan	189	56	4060914	1588024
港澳台商投资股份有限公司	Share－holding Corporations Ltd. with Investment from Hong Kong, Macao and Taiwan	6	－	1197955	950580
外商投资企业	Enterprises with Foreign Investment	666	159	23126456	6530841
中外合资经营企业	Joint－venture Enterprises	361	74	13434674	4113461
中外合作经营企业	Cooperation Enterprises	9	4	106952	8776
外商独资经营企业	Enterprises with Sole Foreign Investment	290	81	9313423	2242291
外商投资股份有限公司	Share－holding Corporations Ltd. with Foreign Investment	4	－	113436	41486

主要经济指标按登记注册类型分（2013 年）
Above Designated Size by Status of Registration(2013)

(10000 yuan)

工业销售产值 Value of Industrial Products Sales	出口交货值 Export delivery value	实收资本 Total Capital Hold	国家资本 State Capital	个人资本 Personal Capital	港澳台资本 Hongkong, Macau and TaiWan Capital	外商资本 Foreign Capital	就业人员年平均人数(人) Annual Average Number of Staff and Workers (person)
85307545	8504472	14237444	1269525	6097922	53441	46146	810027
7115371	21011	253875	248453	–	–		19282
39492	4972	1934	–	272	–	–	652
55414	–	52370	–	7240	–	–	1399
4006	–	100	–	–	–	–	62
–	–	–	–	–	–	–	–
4006	–	100	–	–	–	–	62
–	–	–	–	–	–	–	–
–	–	–	–	–	–	–	–
27546976	1780840	5145277	698634	1148203	18283	9092	224930
3430980	10765	532346	336221	–	–	–	14156
24115996	1770074	4612931	362413	1148203	18283	9092	210774
10184067	1574968	2637259	320983	1092236	10562	30468	85852
40362219	5122682	6146629	1455	3849972	24596	6586	477850
931979	126857	64607	120	46040	–	–	13616
114008	3627	10456	515	8474	–	–	2029
37614142	4764292	5661172	820	3631080	24596	6586	449742
1702091	227907	410394	–	164378	–	–	12463
14299303	3312691	4091512	196531	334394	2641430	108640	162233
9050142	1714469	2122088	22111	164814	1065397	107900	91743
52624	7183	4733	–	407	1212	–	398
4028997	1340421	1508900	–	–	1494501	700	60528
1167540	250618	455791	174420	169173	80321	40	9564
23552373	5228927	5305379	101256	121083	55854	4010049	226468
13692944	2556246	2487461	101256	84798	49675	1303541	123817
104947	31570	41847	–	2181	–	16972	1633
9504304	2594099	2685578	–	–	6179	2661029	97848
113037	47012	23806	–	–	–	20631	2026

4－13 全市规模以上工业企业

Main Economic Indicators of Industrial

单位:万元

项 目	Item	企业单位数(个) Number of Enterprises (unit)	#亏损企业(个) Loss Making Enterprises (unit)	工业总产值(当年价格) Gross Industrial Output Value (current price)	#新产品产值 Output of New Products
按经济组织类型分组	**Grouped by Type of Ownership**				
独资企业	Solely－owned Enterprises	704	155	21499187	4089088
国有企业	State－owned	25	2	7140899	167812
集体企业	Collective－owned	11	1	39776	689
私营独资企业	Private－owned	189	15	944174	90272
港澳台商独资经营企业	Enterprises with Sole Investment from Hong Kong, Macao and Taiwan	189	56	4060914	1588024
外商独资经营企业	Enterprises with Sole Foreign Investment	290	81	9313423	2242291
合作、合伙企业	Cooperation and Partnership Enterprises	－	－	－	－
股份合作企业	Share－holding Cooperative	12	－	56837	3383
国有联营企业	State Joint Ownership	－	－	－	－
集体联营企业	Collective Joint Ownership	1	－	4006	－
国有与集体联营企业	Joint State－collective Ownership	－	－	－	－
其他联营企业	Other Joint Ownership	－	－	－	－
私营合伙企业	Private Partnership	24	3	114739	4338
内地与港澳台合作经营企业	Cooperative Enterprises with funds from Hong Kong, Macao and Taiwan	3	－	52624	26884
中外合作经营企业	Sino－foreign Cooperation Enterprises	9	4	106952	8776
其他企业	Other Enterprises (Domestic Investment)	2	－	157971	124828
股份有限公司	Share－holding Corporations Ltd.	－	－	－	－
股份有限公司(内资)	Share－holding Corporations Ltd. (Domestic Investment)	148	12	10298613	5070942
私营股份有限公司	Private Share－holding Corporations Ltd.	51	13	1710885	606576
港澳台商投资股份有限公司	Share－holding Corporations Ltd. with Investment from Hong Kong, Macao and Taiwan	6	－	1197955	950580
外商投资股份有限公司	Share－holding Corporations Ltd. with Foreign Investment	4	－	113436	41486
有限责任公司	Limited Liability Corporations	5320	749	88866829	24034530
国有独资公司	State－owned	29	2	3403602	201200
私营有限责任公司	Private	3661	479	38332532	9019528
内地与港澳台合资经营企业	Joint Venture Enterprises with funds from Hong Kong, Macao and Taiwan	334	48	9187781	3430994
中外合资经营企业	Sino－foreign Joint Venture	361	74	13434674	4113461
其他有限责任公司	Others	935	146	24508240	7269348

主要经济指标按经济组织类型分(2013 年)

Enterprises Above Designated Size by the Type of Ownership(2013)

(10000 yuan)

工业销售产值 Value of Industrial Products Sales	出口交货值 Export delivery value	实收资本 Total Capital Hold	国家资本 State Capital	个人资本 Personal Capital	港澳台资本 Hongkong, Macau and TaiWan Capital	外商资本 Foreign Capital	就业人员年平均人数(人) Annual Average Number of Staff and Workers (person)
21620143	4087359	4514893	248573	46312	1500680	2661730	191926
7115371	21011	253875	248453	–	–	–	19282
39492	4972	1934	–	272	–	–	652
931979	126857	64607	120	46040	–	–	13616
4028997	1340421	1508900	–	–	1494501	700	60528
9504304	2594099	2685578	–	–	6179	2661029	97848
–	–	–	–	–	–	–	–
55414	–	52370	–	7240	–	–	1399
–	–	–	–	–	–	–	–
4006	–	100	–	–	–	–	62
–	–	–	–	–	–	–	–
	–	–	–	–	–	–	–
114008	3627	10456	515	8474	–	–	2029
52624	7183	4733	–	407	1212	–	398
104947	31570	41847	–	2181	–	16972	1633
137142	–	66689	–	34104	–	7876	1144
–	–	–	–	–	–	–	–
10184067	1574968	2637259	320983	1092236	10562	30468	85852
1702091	227907	410394	–	164378	–	–	12463
1167540	250618	455791	174420	169173	80321	40	9564
113037	47012	23806	–	–	–	20631	2026
87904203	10815846	15415998	822820	5028895	1157951	1427119	890232
3430980	10765	532346	336221	–	–	–	14156
37614142	4764292	5661172	820	3631080	24596	6586	449742
9050142	1714469	2122088	22111	164814	1065397	107900	91743
13692944	2556246	2487461	101256	84798	49675	1303541	123817
24115996	1770074	4612931	362413	1148203	18283	9092	210774

4－14　规模以上工业企业主要经济效益指标(1998－2013)

Main Economic Indicators of Industrial Enterprises Above Designated Size(1998－2013)

单位:亿元　　(100 million yuan)

年份 Year	规模以上工业总产值 Output Value of Industrial Enterprises Above Designated Size	规模以上工业增加值 Added Value of Industrial Enterprises Above Designated Size	资产总计 Total Assets	流动资产合计 Total Current Assets	主营业务收入 Revenne from Principal Business	利润总额 Total Profits	利税总额 Total Profits and Tax
1998	1109.94	274.70	1486.02	732.72	1036.09	38.44	101.36
1999	1200.07	298.90	1620.93	800.60	1132.80	54.47	127.89
2000	1543.57	360.97	1828.35	946.32	1465.49	76.20	161.61
2001	1919.51	444.91	2148.96	1122.07	1828.28	107.56	208.54
2002	2400.30	597.01	2514.19	1313.92	2288.21	145.48	274.98
2003	3202.52	783.51	3258.93	1783.50	3117.46	194.16	359.54
2004	4486.58	1019.47	4118.31	2300.84	4363.27	226.74	427.23
2005	5441.13	1126.54	4781.34	2692.73	5282.80	234.99	450.68
2006	6975.46	1363.17	5564.68	3215.19	6807.64	314.49	576.51
2007	8351.40	1717.65	6573.12	3880.23	8057.03	414.55	730.50
2008	9379.58	1743.20	7506.26	4437.50	8976.46	453.92	802.13
2009	9390.73	1792.00	8405.62	4968.21	9026.32	510.97	882.62
2010	11081.04	2153.83	9937.41	6011.68	10843.24	764.47	1224.48
2011	12352.92	2369.00	10968.69	6709.76	12022.57	795.53	1330.48
2012	12959.68	2492.00	11983.52	7215.40	12525.39	771.68	1339.94
2013	12418.00	2664.13	12680.28	7609.51	12424.15	853.60	1450.55

4－14　续表　continued

年份 Year	资产负债率(%) Rate of Assets and Liabilites	流动资产周转次数(次) the Number of Current Assets Turnover	成本费用利润率(%) Profit Rate of Costs	全员劳动生产率(元/人) All －personnel Labor Productivity (Yuan/Ren)	产品销售率(%) Prodnct Sales Rate(%)
1998	57.02	1.47	3.86	37976	95.91
1999	55.69	1.46	5.06	44307	98.07
2000	58.59	1.62	5.49	52713	97.19
2001	57.20	1.70	6.26	59518	97.40
2002	56.82	1.82	6.84	76402	97.76
2003	58.70	1.87	6.69	91284	97.68
2004	59.80	2.00	5.50	98809	98.10
2005	60.12	2.06	4.69	105786	98.25
2006	59.83	2.23	4.87	120289	98.36
2007	60.43	2.21	5.44	138016	98.17
2008	60.42	2.10	5.34	152070	98.14
2009	59.07	1.86	5.86	151002	98.63
2010	58.34	1.96	7.60	166516	98.83
2011	59.12	1.91	6.96	190110	98.61
2012	49.57	1.74	6.60	232587	98.63
2013	58.09	1.63	7.39	222570	99.18

4-15 主要工业产品生产量(2013年)
Output of Major Industrial Products(2013)

产品名称		Item		全市 Whole City 2013年	为上年(%) As Compared with the Preceding Year(%)	市区 Urban District
铁矿石原矿量	(万吨)	The volume of iron ore	(10000 tons)	4.10	125.1	-
原油加工量	(万吨)	Crude oil processing volume	(10000 tons)	13.78	22.6	13.78
发电量	(亿千瓦小时)	Electricity	(100 million kwh)	196.11	103.7	131.38
罐头	(万吨)	Canned Food	(10000 tons)	7.33	117.8	0.36
乳制品	(吨)	Dairy Products	(ton)	268253	129.1	250353
啤酒	(千升)	Beer	(1000 litres)	987166	108.8	721220
软饮料	(万吨)	Soft Drinks	(10000 tons)	738.35	94.9	439.76
精制茶	(吨)	Tea	(ton)	47026.95	82.7	5132.90
卷烟	(亿支)	Cigarettes	(100 million)	542.86	107.3	542.86
方便面	(吨)	Instant Noodle	(ton)	253981	72.4	253981
化学纤维	(吨)	Chemical Fiber	(ton)	6847039	115.7	6698782
#合成纤维	(吨)	Synthetic Fibre	(ton)	6691769	116.1	6543512
纱	(万吨)	Yarn	(10000 tons)	67.00	106.6	60.40
布	(万米)	Cloth	(10000 m)	416948	101.6	332646
印染布	(万米)	Printed Fabric	(10000 m)	529287	100.8	517560
蚕丝及交织机织物(含蚕丝≥50%)	(万米)	Silk and Woven Fabrics (Containing Greater than or Equal 50% silk)	(10000 m)	5264.55	105.2	4354.91

4－15 续表1 continued 1

产品名称	Item	全市 Whole City 2013年	全市 Whole City 为上年(%) As Compared with the Preceding Year(%)	市区 Urban District
服装 (万件)	Garment (10000 units)	38427.47	97.1	30879.61
皮革鞋靴 (万双)	Leather Footwear (10000 units)	1437.94	92.5	303.57
家具 (万件)	Furniture (10000 units)	3902.02	104.8	3524.62
塑料制品 (吨)	Plastic Membrane (ton)	1636232	102.4	1328637
机制纸及纸板 (万吨)	Machine Made Paper and Paperboard (10000 tons)	691.42	103.8	16.18
焦炭 (万吨)	Coke (10000 tons)	52.01	99.1	52.01
盐酸(含量31%以上)(吨)	Mariatic Acid(above 31% percent) (ton)	96176.00	90.4	96176.00
氢氧化钠(烧碱)(折100%) (吨)	Caustic Soda (ton)	193117	97.3	193117
碳酸钠(纯碱) (吨)	Soda ash (ton)	282607	113.7	282607
初级形态的塑料(塑料树脂及共聚物)(吨)	Plastics in Primary Form(Plastic Resins and Copolymers) (ton)	446577	91.5	364398
合成氨 (吨)	Synthetic Ammonia (ton)	184420	114.4	164691
农用氮、磷、钾化学肥料总计(折纯)(吨)	Chemical Fertilizer (ton)	83548.00	110.8	74978.00
化学农药原药(折有效成分100%)(吨)	Chemical Pesticide (ton)	126694	89.6	17058.59
涂料(油漆) (吨)	Paint (ton)	225938	107.6	119527
合成洗涤剂 (吨)	Synthetic Detergent (ton)	138320	90.2	105278

4－15 续表2 continued 2

产品名称	Item	全市 Whole City 2013 年	全市 Whole City 为上年(%) As Compared with the Preceding Year(%)	市区 Urban District
化学药品原药(化学原料药)（吨）	Original Drug Chemicals (ton)	12413.23	150.7	7860.70
中成药（吨）	Traditional Chinese Medicine (ton)	7980.39	110.8	7552.83
橡胶轮胎外胎(轮胎外胎)（万条）	Rubber Tires (10000 units)	5790.55	110.4	5132.62
水泥（万吨）	Cement (10000 tons)	2162.35	105.0	910.93
粗钢（万吨）	Crude Steel (10000 tons)	378.84	107.2	344.78
生铁（万吨）	Pig Iron (10000 tons)	267.94	104.8	267.94
铁合金（万吨）	Iron Alloy (10000 tons)	6.00	88.4	0.80
钢材（万吨）	Steel Products (10000 tons)	975.75	103.5	844.19
精炼铜(电解铜)（吨）	Refined Copper (ton)	131210	87.1	1946.35
工业锅炉（蒸发量吨）	Industry Boiler (ton)	11756.00	110.8	11756.00
金属切削机床（台）	Metal－cutting Machine Tools (unit)	47475	111.2	39752
金属成形机床(锻压设备)（台）	Metal Forming Machine(Forge Equipment) (Tai)	10718	72.5	8598
泵(液体泵)（万台）	Pump (10000 sets)	70.19	120.0	69.11
滚动轴承(轴承)（万套）	Bearings (10000 units)	15520.50	101.0	14608.50
汽车（辆）	Motor Vehicles (unit)	92996	103.1	92996

4－15 续表3 continued 3

产品名称	Item	全市 Whole City 2013年	为上年(%) As Compared with the Preceding Year(%)	市区 Urban District
叉车 （台）	Forklift (unit)	72235	114.1	1975
两轮自行车(自行车)（万辆）	Bicycles (10000 units)	426.94	73.5	423.63
交流电动机 （万千瓦）	AC Motor (10000 kw)	56.38	105.9	38.64
钢绞线 （吨）	Strand (ton)	56571.76	90.5	56563.00
通信及电子网络用电缆 （万对千米）	Communication Cable (10000 km)	467.61	100.5	21.21
光缆(光纤通讯电缆)（万芯千米）	Electric Power Cable (10000 km)	2429.59	110.9	95.06
家用电冰箱 （万台）	Household Refrigerators (10000 units)	111.75	104.4	111.75
家用洗衣机 （万台）	Household Washing Machines (10000 units)	354.14	103.1	354.14
吸排油烟机 （万台）	Smoke Absorbers (10000 units)	182.73	130.3	182.73
移动通信手持机(手机)（万部）	Mobile Telephone Sets (10000 units)	401.36	100.7	401.36
电工仪器仪表 （万台）	Electric Instrument and Apparatus (10000 units)	2955.34	83.8	2456.85
工业自动调节仪表与控制系统 （万台）	Industrial Automatic Adjustment Meter and Control System (10000 units)	350.96	103.0	350.96
电光源(灯泡) （亿只）	Light Bulbs (100 million units)	15.76	106.7	2.20
彩色电视机 （万部）	Color－Television Sets (10000 units)	68.66	305.8	68.66
微型计算机设备 （万台）	Micro－computer Equipment (10000 units)	164.22	101.9	164.22

4-16 单位 GDP 能耗降低情况(2013 年)

Increase or Decrease of Energy Consumption Per Unit of GDP(2013)

地 区	Region	单位 GDP 能耗(吨标准煤/万元) Energy Consumption Per Unit of GDP (tons of SCE/10000 yuan)		单位 GDP 电耗(千瓦时/万元) Electricity Consumption Per Unit of GDP (kwh/10000 yuan)		单位工业增加值能耗降低率 Decrease Rate of Energy Consumption Per Unit of Industriul Value - Added (±%)
		2013 年	降低率 Decrease Rate (±%)	2013 年	降低率 Decrease Rate (±%)	
杭州市	Hangzhou	0.52	3.5	829	0.06	5.13
#上城区	Shangcheng	-	-	317	-0.49	-6.66
下城区	Xiacheng	-	-	336	1.59	4.10
江干区	Jianggan	-	-	658	-7.57	7.63
拱墅区	Gongshu	-	-	1109	2.21	4.92
西湖区	Xihu	-	-	579	0.10	11.90
高新(滨江)区	Hi-Tech(Binjiang)	-	-	415	-1.88	15.46
下沙经济技术开发区	HEDA	-	-	811	-1.51	2.07
萧山区	Xiaoshan	0.74	0.28	1301	-0.27	3.69
余杭区	Yuhang	0.52	2.51	902	0.43	8.80
桐庐县	Tonglu	0.53	4.31	676	-0.36	7.28
淳安县	Chun'an	0.36	1.02	635	1.35	4.47
建德市	Jiande	0.98	4.81	1089	0.99	4.37
富阳市	Fuyang	0.98	5.74	1271	5.55	5.54
临安市	Lin'an	0.51	4.50	807	3.62	7.93

注:1. 江干区不含杭州经济技术开发区。

2. 本表单位 GDP 能耗、单位 GDP 电耗指标中的 GDP,采用 2010 年价格计算。

a) HEDA is not included in Jianggan district in this table.

b) The GDP in this table was calculated at 2010 prices.

4－17　工业企业主要能源

Energy Consumption of Industrial

行　业	Sector	原煤(吨) Raw Coal(Ton)	洗精煤(吨) Washing Coal(Ton)	焦炭(吨) Coke(Ton)	汽油(吨) Gasoline(Ton)	煤油(吨) Kerosene(Ton)
总　计	**Total**	**13427337**	**689882**	**1241751**	**49705**	**1403**
煤炭开采和洗选业	Coal Mining and Dressing	–	–	–	–	–
黑色金属矿采选业	Ferrous Metals Mining and Dressing	–	–	–	–	–
有色金属矿采选业	Nonferrous Minerals Mining and Dressing	–	–	–	17	–
非金属矿采选业	Nonmetal Minerals Mining and Dressing	40089	–	–	24	–
农副食品加工业	Agricultural Products Processing	32027	–	–	313	3
食品制造业	Food Manufacturing	26678	–	–	1084	–
酒、饮料和精制茶制造业	Wine, Beverage and Tea Manufacturing	24246	–	–	97	–
烟草制品业	Tobacco Processing	–	–	–	42	–
纺织业	Textile Processing	1178813	–	–	4756	1
纺织服装、服饰业	Textile Products and Costume Industry	13013	–	958	2385	–
皮革、毛皮、羽毛及其制品和制鞋业	Leather. Furs. Downand Related and Shoes Products	21241	–	–	1354	–
木材加工和木、竹、藤、棕、草制品业	Timber Processing, Bamboo, Cane, Plam Fiber and Straw Products	474	–	–	128	–
家具制造业	Furniture Manufacturing	387	–	718	537	–
造纸和纸制品业	Paper Making and Paper Products	312424	–	–	811	7
印刷和记录媒介复制业	Printing	457	–	–	875	–
文教、工美、体育和娱乐用品制造业	Cultural, Educational. Industrial Arts. Sports and Entertainment Goods	1717	–	69	1115	1
石油加工、炼焦和核燃料加工业	Petroleum Processing, Coking and Nuclear Fuel Processing	1060	–	–	58	–

消费量按行业分(2013 年)
Enterprises by Sector(2013)

柴油(吨) Diesel oil(Ton)	燃料油(吨) Fuel Oil(Ton)	液化石油气(吨) Liquefied Petroleum Gas(Ton)	天然气(万立方米) Natural Gas (10000 cu. m)	其他石油制品(吨) Other Petroleum Products(Ton)	热力(百万千焦) Heat(Million kilo - joule)	电力(万千瓦时) Electricity (10000 kwh)
162127	**44097**	**13241**	**180077**	**132785**	**92096084**	**3478175**
-	-	-	-	-	-	-
-	-	-	-	-	-	402
28	-	-	-	-	-	2047
7581	-	-	-	56	-	9442
1437	-	13	67	-	111614	13318
1934	291	111	937	-	1175803	21056
863	3604	3	534	-	2098786	61676
489	660	-	567	-	163636	7047
3589	-	73	1924	30	21947800	497371
2042	35	7	23	-	570033	24791
619	-	-	-	-	133318	15221
136	-	-	12	-	-	5585
1239	408	-	481	-	83187	10347
2347	-	-	107	-	27876618	269538
782	-	55	287	-	107424	14756
1015	1	84	49	6	208355	15235
336	2521	-	-	105721	2461	1946

4-17 续表

行 业 Sector	原煤(吨) Raw Coal(Ton)	洗精煤(吨) Washing Coal(Ton)	焦炭(吨) Coke(Ton)	汽油(吨) Gasoline(Ton)	煤油(吨) Kerosene(Ton)
化学原料和化学制品制造业 Raw Chemical Materials and Chemical Products	1501934	–	–	4089	238
医药制造业 Medical and Pharmaceutical Products	69976	–	–	607	–
化学纤维制造业 Chemical Fiber	236246	–	–	965	–
橡胶和塑料制品业 Rubber and Plastic Products	304996	–	–	2945	24
非金属矿物制品业 Nonmetal Minerals Products	2296601	–	–	2918	–
黑色金属冶炼和压延加工业 Smelting and Processing of Ferrous Metals	566661	689882	1218101	793	–
有色金属冶炼和压延加工业 Smelting and Processing of Nonferrous Metals	25351	–	18710	301	2
金属制品业 Metal Products	47154	–	831	2251	30
通用设备制造业 Ordinary Machinery	6778	–	879	5332	453
专用设备制造业 Special Purpose Equipment	6904	–	719	1839	3
汽车制造业 Automobile Manufacturing	5589	–	528	3013	593
铁路、船舶、航空航天和其他运输设备制造业 Railway. watercraft. Avigation spaceflight and other Equipment Manufacturing	1720	–	–	430	–
电气机械和器材制造业 Electric Equipment and Machinery	4789	–	105	3477	1
计算机、通信和其他电子设备制造业 Computers. Telecommunications and Other Electronic Equipment Manufacturing	4064	–	8	2847	–
仪器仪表制造业 Instruments and Meters Manufacturing	1785	–	–	1622	48
其他制造业 Other Manufacturing	–	–	–	142	–
废弃资源综合利用业 Multiple Utilization of Waste Resouces	2525	–	124	133	–
金属制品、机械和设备修理业 Metal Products, Machinery and Equipment Repair	–	–	–	–	–
电力、热力生产和供应业 Production and Supply of Electric Power and Hot Water	6691638	–	–	1777	–
燃气生产和供应业 Production and Supply of Gas	–	–	–	288	–
水的生产和供应业 Production and Supply of Tap Water	–	–	–	339	–

continued

柴油(吨) Diesel oil(Ton)	燃料油(吨) Fuel Oil(Ton)	液化石油气(吨) Liquefied Petroleum Gas(Ton)	天然气(万立方米) Natural Gas (10000 cu. m)	其他石油制品(吨) Other Petroleum Products(Ton)	热力(百万千焦) Heat(Million kilo – joule)	电力(万千瓦时) Electricity (10000 kwh)
9934	10188	–	2657	24441	17775256	376042
2080	158	45	1546	46	669908	47614
1448	5699	81	252	394	11385941	350177
3253	2418	2788	863	–	4546834	189667
84070	8994	1162	9633	–	274273	252494
3270	–	946	2762	6	873887	327828
1366	6125	99	1815	31	59177	36251
3978	2593	161	4243	282	468163	90570
10198	292	148	991	690	69380	96695
1183	–	670	371	67	186903	23933
5114	6	228	805	987	220803	86565
615	101	413	125	–	–	7025
3561	–	5507	1020	11	409257	128411
2706	–	633	588	–	254358	89165
741	3	2	267	10	6291	20128
963	–	–	2	–	–	1556
380	–	–	–	–	–	8759
–	–	–	–	–	–	15
2113	–	–	147112	6	416621	308842
410	–	–	39	–	–	632
304	–	13	3	–	–	66030

4-18 电力消费量(2013年)
Electricity Consumption(2013)

单位:万千瓦时 (10000 kwh)

项目	Item	2013年	2012年
总计	**Total**	**6385463**	**5917172**
#线路损失电量	#Losses in Transmission	196243	115938
农林牧渔业	Farming, Forestry, Animal Husbandry and Fishery Conservancy	52712	49325
工业	Industry	4171529	3961931
#轻工业	Light Industry	2026093	1996773
重工业	Heavy Industry	2145437	1965158
#采矿业	#Mining and Quarrying	38510	39637
制造业	Manufacturing Industry	3768395	3641169
电力、燃气及水的生产和供应业	Produotion and supply of electricity, gas & water	364624	281125
建筑业	Construction	128250	115795
交通运输、仓储及邮政业	Transportation, Storage, Post & Telecommunications	98035	69283
信息传输、计算机服务和软件业	Information Transmission, Computer Services and Software	110965	96521
商业、住宿和餐饮业	Commerce, Catering and lodging	324596	290646
金融、房地产、商务及居民服务业	Finance, Real Estate Commerce and Service for the Residents	256362	220976
公共管理和社会组织	Public Management and Social Organizations	347776	319450
城乡居民生活用电	Residential Consumption	895236	793246
#城市	Cities	546921	488294
乡村	#Rural Areas	348315	304952

4－19 水资源量和总用水量(2001－2013)

Total Water Resources and Water Consumption(2001－2013)

单位:亿立方米 (100 million Cubic Meters)

		全市 Whole City	市区 Urban District	桐庐 Tonglu	淳安 Chan'an	建德 Jiangde	富阳 Fuyang	临安 Lin'an
2001 年	水资源量 Water Resources	156.37	18.87	14.28	41.14	18.54	14.23	26.76
	用水量 Water Consumption	40.29	28.05	2.01	1.03	2.11	4.17	2.92
2002 年	水资源量 Water Resources	213.00	30.21	24.30	65.46	31.59	23.54	37.90
	用水量 Water Consumption	39.92	27.51	2.01	1.05	2.18	4.35	2.82
2003 年	水资源量 Water Resources	102.65	9.31	10.32	41.43	15.57	8.13	17.90
	用水量 Water Consumption	44.72	29.13	1.98	1.38	2.30	7.12	2.81
2004 年	水资源量 Water Resources	85.28	12.04	10.35	27.82	11.34	9.15	14.58
	用水量 Water Consumption	48.90	32.89	2.21	1.09	2.35	7.17	3.19
2005 年	水资源量 Water Resources	90.65	14.32	9.46	26.66	10.36	10.31	19.54
	用水量 Water Consumption	49.58	32.95	2.25	1.24	2.38	7.16	3.61
2006 年	水资源量 Water Resources	109.80	15.14	11.70	38.42	13.41	10.36	20.75
	用水量 Water Consumption	48.73	31.39	2.39	1.42	2.68	7.13	3.72
2007 年	水资源量 Water Resources	104.13	20.28	10.12	29.88	11.72	11.76	20.36
	用水量 Water Consumption	49.56	32.57	2.53	1.53	3.09	6.45	3.39
2008 年	水资源量 Water Resources	154.38	24.58	14.95	49.22	18.52	14.20	32.92
	用水量 Water Consumption	56.70	39.57	2.90	1.32	2.69	6.49	3.70
2009 年	水资源量 Water Resources	141.50	23.38	16.67	37.46	15.63	16.33	32.03
	用水量 Water Consumption	54.28	39.24	2.52	1.46	2.81	5.18	3.07
2010 年	水资源量 Water Resources	190.40	29.58	19.03	63.61	30.36	17.92	29.91
	用水量 Water Consumption	54.95	39.00	2.79	1.61	2.88	4.80	3.87
2011 年	水资源量 Water Resources	136.70	20.21	15.81	41.00	19.11	13.43	27.13
	用水量 Water Consumption	57.71	40.40	2.98	1.37	2.92	5.83	4.21
2012 年	水资源量 Water Resources	221.26	36.20	24.89	66.73	31.08	23.57	38.83
	用水量 Water Consumption	56.45	39.69	2.67	1.40	2.84	5.75	4.10
2013 年	水资源量 Water Resources	141.15	28.82	15.63	35.29	19.21	15.33	26.87
	用水量 Water Consumption	57.77	41.07	2.53	1.42	2.74	6.22	3.79

主要统计指标解释

工业总产值 是以货币表现的工业企业在报告期内生产的已出售或可供出售工业产品总量,它反映一定时间内工业生产的总规模和总水平,它包括:在本企业内不再进行加工,经检验、包装入库(规定不需包装的产品除外)的成品价值,对外加工费收入,自制半成品,在产品期末初差额价值。工业总产值采用"工厂法"计算,即以工业企业作为一个整体,按企业工业生产活动的最终成果来计算,企业内部不允许重复计算,不能把企业内部各个车间(分厂)生产的成果相加。

工业销售产值 是以货币表现的工业企业在一定时期内销售的本企业生产的工业产品总量。包括已销售的成品、半成品价值,对外提供的工业性作业和对本单位基本建设部门、生活福利部门等提供的产品和工业性作业及自制设备的价值。已销售的成品、半成品不论是本期生产的、还是上期生产的,只要是本期销售出去的均包括在内。对外提供的工业性作业是指企业按合同对外提供的工业性劳务。企业为本单位基本建设部门、生活福利部门等提供的产品和工业性作业及自制设备也应视同销售,这部分也作为销售统计。工业销售产值的计算范围、计算价格和计算方法与工业总产值一致,但两者计算的基础不同;工业销售产值计算的基础是产品销售总量,工业总产值计算的基础是工业产品生产总量。

工业增加值 是指工业行业在报告期内以货币表现的工业生产活动的最终成果。

固定资产原价 固定资产原值指企业在建造、购置、安装、改建、扩建、技术改造某项固定资产时所支出的全部货币总额。它一般包括买价、包装费、运杂费和安装费等。

固定资产净值 是指固定资产原价减去历年已提折旧额后的净额。

利税总额 指企业利润总额、产品销售税金及附加和应交增值税之和。

主营业务收入 指企业销售产品的销售收入和提供劳务等主要经营业务取得的收入总额。

主营业务成本 指企业销售产品和提供劳务等主要经营业务的实际成本。

主营业务税金及附加 指企业销售产品和提供工业性劳务等主要经营业务应负担的城市维护建设税、消费税、资源税和教育费附加。

主营业务利润 指企业销售产品和提供工业性劳务等主要经营业务收入和除其成本、费用、税金后的利润。

利润总额 指企业实现的利润。

应交增值税 指企业在报告期内应交纳的增值税额。

总资产 指企业拥有或控制的全部资产。包括流动资产、长期投资、固定资产、无形及递延资产、其他长期资产、递延税项等,即为企业资产负债表的资产总计项。

(1)流动资产指企业可以在一年内或者超过一年的一个生产周期内变现或耗用的资产合计。包括现金及各种存款、短期投资、应收及预付款项、存货等。

(2)固定资产指企业固定资产净值、固定资产清理、在建工程、待处理固定资产损失所占用的资金合计。

(3)无形资产指企业长期使用而没有实物形态的资产。包括专利权、非专利技术、商标权、著作权、土地使用权、商誉等。

总负债 指企业承担并需要偿还的全部债务。包括流动负债和长期负债、递延税项等,即为企业资产负债表的负债合计项。

(1)流动负债指企业在一年内或者超过一年的一个营业周期内需要偿还的债务合计,其中包括短期借款、应付及预收款项、应付工资、应交税金和应交利润等。

(2)长期负债指企业在一年以上或者超过一年的一个生产周期以上需要偿还的债务合计,其中包括长期借款、应付债务、长期应付款项等。

所有者权益 指企业投资人对企业净资产的所有权。企业净资产等于企业全部资产减去全部负债后的余额。其中包括投资者对企业的最初投入,以及资本公积金、盈余公积金和未分配利润,对股份制企业即为股东权益。

Explanatory Notes on Main Statistical Indicators

Gross Industrial Output Value is the total volume of industrial products sold or available for sale in value terms which reflects the total achievements and overall scale of industrial production during a given period. It includes the value of the finished products, which are not to be further processed in the enterprises and have been inspected, packed and put in storage, the value of industrial services rendered to other units, and the changes in the value of the semi – finished products and products in process between the beginning and closing of the period. The gross industrial output value is calculated with "factory method". No double calculations are to be made within the same enterprise. However, double counting does occur among different enterprises.

Industrial Sales Output Value is the total volume of industrial products sold in value term of an industrial enterprise during a given period. It includes the value of finished products, semi – finished products, industrial operations rendered to other units, products industrial operations & self – made equipment provided to the basic construction department, welfare department, etc. of the enterprise. For finished products & semi – finished products, whether produced in this calculation period or the previous one, if they are sold in this calculation period, they should be included. Industrial operations are industrial services rendered to other units according to contracts. Products, industrial operations & self – made equipment provided to basic construction department, welfare department, etc. of the enterprise should be regarded as act of sale, and included in sales statistics.

The scope , price and method of calculation of industrial sales output value are the same as those for gross industrial output value. But the calculation bases are different: the base for sales output value is the total volume of products sold; the base for gross industrial output value is total volume of production of industrial products.

Value – added of Industry refers to the final results of industrial production of the industrial trade in money terms during the reference period.

Original Value of Fixed Assets refers to the original value of all assets owned by industrial enterprises, calculated at the cost paid at the time of purchase, installation, reconstruction, expansion, and technical innovation and transformation of the said assets, which includes expenses on purchase, package, transportation, and installation, etc.

Net Value of Fixed Assets is obtained by deducting depreciation over years from the original value of fixed assets.

Total Pre – tax Profits refers to the sum of sales tax and extra charges adding total profits.

Sales Revenue of Industrial Products refers to the revenue from the sales of products by industrial enterprises and the revenue from services provided and etc.

Sales Cost of Industrial Products refers to the actual cost of products of industrial enterprises and industrial services provided, etc.

Tax and Extra Charges on Sales of Products refer to the tax on city maintenance and construction, consumption tax, resources tax and extra charges for education , which should be borne by the enterprises in selling products and providing industrial services.

Sales Profit of Products refers to the profit gained by the enterprises by deducting cost, charges and taxes from the business income of the enterprises obtained in selling products and providing industrial services.

Total Profits refer to the profits gained by the enterprises.

Value – added Tax Payable refers to the amount of the value added tax which should be paid by the enterprises in the reporting period.

Total Assets refer to all assets which are owned or controlled by enterprises, including circulating assets, long term investment, fixed assets, intangible assets and deferred assets, other long term assets, and deferred taxes, etc. The summation of above items is equal to total assets shown in the balance sheets of the enterprises.

(1) Circulating assets (working capital) refer to assets which can be cashed in or spent or consumed in an operating cycle of one year or over one year, including cash, all kinds of deposits, short term investment, receivables, advance payment, stock, etc.

(2) Fixed assets refer to the net value of fixed assets, clearance of fixed assets, project under construction, fixed assets losses in suspense. These are corporations' fund holdings.

(3) Intangible assets refer to assets without material form used by enterprises over a lone time, such as patents, non – patent technologies, trade marks, copyright, land use right, business reputation, etc.

Total Liabilities refer to the debts that enterprises are responsible for repayment, including liquid liabilities, long – term liabilities and deferred taxes, etc. Total liabilities correspond to the summation item of liabilities shown in the balance sheets of the enterprises.

(1) Liquid liabilities (also called quick liabilities or immediate liabilities) refer to enterprises' total debt payable within an operating cycle of one year or over one year, including short term loans, payables and advance payments, wages payable, taxes payable and profit payable, etc.

(2) Long term liabilities refers to total debt payable within an operating cycle of one year or over one year, including long – term loans, payable liabilities, long – term payables, etc.

Creditors' Equity refers to investors' ownership of net assets of the enterprise. It is equal to the total assets of the enterprise minus its total liabilities, including the primary input from investors, capital accumulation fund, surplus accumulation fund and undistributed profit. It is the shareholder's equity in share – holding companies.

五、建筑业

V.CONSTRUCTION

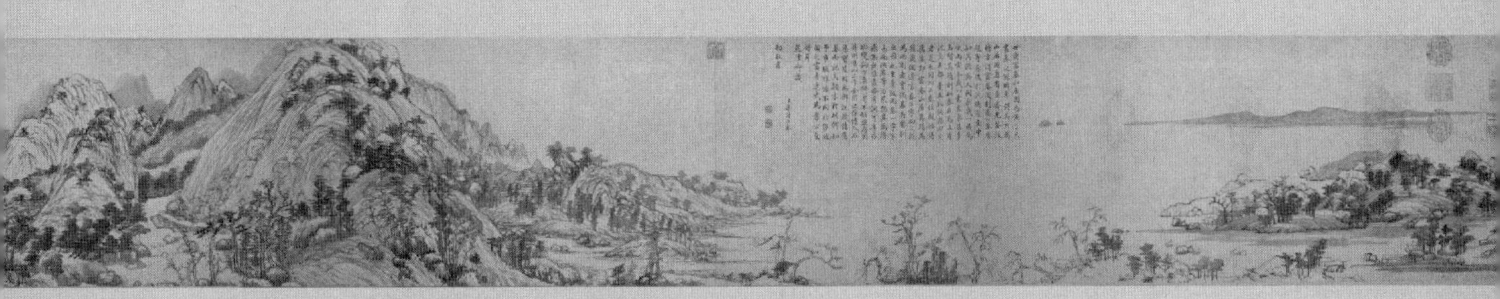

建筑业
Construction

主 要 统 计 指 标
Major Statistical Indicators

建筑业总产值	Gross Output Value of Construction	3755.47	亿元	(100 million yuan)
为上年	As Compared with the Preceding Year	113.5	%	(%)
房屋建筑施工面积	Floor Space of Buildings Under Construction	29538	万平方米	(10, 000 sq.m)
为上年	As Compared with the Preceding Year	112.0	%	(%)
房屋建筑竣工面积	Floor Space of Buildings Completed	9613	万平方米	(10, 000 sq.m)
为上年	As Compared with the Preceding Year	114.6	%	(%)

5－01 建筑业总产值(2013 年)

Gross Output Value of Construction(2013)

单位:万元 (10000 yuan)

地 区	Region	建筑企业单位数(个) Number of Construction Enterprises (unit)	建筑业总产值 Gross Output Value of Construction			
				建筑工程产值 Output Value of Construction Projects	安装工程产值 Output value of Installation Projects	其他产值 Other Output Values
全 市	**Total**	**1515**	**37554704**	**33244948**	**3270944**	**1038812**
市 区	Urban District	1200	34423172	30509156	3040773	873243
#上城区	Shangcheng	89	2265042	1527464	676939	60639
下城区	Xiacheng	81	1190531	958927	216083	15521
江干区	Jianggan	131	2408802	2065162	328356	15284
拱墅区	Gongshu	168	2887814	2384028	428809	74977
西湖区	Xihu	173	7853400	7197665	348717	307018
高新(滨江)区	Hi－Tech (Binjiang)	56	3865798	3712853	56320	96625
萧山区	Xiaoshan	305	11555552	10434963	821787	298802
余杭区	Yuhang	176	1758819	1630429	125797	2593
桐庐县	Tonglu	46	440111	399258	26791	14062
淳安县	Chun'an	44	280494	240485	30724	9285
建德市	Jiande	46	232978	197096	25628	10254
富阳市	Fuyang	122	1457854	1225269	113914	118671
临安市	Lin'an	57	720096	673684	33115	13297

5-02 建筑总专包

Financial Indicators on Construction Enterprises of

单位:万元

指标名称	Item	二、年末资产 Asset and Liabilities		
		流动资产合计 Circulating Funds	固定资产合计 Fixed Assets	资产合计 Total Assets
总　计	**Total**	**19959672**	**2371260**	**26205266**
#特、一、二级企业	of Which: Special Grade, First Grade, Second Grade	17631502	1975322	23234975
#国有及国有控股企业	of Which: State - owned and State Holding Enterprises	3632216	255287	4524262
一、按登记注册类型分组	**Grouped by Registration Status**			
内资企业	Domestic Funded	19722322	2329967	25907254
国有企业	State - owned	394404	57977	511060
集体企业	Collective - owned	23910	1701	26941
股份合作企业	Share - holding Cooperative Enterprises	24	90	114
联营企业	Joint Venture	8958	3959	13982
有限责任公司	Limited Liability Corporations	9271315	724095	11360296
股份有限公司	Share - holding Corporations Ltd.	1420326	297158	1938166
私营企业	Private Enterprises	8603386	1244989	12056696
其他企业	Other Enterprises			
港、澳、台商投资企业	Funded from Hong Kong, Macao and Taiwan	214747	38218	270741
外商投资企业	Foreign Funded	22602	3074	27271
二、按国民经济行业分组	**Grouped by Sector**			
房屋建筑业	Housing Construction	11509477	1296656	14498944
土木工程建筑业	Civil Engineering Construction	6339936	814393	8088983
建筑安装业	Installation of Lines, Pipelines and Equipment	847604	118627	1061534
建筑装饰和其他建筑业	Fitting、Decoration of Building and Others Construction	1262654	141584	2555804

企业财务指标(2013 年)

General Contractors and Specialist Contractors(2013)

(10000 yuan)

负债 at Year - end		所有者权益合计 Owners´Equity		
流动负债合计 Liquid Liabilities	负债合计 Total Liabilities		#实收资本 of Which: Paid - in Capitals	#国家资本 of Which: State Capital
16473990	**17591701**	**8559878**	**5019389**	**232890**
14994875	16058630	7137624	3965312	226139
3275685	3630169	894094	551913	230089
16236987	17354688	8498879	4987985	232890
363112	383685	127375	72955	24955
20579	21021	5920	4039	-
63	63	51	116	-
8028	8028	5953	3010	3010
7621580	8199245	3157533	1642240	204925
1290136	1358546	578631	273291	-
6933488	7384100	4623417	2992334	-
220683	220683	50058	23760	-
16321	16330	10941	7644	-
9128345	9798366	4685267	2631578	41212
4836085	5142489	2911638	1728249	178605
654215	675840	382454	262238	5080
1855346	1975007	580519	397325	7992

指标名称	Item	三、损益 Expenditure, Income	
		工程结算收入 Revenue of Project Settlement Accounts	工程结算成本 Costs of Project Settlement Accounts
总　计	**Total**	**33375924**	**30159197**
#特、一、二级企业	of Which: Special Grade, First Grade, Second Grade	30440473	27646306
#国有及国有控股企业	of Which: State－owned and State Holding Enterprises	6358548	5862050
一、按登记注册类型分组	**Grouped by Registration Status**		
内资企业	Domestic Funded	33153926	29967346
国有企业	State－owned	876433	783386
集体企业	Collective－owned	17524	16412
股份合作企业	Share－holding Cooperative Enterprises	8	4
联营企业	Joint Venture	18139	16770
有限责任公司	Limited Liability Corporations	16056180	14790730
股份有限公司	Share－holding Corporations Ltd.	2482104	2124145
私营企业	Private Enterprises	13703539	12235900
其他企业	Other Enterprises		
港、澳、台商投资企业	Funded from Hong Kong, Macao and Taiwan	170979	145849
外商投资企业	Foreign Funded	51020	46001
二、按国民经济行业分组	**Grouped by Sector**		
房屋建筑业	Housing Construction	21123390	19341367
土木工程建筑业	Civil Engineering Construction	8563230	7523220
建筑安装业	Installation of Lines, Pipelines and Equipment	1376758	1210782
建筑装饰和其他建筑业	Fitting、Decoration of Building and Others Construction	2312547	2083828

continued (10000 yuan)

及分配 and Distribution					
工程结算税金及附加 Taxes and Extra Charges Project Settlement Accounts	销售费用 Sales Expenses	管理费用 Management Expenditure	财务费用 Financial Expenditure	利润总额 Total Profits	应交所得税 Income Taxes Payable
987132	**95255**	**905194**	**318198**	**883887**	**190485**
894254	68385	724790	287479	783114	165100
167595	5430	199871	18769	139184	26979
984053	92164	894222	309656	877452	189457
19603	353	63537	1460	14223	5453
568	2	1221	-568	345	66
-	-	15	-	-11	-
469	-	816	-6	76	19
466719	19285	360406	117724	400010	80794
68132	6349	60568	35721	59285	12623
428562	66175	407660	155325	403525	90502
1798	2835	8782	8083	5703	760
1282	256	2190	460	732	268
615579	52715	381077	205797	477918	100480
265520	30925	357031	82569	318845	68770
38659	6599	83165	9892	31423	7771
67374	5016	83920	19939	55701	13464

5－03 建筑业企业生产情况（2007－2013）

Statistics on Production of Construction Enterprises（2007－2013）

指标名称	Item	2007	2008	2009	2010	2011	2012	2013
一、建筑业合同情况	**Contract of Construction**							
签订的合同额（万元）	Total Value of Contracts （10000 yuan）	24696898	30088537	36623552	46427916	55290611	59279520	66234009
上年结转合同额（万元）	Value from Contracts Signed in 2012 （10000 yuan）	9290912	11210961	14824477	17396267	22189586	25205183	26548398
本年新签合同额（万元）	Value from New Contracts Signed in 2013 （10000 yuan）	15405986	18877576	21799075	29031649	33101025	34074337	39685611
二、承包工程完成情况	**Completion of Contracted Projects**							
直接从建设单位承揽工程完成的产值（万元）	Complete Output Value of Projects Contacted Directly from Investors （10000 yuan）	14853868	17871119	20791153	26259274	29993008	32845834	37176277
自行完成施工产值（万元）	Own－completed Output Value （10000 yuan）	14495495	17427692	20424041	25689110	29339695	31586124	35973925
分包出去工程的产值（万元）	Output Value of Out－sourced Projects （10000 yuan）	358373	443427	367112	570163	653313	1259710	1202352
从建设单位以外承揽工程完成的产值（万元）	Completed Output Value of Projects Contacted from Non－investors （10000 yuan）	349254	576832	677632	949202	985280	1489749	1580779
建筑业总产值（万元）	Gross Output Value （10000 yuan）	14844749	18004524	21101673	26638312	30324975	33075873	37554704
#装饰装修产值（万元）	of Which：Output Value of Fitting and Decoration of Buildings （10000 yuan）	1149597	1404589	1641467	2177414	2556382	2821922	3216682
#在外省完成的产值（万元）	of Which：Completed Output Value outside of Zhejiang Province （10000 yuan）	3489987	4971040	5828938	8882553	10267000	11179195	12048961
按构成分	by Structure							
建筑工程产值（万元）	Output Value of Construction Projects （10000 yuan）	12768968	15351303	18280567	23307310	26308977	28976550	33244948
安装工程产值（万元）	Output value of Installation Projects （10000 yuan）	1729043	2083405	2193971	2557314	2801907	3092140	3270944
其他产值（万元）	Other Output Values （10000 yuan）	346738	569816	627135	773688	1214091	1007183	1038812
竣工产值（万元）	Output Value of Buildings Completed （10000 yuan）	9344723	10976179	12919145	16373795	16286512	17563992	21021307
房屋建筑施工面积（万平方米）	Floor Space of Buildings Under Construction （10000 sq. m）	15108.93	16059.15	19433.82	22650.40	26104.43	26362.73	29537.59
#本年新开工面积（万平方米）	of Which：Beginning Projects in this Year （10000 sq. m）	7516.70	7281.49	7839.32	11063.95	12024.02	10540.82	11963.98
#实行投标承包面积（万平方米）	of Which：Floor Space of Biding System （10000 sq. m）	13865.27	14725.56	18133.40	19792.30	23648.69	22684.32	24705.47
#本年新开工（万平方米）	of Which：Beginning Projects in this Year （10000 sq. m）	7064.70	6646.09	7390.40	9705.96	11256.35	9546.57	10685.96
房屋建筑竣工面积（万平方米）	Floor space of Buildings Completed （10000 sq. m）	5380.57	5799.98	6610.35	8219.87	8556.11	8388.44	9613.09
三、年末自有施工机械设备	**Machinery and Equipment Owned（year－end）**							
年末自有施工机械设备净值（万元）	Net Value of Machinery and Equipment Owned （10000 yuan）	462157	559442	683528	798573	825813	799293	832466
年末自有施工机械设备总台数（台）	Number of Machinery and Equipment Owned （set）	148722	157385	178586	205574	204139	178639	185792
年末自有施工机械设备总功率（千瓦）	Total Power of Machinery and Equipment Owned （1000 kw）	1958612	2435575	2748357	3261216	3611172	3355223	3460437
四、就业人员情况	**Number of Employed Persons**							
计算劳动生产率的平均人数（人）	Average Employed Persons Overall Labor Productivity （person）	775498	863862	966098	1149924		1203387	1259282
年末就业人员数（人）	Employed Persons（year－end） （person）	758171	801246	923046	1117287		1002886	1274082

主要统计指标解释

建筑业总产值　建筑业总产值是以货币表现的建筑业企业在一定时期内生产的建筑业产品和服务的总和。建筑业总产值包括建筑工程产值、安装工程产值和其他产值三部分内容。

房屋建筑施工面积　指报告期内施过工的全部房屋建筑面积,它包括本期新开工的面积、上期跨入本期继续施工的房屋面积、上期停缓建在本期恢复施工的房屋面积、本期竣工的房屋面积以及本期施工后又停缓建的房屋面积。

房屋建筑竣工面积　指在报告期内房屋建筑按照设计要求已全部完工,达到了使用条件,经检查验收鉴定合格的房屋建筑面积。

工程结算收入(主营业务收入)　指本企业承包工程实现的工程价款结算收入以及向发包单位收取的除工程价款以外按规定列作营业收入的各种款项,如临时设施费、劳动保险费、施工机构调迁费等以及向发包单位收取的各种索赔款。

工程结算成本(主营业务成本)　指在报告期内与发包单位办理工程价款结算的已完工程实际成本。

Explanatory Notes on Main Statistical Indicators

Gross Output Value of Construction refers to total of construction products and services, expressed in money terms, produced or rendered by construction and installation enterprises during a given period of time. It includes: output value of construction projects, output value of installation projects and other output values.

Floor Space of Buildings Under Construction refers to floor space of buildings under construction during the reference period, including the floor space of buildings for which construction has newly started; buildings for which construction has started earlier and is continuing during the reference period; and buildings for which construction has been suspended earlier but has restarted during the reference period; buildings completed during the reference period; and buildings under construction but construction has subsequently been during the reference period.

Floor Space of Buildings Completed refers to the floor space of buildings that are completed in the reference period in accordance with the requirements of the design, up to the standard for being put into use, and having been checked and accepted by departments concerned as qualified ones.

Income from Settlement of Projects refers to the income received by the construction enterprise from the contracted project through settlement procedures, and other charges to the contractor as operational costs in addition to the value of the project, such as temporary facility fee, labor insurance premium, moving cost of construction equipment, as well as various types of claims to the contractor.

Project Settlement Costs refers to the contracting process works price of the actual settlement costs of projects have been completed during the reporting period.

六、交通运输、邮电

Ⅵ.TRANSPORTATION, POST AND TELECOMMUNICATIONS

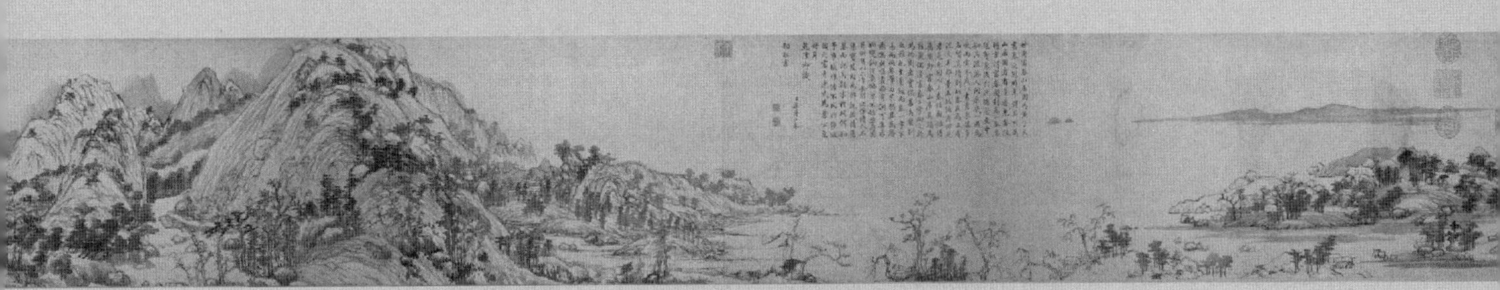

交通运输、邮电
Transportation, Post and Telecommunications

主要统计指标
Major Statistical Indicators

客运量	Passenger Traffic	36409	万人次	(10, 000 person-times)
为上年	As Compared with the Preceding Year	101.6	%	(%)
货运量	Freight Traffic	30734	万吨	(10, 000 tons)
为上年	As Compared with the Preceding Year	102.1	%	(%)
邮电业务收入	Business Income of Post & Telecommunication Service	245.50	亿元	(100 million yuan)
为上年	As Compared with the Preceding Year	115.2	%	(%)
年末固定电话用户数	Number of Local Telephone Subscribers(year-end)	334.87	万户	(10, 000 subscribers)
为上年	As Compared with the Preceding Year	96.7	%	(%)
年末移动电话用户数	Number of Mobile Telephone Subscribers(year-end)	1546.83	万户	(10, 000 subscribers)
为上年	As Compared with the Preceding Year	107.5	%	(%)
年末宽带业务户数	Broadband Subscribers of Internet(year-end)	338.63	万户	(10, 000 subscribers)
为上年	As Compared with the Preceding Year	122.7	%	(%)

6－01　全市客运量(1978－2013)

Total Passenger Traffic（1978－2013)

单位:万人次　　(10,000 person－times)

年　份 Year	合　计 Total	铁　路 Railways	公　路 Highways	水　路 Waterways	民　航 Civil Aviation
1978	2878	485	－	－	3
1979	3122	560	1829	729	4
1980	3905	672	2358	870	5
1981	4484	769	2857	850	8
1982	5263	813	3377	1064	9
1983	5451	878	3530	1035	8
1984	6056	983	3912	1151	10
1985	6724	1004	4595	1111	14
1986	6765	1034	4768	941	22
1987	6905	1127	4852	896	30
1988	6593	1237	4445	877	34
1989	7493	1182	5488	801	22
1990	8119	1056	6350	691	22
1991	10701	1062	8876	710	53
1992	13358	1083	11538	670	67
1993	13070	1139	11403	454	74
1994	13373	1230	11669	390	84
1995	16620	1242	14921	339	118
1996	16714	1112	15184	273	145
1997	17034	1040	15623	260	111
1998	17395	1120	15925	235	115
1999	17882	1168	16369	235	110
2000	18607	1202	17102	179	124
2001	20342	1342	18707	148	145
2002	21089	1574	19213	108	194
2003	21348	1534	19510	89	215
2004	22833	1908	20372	237	316
2005	24124	2011	21431	304	378
2006	25810	2124	22961	267	458
2007	28026	2255	24836	306	629
2008	29084	2498	25630	277	679
2009	30116	2494	26454	372	796
2010	33772	2741	29671	456	904
2011	34778	2962	30305	595	916
2012	35819	3112	31126	592	989
2013	36409	3717	30994	547	1151

注:1990 年以前为交通系统数,客运量全市数自 1990 年起为全社会数。

a) Before 1990 the data in the table included transportation system, while date included non－transportation system.

6－02　全市货运量(1978－2013)

Total Freight Traffic (1978－2013)

单位:万吨　　(10000 tons)

年　份 Year	合　计 Total	铁　路 Railways	公　路 Highways	水　路 Waterways	民　航 Civil Aviation
1978	1706	418	633	655	
1979	1983	440	771	772	
1980	2070	444	762	864	
1981	1972	449	886	637	
1982	2261	485	795	981	
1983	2299	488	838	973	
1984	2385	510	888	987	
1985	2488	524	890	1074	
1986	2558	551	874	1133	
1987	2515	574	899	1041	1
1988	2416	555	823	1037	1
1989	7377	539	5095	1743	
1990	6522	449	4479	1594	
1991	7017	451	4891	1675	
1992	8434	534	6063	1836	1
1993	9082	580	6353	2148	1
1994	8962	491	6563	1907	1
1995	10347	482	7021	2842	2
1996	10962	445	7735	2780	2
1997	11015	406	7932	2676	1
1998	11329	418	8196	2713	2
1999	11684	403	8037	3241	3
2000	11459	417	7865	3173	4
2001	12443	452	8588	3398	5
2002	14347	446	10391	3504	6
2003	16815	438	12118	4253	6
2004	18895	480	13117	5289	9
2005	19909	525	13539	5833	12
2006	20924	569	14588	5754	13
2007	22569	573	16484	5500	12
2008	22550	483	16822	5232	13
2009	22372	427	16536	5396	13
2010	25915	379	19148	6371	17
2011	28831	331	21755	6727	18
2012	30089	322	23243	6503	20
2013	30734	284	23884	6545	22

注:1990 年以前为交通系统数,货运量全市数自 1990 年起为全社会数。

a) The date in the table in cluded transportation system before 1990, while it included the whole society since 1990.

6-03 全社会客货运输量(2013年)
Total Passenger and Freight Traffic(2013)

项 目	Item	全市 Whole City	为上年(%) As Compared with the Preceding Year(%)
一、客运量合计(万人次)	**Passenger Traffic(10000 person-times)**	**36409**	**101.6**
铁路客运量	Passenger Railways	3717	119.4
民航客运量	Passenger Civil Aviation	1151	116.4
公路客运量	Passenger Highways	30994	99.6
水路客运量	Passenger Waterways	547	92.4
二、旅客周转量合计(万人公里)	**Total Passenger-kilometers(10000 passenger-km)**	**1573289**	**98.5**
公路旅客周转量	Passenger-kilometers Highways	1566046	98.5
水路旅客周转量	Passenger-kilometers Waterways	7243	89.5
三、货运量合计(万吨)	**Total Freight Traffic(10000 tons)**	**30734**	**102.1**
铁路货运量	Freight Railways	284	88.1
民航货运量	Freight Civil Aviation	22	106.5
公路货运量	Freight Highways	23884	102.8
水路货运量	Freight Waterways	6545	100.6
四、货运周转量合计(万吨公里)	**Total Freight Ton-kilometers(10000 ton-km)**	**4724588**	**103.5**
公路货物周转量	Freight Ton-kilometers Highways	2719204	102.9
水路货物周转量	Freight Ton-kilometers Waterways	2005384	104.4

6－04 分地区交通
Traffic and Transport

项 目		Item		全市 Whole City	市区 Urban District
铁路旅客运量	（万人）	Passenger Railways	(10,000 Persons)	3717	3717
铁路货物运量	（万吨）	Freight Railways	(10,000 tons)	284	211
公路客运量(全社会)	（万人）	Passenger Highways(Whole Society)	(10,000 Persons)	30994	19315
公路货运量(全社会)	（万吨）	Freight Highway(Whole Society)	(10,000 tons)	23884	17884
民用航空客运量	（万人）	Passenger Civil Aviation	(10,000 Persons)	1151	1151
民用航空货邮运量	（万吨）	Freight Civil Aviation	(10,000 tons)	22	22
水运客运量(全社会)	（万人）	Passenger Waterways(Whole Society)	(10,000 Persons)	547	265
水运货运量(全社会)	（万吨）	Freight Waterways(Whole Society)	(10,000 tons)	6545	5780
民用汽车拥有量	（辆）	Possession of Civil Vehicles	(Unit)	2045618	1734678
#私人汽车拥有量	（辆）	in which:Possession of Private Vehicles	(Unit)	1678453	1414108

运输情况(2013 年)
Situation by Region(2013)

萧山区 Xiaoshan	余杭区 Yuhang	桐庐县 Tonglu	淳安县 Chun'an	建德市 Jiande	富阳市 Fuyang	临安市 Lin'an
382	76	–	–	–	–	–
43	21	–	73	–	–	–
7180	5513	2551	980	2196	3150	2802
5972	1902	814	499	1307	1449	1931
1151	–	–	–	–	–	–
22	–	–	–	–	–	–
15	–	23	211	13	5	30
1447	3062	99	98	84	371	112
356733	256317	53303	22714	39679	105299	89945
297256	218963	44986	19226	32647	90164	77322

6-05 社会机动车辆年末拥有量(2013 年)

Total Number of Motor Vehicles End of the Year(2013)

单位:辆 (unit)

项　目	Item	全市 Whole City	为上年(%) As Compared with the Preceding Year(%)
总计	**Total**	**2542976**	**112.2**
#民用汽车拥有量	**Possession of Civilian Vehicles**	**2045618**	**116.2**
#私人汽车	Private Vehicles	1678453	119.2
载客汽车	**Passenger Vehicles**	**1860794**	**118.5**
大型载客汽车	Large	17078	106.0
中型载客汽车	Medium	17849	98.6
小型载客汽车	Small	1794017	119.7
微型载客汽车	Minicar	31850	87.4
载货汽车	**Trucks**	**173227**	**96.6**
重型载货汽车	Heavy	35917	115.3
中型载货汽车	Light - heavy	17530	69.5
轻型载货汽车	Light	119205	97.5
微型载货汽车	Mini	575	83.7
其他汽车	**Else**	**11597**	**100.8**
摩 托 车	**Motorcycles**	**490884**	**98.2**
普通摩托车	Genera Motorcycles	466625	99.1
轻便摩托车	Light Motorcycles	24259	82.8

6－06　邮政、电信主要指标

Post and Telecommunications

项目		Item		2013 年	2012 年
邮政业务总收入	（万元）	Total Business Income of Postal Service	(10,000 yuan)	702664	533059
电信业务收入	（万元）	Total Business Income of Telecommunications Services	(10,000 yuan)	1752286	1597344
函件	（万件）	Number of Letters	(10,000 pcs)	20132.99	21226.35
包裹	（万件）	Number of Parcels	(10,000 pcs)	133.36	128.76
快递	（万份）	Pieces of Express Mail Service	(10,000 copies)	46852	25536
#国际及港澳台快递	（万份）	Pieces of Express to overseas and HongKong, macao, Taiwan	(10,000 copies)	738	525
快递业务收入	（万元）	Business Income of Express Mail Service	(10,000 yuan)	563459	427356
纪特邮票	（万枚）	Stamps for Collettion	(10,000 pcs)	1412.39	1744.06
年末固定电话用户数	（万户）	Number of Local Telephone Subscribers (year－end)	(10,000 subscribers)	334.87	346.22
年末移动电话用户数	（万户）	Number of Subscribers of Mobile Telephone (year－end)	(10,000 subscribers)	1546.83	1438.67
年末宽带业务户数	（万户）	Number of Wide Band Subscribers	(10,000 subscribers)	338.63	275.91

注：邮政业务总收入含规模以上快递企业。

a) The total business income of postal services included the express enterprises above designated sice.

主要统计指标解释

货(客)运量　指在一定时期内,各种运输工具实际运送的货物(旅客)数量。是反映运输业为国民经济和人民生活服务的数量指标,也是制定和检查运输生产计划、研究运输发展规模和速度的重要指标。货运按吨计算,客运按人计算。货物不论运输距离长短、货物类别,均按实际重量统计。旅客不论行程远近或票价多少,均按一人一次作为客运量统计;半价票、小孩票也按一人统计。

货物(旅客)周转量　指在一定时期内,由各种运输工具运送的货物(旅客)数量与其相应运输距离的乘积之总和。是反映运输业生产总成果的重要指标,也是编制和检查运输生产计划,计算运输效率、劳动生产率以及核算运输单位成本的主要基础资料。通常以吨公里和人公里为计算单位。计算货物周转量通常按发出站与到达站之间的最短距离,也就是计费距离计算。

移动电话用户　指在邮电部门登记,通过移动电话交换机进入移动电话网,占有移动电话号码的电话用户。用户数量以实际办理登记手续进入邮电部门移动电话网的户数进行计算,一部或一台移动电话统计为一户。

Explanatory Notes on Main Statistical Indicators

Freight(passenger) Traffic refers to the volume of freight (passenger) transported with various means. Freight transport is calculated in tons and passenger traffic is calculated in the number of persons. Despite the type of freight and traveling distance, the freight transport is calculated in the actual weight of the goods; and despite the traveling distance and ticket price, the passenger traffic is calculated by the principle that one person can be counted only once in one travel. The passenger who travel with a half – price ticket or a child ticket is also calculated as one person. The freight (passenger) traffic provides a quantitative measure to show how the transport industry serves the national economy and people, and is also an important indicator for plan the transport industry and for studying the development scale and speed of the transport industry.

Freight Ton – kilometers(Passenger – kilometers) refers to the sum of the products of the volume of transported cargo (passengers) multiplying by the transport distance, usually using ton – kilometer and passenger – kilometer as units for measurement . Normally, the shortest distance between the departure station and the terminal station (i. e. , the payable distance) is the basis to calculate the freight ton – kilometers. This is an important indicator to show the total results of the transport industry, to prepare and examine the transport plan and to measure the efficiency, the labour productivity and the unit cost of transport.

Mobile Telephone Subscribers refer to the persons who own mobile telephone number connected with the mobile telephone communication network and registered by post and telecommunications organization. The number of subscribers is calculated only when the subscribers who have gone through all the register formalities and entered into the mobile telephone network. One mobile telephone is treated as a subscriber.

七、固定资产投资

Ⅶ.INVESTMENT IN FIXED ASSETS

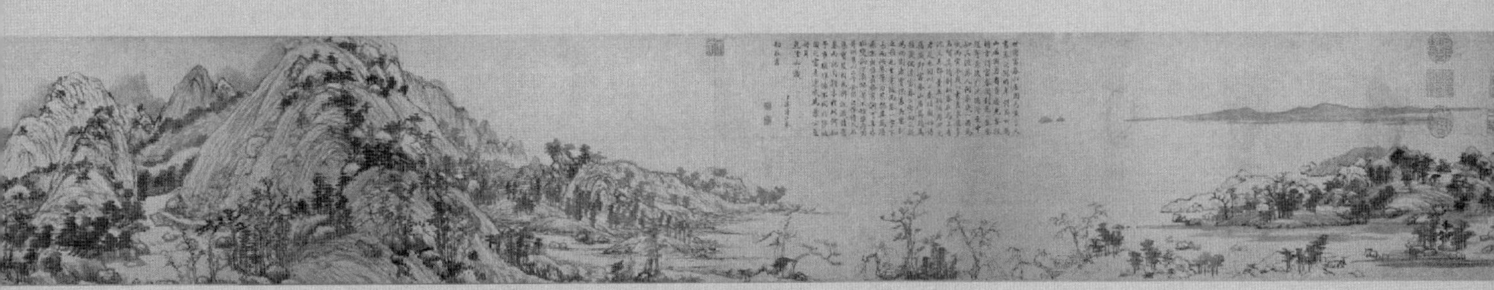

固定资产投资
Investment in Fixed Assets

主要统计指标
Major Statistical Indicators

固定资产投资额	Investment in Fixed Assets	4263.87	亿元	(100 million yuan)
为上年	As Compared with the Preceding Year	114.5	%	(%)
#第一产业	Primary Industry	8.40	亿元	(100 million yuan)
为上年	As Compared with the Preceding Year	196.9	%	(%)
#第二产业	Secondary Industry	912.53	亿元	(100 million yuan)
为上年	As Compared with the Preceding Year	107.0	%	(%)
#第三产业	Tertiary Industry	3342.94	亿元	(100 million yuan)
为上年	As Compared with the Preceding Year	116.7	%	(%)
房地产企业营业收入	Operating Revenue of Real Estate Enterprise	1595.71	亿元	(100 million yuan)
为上年	As Compared with the Preceding Year	143.8	%	(%)
房地产企业单位数	Number of Enterprises for Real Estate Developement	1437	个	(unit)
为上年	As Compared with the Preceding Year	95.4	%	(%)

7－01 全市固定资产投资总额(1978－2013)

Investment in Fixed Assets (1978－2013)

单位:万元 (10000 yuan)

年份 Year	全社会固定资产投资 Total Investment in Fixed Assets	固定资产投资 Investment in Fixed Assets	房地产开发投资 Investment in Real Estate Development	项目投资 Projects Investment	#基础设施投资 Infrastructural Investment	工业投资 Industrial Investment	#民间投资 Nongovernment Investment
1978	48307						
1979	55828						
1980	70936						
1981	79791						
1982	97895						
1983	102413						
1984	148601						
1985	229746						
1986	284936						
1987	350033						
1988	370954						
1989	345548						
1990	366296		20409				
1991	418845		25247				
1992	654537		41886				
1993	1310914		218006				
1994	1620301		320532				
1995	2323355		527985				
1996	2611772		572749				
1997	3033904		572686				
1998	3636607		666244				
1999	4354770		848441				
2000	5154923		1015347				
2001	6309723		1409132				
2002	7697578		1982517				
2003	10067440	8952090	2588452	6363638	2907234	3194960	4192567
2004	12022243	11081993	3285409	7796584	3254648	4357950	5761350
2005	13866833	12777972	4105706	8672266	3715525	4438723	6723758
2006	14607422	13734482	4426534	9307948	3871462	4640261	7551249
2007	16841298	15837775	5187904	10649871	4056241	5271141	8215570
2008	19805018	18822936	6154060	12668876	5410313	5693385	9450542
2009	22916543	21951706	7046752	14904954	6018416	6091653	11127373
2010	27531348	26518839	9561970	16956869	6452236	6855587	13680327
2011	–	31000218	13027234	17972984	6437025	7474806	17507040
2012	–	37227544	15973611	21253933	7785196	8518653	20595909
2013	–	42638732	18532841	24105891	8524663	9104614	22560292

注:2011 年开始固定资产投资口径由计划总投资 500 万元以上项目投资及房地产开发投资构成。

a) From 2011, the date of investment in fixed Assets was composed by investment projects which each of them over 5 million yuan and Investment in real estate.

7-02 市区固定资产投资总额(1978-2013)

Investment in Fixed Assets of Urban District (1978-2013)

单位:万元 (10000 yuan)

年份 Year	全社会固定资产投资 Total Investment in Fixed Assets	固定资产投资 Investment in Fixed Assets	房地产开发投资 Investment in Real Estate Development	项目投资 Projects Investment	#基础设施投资 Infrastructural Investment	工业投资 Industrial Investment	民间投资 Nongovernment Investment
1978	22468						
1979	26793						
1980	35925						
1981	41729						
1982	52541						
1983	57191						
1984	88074						
1985	125927						
1986	154417						
1987	163067						
1988	159599						
1989	150113						
1990	170878		12750				
1991	176914		16509				
1992	231616		29784				
1993	499373		115116				
1994	717285		189357				
1995	1148688		375816				
1996	1485008		439245				
1997	1821969		445316				
1998	2260918		538499				
1999	2672757		636705				
2000	3009630		737950				
2001	5381284		1255605				
2002	6388204		1724128				
2003	7971044	7409538	2176433	5233105	2535843	2424383	3316886
2004	9648206	8963515	3088508	6153009	2624214	3299235	5238005
2005	10787387	10358519	3485810	6872709	3071506	3247399	5802542
2006	11169155	10944075	3653393	7290682	3150192	3289532	5559199
2007	13150724	12630099	4298687	8331412	3396807	3617512	6218211
2008	15634404	15184281	5269947	9914334	4726734	3676567	7076219
2009	18172403	17797778	6261562	11536216	5070500	3821313	8632900
2010	21827468	21437496	8486495	12951001	5438685	4293707	10332997
2011	-	25202394	11409566	13792828	5451654	4801419	13302115
2012	-	30160782	13749412	16411370	6495070	5554286	15669790
2013	-	34029665	15978470	18051195	6728552	5787728	16759259

注:2011 年开始固定资产投资口径由计划总投资 500 万元以上项目投资及房地产开发投资构成。

a) From 2011, the date of investment in fixed Assets was composed by investment projects which each of them over 5 million yuan and Investment in real estate.

7-03 三次产业固定资产投资(1978-2013)

Investment in Fixed Assets Grouped by Three Industries (1978-2013)

单位:万元 (10000 yuan)

年 份 Year	绝对数(万元) Absolute Figure(10000 yuan)				比重(以投资总额为 100) Proportion(%)		
	合 计 Total	第一产业 Primary Industry	第二产业 Secondary Industry	第三产业 Tertiary Industry	第一产业 Primary Industry	第二产业 Secondary Industry	第三产业 Tertiary Industry
1978	23941	2174	14455	7312	9.1	60.4	30.5
1979	34407	2454	19927	12026	7.1	57.9	35.0
1980	45752	1608	26211	17933	3.5	57.3	39.2
1981	51538	850	29176	21512	1.6	56.6	41.8
1982	66123	1352	37648	27123	2.0	57.0	41.0
1983	68306	1297	37823	29186	1.9	55.4	42.7
1984	93244	2831	46619	43794	3.0	50.0	47.0
1985	141889	3207	71608	67074	2.3	50.5	47.2
1986	182398	2265	94394	85739	1.2	51.8	47.0
1987	200516	2994	106600	90922	1.5	53.2	45.3
1988	205967	4746	118736	82485	2.3	57.6	40.1
1989	202131	3038	117651	81442	1.5	58.2	40.3
1990	229214	2181	126263	100770	1.0	55.1	43.9
1991	255696	3204	132303	120189	1.3	51.7	47.0
1992	384136	4424	206659	173053	1.2	53.8	45.0
1993	825382	5650	346416	473316	0.7	42.0	57.3
1994	1059437	3905	354672	700860	0.4	33.5	66.1
1995	1566280	5821	534687	1025772	0.4	34.1	65.5
1996	1819333	3100	640273	1175960	0.2	35.2	64.6
1997	2139012	1712	595966	1541334	-	27.9	72.1
1998	2681740	4053	706948	1970739	0.2	26.4	73.4
1999	3233609	23546	764309	2445754	0.7	23.6	75.7
2000	3766473	774	844334	2921365	0.2	22.4	77.4
2001	4634929	595	953494	3680840	-	20.6	79.4
2002	5623366	6514	1104212	4512640	0.1	19.6	80.3
2003	8952090	10489	3208885	5732716	0.1	35.9	64.0
2004	11081993	15992	4369015	6696986	0.1	39.4	60.5
2005	12777972	13982	4451936	8312054	0.1	34.8	65.1
2006	13734482	17892	4651420	9065170	0.1	33.9	66.0
2007	15837775	23278	5286340	10528157	0.1	33.4	66.5
2008	18822936	30810	5705736	13086390	0.2	30.3	69.5
2009	21951706	31335	6115482	15804889	0.1	27.9	72.0
2010	26518839	41959	6875840	19601040	0.2	25.9	73.9
2011	31000218	76931	7486832	23436455	0.2	24.2	75.6
2012	37227544	42668	8531598	28653278	0.1	22.9	77.0
2013	42638732	84018	9125316	33429398	0.2	21.4	78.4

注:2002 年以前为全部城镇及以上投资,不包括农村集体及私人投资。从 2003 年开始为计划总投资 500 万元以上项目投资及房地产开发投资。

a) Before year 2002, data in this table refer to urban investments and the rural investments are excluded. From 2003, the Investment in Fixed Assets was composed by investment projects which each of them over 5 million yuan and Investment in real estate.

7－04 全市固定资产投资房屋建筑面积及造价(1978－2013)

Floor Space of Buildings and Their Cost (1978－2013)

年份 Year	施工面积(万平方米) Floor Space of Buildings Under Construction (10000sq. m)	#住宅 Residential Buildings	竣工面积(万平方米) Floor Space of Buildings Completed (10000 sq. m)	#住宅 Residential Buildings	竣工房屋价值(万元) Value of Buildings Completed (10000 yuan)	#住宅 Residential Buildings	每平方米造价(元) Cost Per Square (yuan)	#住宅 Residential Buildings
1978			101.95	39.58	8869	2810	87	71
1979			150.26	68.01	13223	4965	88	73
1980	456.54		202.58	104.44	19448	8564	96	82
1981	507.94		232.25	120.35	26709	12396	115	103
1982	554.89	258.09	281.63	148.66	34095	16470	121	111
1983	531.79	244.36	247.07	125.86	33938	15494	137	123
1984	620.71	293.21	267.85	138.71	42740	18398	160	133
1985	741.47	333.72	327.75	157.85	56561	22825	173	145
1986	674.58	278.19	338.19	160.19	50561	27338	238	170
1987	544.64	149.07	254.73	73.16	68801	14944	270	204
1988	526.70	156.92	230.21	75.44	68407	17820	297	236
1989	420.81	116.12	202.15	64.15	69750	18200	345	284
1990	472.59	209.50	236.44	112.77	93557	34266	396	304
1991	459.00	205.41	226.84	92.72	93158	28599	411	308
1992	604.85	301.21	262.11	114.97	116169	39834	452	350
1993	958.91	533.01	380.29	199.96	224251	105107	589	525
1994	1069.68	613.62	460.20	274.19	375211	212705	815	776
1995	1320.68	737.79	524.58	319.41	491705	274314	937	859
1996	1399.70	758.00	582.70	354.50	688569	370485	1182	1045
1997	1363.80	660.70	642.10	338.00	871361	449235	1357	1329
1998	1456.02	743.59	515.16	271.91	709730	390624	1378	1437
1999	1681.71	956.15	709.10	411.44	1119141	641717	1578	1560
2000	1721.58	949.32	744.42	419.80	1207767	709044	1622	1689
2001	2318.95	1251.92	830.05	402.46	1310380	679449	1579	1688
2002	2713.02	1586.28	890.05	492.95	1623662	956643	1820	1941
2003	4392.79	2083.58	1618.01	651.58	2732763	1353422	1689	2077
2004	5731.48	2909.03	1865.83	717.46	2791115	1313596	1496	1831
2005	6671.39	3628.34	1856.34	801.34	3265491	1865538	1759	2328
2006	7260.08	3747.60	1737.51	706.13	2900836	1580689	1670	2239
2007	7942.07	4040.54	1849.24	858.99	3750264	2329184	2028	2712
2008	9471.42	4160.27	2057.86	846.34	4113211	2171525	1999	2566
2009	10308.45	4441.84	2009.90	700.63	3626421	1684092	1804	2404
2010	12971.81	5534.10	2695.90	902.57	5274936	2285285	1957	2532
2011	15982.64	6442.52	3108.57	991.72	6209320	2498468	1997	2519
2012	17329.23	6938.29	2952.06	1048.95	6015778	2485123	2038	2369
2013	19226.78	7392.23	3666.67	1308.83	7744168	3530744	2112	2698

注:2002 年以前为全部城镇及以上投资,不包括农村集体及私人投资。从 2003 年开始为计划总投资 500 万元以上项目投资及房地产开发投资。

a) Before year 2002, data in this table refer to urban investments and the rural investments are excluded. From 2003, the Investment in Fixed Assets was composed by investment projects which each of them over 5 million yuan and Investment in real estate.

7－05　市区固定资产投资房屋建筑面积及造价（1978－2013）

Urban District Floor Space of Buildings and Their Cost （1978－2013）

年　份 Year	施工面积（万平方米）Floor Space of Buildings Under Construction（10000 sq. m）	#住　宅 Residential Buildings	竣工面积（万平方米）Floor Space of Buildings Completed（10000sq. m）	#住　宅 Residential Buildings	竣工房屋价值（万元）Value of Buildings Completed（10000 yuan）	#住　宅 Residential Buildings	每平方米造价（元）Cost Per Square（yuan）	#住　宅 Residential Buildings
1978			71.56	29.06	6941	2237	97	77
1979			109.23	53.37	10267	4056	94	76
1980			137.11	76.73	14396	6752	105	88
1981			163.36	90.12	20093	9643	123	107
1982	378.88	172.11	189.92	100.07	25200	11980	133	120
1983	376.32	169.17	157.14	81.68	24029	11045	153	135
1984	465.27	221.72	191.13	104.55	33863	14658	177	140
1985	532.66	258.19	219.79	114.26	40344	17489	184	153
1986	465.75	203.22	219.33	116.70	58619	21149	267	181
1987	336.85	86.05	150.59	41.72	46530	9513	309	228
1988	315.80	90.98	117.71	37.63	38501	10117	330	269
1989	253.41	56.39	99.86	28.89	38680	9087	387	315
1990	301.82	128.50	137.88	62.47	60551	20361	439	326
1991	265.61	118.99	114.19	42.31	53819	12892	471	305
1992	329.16	190.55	115.59	57.36	55758	19706	483	344
1993	500.08	266.80	175.22	104.83	101528	53540	579	511
1994	618.91	352.16	212.06	123.74	182730	102924	862	832
1995	821.03	463.98	244.94	152.10	250073	139666	1021	918
1996	969.10	538.50	350.10	229.00	437239	274244	1249	1196
1997	1017.30	485.20	442.00	232.70	675762	357624	1529	1537
1998	1055.24	541.41	321.17	184.18	516400	317402	1608	1723
1999	1204.30	656.07	489.23	294.85	908844	533675	1858	1810
2000	1176.29	617.80	497.64	269.94	916212	528385	1841	1957
2001	2053.02	1085.30	698.29	325.64	1193818	615802	1710	1891
2002	2330.97	1335.78	744.48	404.35	1483862	869969	1993	2152
2003	3637.82	1699.61	1325.48	516.33	2395039	1174735	1807	2275
2004	4740.42	2453.87	1389.30	528.26	2257386	1068708	1625	2023
2005	5533.58	3039.08	1478.07	661.56	2804402	1626514	1897	2459
2006	5898.15	3114.45	1327.37	580.22	2365342	1357671	1782	2340
2007	6496.01	3357.18	1355.43	674.97	3063585	1992874	2260	2953
2008	7812.71	3466.88	1537.69	668.13	3372465	1827426	2193	2735
2009	8558.17	3807.67	1398.49	537.39	2725150	1321357	1949	2459
2010	10738.49	4759.75	1983.33	732.55	4255543	1927150	2146	2631
2011	13259.13	5451.45	2091.12	797.96	4736356	2122126	2265	2659
2012	14385.57	5680.08	2169.11	889.73	4966296	2207085	2290	2481
2013	15693.30	5910.71	2637.83	986.35	6074353	2822878	2303	2862

注：2002 年以前为全部城镇及以上投资，不包括农村集体及私人投资。从 2003 年开始为计划总投资 500 万元以上项目投资及房地产开发投资。

a) Before year 2002, data in this table refer to urban investments and the rural investments are excluded. From 2003, the Investment in Fixed Assets was composed by investment projects which each of them over 5 million yuan and Investment in real estate.

7-06 分地区固定

Investment in Fixed Assets

单位:万元

指　　标	Item	全　市 Total 2013 年	为上年(%) As Compared with the Preceding Year(%)	市　区 Urban District 2013 年
固定资产投资额	**Investment in Fixed Assets**	**42638732**	**114.5**	**34029665**
#民间投资	#Residential Buildings	22560292	109.5	16759259
#工业投资	Industrial Investment	9104614	106.9	5787728
#基础设施投资	Infrastructural Investment	8524663	109.5	6728552
一、按投资、房地产分	**Grouped by Sector**			
投资项目完成额	Investment Projects	24105891	113.4	18051195
房地产开发完成额	Real Estate	18532841	116.0	15978470
二、按登记注册类型分	**Grouped by Status of Registration**			
内资	Domestic - funded	36663683	110.9	28826103
国有	State - owned	9199618	105.5	7813506
集体	Collective - owned	828579	131.8	622122
股份合作	Cooperative	90068	105.4	83569
国有联营企业	State Joint Ownership	3480	-	-
国有与集体联营	Joint State - collective Ownership	1329	75.1	1072
国有独资公司	State - owned Corporations	2260148	184.9	1671818
其他有限责任公司	Other Limited Liability Corporations	15065222	104.7	12812824
股份有限公司	Share - holding Corporations Ltd.	1006009	81.3	766328
私营	Private	7978376	120.1	4989969
其他	Other	230854	169.6	64895
港、澳、台商投资	Investment from Hong Kong, Macao and Taiwan	4089666	137.3	3557500
外商投资	Foreign Investment	1865713	159.1	1644323
个体经营	Individual	19670	138.9	1739

资产投资(2013 年)
by Region(2013)

(10000 yuan)

为上年(%) As Compared with the Preceding Year(%)	#萧山区 Xiaoshan	#余杭区 Yuhang	桐庐县 Tonglu	淳安县 Chun'an	建德市 Jiande	富阳市 Fuyang	临安市 Lin'an
112.8	**7307304**	**6312261**	**1725986**	**1193796**	**1176467**	**2868320**	**1644498**
107.0	4130840	4098317	1262219	690728	827357	1799218	1221511
104.2	2701679	1307968	592006	293533	529546	1223911	677890
103.6	1515009	787937	440693	395239	235042	467876	257261
110.0	4828980	3664315	1221975	841229	901463	2082659	1007370
116.2	2478324	2647946	504011	352567	275004	785661	637128
108.4	5949115	5693169	1600070	1157815	1032901	2526543	1520251
103.2	1227300	914956	270831	367608	252456	291684	203533
131.8	76055	216874	120187	5139	1376	79755	–
100.2	–	10774	318	–	–	6181	–
–	–	–	3480	–	–	–	–
63.5	–	1072	–	–	–	257	–
176.0	540349	563685	105185	87550	66900	306112	22583
107.4	1967809	2212539	250553	350493	239801	687684	723867
72.7	94523	77221	44171	6517	42028	69133	77832
112.8	2001686	1690892	805345	308135	363495	1022981	488451
67.3	41393	5156	–	32373	66845	62756	3985
135.7	674343	399468	83530	11952	110288	251786	74610
172.0	683396	218335	35367	20258	26137	89991	49637
63.7	450	1289	7019	3771	7141	–	–

指　　标	Item	全　　市 Total		市　　区 Urban District
		2013 年	为上年(%) As Compared with the Preceding Year(%)	2013 年
三、按行业分	**Grouped by Sector**			
农林牧渔业	Agricultare, Forestry, Animal Husbandry and Fishery	84018	196.9	4932
采矿业	Mining	50924	140.4	-
制造业	Manufacturing	7886618	109.4	4900090
电力、热力、燃气及水的生产和供应业	Production and Supply of Electric Power, Heat Power, Gas and Tap Water	1167072	91.5	887638
建筑业	Construction	20702	159.9	20702
批发和零售业	Wholesale & Retail Trades	1133166	112.5	984519
交通运输、仓储和邮政业	Transportation, Storage and Post	2375342	92.3	1879803
住宿和餐饮业	Hotels and Catering Services	541380	127.3	294948
信息传输、软件和信息技术服务业	Information Transmission, Softuare and Information Technology	526553	149.7	495207
金融业	Financial Intertnediation	307335	70.9	300426
房地产业	Real Estate	22277214	117.0	19219972
租赁和商务服务业	Leasing and Business Services	890060	165.2	846646
科学研究和技术服务业	Scientific Research and Technical Service	341225	149.9	254655
水利、环境和公共设施管理业	Management of Water Conservancy, Environment and Public Facilities	3486809	127.9	2762113
居民服务、修理和其他服务业	Residentid Service, Repairs and Other Service	14583	37.9	3582
教育	Education	643681	112.5	502420
卫生和社会工作	Health Care and Social Welfare	313997	127.6	241256
文化、体育和娱乐业	Culture, Sports and Entertainment	416071	126.3	308043
公共管理、社会保障和社会组织	Public Management, Social Security and Social Organizations	161982	117.6	122713

continued (10000 yuan)

为上年(%) As Compared with the Preceding Year(%)	#萧山区 Xiaoshan	#余杭区 Yuhang	桐庐县 Tonglu	淳安县 Chun'an	建德市 Jiande	富阳市 Fuyang	临安市 Lin'an
42.2	2900	2032	28487	4340	19975	9561	16723
–	–	–	–	9871	13539	19241	8273
108.7	2548404	1167264	550546	237466	474926	1135673	587917
85.1	153275	140704	41460	46196	41081	68997	81700
159.9	2500	3157	–	–	–	–	–
110.2	23794	319399	1821	22735	17954	88361	17776
83.1	595706	223396	32389	167942	105592	128337	61279
106.2	54544	69114	80081	102447	25238	15695	22971
142.3	28919	99429	1083	10210	901	19152	–
72.5	–	6220	318	–	–	6181	410
117.0	2783970	3507428	612205	379600	378204	1045487	641746
157.1	286720	147518	651	–	–	36358	6405
131.0	12426	147015	–	15008	388	199	70975
124.7	525412	253270	274731	142192	73740	167691	66342
33.3	3582	–	670	–	5050	5281	–
109.7	100867	118327	29853	24204	7455	61040	18709
125.6	69835	44800	16631	9372	6615	30097	10026
127.5	75525	26010	47956	15674	3964	18850	21584
116.1	38925	37178	7104	6539	1845	12119	11662

7－07　分地区工业
Investment in Industrial

单位:万元

指　　标	Item	全　　市 Total		市　　区 Urban District
		2013 年	为上年(%) As Compared with the Preceding Year(%)	2013 年
总计	**Total**	**9104614**	**106.9**	**5787728**
#技术改造投资	**Investment in Technique Innovation**	**7373058**	**112.0**	**4641532**
一、按登记注册类型分	**Total Investment**			
内资	Domestic－funded	7139112	100.2	4135844
国有	State－owned	979637	98.4	861188
集体	Collective－owned	37275	59.6	31734
股份合作	Cooperative	2105	19.7	2105
国有联营企业	State Joint Ownership	3480	－	－
国有独资公司	State－funded Corporations	183290	116.2	129848
其他有限责任公司	Other Limited Liability Corporations	1932283	75.7	1098606
股份有限公司	Share－holding Corporations Ltd.	476613	88.6	308966
私营	Private	3522840	125.6	1701808
其他	Other	1589	63.0	1589
港、澳、台商投资	Investment from Hong Kong, Macao and Taiwan	605211	101.8	508188
外商投资	Foreign Investment	1346581	169.8	1142407
个体经营	Individual	13710	195.9	1289
二、按行业分	**Grouped by Sector**			
采矿业	Mining	50924	140.4	－
制造业	Manufacturing	7886618	109.4	4900090
#农副食品加工业	Processing of Food from Agricultural Products Processing	127477	116.7	48580
食品制造业	Food Manufacturing	202435	159.7	136042
酒、饮料和精制茶制造业	Wine, Beverage and Tea Manufacturing	138956	66.9	48944
烟草制品业	Tobacco Processing	99593	95.6	99593
纺织业	Textile Processing	581488	99.5	477948
纺织服装和服饰业	Textile Products and Costume Industry	163937	151.5	88898

投资(2013 年)

Sector by Region(2013)

(10000 yuan)

			桐庐县 Tonglu	淳安县 Chun'an	建德市 Jiande	富阳市 Fuyang	临安市 Lin'an
为上年(%) As Compared with the Preceding Year(%)	#萧山区 Xiaoshan	#余杭区 Yuhang					
104.2	**2701679**	**1307968**	**592006**	**293533**	**529546**	**1223911**	**677890**
112.7	**2207759**	**1100338**	**407836**	**199301**	**503107**	**1053012**	**568270**
93.2	1793084	1044157	535423	278216	461664	1098066	629899
98.0	121900	121901	27796	33989	26674	17111	12879
70.5	11520	20033	2656	2885	–	–	–
19.7	–	2105	–	–	–	–	–
–	–	–	3480	–	–	–	–
96.1	35593	31201	–	15522	5644	31470	806
76.6	609978	108843	48531	47133	157005	301872	279136
73.5	94523	68620	42166	2608	19803	62128	40942
112.8	917981	691454	410794	176079	252538	685485	296136
80.9	1589	–	–	–	–	–	–
105.3	261225	131139	19374	3443	35262	35854	3090
179.7	647370	131383	33347	9798	26137	89991	44901
172.8	–	1289	3862	2076	6483	–	–
–	–	–	–	9871	13539	19241	8273
108.7	2548404	1167264	550546	237466	474926	1135673	587917
108.2	9609	34429	13826	21131	16712	–	27228
146.5	76264	12431	20245	13930	6788	6517	18913
58.0	12017	7189	3519	20954	65539	–	–
95.6	–	14057	–	–	–	–	–
104.8	389580	81304	26040	27798	21266	14698	13738
133.1	18734	39215	60450	–	–	14589	–

指 标	Item	全市 Total 2013 年	为上年(%) As Compared with the Preceding Year(%)	市区 Urban District 2013 年
皮革、毛皮、羽毛(绒)及其制造业	Leather, Furs, Down and Related Products	35040	67.2	25210
木材加工及木、竹、藤、棕、草制品业	Timber Processing, Bamboo, Cane, Palm Fiber and Straw Products	40245	102.7	17888
家具制造业	Furniture Manufacturing	75696	99.4	48846
造纸及纸制品业	Paper Making and Paper Products	215487	107.6	38188
印刷业和记录媒介的复制业	Printing and Reproduction of Recording media	53971	89.3	33245
文教体育用品制造业	Cultural, Educational and Sports Goods	142208	142.0	88909
石油加工、炼焦及核燃料加工业	Petroleum and Nuclear Fuel Processing	3642	39.4	1057
化学原料及化学制品制造业	Raw Chemical Material and Chemical Products	506378	81.3	350851
医药制造业	Medical and Pharmaceutical Products	243216	94.4	111770
化学纤维制造业	Chemical Fiber	297637	139.3	271950
橡胶和塑料制造业	Rubber and Plastic Products	583767	119.7	268353
非金属矿制品业	Nonmetal Mineral Products	323129	99.9	114014
黑色金属冶炼和压延加工业	Smelting and Pressing of Ferrous Metals	67968	63.1	55134
有色金属冶炼和压延加工业	Smelting and Pressing of Nonferrous Metal	145417	73.0	52715
金属制品业	Metal Products	415545	120.5	225001
通用设备制造业	General Purpose Machinery	762122	105.7	477515
专业设备制造业	Special Purpose Machinery	248283	92.5	161374
汽车制造业	Automobile Manufacturing	782053	220.4	679113
铁路、船舶、航空航天等制造业	Railway, Watercraft, Avigation Spaceflight and other Equipment Manufacturing	70555	78.9	55179
电气机械及器材制造业	Electric Equipment and Machinery	723493	99.3	331371
计算机、通信和其他电子设备制造业	Computers, Telecommunications and other Electronic Equipment Manufacturing	510755	112.1	392174
仪器仪表制造业	Instruments and Meters Manufacturing	167355	126.4	122355
其他制造业	Other Manufacturing	112425	131.0	70960
废弃资源综合利用业	Multiple Utilization of Waste Resouces	41100	145.0	1668
金属制品、机械和设备修理业	Metal Products, Machinery and Equipment Repair	5245	76.2	5245
电力、热力、燃气及水的生产和供应业	Production and Supply of Electric Power, Heat Power, Gas and Tap Water	1167072	91.5	887638

continued (10000 yuan)

为上年(%) As Compared with the Preceding Year(%)	#萧山区 Xiaoshan	#余杭区 Yuhang	桐庐县 Tonglu	淳安县 Chun′an	建德市 Jiande	富阳市 Fuyang	临安市 Lin′an
74.1	20553	4657	2106	701	3438	2224	1361
132.4	16915	973	–	14892	662	2419	4384
79.6	40781	7765	5999	10729	4118	2546	3458
113.1	15763	18518	12869	–	6297	118178	39955
66.5	13737	8500	9962	1350	3448	3947	2019
158.5	34936	41538	38753	3017	3945	4958	2626
18.8	–	–	–	–	–	550	2035
73.6	288166	29909	16238	8159	34208	64609	32313
81.2	2201	42217	10024	5262	3329	111401	1430
127.8	262313	2100	–	–	–	22710	2977
123.4	53582	45281	24911	952	120246	155775	13530
75.1	47764	43864	41705	18569	86372	32472	29997
105.8	22581	22845	3076	–	1237	7008	1513
61.7	26304	26269	18475	2854	–	62252	9121
94.7	111453	75666	30860	10401	19189	106395	23699
109.7	201245	221972	50446	16057	30261	126202	61641
93.8	85252	58016	31459	18744	5003	29434	2269
239.2	630008	27548	20121	–	2517	34798	45504
88.2	38117	16150	2138	833	2606	7271	2528
89.5	39329	144704	41900	8188	24594	107814	209626
111.0	28974	92770	32623	11283	936	44012	29727
125.4	21766	44294	4707	8236	–	30221	1836
140.4	40460	2233	10115	8651	5683	12527	4489
48.1	–	850	17979	4775	6532	10146	–
88.9	–	–	–	–	–	–	–
85.1	153275	140704	41460	46196	41081	68997	81700

7－08 分地区房地产开发
Investment in Real Estate

指 标	Item	全市 Total 2013 年	全市 Total 为上年(%) As Compared with the Preceding Year(%)	市区 Urban District 2013 年
房地产开发投资额 （万元）	**Investment in Real Estate Development (10000 yuan)**	**18532841**	**116.0**	**15978470**
住宅 （万元）	Residential Buildings (10000 yuan)	11695643	116.8	9890618
办公楼 （万元）	Office Buildings (10000 yuan)	1687874	119.0	1613616
商业营业用房 （万元）	Buildings for Business Use (10000 yuan)	1748301	126.9	1442716
其他 （万元）	Others (10000 yuan)	3401023	107.6	3031520
房屋建筑面积	**Floor space of Buildings**			
施工面积 （万平方米）	Under Construction (10000 sq. m)	9327.52	112.6	7746.86
#住宅 （万平方米）	#Residential Buildings (10000 sq. m)	5509.11	109.7	4374.30
新开工面积 （万平方米）	Started This Year (10000 sq. m)	2039.06	112.3	1637.34
#住宅 （万平方米）	#Residential Buildings (10000 sq. m)	1143.75	111.3	868.09
竣工面积 （万平方米）	Construction Completed (10000 sq. m)	1172.24	111.1	923.74
#住宅 （万平方米）	#Residential Buildings (10000 sq. m)	845.12	125.4	646.35
商品房销售情况	**Selling of Commercialized Buildings**			
销售金额 （万元）	Total Sales of Buildings (10000 yuan)	17111998	116.8	15307975
#住宅 （万元）	#Residential Buildings (10000 yuan)	14220307	116.3	12625458
现房销售额 （万元）	Selling of Completed Buildings (10000 yuan)	1961653	182.8	1663408
#住宅 （万元）	#Residential Buildings (10000 yuan)	1338904	264.2	1102846
期房销售金额 （万元）	Selling of Futures Buildings (10000 yuan)	15150345	111.6	13644567
#住宅 （万元）	#Residential Buildings (10000 yuan)	12881403	109.9	11522612
销售面积 （万平方米）	Floor Space of Buildings Sold (10000 sq. m)	1139.13	104.5	922.11
#住宅 （万平方米）	#Residential Buildings (10000 sq. m)	968.78	105.3	774.78
现房销售面积 （万平方米）	Floor Space of Completed Buildings Sold (10000 sq. m)	163.35	202.9	113.97
#住宅 （万平方米）	#Residential Buildings (10000 sq. m)	123.15	262.4	81.96
期房销售面积 （万平方米）	Floor Space of Futures Buildings Sold (10000 sq. m)	975.79	96.7	808.14
#住宅 （万平方米）	#Residential Buildings (10000 sq. m)	845.63	96.8	692.82

投资(2013 年)
Development by Region(2013)

为上年(%) As Compared with the Preceding Year(%)	#萧山区 Xiaoshan	#余杭区 Yuhang	桐庐县 Tonglu	淳安县 Chun'an	建德市 Jiande	富阳市 Fuyang	临安市 Lin'an
116.2	**2478324**	**2647946**	**504011**	**352567**	**275004**	**785661**	**637128**
117.6	1660830	2042253	378145	186761	173930	545498	520691
119.3	242513	47076	17686	3244	3494	45549	4285
121.8	191440	125840	61760	32041	76878	91045	43861
108.3	383541	432777	46420	130521	20702	103569	68291
111.6	1273.75	1979.51	420.02	236.66	165.64	304.34	453.99
107.8	637.41	1467.40	310.53	149.72	125.85	204.88	343.83
115.0	260.13	441.80	88.14	68.62	41.87	71.17	131.93
118.1	131.19	325.49	64.34	43.01	33.09	44.76	90.46
100.7	182.27	210.46	89.68	42.62	0.85	56.61	58.74
112.9	136.83	160.87	74.63	33.67	0.54	40.46	49.46
115.2	1738186	3374852	378181	204443	144200	631472	445727
113.6	1491184	3242935	321757	192847	115173	550633	414439
178.5	150802	383804	75037	63183	6838	76597	76590
276.8	103618	339748	57849	56313	4277	52683	64936
110.4	1587384	2991048	303144	141260	137362	554875	369137
107.5	1387566	2903187	263908	136534	110896	497950	349503
100.0	114.83	323.22	59.79	25.95	19.31	49.98	61.99
98.0	93.18	307.74	52.13	24.47	16.01	43.43	57.95
185.6	15.34	44.18	16.50	12.93	0.93	6.48	12.53
254.9	11.65	40.20	13.36	11.99	0.67	4.52	10.64
93.9	99.48	279.04	43.29	13.02	18.38	43.50	49.45
91.4	81.53	267.54	38.77	12.48	15.34	38.91	47.31

7－09 分地区农村

Rural Investment

单位:万元

指标	Item	全市 Total		市区 Urban District
		2013 年	为上年(%) As Compared with the Preceding Year(%)	2013 年
本年完成投资额	**Total Investment of the Year**	**6903071**	**95.6**	**3827356**
按行业分	**Grouped by Sector**			
农林牧渔业	Agriculture, Forestry, Animal Husbandry and Fishery	67945	197.4	1508
采矿业	Mining	43171	119.0	–
制造业	Manufacturing	3553171	89.9	1854323
电力、热力、燃气及水的生产和供应业	Production and Supply of Electric Power, Heat Power, Gas and Tap Water	358579	74.6	220110
建筑业	Construction	5300	–	5300
批发和零售业	Wholesale & Retail Trades	224386	119.7	144317
交通运输、仓储和邮政业	Transportation, Storage and Post	845463	109.4	519555
住宿和餐饮业	Hotels and Catering Services	160901	135.9	100328
信息传输、软件和信息技术服务业	Information Transmission, Software and Information Technology	66897	228.3	45761
金融业	Financial Intermediation	728	73.9	–
房地产业	Real Estate	691105	85.7	476459
租赁和商务服务业	Leasing and Busyness Services	64600	212.8	27591
科学研究和技术服务业	Scientific Research and Technical Service	12087	112.1	11500
水利、环境和公共设施管理业	Management of Water Conservancy, Enviroment and Public Facilities	507126	131.9	216372
居民服务、修理和其他服务业	Residentid Service, Repairs and Other Services	9539	32.7	–
教育	Education	105859	54.7	88393
卫生和社会工作	Health Care and Social Welfare	63233	187.4	52442
文化、体育和娱乐业	Culture, Sports and Entertainment	71425	90.9	34944
公共管理、社会保障和社会组织	Public Management, Social Security and Social Organizations	51556	134.7	28453
房屋建筑施工面积(万平方米)	**Floor Space of Buildings Under Construction (10000sq. m)**	**2847.78**	**96.4**	**1880.98**
其中:住宅	Residential Buildings	346.19	101.2	169.40
房屋建筑竣工面积(万平方米)	**Floor Space of Buildings Completed (10000sq. m)**	**955.18**	**117.2**	**549.10**
其中:住宅	Residential Buildings	87.82	95.9	30.25

固定资产投资(2013 年)
by Region(2013)

(10000 yuan)

为上年(%) As Compared with the Preceding Year(%)	#萧山区 Xiaoshan	#余杭区 Yuhang	桐庐县 Tonglu	淳安县 Chun'an	建德市 Jiande	富阳市 Fuyang	临安市 Lin'an
80.5	**2208520**	**1395301**	**632573**	**295181**	**632616**	**1163616**	**351729**
18.7	–	1508	19743	3861	18859	9561	14413
–	–	–	–	9030	6627	19241	8273
80.1	1334436	516075	318418	64803	385825	710005	219797
62.9	55089	12832	23507	12445	38255	48349	15913
–	2500	2800	–	–	–	–	–
83.5	15520	111764	716	1383	–	69306	8664
83.8	386372	133183	26877	132871	79923	50807	35430
126.6	45261	35487	30918	8186	3627	6442	11400
156.2	–	35738	1083	–	901	19152	–
–	–	–	318	–	–	–	410
76.2	85138	372290	25439	5340	59127	124740	–
90.9	17340	10251	651	–	–	36358	–
108.9	–	11500	–	–	388	199	–
103.7	160856	55516	161668	45268	21777	41951	20090
–	–	–	–	–	4258	5281	–
49.3	16301	72092	–	6473	5554	5059	380
192.2	34538	16037	597	1022	2494	3168	3510
54.1	34944	–	18376	3529	3482	4900	6194
93.7	20225	8228	4262	970	1519	9097	7255
87.2	**708.39**	**1140.17**	**164.16**	**56.72**	**190.56**	**479.35**	**76.01**
101.4	54.02	111.86	15.34	5.05	51.78	104.57	0.05
120.9	**291.36**	**256.53**	**74.37**	**21.03**	**108.95**	**158.67**	**43.06**
61.8	14.57	15.69	4.73	5.05	23.24	24.55	–

7－10 房屋建筑面积及造价(2013年)
Floor Space of Buildings and Their Cost(2013)

指 标	Item	施工面积(万平方米) Floor Space of Buildings Under Construction (10000 sq. m)	竣工面积(万平方米) Floor Space of Buildings Completed (10000 sq. m)	竣工房屋的价值(万元) Value of Buildings Completed (10000 yuan)	每平方米造价(元) Cost Per Square Meter (yuan)
全 市	**Total**				
房屋建筑面积合计	**Floor Space of Buildings**	**19226.78**	**3666.67**	**7744168**	**2112**
#住宅	#Residential Buildings	7392.23	1308.83	3530744	2698
房地产开发	Real Estate Development	9327.52	1172.24	3698881	3155
#住宅	#Residential Buildings	5509.11	845.12	2703723	3199
市 区	**Urban District**				
房屋建筑面积合计	**Floor Space of Buildings**	**15693.30**	**2637.83**	**6074353**	**2303**
#住宅	#Residential Buildings	5910.71	986.35	2822878	2862
房地产开发	Real Estate Development	7746.86	923.74	3016961	3266
#住宅	#Residential Buildings	4374.30	646.35	2142145	3314
#萧山区	**Xiaoshan**				
房屋建筑面积合计	**Total Floor Space of Buildings**	**2787.85**	**627.50**	**1066750**	**1700**
#住宅	#Residential Buildings	769.30	160.49	441098	2748
房地产开发	Real Estate Development	1273.75	182.27	535653	2939
#住宅	#Residential Buildings	637.41	136.83	414219	3027
余杭区	**Yuhang**				
房屋建筑面积合计	**Total Floor Space of Buildings**	**4504.89**	**776.24**	**1336828**	**1722**
#住宅	#Residential Buildings	1745.60	217.92	410590	1884
房地产开发	Real Estate Development	1979.51	210.46	412710	1961
#住宅	#Residential Buildings	1467.40	160.87	314213	1953

7-10 续表 continued

指 标	Item	施工面积（万平方米）Floor Space of Buildings Under Construction (10000 sq. m)	竣工面积（万平方米）Floor Space of Buildings Completed (10000 sq. m)	竣工房屋的价值（万元）Value of Buildings Completed (10000 yuan)	每平方米造价（元）Cost Per Square Meter (yuan)
桐庐县	**Tonglu**				
房屋建筑面积合计	**Total Floor Space of Buildings**	**779.24**	**244.42**	**440152**	**1801**
#住宅	#Residential Buildings	343.95	84.72	232395	2743
房地产开发	Real Estate Development	420.02	89.68	242898	2709
#住宅	#Residential Buildings	310.53	74.63	205584	2755
淳安县	**Chun'an**				
房屋建筑面积合计	**Total Floor Space of Buildings**	**468.43**	**121.69**	**163427**	**1343**
#住宅	#Residential Buildings	163.35	43.30	65335	1509
房地产开发	Real Estate Development	236.66	42.62	74306	1744
#住宅	#Residential Buildings	149.72	33.67	55915	1660
建德市	**Jiande**				
房屋建筑面积合计	**Total Floor Space of Buildings**	**438.57**	**145.16**	**144021**	**992**
#住宅	#Residential Buildings	210.00	42.73	45021	1054
房地产开发	Real Estate Development	165.64	0.85	2108	2489
#住宅	#Residential Buildings	125.85	0.54	1340	2489
富阳市	**Fuyang**				
房屋建筑面积合计	**Total Floor Space of Buildings**	**1164.05**	**342.12**	**582978**	**1704**
#住宅	#Residential Buildings	420.33	102.26	223993	2190
房地产开发	Real Estate Development	304.34	56.61	194434	3434
#住宅	#Residential Buildings	204.88	40.46	157617	3895
临安市	**Lin'an**				
房屋建筑面积合计	**Total Floor Space of Buildings**	**683.19**	**175.44**	**339237**	**1934**
#住宅	#Residential Buildings	343.88	49.46	141122	2853
房地产开发	Real Estate Development	453.99	58.74	168174	2863
#住宅	#Residential Buildings	343.83	49.46	141122	2853

7－11 分注册类型和资质等级

Financial Statistics of Enterprises for Real Estate Development

单位:万元

项　　目	Item	法人企业数(个) Number of Enterprises (unit)	年末 Asset and		
			流动资产合　计 Circulating Funds	应收账款 Account Receivable	固定资产合　计 Fixed Assets
总计	**Total**	**1437**	**96037740**	**1115014**	**1848946**
一、按登记注册类型分组	**Grouped by Registration Status**				
内资企业	Domestic Funded	1339	78895197	1059580	1774590
国有企业	State－owned	19	1357028	62348	9093
集体企业	Collective－owned	2	156565	－	5
股份合作企业	Share－holding Cooperative Enterprises	－	－	－	－
联营企业	Joint Venture	1	7842	－	228
有限责任公司	Limited Liability Corporations	771	59429408	523502	1223505
股份有限公司	Share－holding Corporations Ltd.	28	2398998	29344	33901
私营企业	Private Enterprises	517	15539698	444386	507857
其他企业	Other Enterprises	1	5658	－	－
港澳台商投资企业	Funded from Hong Kong, Macao and Taiwan	75	12218277	46426	42542
外商投资企业	Foreign Funded	23	4924266	9009	31815
二、按企业资质等级分	**Grouped by Quali Fication Grade**				
一级	Grade Ⅰ	49	10758714	35696	126421
二级	Grade Ⅱ	163	11612467	164826	226024
三级	Grade Ⅲ	265	9323105	245815	519808
四级	Grade Ⅳ	86	1242724	56126	22356
暂定	Tentatine	595	47401650	524254	756511
其他	Others	279	15699081	88297	197827

房地产开发企业财务状况(2013 年)

Grouped by Registration Status and Qualification Grade(2013)

(10000 yuan)

资产负债 Liabilities at Year - end						所有者权益合计 Creditors´ Equity	
固定资产原价 Orginal Value of Fixed Assets	累计折旧 Accumulated Depreciation	#本年折旧 Depreciation This Year	在建工程 Projects wnder Construction	资产总计 Total Assets	负债合计 Total Liabilities		#实收资本 Capital Hold
1826869	**488225**	**118030**	**2121117**	**113091962**	**86357649**	**26734313**	**23022713**
1718427	452676	110331	1988811	94037821	74217327	19820494	17216679
12111	5302	598	5193	1689405	1258088	431317	164304
94	90	–	–	163138	161298	1840	2000
–	–	–	–	–	–	–	–
410	288	75	–	8733	5476	3257	1000
1048960	261416	66260	1830261	70488700	56354465	14134235	9070502
51968	21209	5585	–	3913970	1919978	1993992	540079
604884	164373	37813	153358	17767997	14517974	3250023	7432895
–	–	–	–	5879	48	5831	5900
61127	20059	4268	104573	12650108	7247234	5402874	4993800
47315	15490	3432	27733	6404033	4893089	1510944	812234
192825	70129	14711	108	17045028	12676508	4368520	1258456
324663	113189	20419	834244	16064927	12001911	4063015	2040625
561885	120006	30831	125598	11646660	8567175	3079484	1653757
49054	19563	5797	333065	1741911	1344133	397778	196718
482687	109769	32159	545844	49668325	38568903	11099422	14763054
215755	55569	14114	282259	16925112	13199019	3726093	3110103

单位:万元　　7－11　续表

项　　目	Item	营业收入 Revenue of Business	#主营业务收入 Main Revenue of Business	营业成本 Operating Costs	#主营业务成本 Main Cost of Business
总计	**Total**	**15957146**	**15717837**	**11211881**	**11003051**
一、按登记注册类型分组	**Grouped by Registration Status**				
内资企业	Domestic Funded	13528586	13290053	9674969	9466139
国有企业	State－owned	60001	59806	34320	33123
集体企业	Collective－owned	－	－	－	－
股份合作企业	Share－holding Cooperative Enterprises	－	－	－	－
联营企业	Joint Venture	568	568	－	－
有限责任公司	Limited Liability Corporations	10295052	10066037	7409314	7216698
股份有限公司	Share－holding Corporations Ltd.	602680	602680	324928	324928
私营企业	Private Enterprises	2570286	2560963	1906408	1891389
其他企业	Other Enterprises	－	－	－	－
港澳台商投资企业	Funded from Hong Kong, Macao and Taiwan	2143897	2143534	1372938	1372938
外商投资企业	Foreign Funded	284664	284250	163974	163974
二、按企业资质等级分	**Grouped by Quali Fication Grade**				
一级	Grade Ⅰ	1161318	1125630	602896	593478
二级	Grade Ⅱ	2277526	2268138	1510930	1438064
三级	Grade Ⅲ	2509507	2503863	1860221	1857789
四级	Grade Ⅳ	231629	231532	162490	162433
暂定	Tentatine	7478648	7293076	5496222	5384694
其他	Others	2298520	2295598	1579123	1566592

continued (10000 yuan)

营业税金及附加 Main Sales Tax and Extra Charges	销售费用 Cost of Sales	管理费用 Administration Cost	财务费用 Financil Cost	#利息支出 Interest Expenditure	营业利润 Management Profits	利润总额 Total Profits	应交所得税 Income Tax	就业人员年平均人数(人) Annual Average Number of Employed Persons(Person)
1351166	**499083**	**693236**	**365212**	**297057**	**2649370**	**2770300**	**474712**	**30618**
1100429	409126	608893	378884	309511	2153422	2273452	345609	26919
6590	3034	11368	4338	15805	12887	12833	1737	273
–	27	327	-254	-254	-99	-130	–	6
–	–	–	–	–	–	–	–	–
50	4	698	–	–	-66	-100	–	33
838654	310190	404316	271209	217347	1601014	1679444	274257	18706
51375	8955	23805	27374	12131	365489	371733	8387	995
203760	86916	168363	76217	64484	174213	209688	61227	6899
–	–	16	–	–	-16	-16	–	7
231390	70690	46403	7213	8180	392498	393516	118741	2596
19347	19268	37940	-20885	-20634	103449	103331	10362	1103
97007	30277	105934	130587	106749	713950	743336	29066	3146
205914	46653	126555	91170	83889	587911	644988	91800	4991
174937	51020	127072	40853	16239	278393	294564	51185	5431
18579	5327	12124	2631	7898	31295	31877	7445	1068
655772	293470	235115	73409	60103	671039	669636	195962	12002
198958	72336	86436	26561	22179	366782	385899	99254	3980

主要统计指标解释

固定资产投资完成额 固定资产投资完成额是以货币表现的建造和购置固定资产的工作量以及与此有关的费用的总称。它是反映固定资产投资规模、速度、比例关系和使用方向的综合性指标。

房地产开发投资 包括各种经济类型的房地产开发公司、商品房建设公司及其他房地产开发单位统一开发的包括统代建、拆迁还建的住宅、厂房、仓库、饭店、宾馆、度假村、写字楼、办公楼等房屋建筑物和配套的服务设施、土地开发工程,如道路、给水、排水、供电、供热、通讯、平整场地等基础设施工程的投资。包括非房地产企业实际从事房地产开发或经济活动,不包括单纯的土地交易活动。

施工和竣工房屋建筑面积 房屋建筑面积是从房屋外墙线算起的各层平面面积的总和,包括房屋结构(如柱、墙)占用的面积和地下室面积。多层建筑按各自然层面积总和计算,包括房屋内的楼隔层,突出墙面的眺望间、门斗、有柱雨罩的面积。不包括突出墙面结构的构件、艺术装饰等所占的面积,如台阶等。凹阳台、挑阳台按其水平投影面积一半计算建筑面积。

房屋新开工面积 指在报告期内新开工建设的房屋面积。不包括上期跨入报告期继续施工的房屋面积和上期停缓建而在本期恢复施工的房屋面积。房屋的开工应以房屋正式开始破土刨槽(地基处理或打永久桩)的日期为准。

商品房销售面积 指报告期内出售商品房屋的合同总面积(即双方签署的正式买卖合同中所确定的建筑面积)。由现房销售建筑面积和期房销售建筑面积两部分组成。

(1)现房销售面积:是指在报告期内正式签订买卖合同、已经竣工达到入住条件的商品房屋建筑面积。包括以一次性付款方式和分期付款方式销售的现房建筑面积。

(2)期房销售面积:是指在报告期内正式签订买卖合同、正在建设尚未竣工交付使用的商品房屋建筑面积。包括以一次性付款方式和分期付款方式销售的商品房屋建筑面积。期房销售建筑面积竣工后不再转为现房销售建筑面积。

新增固定资产 指通过投资活动所形成的新的固定资产价值。包括已经建成投入生产或交付使用的工程价值和达到固定资产标准的设备、工具、器具的价值及有关应摊入的费用。它是以价值形式表示的固定资产投资成果的综合性指标,可以综合反映不同时期、不同部门、不同地区的固定资产投资成果。

Explanatory Notes on Main Statistical Indicators

Total Investment in Fixed Assets refer to the volume of activities in construction and purchases of fixed assets in monetary terms and other relative expenses. It is a comprehensive indicator which shows the size, pace, proportional relations and use orientation of investment in fixed assets.

Investment in Real Estate Development include the investment by the real estate development companies, commercial buildings construction companies and other real estate development units of various types of ownership in the construction of house buildings, such as residential buildings, factory buildings, warehouses, hotels, guesthouses, holiday supply, water drainage, power supply, heating, telecommunications, land leveling and other projects of infrastructure, it excludes the activities in simple land transaction.

Floor space of Building Under Construction and Completed refer to total floor space in each story of buildings calculate from the outside line of building walls, including the space occupied by construction like pillars or walls and basements. The floor space of multi – story building includes the total floor space of each story, including area occupied by separating walls, watching rooms, door – ways, and pillars, but excluding protruding wall structures, artistic decoration, etc. (for example, flight of steps). The space of balcony is counted by half of the projection area.

Beginning to Construction Floor Space of Building refer to the area space which constructed in report period, not including the floor whose construction lasted to report period and which stopped in the last period to continue construction in the report period. And the beginning of construction of floor space should base on the date of breaking the earth(disposal the basement or piling).

Selling of the Commercial Building refer to the total area that sold by contract(which reflected in the contract), which include completed and future buildings.

(1) Floor Space of Completed Building: refer to the area which formal contract has been signed and which has been completed and reached the condition of living, including payment in one time and installment payment.

(2) Floor Space of Future Building: refer to the area which signed by formal contract and under constructing, including payment in one time and installment payment. Which can not be turned into completed building's sale when they completed.

Newly Increased Fixed Assets refer to the newly increased value of fixed assets through investment, including the value of projects completed and put into production, the value of equipment, tools, and vessels considered as fixed assets, as well as the relevant expenses as investment in fixed assets. This is a comprehensive indicator of investment in fixed assets, reflecting the achievements of investment in fixed assets in different periods, different sectors, and different regions.

八、国内贸易

Ⅷ.DOMESTIC TRADE

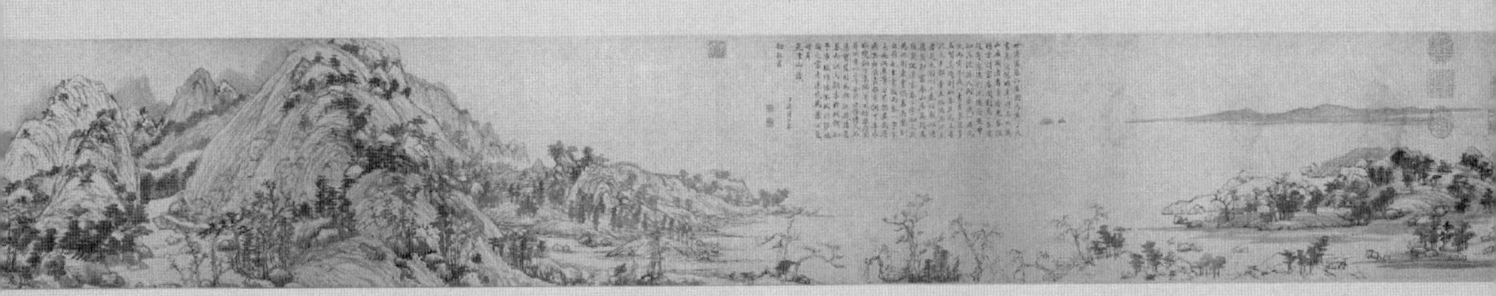

国 内 贸 易
Domestic Trade

主 要 统 计 指 标
Major Statistical Indicators

社会消费品零售总额	Total Retail Sales of Consumer Goods	3531.17	亿元	(100 million yuan)
为上年	As Compared with the Preceding Year	113.0	%	(%)
批发和零售贸易业	Wholesale and Retail Trades	3161.97	亿元	(100 million yuan)
为上年	As Compared with the Preceding Year	114.3	%	(%)
住宿和餐饮业	Hotels and Catering Services	369.21	亿元	(100 million yuan)
为上年	As Compared with the Preceding Year	103.3	%	(%)

8－01 社会消费品零售总额(1978－2013)
Total Retail Sale of Consumer Goods(1978－2013)

单位:万元 (10,000 yuan)

年　份 Year	全　市 Total	市　区 Urban District	县(市)合计 All Counties
1978	119509	73653	45856
1979	150462	93342	57120
1980	205381	128440	76941
1981	236188	148152	88036
1982	251068	154582	96486
1983	273664	169508	104156
1984	343722	215901	127821
1985	478117	308901	169216
1986	557963	360479	197484
1987	657838	426745	231093
1988	866373	557374	308999
1989	927019	600816	326203
1990	981713	650278	331435
1991	1155476	777559	377917
1992	1408525	928586	479939
1993	1901509	1300037	601472
1994	2616477	1733572	882905
1995	2993250	1930140	1063110
1996	3478156	2310619	1167537
1997	3815537	2537537	1278000
1998	4178013	2794171	1383842
1999	4574924	3053983	1520941
2000	5146789	3436536	1710253
2001	5790138	4993078	797060
2002	6606548	5701707	904841
2003	7425760	6401970	1023790
2004	8554476	7385662	1168814
2005	9784275	8440559	1343716
2006	11191900	9630210	1561690
2007	13082930	11247539	1835391
2008	15775872	13542665	2233207
2009	18049303	15498990	2550313
2010	21460790	18432319	3028471
2011	25483599	21877831	3605768
2012	29446266	25216914	4229352
2013	35311732	30419033	4892699

注:从2001年起市区数据包括萧山区和余杭区。

a) Data of urban district include Xiaoshan and Yuhang district since 2001.

8-02 分地区社会

Total Retail Sale of Consumer Goods

单位:万元

年 份 Year	全 市 Whole City		市 区 Urban District		#萧山区 Xiaoshan
	合 计 Total	为上年(%) As Compared with the Preceding Year(%)	合 计 Total	为上年(%) As Compared with the Preceding Year(%)	
1978	119509	112.5	73653	115.8	12985
1979	150462	125.9	93342	127.2	16270
1980	205381	136.5	128440	138.1	22292
1981	236188	115.0	148152	115.6	25297
1982	251068	106.3	154582	103.3	29007
1983	273664	109.0	169508	110.1	32136
1984	343722	125.6	215901	128.4	41210
1985	478117	139.1	308901	145.2	51879
1986	557963	116.7	360479	116.8	61421
1987	657838	117.9	426745	118.6	73159
1988	866373	131.7	557374	130.1	101227
1989	927019	107.0	600816	108.3	103419
1990	981713	105.9	650278	109.5	111757
1991	1155476	117.7	777559	120.4	123753
1992	1408525	121.9	928586	118.3	153254
1993	1901509	135.0	1300037	134.4	195472
1994	2616477	137.6	1733572	132.2	299072
1995	2993250	114.4	1930140	118.2	339447
1996	3478156	116.2	2310619	120.9	390364
1997	3815537	109.7	2537537	109.9	431742
1998	4178013	109.5	2794171	110.5	470599
1999	4574924	109.5	3053983	109.3	520482
2000	5146789	112.5	3436536	112.8	602198
2001	5790138	113.6	4993078	113.9	690721
2002	6606548	114.1	5701707	114.2	795711
2003	7425760	112.4	6401970	112.3	929390
2004	8554476	115.2	7385662	115.4	1069728
2005	9784275	114.4	8440559	114.3	1234568
2006	11191900	114.4	9630210	114.1	1462157
2007	13082930	116.9	11247539	116.8	1721511
2008	15775872	120.6	13542665	120.4	2059811
2009	18049303	114.4	15498990	114.4	2376949
2010	21460790	119.9	18432319	120.1	2839433
2011	25483599	118.7	21877831	118.7	3369839
2012	29446266	115.5	25216914	115.3	3941364
2013	35311732	113.0	30419033	112.6	4455510

注:从2001年起市区数据包括萧山区和余杭区。

消费品零售总额(1978 -2013)
by Region(1978 -2013)

(10000 yuan)

#余杭区 Yuhang	桐庐县 Tonglu	淳安县 Chun'an	建德市 Jiande	富阳市 Fuyang	临安市 Lin'an
11472	3536	3507	4390	5209	4757
14439	4283	4274	5300	6435	6119
19917	5501	5225	7119	8661	8226
22172	6456	6201	7970	10226	9714
23435	7101	6663	8562	11016	10702
23496	7694	7168	9380	12307	11975
29292	9235	8331	10770	14972	14011
39798	11826	11081	14687	21013	18932
47499	13217	12525	15832	23400	23590
53005	17394	14449	18076	27939	27071
64653	24390	18944	23545	42601	33639
74044	23029	19014	23138	48836	34723
69360	23141	18764	23820	45364	39229
84399	26350	20950	25107	52807	44551
110075	34110	23983	30770	74865	52882
149128	44909	28038	40237	76162	67526
212955	69025	34179	54562	101829	111283
255972	93736	42143	70570	127592	133650
266467	104234	51794	77620	146348	130710
294446	114032	58994	83837	163324	131625
321241	123154	67136	93169	171654	136889
352723	135223	74293	103417	185730	149073
397166	148745	81054	115062	198917	167111
446812	166892	90133	128754	223782	187499
508919	188087	101581	144849	254887	215437
584748	209153	114990	163244	289297	247106
674799	237598	130974	185772	331534	282936
778848	272394	149456	212138	382960	326768
906960	317484	173272	247425	450365	373144
1064956	371057	201769	288873	526750	446942
1302135	451356	244069	350854	643169	543759
1499377	516037	278356	400157	734925	620838
1767194	608722	328351	484678	871296	735424
2100841	724257	391658	575700	1038410	875743
2389916	851437	460041	673339	1217640	1026896
2778302	977884	528822	772663	1421606	1191724

a) Data of urban district include Xiaoshan and Yuhang district since 2001.

8－03 社会消费品
Total Retail Sale of

单位:万元

地 区	Region	合 计 Total
全 市	**Total**	**35311732**
市 区	Urban District	30419033
#上城区	Shangcheng	2819973
下城区	Xiacheng	7000001
江干区	Jianggan	2867884
拱墅区	Gongshu	3602259
西湖区	Xihu	3646931
高新(滨江)区	Hi－Tech(Binjiang)	617775
萧山区	Xiaoshan	4455510
余杭区	Yuhang	2778302
桐庐县	Tonglu	977884
淳安县	Chun'an	528822
建德市	Jiande	772663
富阳市	Fuyang	1421606
临安市	Lin'an	1191724

零售总额(2013 年)
Consumer Goods(2013)

(10000 yuan)

按经营地分 By Location		按行业分 By sector	
城镇 Urban Areas	乡村 Rural Areas	批发和零售贸易业 Wholesale and Retail Trades	住宿和餐饮业 Hotels and Catering Services
33541219	**1770513**	**31619665**	**3692067**
30419033	–	27447171	2971862
2819973	–	2440888	379085
7000001	–	6493604	506398
2867884	–	2664934	202950
3602259	–	3448653	153606
3646931	–	3319734	327196
617775	–	531102	86673
4455510	–	3915390	540120
2778302	–	2508926	269375
603893	373991	829950	147934
319773	209049	405779	123042
538349	234314	638207	134456
971105	450501	1259464	162142
689066	502658	1039093	152631

8-04 按登记注册类型分限额以上批发零售贸易企业商品销售总额(2013年)

Sales of Wholesale and Retail Trades Above Designated Size by Status of Registration(2013)

单位:万元 (10000 yuan)

项　目	Item	法人企业(个) Number of Enterprises (unit)	销售总额 Total Sales	批发额 Wholesale	零售额 Retail
总　计	**Total**	**3684**	**158597327**	**129600126**	**28997201**
1.内资企业	**Domestic - funded Enterprises**	**3580**	**150792807**	**125406488**	**25386318**
国有企业	State - owned Enterprises	25	4188617	4168557	20060
集体企业	Collective - owned Enterprises	15	162278	98696	63582
股份合作企业	Cooperative Enterprises	3	4208	-	4208
联营企业	Joint Ownership Enterprises	7	56075	1697	54378
国有联营企业	State Joint Ownership Enterprises	-	-	-	-
集体联营企业	Collective Joint Ownership Enterprises	-	-	-	-
国有与集体联营企业	Joint State - collective Enterprises	7	56075	1697	54378
其他联营企业	Other Joint Ownership Enterprises	-	-	-	-
有限责任公司	Limited Liability Corporations	1070	73436609	62248204	11188405
国有独资公司	State - funded Corporations	44	4720357	4565967	154390
其他有限责任公司	Other Limited Liability Corporations	1026	68716252	57682237	11034015
股份有限公司	Share - holding Corporations Ltd.	96	28220037	18068012	10152025
私营企业	Private Enterprises	2331	44615870	40734209	3881661
私营独资企业	Private - funded Enterprises	29	132646	87367	45278
私营合伙企业	Private Partnership Enterprises	-	-	-	-
私营有限责任公司	Private Limited Liability Corporations	2262	43719818	40069182	3650637
私营股份有限公司	Private Share - holding Corporations Ltd.	40	763406	577660	185746
其他企业	Other Enterprises	33	109113	87113	22000
2.港、澳、台商投资企业	**Enterprises With Investment from Hong Kong, Macao and Taiwan**	**48**	**2598570**	**993798**	**1604772**
合资经营企业(港或澳、台资)	Joint - venture Enterprises (With Funds from Hong Kong, Macao and Taiwan)	19	1605797	673166	932631
合作经营企业(港或澳、台资)	Coorperative Enterprises (With Funds from Hong Kong, Macao and Taiwan)	1	72427	-	72427
港、澳、台商独资经营企业	Enterprises With Sole Investment from Hong Kong, Macao and Taiwan	27	915025	320632	594393
港、澳、台商投资股份有限公司	Share - holding Corporations Ltd. With Investment from Hong Kong, Macao and Taiwan	1	5321	-	5321
3.外商投资企业	**Enterprises With Foreign Investment**	**56**	**5205951**	**3199840**	**2006111**
中外合资经营企业	Joint - venture Enterprises	14	3569198	2897644	671555
中外合作经营企业	Cooperation Enterprises	1	7873	-	7873
外资企业	Enterprises With Sole Foreign Investment	39	1476742	150059	1326683
外商投资股份有限公司	Share - holding Corporations Ltd. With Foreign Investment	1	105603	105603	-

8-05 按国民经济行业分限额以上批发零售贸易企业商品销售总额(2013年)

Sales of Wholesale and Retail Trades Above Designated Size by Sector(2013)

单位:万元 (10000 yuan)

项目	Item	法人企业(个) Number of Enterprises (unit)	销售总额 Total Sales	批发额 Wholesale	零售额 Retail
总计	**Total**	**3684**	**158597327**	**129600126**	**28997201**
一、批发业	**Wholesale**	**2761**	**139719495**	**127887999**	**11831496**
农、林、牧产品批发	Wholesale of Farm, Forestry and Animal Husbandry Products	36	691875	684602	7273
食品、饮料及烟草制品批发	Wholesale of Food, Beverages and Tobaccos	163	9967029	9901354	65675
纺织、服装及家庭用品批发	Wholesale of Textile Products, Garments and Household Articles	562	15007163	14780615	226548
文化、体育用品及器材批发	Wholesale of Cultural and Sports Goods	87	2600864	2545017	55847
医药及医疗器材批发	Wholesale of Medicines and Medical Appliances	102	6870469	4365099	2505371
矿产品、建材及化工产品批发	Wholesale of Mineral Products, Building and Chemical Materials	1314	91429644	82836935	8592709
机械设备、五金产品及电子产品批发	Wholesale of Machinery, Hardware and Electronic Products	407	11487665	11109935	377730
#汽车、摩托车及零配件批发	Wholesale of Automobiles, Motorcycle and Parts	75	4469226	4367448	101778
其他批发业	Other	89	1640306	1639963	343
二、零售业	**Retail Trade**	**923**	**18877832**	**1712127**	**17165705**
综合零售	Comprehensive Retail Trade	116	5599085	796310	4802775
食品、饮料及烟草制品专门零售	Specialism Retail of Food, Beverages and Tobaccos	60	282895	43028	239867
纺织、服装及日用品专门零售	Specialism Retail of Textile Products, Garments, Shoes and Caps	59	596272	53910	542362
文化、体育用品及器材专门零售	Specialism Retail of Cultural and Sports Goods	46	639321	152959	486363
医药及医疗器材专门零售	Specialism Retail of Medicines and Medical Appliances	54	527154	21287	505867
汽车、摩托车、燃料及零配件专门零售	Specialism Retail of Automobiles, Motorcycle, Fuels and Parts	427	9532395	441211	9091184
#汽车零售	Specialism Retail of Automobiles	282	8190768	387320	7803448
家用电器及电子产品专门零售	Specialism Retail of Household Electric Applianes, and Electronic Products	90	948801	123901	824900
五金、家具及室内装饰材料专门零售	Specialism Retail of Hardware and Upholstery Materials	38	252526	42496	210031
货摊、无店铺及其他零售业	Stall, Non-shop and Other Retails	33	499382	37025	462357

8－06 按登记注册类型分限额以上

Main Financial Indicators of Enterprises Above Designated Size in

单位：万元

项　　目	Item	法人企业数(个) Number of Enterprises (unit)	年末资产负债 Assets and Liabilities		
			流动资产合计 Circulating Funds	# 存　货 Inventory	固定资产原价 Orginal Value of Fixed Assets
批发零售贸易业企业合计	**Total**	**3684**	**49288544**	**7508471**	**4391705**
1. 内资企业	**Domestic－funded Enterprises**	**3580**	**46464853**	**7043897**	**3875152**
国有企业	State－owned Enterprises	25	1301916	180042	143586
集体企业	Collective－owned Enterprises	15	74392	2148	8171
股份合作企业	Cooperative Enterprises	3	8912	242	2020
联营企业	Joint Ownership Enterprises	7	4345	408	1893
国有联营企业	State Joint Ownership Enterprises	－	－	－	－
集体联营企业	Collective Joint Enterprises	－	－	－	－
国有与集体联营企业	Joint State－collective Enterprises	7	4345	408	1893
其他联营企业	Other Joint Ownership Enterprises	－	－	－	－
有限责任公司	Limited Liability Corporations	1070	21824205	3805174	1411822
国有独资公司	State－funded Corporations	44	1546574	308548	116273
其他有限责任公司	Other Limited Liability Corporations	1026	20277631	3496626	1295549
股份有限公司	Share－holding Corporations Ltd.	96	5059673	941700	1182034
私营企业	Private Enterprises	2331	18166266	2110650	1116671
私营独资企业	Private－funded Enterprises	29	46987	9192	6795
私营合伙企业	Private Partnership Enterprises	－	－	－	－
私营有限责任公司	Private Limited Liability Corporations	2262	17664504	2054441	1093053
私营股份有限公司	Private Share－holding Corporations Ltd.	40	454775	47018	16823
其他企业	Other Enterprises	33	25145	3534	8955
2. 港、澳、台商投资企业	**Enterprises With Investment from Hong Kong, Macao and Taiwan**	**48**	**983490**	**132259**	**192110**
合资经营企业(港或澳、台资)	Joint－venture Enterprises (With Funds from Hong Kong, Macao and Taiwan)	19	505048	50378	110451
合作经营企业(港或澳、台资)	Cooperative Enterprises (With Funds from Hong Kong, Macao and Taiwan)	1	18552	882	18977
港、澳、台商独资经营企业	Enterprises With Sole Investment from Hong Kong, Macao and Taiwan	27	459151	80568	61030
港、澳、台商投资股份有限公司	Share－holding Corporations Ltd. With Investment from Hong Kong, Macao and Taiwan	1	739	431	1653
3. 外商投资企业	**Enterprises With Foreign Investment**	**56**	**1840200**	**332314**	**324442**
中外合资经营企业	Joint－venture Enterprises	14	716657	225882	188979
中外合作经营企业	Cooperation Enterprises	1	7205	854	7204
外资企业	Enterprises With Sole Foreign Investment	39	1078959	99443	126452
外商投资股份有限公司	Share－holding Corporations Ltd. With Foreign Investment	1	35804	4991	1806

批发零售贸易企业财务状况(2013 年)

Wholesale and Retail Trades by Status of Registration(2013)

(10000 yuan)

累计折旧 Accumulated Depreciation	#本年折旧 Depreciation	资产总计 Total Assets	负债合计 Total Liabilities	所有者权益合计 Creditors´ Equity	实收资本 Capital Hold	#国家资本 State Capital
1589631	**278331**	**64452281**	**48847291**	**15604990**	**8972858**	**1930507**
1411666	**247228**	**60816889**	**46318763**	**14498125**	**8265476**	**1890602**
73940	7174	1554010	604417	949593	210573	189128
2848	404	88499	82816	5684	5788	–
570	44	13352	11969	1383	335	–
847	157	5458	3100	2358	907	317
–	–	–	–	–	–	–
–	–	–	–	–	–	–
847	157	5458	3100	2358	907	317
–	–	–	–	–	–	–
511752	90149	27811943	21673042	6138901	3195687	433463
40439	6349	2098853	1441541	657312	261363	185483
471313	83800	25713090	20231501	5481589	2934324	247980
411291	62548	8893159	5531046	3362113	1925237	1267395
408244	86378	22412182	18390326	4021856	2921736	300
1792	430	52106	42585	9521	3096	–
–	–	–	–	–	–	–
399061	84765	21884601	17943887	3940714	2875494	300
7391	1183	475475	403854	71621	43146	–
2173	374	38285	22048	16237	5213	–
64272	**12399**	**1250101**	**797084**	**453017**	**278677**	**4250**
36798	6202	666526	419525	247002	75153	4250
9008	664	35674	5337	30336	18975	–
17739	4806	546111	371132	174979	183611	–
727	727	1790	1090	700	937	–
113693	**18704**	**2385291**	**1731444**	**653848**	**428705**	**35655**
48447	6951	1036159	841428	194731	152306	35655
3904	253	13963	5059	8904	12916	–
60636	11394	1281619	852266	429354	257295	–
706	105	51933	32264	19669	5188	–

项　目	Item	营业收入 Revenue of Business	#主营业务收入 Main Revenue of Business	主营业务成本 Main Cost of Business	主营业务税金及附加 Main Sales Tax and Extra Charges
批发零售贸易业企业合计	**Total**	**139095539**	**137552620**	**130967579**	**270464**
1.内资企业	**Domestic－funded Enterprises**	**132287199**	**130858756**	**124881575**	**247100**
国有企业	State－owned Enterprises	3636738	3627289	3204567	83424
集体企业	Collective－owned Enterprises	143567	143131	138097	419
股份合作企业	Cooperative Enterprises	3953	3601	3269	8
联营企业	Joint Ownership Enterprises	47929	47928	44636	58
国有联营企业	State Joint Ownership Enterprises	－	－	－	－
集体联营企业	Collective Joint Enterprises	－	－	－	－
国有与集体联营企业	Joint State－collective Enterprises	47929	47928	44636	58
其他联营企业	Other Joint Ownership Enterprises	－	－	－	－
有限责任公司	Limited Liability Corporations	65205468	64421282	61608948	82628
国有独资公司	State－funded Corporations	4110391	4101466	4027860	1644
其他有限责任公司	Other Limited Liability Corporations	61095077	60319817	57581088	80984
股份有限公司	Share－holding Corporations Ltd.	23197086	22804231	21665730	31336
私营企业	Private Enterprises	39946516	39705392	38113319	49132
私营独资企业	Private－funded Enterprises	119666	119442	108086	215
私营合伙企业	Private Partnership Enterprises	－	－	－	－
私营有限责任公司	Private Limited Liability Corpora tions	39151811	38913542	37400646	47388
私营股份有限公司	Private Share－holding Corporations Ltd.	675039	672408	604588	1529
其他企业	Other Enterprises	105943	105902	103008	95
2.港、澳、台商投资企业	**Enterprises With Investment from Hong Kong,Macao and Taiwan**	**2170534**	**2150892**	**1841154**	**9612**
合资经营企业(港或澳、台资)	Joint－venture Enterprises (With Funds from Hong Kong,Macao and Taiwan)	1282825	1269372	1098711	5857
合作经营企业(港或澳、台资)	Coorperative Enterprises (With Funds from Hong Kong,Macao and Taiwan)	61864	61864	51968	254
港、澳、台商独资经营企业	Enterprises With Sole Investment from Hong Kong,Macao and Taiwan	820525	814335	686963	3475
港、澳、台商投资股份有限公司	Share－holding Corporations Ltd. With Investment from Hong Kong,Macao and Taiwan	5321	5321	3513	26
3.外商投资企业	**Enterprises With Foreign Investment**	**4637806**	**4542973**	**4244851**	**13752**
中外合资经营企业	Joint－venture Enterprises	3152108	3099320	3023083	4924
中外合作经营企业	Cooperation Enterprises	8138	6729	5428	26
外资企业	Enterprises With Sole Foreign Investment	1346444	1305809	1095182	8630
外商投资股份有限公司	Share－holding Corporations Ltd. With Foreign Investment	91367	91367	81385	169

continued (10000 yuan)

销售费用 Cost of Sales	管理费用 Administration Cost	财务费用 Financil Cost	营业利润 Management Profits	利润总额 Total Profits	应交所得税 Income Tax	就业人员期末人数(人) Employed Persons at year - end (person)
3400379	**1696090**	**677244**	**1467686**	**1707690**	**476628**	**240898**
3038153	**1494571**	**655885**	**1329592**	**1569842**	**411730**	**219743**
33936	71007	-14550	254244	255349	65297	2503
1397	1611	1668	423	1624	430	245
52	517	35	70	260	66	69
1195	212	-10	1838	2049	179	132
-	-	-	-	-	-	-
-	-	-	-	-	-	-
1195	212	-10	1838	2049	179	132
-	-	-	-	-	-	-
1570673	606589	218595	779893	905508	198977	91088
29442	32954	5534	57043	72839	7588	2218
1541231	573635	213061	722849	832669	191389	88870
639896	284945	121903	230065	319403	99709	53673
790544	528646	328027	61893	84589	47042	71358
3181	3772	916	3497	3482	904	797
-	-	-	-	-	-	-
738141	514664	322434	50137	71802	44343	68825
49222	10210	4677	8259	9305	1794	1736
460	1044	218	1168	1062	31	675
192103	**83996**	**3671**	**31432**	**31992**	**17216**	**10173**
119246	34682	-1570	29207	29358	13474	4277
2936	6313	127	267	1889	69	366
69822	41219	5092	2081	868	3673	5468
100	1782	23	-122	-124	-	62
170123	**117523**	**17688**	**106661**	**105856**	**47683**	**10982**
65261	39069	10352	48041	51611	16262	4193
1635	59	2	606	825	206	50
102533	73597	7098	53656	49111	31215	6365
675	4771	155	4513	4480	-	374

8－07 按国民经济行业分限额以上

Main Financial Indicators of Enterprises Above Designated

单位：万元

项　目	Item	法人企业数(个) Number of Enterprises (unit)	年末资产负债 Assets and Liabilities		
			流动资产合计 Circulating Funds	# 存　货 Inventory	固定资产原价 Orginal Value of Fixed Assets
总　计	**Total**	**3684**	**49288544**	**7508471**	**4391705**
一、批发业	**Wholesale**	**2761**	**42287864**	**6000682**	**2873303**
农、林、牧产品批发	Wholesale of Farm, Forestry and Animal Husbandry Products	36	250579	41708	31448
食品、饮料及烟草制品批发	Wholesale of Food, Beverages and Tobaccos	163	3831609	424708	299972
纺织、服装及家庭用品批发	Wholesale of Textile Products, Garments and Household Articles	562	6306372	1237438	371294
文化、体育用品及器材批发	Wholesale of Cultural and Sports Goods	87	1019748	383937	78369
医药及医疗器材批发	Wholesale of Medicines and Medical Appliances	102	2269294	497159	130440
矿产品、建材及化工产品批发	Wholesale of Mineral Products, Building and Chemical Materials	1314	24190111	2904865	1701830
机械设备、五金产品及电子产品批发	Wholesale of Machinery, Hardware and Electronic Products	407	3852395	449516	245031
#汽车、摩托车及零配件批发	Wholesale of Automobiles, Motorcycle and Parts	75	991338	119582	45566
其他批发业	Other	89	564315	61342	14600
二、零售业	**Retail Trade**	**923**	**7000680**	**1507789**	**1518402**
综合零售	Comprehensive Retail Trade	116	2950376	263272	673141
食品、饮料及烟草制品专门零售	Specialism Retail of Food, Beverages and Tobaccos	60	118879	27258	22766
纺织、服装及日用品专门零售	Specialism Retail of Textile Products, Garments, Shoes and Caps	59	411612	157216	128025
文化、体育用品及器材专门零售	Specialism Retail of Cultural and Sports Goods	46	293388	136577	122779
医药及医疗器材专门零售	Specialism Retail of Medicines and Medical Appliances	54	204470	54767	22665
汽车、摩托车、燃料及零配件专门零售	Specialism Retail of Automobiles, Motorcycle, Fuels and Parts	427	2356875	738179	420225
#汽车零售	Specialism Retail of Automobiles	282	2250473	715802	356141
家用电器及电子产品专门零售	Specialism Retail of Household Electric Applianes, and Electronic Products	90	395614	87076	46601
五金、家具及室内装饰材料专门零售	Specialism Retail of Hardware and Upholstery Materials	38	140689	16018	49574
货摊、无店铺及其他零售业	Stall, Non－shop and Other Retails	33	128777	27424	32625

批发零售贸易企业财务状况(2013 年)
Size in Wholesale and Retail Trades by Sector(2013)

(10000 yuan)

累计折旧 Accumulated Depreciation	#本年折旧 Depreciation	资产总计 Total Assets	负债合计 Total Liabilities	所有者权益合计 Creditors´ Equity	实收资本 Capital Hold	#国家资本 State Capital
1589631	**278331**	**64452281**	**48847291**	**15604990**	**8972858**	**1930507**
1069220	**187399**	**55378835**	**41918909**	**13459926**	**7543996**	**1861587**
9753	1747	316300	254260	62040	38412	3424
128942	18262	4752106	3086840	1665265	430385	114700
152311	36132	7670512	6113313	1557199	820338	14465
32666	4166	1358851	892440	466411	179778	10230
50940	10012	2636083	1897288	738795	252335	33323
596688	98138	33123462	25536351	7587110	5039084	1643033
92846	17993	4886049	3621368	1264681	673905	42411
11915	3908	1212253	1056430	155823	152685	1700
4963	906	631787	513938	117848	109379	–
520411	**90932**	**9073446**	**6928381**	**2145064**	**1428862**	**68920**
265313	34673	3793095	2821024	972071	443806	22839
7800	2458	162930	115050	47881	32149	465
22922	4131	560077	473358	86719	147812	105
28206	4080	452530	345309	107221	93040	10488
10399	2263	235282	178916	56366	28370	1326
134671	35494	3031854	2393962	637892	460217	31198
109961	30076	2827835	2302355	525480	397200	24191
16124	2438	486860	345409	141451	113324	–
20567	3411	187485	106974	80511	62333	–
14410	1984	163333	148380	14953	47811	2500

项　目	Item	营业收入 Revenue of Business	其中:主营业务收入 Main Revenue of Business	主营业务成本 Main Cost of Business	主营业务税金及附加 Main Sales Tax and Extra Charges
总　计	**Total**	**139095539**	**137552620**	**130967579**	**270464**
一、批发业	**Wholesale**	**122390223**	**121182107**	**116383037**	**202554**
农、林、牧产品批发业	Wholesale of Farm , Forestry and Animal Husbandry Products	645744	644594	622717	555
食品、饮料、烟草制品批发	Wholesale of Food, Beverages and Tobaccos	9146989	8921135	7712709	98257
纺织、服装及家庭用品批发	Wholesale of Textile Products, Garments and Household Articles	14034704	13883992	12980969	25244
文化、体育用品及器材批发	Wholesale of Cultural and Sports Goods	2306918	2295942	2197225	3435
医药及医疗器材批发	Wholesale of Medicines and Medical Appliances	5941751	5931520	5484143	8717
矿产品、建材及化工产品批发	Wholesale of Mineral Products, Building and Chemical Materials	78515916	77767733	76311449	44571
机械设备、五金产品及电子产品批发	Wholesale of Machinery, Hardware and Electronic Products	10345965	10285979	9653392	14109
#汽车、摩托车及零配件批发	Wholesale of Automobiles, Motorcycle and Parts	3840208	3834906	3664826	3524
其他批发业	Other	1427759	1426740	1396820	7635
二、零售业	**Retail Trade**	**16705316**	**16370513**	**14584542**	**67910**
综合零售	Comprehensive Retail Trade	4914014	4675794	4006537	35249
食品、饮料及烟草制品专门零售	Specialism Retail of Food, Beverages and Tobaccos	249731	248768	194059	1062
纺织、服装及日用品专门零售	Specialism Retail of Textile Products, Garments, Shoes and Caps	530313	526004	341730	3816
文化、体育用品及器材专门零售	Specialism Retail of Cultural and Sports Goods	553749	549993	473407	8649
医药及医疗器材专门零售	Specialism Retail of Medicines and Medical Appliances	464070	460350	370444	1706
汽车、摩托车、燃料及零配件专门零售	Specialism Retail of Automobiles, Motorcycle, Fuels and Parts	8457182	8396912	7914860	12060
#汽车零售	Specialism Retail of Automobiles	7288866	7231686	6810676	10833
家用电器及电子产品专门零售	Specialism Retail of Household Electric Applianes, and Electronic Products	827028	810282	694806	2811
五金、家具及室内装饰材料专门零售	Specialism Retail of Hardware and Upholstery Materials	232784	228557	182201	1130
货摊、无店铺及其他零售业	Stall, Non - shop and Other Retails	476445	473854	406498	1426

continued (10000 yuan)

销售费用 Cost of Sales	管理费用 Administration Cost	财务费用 Financil Cost	营业利润 Management Profits	利润总额 Total Profits	应交所得税 Income Tax	就业人员期末人数(人) Employed Persons at year - end (person)
3400379	**1696090**	**677244**	**1467686**	**1707690**	**476628**	**240898**
2301252	**1192095**	**596393**	**1194689**	**1430195**	**370464**	**140950**
6453	8798	7666	-627	3788	2054	709
611118	150971	5030	463596	514928	122200	28269
413286	264558	90154	200017	229805	44428	29597
40782	34527	11136	33490	34857	2132	3679
187852	93257	25847	189699	195817	38105	9457
677927	461414	373469	248313	367129	128451	48348
359037	169539	53506	77664	88725	32075	19728
168980	21169	6657	-28082	-27692	2268	3315
4487	8782	29281	-17433	-4873	1015	1142
1099127	**503995**	**80852**	**272996**	**277495**	**106165**	**99948**
496605	191521	-5819	166530	186394	72637	39434
38401	14215	1808	287	2246	1123	4284
120498	49511	7559	-3749	-3860	3460	9359
47583	21925	11263	-8433	-6279	426	5016
48315	23164	2377	19350	19988	5292	6345
207089	157688	55607	83293	58461	18872	24720
179123	149517	53095	61199	37088	15062	21349
70457	22880	4706	-517	-235	1624	6561
12397	9082	2181	23395	23511	1087	1204
57784	14007	1171	-7160	-2731	1643	3025

8－08　分地区限额以上

The Situation of Wholesale

单位:万元

地　区	Region	企业法人数(个) Number of Enterprises (unit)	商品销售总额 Total Sales of Commodities	主营业务收入 Main Revenue of Business	主营业务成本 Main Cost of Business	主营业务税金及附加 Main Sales Tax and Extra Charges
全　市	**Total**	**3684**	**158597327**	**137552620**	**130967579**	**270464**
市　区	Urban District	3150	152568106	132096309	125861659	254568
#上城区	Shangcheng	312	29690166	25811682	24321778	110845
下城区	Xiacheng	489	37364280	32679992	31450715	48317
江干区	Jianggan	336	14602379	12882466	12288146	14801
拱墅区	Gongshu	487	18906436	16324022	15774371	17209
西湖区	Xihu	272	12422276	9117132	8485529	14674
高新(滨江)区	Hi－Tech(Binjiang)	180	10793711	9442872	9070074	9066
萧山区	Xiaoshan	614	19196099	17020773	16216537	24655
余杭区	Yuhang	407	7049152	6385037	6131120	8031
桐庐县	Tonglu	104	988523	879500	834309	1998
淳安县	Chun'an	49	464682	409601	346776	1030
建德市	Jiande	52	546785	502412	473378	966
富阳市	Fuyang	224	2840793	2575022	2400742	10417
临安市	Lin'an	105	1188438	1089777	1050716	1485

批发零售业主要指标(2013 年)

and Retail Trades by Region(2013)

(10000 yuan)

销售费用 Cost of Sales	管理费用 Administration Cost	财务费用 Financil Cost	利润总额 Total Profits	本年应交增值税 Value Added Tax Payable	就业人员期末人数(人) Employed Persons at year－end (person)
3400379	**1696090**	**677244**	**1707690**	**965533**	**240898**
3240814	1613696	610912	1646856	841147	222055
538036	337524	52663	616485	252296	46681
620009	386661	95758	403202	139350	40319
313987	170526	45232	171885	82146	25709
283800	164742	64321	52733	71049	23353
492953	172984	131465	－20767	55015	30218
200978	103845	53518	152788	53647	9267
441607	147353	110595	175555	96909	25703
133483	92544	53392	－8361	37573	14399
17212	15658	7946	6131	17654	2999
55048	5096	1560	3634	8580	3868
23715	7795	4490	－5948	8289	1968
43680	40545	46432	52186	84053	6706
19910	13300	5905	4830	5810	3302

8－09 按注册类型、行业分限额以上

Main Financial Indicators of Hotels and Catering Services

单位：万元

项　目	Item	法人企业数(个) Number of Enterprises (unit)	年末资产负债 Assets and Liabilities 流动资产合计 Circulating Funds	# 存货 Inventory	固定资产原价 Orginal Value of Fixed Assets
总　计	**Total**	**874**	**1534315**	**107170**	**2629171**
(一)按登记注册类型分组	**Grouped By Registered Type**				
1. 内资企业	**Domestic－funded Enterprises**	**837**	**1231510**	**62573**	**2088051**
国有企业	State－owned Enterprises	45	88553	3666	201659
集体企业	Collective－owned Enterprises	19	22116	1399	90667
股份合作企业	Cooperative Enterprises	2	1085	234	1910
联营企业	Joint Ownership Enterprises	1	3950	77	4872
有限责任公司	Limited Liability Corporations	240	490457	23204	1144539
股份有限公司	Share－holding Corporations Ltd.	11	77216	2908	92480
私营企业	Private Enterprises	518	547071	31046	549024
其他企业	Other Enterprises	1	1062	39	2899
2. 港、澳、台商投资企业	**Enterprises With Investment from Hong Kong, Macao and Taiwan**	**17**	**142227**	**28336**	**299734**
3. 外商投资企业	**Enterprises With Foreign Investment**	**20**	**160578**	**16261**	**241387**
(二)按国民经济行业分组	**Grouped By Sector**				
1. 住宿业	**Lodging**	**413**	**1036123**	**51947**	**2079654**
旅游饭店	Restaurants for Junketing	255	925104	48515	1913977
一般旅馆	General Hotel	157	110896	3431	165305
其他住宿服务	Other Lodging	1	123	2	372
2. 餐饮	**Catering Services**	**461**	**498192**	**55223**	**549517**
正餐服务	Dinner Services	417	432411	40107	448472
快餐服务	Short Order Services	21	45854	13942	92601
饮料及冷饮服务	Beverages and Services	13	5263	875	1342
其他餐饮业	Others Catering Services	10	14664	299	7101

住宿业和餐饮业财务状况（2013 年）

Enterprises Above Designated Size by Status of Registration and Sector(2013)

(10000 yuan)

累计折旧 Accumulated Depreciation	#本年折旧 Depreciation	资产总计 Total Assets	负债合计 Total Liabilities	所有者权益合计 Creditors' Equity	实收资本 Capital Hold	#国家资本 State Capital
980767	**136004**	**4146213**	**3060380**	**1085833**	**1152102**	**335257**
753634	**96576**	**3344965**	**2425613**	**919352**	**955102**	**317321**
106715	8367	202429	84391	118038	63647	60006
43382	3808	85311	64743	20568	29953	–
1451	100	1544	1188	356	150	–
3160	195	5883	980	4903	120	120
356805	52955	1686349	1253300	433050	482136	195174
42912	3634	211796	88642	123154	104590	61000
199188	27511	1147419	931791	215628	273506	21
21	7	4234	578	3656	1000	1000
147025	**10831**	**326751**	**207309**	**119441**	**81467**	**17937**
80108	**28597**	**474498**	**427458**	**47039**	**115533**	**–**
814976	**89995**	**2994444**	**2146243**	**848202**	**899906**	**332033**
760663	80319	2698564	1948536	750028	817852	327986
54313	9676	295387	197707	97679	81553	4047
–	–	494	–	494	500	–
165791	**46009**	**1151769**	**914138**	**237631**	**252197**	**3224**
114654	25961	951301	760405	190896	202401	3079
46520	19045	175190	141879	33311	44782	100
959	134	6290	3714	2576	1289	25
3660	869	18989	8140	10849	3725	21

项　目	Item	营业收入 Revenue of Business	主营业务收入 Main Revenue of Business	主营业务税金及附加 Business Tax and Extra Charges
总　计	**Total**	**2300265**	**2271451**	**125036**
(一)按登记注册类型分组	**Grouped By Registered Type**			
1. 内资企业	**Domestic - funded Enterprises**	**1613742**	**1594212**	**87168**
国有企业	State - owned Enterprises	135210	132540	6656
集体企业	Collective - owned Enterprises	32213	32182	1868
股份合作企业	Cooperative Enterprises	3477	3477	195
联营企业	Joint Ownership Enterprises	4013	4013	222
有限责任公司	Limited Liability Corporations	565265	553695	30824
股份有限公司	Share - holding Corporations Ltd.	82367	82157	4074
私营企业	Private Enterprises	790580	785530	43279
其他企业	Other Enterprises	617	617	52
2. 港、澳、台商投资企业	**Enterprises With Investment from Hong Kong, Macao and Taiwan**	**146545**	**140766**	**8754**
3. 外商投资企业	**Enterprises With Foreign Investment**	**539979**	**536473**	**29115**
(二)按国民经济行业分组	**Grouped By Sector**			
1. 住宿业	**Lodging**	**1007090**	**983668**	**55698**
旅游饭店	Restaurants for Junketing	853849	832384	47050
一般旅馆	General Hotel	153017	151059	8644
其他住宿服务	Other Lodging	225	225	4
2. 餐饮	**Catering Services**	**1293175**	**1287783**	**69338**
正餐服务	Dinner Services	755661	751121	40615
快餐服务	Short Order Services	497455	497095	26913
饮料及冷饮服务	Beverages and Services	10379	10106	556
其他餐饮业	Others Catering Services	29680	29460	1254

continued (10000 yuan)

销售费用 Cost of Sales	管理费用 Administration Cost	财务费用 Financil Cost	营业利润 Management Profits	利润总额 Total Profits	应交所得税 Income Taxes Payable	就业人员期末人数(人) Employed Persons at year - end (person)
742633	**496614**	**83583**	**-38919**	**-19318**	**19828**	**105111**
527621	**397351**	**71629**	**-64884**	**-45469**	**8817**	**75226**
44153	41670	366	8666	9726	2054	5453
11504	10534	769	-1348	-1222	95	1405
926	565	8	118	119	17	185
1576	1524	-67	44	31	8	160
189266	184327	36781	-46038	-38737	2105	27937
29138	15124	934	8918	11526	955	3817
250730	142671	32839	-34303	-27289	3583	36160
331	936	-	-941	377	-	109
38598	**35385**	**6306**	**19084**	**17233**	**4238**	**4333**
176414	**63878**	**5647**	**6882**	**8919**	**6774**	**25552**
340067	**347903**	**62453**	**-39397**	**-27576**	**8373**	**43722**
286581	295020	57038	-33604	-23646	7365	36564
53486	52878	5414	-5823	-3960	1001	7138
-	5	-	30	30	8	20
402566	**148711**	**21130**	**478**	**8258**	**11455**	**61389**
233673	102394	18816	-25492	-19889	3367	35708
161078	41467	2335	22790	24740	7173	23532
2844	2470	91	485	480	142	477
4971	2380	-112	2695	2927	774	1672

8-10 按登记注册类型和国民经济行业分限额以上住宿业和餐饮业经营情况(2013 年)

Management Conditions of Hotels and Catering Services Enterprises Above Designated Size by Status of Registration and Sector(2013)

单位:万元　　(10000 yuan)

项　目	Item	法人企业(个) Number of Enterprises (unit)	营业额 Revenue of Business	#客房收入 Revenue of Guest Rooms	#餐饮收入 Revenue of Catering Services	#商品销售收入 Revenue of Goods Sales
一、按登记注册类型分	**Grouped By Registered Type**					
总　计	**Total**	**874**	**2268902**	**524421**	**1609138**	**14842**
1. 内资企业	**Domestic - funded Enterprises**	**837**	**1603890**	**454689**	**1033423**	**11753**
国有企业	State - owned Enterprises	45	132874	60439	56378	878
集体企业	Collective - owned Enterprises	19	32144	19521	7918	244
股份合作企业	Cooperative Enterprises	2	3477	1214	2022	25
联营企业	Joint Ownership Enterprises	1	4013	1934	1281	-
国有联营企业	State Joint Ownership Enterprises	-	-	-	-	-
集体联营企业	Collective Joint Enterprises	-	-	-	-	-
国有与集体联营企业	Joint State - collective Enterprises	1	4013	1934	1281	-
其他联营企业	Other Joint Ownership Enterprises	-	-	-	-	-
有限责任公司	Limited Liability Corporations	240	559294	211349	288981	4989
国有独资公司	State - funded Corporations	13	45906	17164	21336	515
其他有限责任公司	Other Limited Liability Corporations	227	513389	194185	267646	4474
股份有限公司	Share - holding Corporations Ltd.	11	82454	13119	64516	1912
私营企业	Private Enterprises	518	789105	146886	612024	3705
私营独资企业	Private - funded Enterprises	28	17352	1675	15344	165
私营合伙企业	Private Partnership Enterprises	6	2714	-	2714	-
私营有限责任公司	Private Limited Liability Corporations	471	656652	138912	489108	3495
私营股份有限公司	Private Share - holding Corporations Ltd.	13	112388	6300	104858	45
其他企业	Other Enterprises	1	529	227	303	-

项　目	Item	法人企业(个) Number of Enterprises (unit)	营业额 Revenue of Business	#客房收入 Revenue of Guest Rooms	#餐饮收入 Revenue of Catering Services	#商品销售收入 Revenue of Goods Sales
2. 港、澳、台商投资企业	**Enterprises With Investment from Hong Kong, Macao and Taiwan**	**17**	**123182**	**46241**	**68019**	**185**
合资经营企业(港或澳、台资)	Joint – venture Enterprises (With Funds from Hong Kong, Macao and Taiwan)	9	101992	38702	54945	136
合作经营企业(港或澳、台资)	Coorperative Enterprises (With Funds from Hong Kong, Macao and Taiwan)	–	–	–	–	–
港、澳、台商独资经营企业	Enterprises With Sole Investment from Hong Kong, Macao and Taiwan	8	21191	7540	13074	49
港、澳、台商投资股份有限公司	Share – holding Corporations Ltd. With Investment from Hong Kong, Macao and Taiwan	–	–	–	–	–
3. 外商投资企业	**Enterprises With Foreign Investment**	**20**	**541829**	**23491**	**507695**	**2904**
中外合资经营企业	Joint – venture Enterprises	7	424942	10772	408375	2793
中外合作经营企业	Cooperation Enterprises	2	3996	2777	784	106
外资企业	Enterprises With Sole Foreign Investment	9	111530	9092	98025	4
外商投资股份有限公司	Share – holding Corporations Ltd. With Foreign Investment	2	1361	849	511	1
二、按国民经济行业分	**Grouped By Sector**					
总　计	**Total**	**874**	**2268902**	**524421**	**1609138**	**14842**
1. 住宿业	**Lodging**	**413**	**978047**	**491650**	**377819**	**7800**
旅游饭店	Restaurants for Junketing	255	826768	391429	339309	7243
一般旅馆	General Hotel	157	151054	100094	38411	556
其他住宿服务	Other Lodging	1	225	127	98	–
2. 餐饮业	**Catering Services**	**461**	**1290854**	**32772**	**1231319**	**7042**
正餐服务	Dinner Services	417	749415	32772	698258	6839
快餐服务	Short Order Services	21	501058	–	494075	–
饮料及冷饮服务	Beverages and Services	13	10404	–	9637	203
其他餐饮业	Others Catering Services	10	29978	–	29350	–

8－11 分地区限额以上

The Situation of Lodging

单位：万元

地 区	Region	企业法人数（个）Number of Enterprises (unit)	营业额 Revenue of Business	#客房收入 Revenue of Guest Rooms	#餐饮收入 Revenue of Catering Services	主营业务收入 Main Revenue of Business
全 市	**Total**	**874**	**2268902**	**524421**	**1609138**	**2271451**
市 区	Urban District	727	2101170	464564	1513135	2113694
#上城区	Shangcheng	144	373286	112069	242426	391934
下城区	Xiacheng	111	279427	67378	194577	279698
江干区	Jianggan	81	149890	49278	80579	146933
拱墅区	Gongshu	62	99610	24351	66789	98315
西湖区	Xihu	128	640648	80215	534202	641084
高新（滨江）区	Hi－Tech (Binjiang)	23	44610	14169	28854	44403
萧山区	Xiaoshan	67	247562	39105	202325	250262
余杭区	Yuhang	42	62618	15335	40059	62105
桐庐县	Tonglu	19	26174	8998	15823	24982
淳安县	Chun'an	45	63017	27800	29859	55961
建德市	Jiande	16	15323	3577	10510	15152
富阳市	Fuyang	32	37059	9565	25086	35734
临安市	Lin'an	35	26159	9917	14725	25928

住宿餐饮业主要指标(2013 年)
and Catering by Region(2013)

(10000 yuan)

主营业务税金及附加 Business Tax and Extra Charges	销售费用 Cost of Sales	管理费用 Administration Cost	财务费用 Financil Cost	利润总额 Total Profits	就业人员期末人数(人) Employed Persons at year - end (person)
125036	**742633**	**496614**	**83583**	**- 19318**	**105111**
116170	691085	446114	69657	3193	95266
22284	124556	88798	14385	23416	14728
15433	115462	56500	7519	- 5822	11548
8201	48716	46317	5488	- 4697	6562
5476	33859	18934	2917	- 1114	3794
35230	180541	102798	9463	19429	30745
2631	13800	9692	2594	- 675	1978
13056	89091	38617	21132	- 13857	14348
3415	16953	23583	2238	- 9434	4004
1557	10032	8943	2014	- 6352	1494
3161	20688	20565	4787	- 7299	3262
817	6738	2474	1306	- 1799	880
1950	7342	11038	3921	- 4439	2608
1381	6748	7480	1898	- 2622	1601

8－12 个体工商业登记注册情况(2013年末)

Statistics of Individual Owned Business(End of 2013)

项目	Item	全市 Whole City		市区 Urban District	
		合计 Total	#城镇 Urban	合计 Total	#城镇 Urban
户数(户)	**Number of Households (household)**	**327961**	**234010**	**225113**	**179091**
农、林、牧、渔业	Farming, Forestry, Animal Husbandry and Fishery	4820	1708	3118	1326
采矿业	Mining and Quarrying	67	17	9	1
制造业	Manufacturing	19062	6781	9743	3717
电力、热力、燃气及水生产和供应业	Production and Supply of Electricity, Gas and Water	60	31	19	11
建筑业	Construction	1075	454	546	319
批发和零售业	Wholesale and Retail Trade & Catering Services	230874	171839	165421	135597
交通运输、仓储和邮政业	Transportation, Storage and Post	5974	3558	3175	2276
住宿和餐饮业	Lodging and Catering	26937	20306	16951	14229
信息传输、软件和信息技术服务业	Information Transmission, Computer Services and Software	526	412	396	354
金融业	Banking and Insurance	7	5	2	2
房地产业	Real Estate	156	146	137	132
租赁和商务服务业	Renting and Business Service	3395	2509	2499	1829
科学研究和技术服务业	Scientific Research and Technical Service	1089	860	778	649
水利、环境和公共设施管理业	Water Conservancy, Environment and Public Utility	40	22	28	15
居民服务、修理和其他服务业	Service for the Residents and Other Service Sector	31931	23796	21074	17581
教育	Education	235	205	192	170
卫生和社会工作	Health Care, Sports & Social Welfare	406	278	172	132
文化、体育和娱乐业	Culture, Sports and Entertainment	1304	1082	851	750
其他	Others	3	1	2	1
从业人员(人)	**Employed Persons(person)**	**661324**	**469926**	**423118**	**344109**
农、林、牧、渔业	Farming, Forestry, Animal Husbandry and Fishery	12845	3859	6550	2504
采矿业	Mining and Quarrying	383	89	25	1
制造业	Manufacturing	68794	21792	23302	7582
电力、热力、燃气及水生产和供应业	Production and Supply of Electricity, Gas and Water	118	67	25	15
建筑业	Construction	4118	1133	1474	587
批发和零售业	Wholesale and Retail Trade & Catering Services	365256	274134	252819	209120
交通运输、仓储和邮政业	Transportation, Storage and Post	9398	5675	4603	3390
住宿和餐饮业	Lodging and Catering	76168	60690	46040	40380
信息传输、软件和信息技术服务业	Information Transmission, Computer Services and Software	1005	821	754	688

8－12 续表 continued

项　目	Item	全市 Whole City		市区 Urban District	
		合计 Total	#城镇 Urban	合计 Total	#城镇 Urban
金融业	Banking and Insurance	16	11	2	2
房地产业	Real Estate	254	236	215	206
租赁和商务服务业	Renting and Business Service	39303	37521	37095	35920
科学研究和技术服务业	Scientific Research and Technical Service	2350	1983	1525	1337
水利、环境和公共设施管理业	Water Conservancy, Environment and Public Utility	138	69	80	33
居民服务、修理和其他服务业	Service for the Residents and Other Service Sector	75439	57292	45315	39502
教育	Education	619	540	494	442
卫生和社会工作	Health Care, Sports & Social Welfare	1030	725	506	400
文化、体育和娱乐业	Culture, Sports and Entertainment	4085	3287	2292	1998
其他	Others	5	2	2	2
注册资金(万元)	**Capital Registered(10000 yuan)**	**2392950**	**1695931**	**1435400**	**1168911**
农、林、牧、渔业	Farming, Forestry, Animal Husbandry and Fishery	143048	48254	74826	34786
采矿业	Mining and Quarrying	3826	967	58	1
制造业	Manufacturing	192184	68107	73339	29496
电力、热力、燃气及水生产和供应业	Production and Supply of Electricity, Gas and Water	348	182	153	118
建筑业	Construction	29435	6141	8254	3546
批发和零售业	Wholesale and Retail Trade & Catering Services	1316965	1017406	853427	724533
交通运输、仓储和邮政业	Transportation, Storage and Post	72592	49657	42676	36347
住宿和餐饮业	Lodging and Catering	291432	244845	171254	156509
信息传输、软件和信息技术服务业	Information Transmission, Computer Services and Software	2585	2012	1719	1556
金融业	Banking and Insurance	108	38	16	16
房地产业	Real Estate	554	499	417	371
租赁和商务服务业	Renting and Business Service	37218	26009	24847	17811
科学研究和技术服务业	Scientific Research and Technical Service	6225	5374	4177	3633
水利、环境和公共设施管理业	Water Conservancy, Environment and Public Utility	373	257	253	166
居民服务、修理和其他服务业	Service for the Residents and Other Service Sector	263196	198467	161630	144093
教育	Education	1611	1477	1314	1207
卫生和社会工作	Health Care, Sports & Social Welfare	4726	3398	2210	1852
文化、体育和娱乐业	Culture, Sports and Entertainment	26520	22840	14828	12869
其他	Others	4	1	2	1

8－13　私营企业登记注册情况(2013 年末)

Statistics of Private Owned Business(End of 2013)

项　目	Item	全市 Whole City		市区 Urban District	
		合计 Total	#城镇 Urban	合计 Total	#城镇 Urban
户数(户)	**Number of Households (household)**	**225219**	**162902**	**188457**	**149727**
农、林、牧、渔业	Farming, Forestry, Animal Husbandry and Fishery	4257	1425	2264	1037
采矿业	Mining and Quarrying	163	32	31	14
制造业	Manufacturing	43370	14549	28894	11581
电力、热力、燃气及水生产和供应业	Production and Supply of Electricity, Gas and Water	373	91	93	45
建筑业	Construction	11208	8354	9508	7617
批发和零售业	Wholesale and Retail Trade & Catering Services	81814	65556	70901	60802
交通运输、仓储和邮政业	Transportation, Storage and Post	3648	2483	3070	2215
住宿和餐饮业	Lodging and Catering	3485	2684	2924	2356
信息传输、软件和信息技术服务业	Information Transmission, Computer Services and Software	11146	10259	10604	9939
金融业	Banking and Insurance	637	438	520	382
房地产业	Real Estate	5269	4048	4245	3367
租赁和商务服务业	Renting and Business Service	29231	26518	27316	25265
科学研究和技术服务业	Scientific Research and Technical Service	16389	15045	15631	14669
水利、环境和公共设施管理业	Water Conservancy, Environment and Public Utility	503	353	367	292
居民服务、修理和其他服务业	Service for the Residents and Other Service Sector	10341	8046	9064	7370
教育	Education	604	533	553	500
卫生和社会工作	Health Care, Sports & Social Welfare	388	281	338	247
文化、体育和娱乐业	Culture, Sports and Entertainment	2388	2203	2131	2027
其他	Others	5	4	3	2
就业人员(人)	**Employed Persons(person)**	**1867608**	**1361005**	**1486790**	**1246840**
农、林、牧、渔业	Farming, Forestry, Animal Husbandry and Fishery	25192	7954	11503	5158
采矿业	Mining and Quarrying	2608	537	670	170
制造业	Manufacturing	443491	141511	217961	106858
电力、热力、燃气及水生产和供应业	Production and Supply of Electricity, Gas and Water	2822	836	589	414
建筑业	Construction	96022	79365	80399	70935
批发和零售业	Wholesale and Retail Trade & Catering Services	603115	515691	536934	484678
交通运输、仓储和邮政业	Transportation, Storage and Post	28042	21048	21015	16612
住宿和餐饮业	Lodging and Catering	34157	25282	29066	21633
信息传输、软件和信息技术服务业	Information Transmission, Computer Services and Software	97145	91964	94269	90070

8－13 续表 continued

项 目	Item	全市 Whole City 合计 Total	全市 Whole City #城镇 Urban	市区 Urban District 合计 Total	市区 Urban District #城镇 Urban
金融业	Banking and Insurance	5691	4749	4841	4166
房地产业	Real Estate	41838	36742	33887	30580
租赁和商务服务业	Renting and Business Service	252968	229063	239826	219637
科学研究和技术服务业	Scientific Research and Technical Service	128265	118874	122128	115755
水利、环境和公共设施管理业	Water Conservancy, Environment and Public Utility	4040	3099	3100	2721
居民服务、修理和其他服务业	Service for the Residents and Other Service Sector	74598	59581	66146	54899
教育	Education	4550	4017	4122	3701
卫生和社会工作	Health Care, Sports & Social Welfare	3122	2467	2736	2179
文化、体育和娱乐业	Culture, Sports and Entertainment	19915	18207	17577	16662
其他	Others	27	18	21	12
注册资金(万元)	**Capital Registered(10000 yuan)**	**70699701**	**53996178**	**59103281**	**48622347**
农、林、牧、渔业	Farming, Forestry, Animal Husbandry and Fishery	843926	261330	456762	190671
采矿业	Mining and Quarrying	137789	44022	30635	28340
制造业	Manufacturing	14006386	5291844	9223215	3921066
电力、热力、燃气及水生产和供应业	Production and Supply of Electricity, Gas and Water	174907	77346	101365	63565
建筑业	Construction	4957869	3882355	4167764	3371036
批发和零售业	Wholesale and Retail Trade & Catering Services	14242672	12012931	12430433	11156301
交通运输、仓储和邮政业	Transportation, Storage and Post	847595	542869	681172	456159
住宿和餐饮业	Lodging and Catering	675202	517137	477523	424265
信息传输、软件和信息技术服务业	Information Transmission, Computer Services and Software	2467965	2360253	2390601	2324504
金融业	Banking and Insurance	2115252	1987078	1593819	1551433
房地产业	Real Estate	7250293	5999026	6098493	5129990
租赁和商务服务业	Renting and Business Service	16267226	15212754	15465685	14600526
科学研究和技术服务业	Scientific Research and Technical Service	4119184	3712175	3754358	3498442
水利、环境和公共设施管理业	Water Conservancy, Environment and Public Utility	259999	204852	180143	162772
居民服务、修理和其他服务业	Service for the Residents and Other Service Sector	1820935	1424529	1599580	1305022
教育	Education	45073	23450	28244	21995
卫生和社会工作	Health Care, Sports & Social Welfare	86182	84923	82207	81488
文化、体育和娱乐业	Culture, Sports and Entertainment	376096	352154	336282	329772
其他	Others	5150	5150	5000	5000

主要统计指标解释

社会消费品零售额 指各种经济类型的批发零售贸易业、住宿餐饮业对城乡居民和社会集团的消费品零售额总和。这个指标反映通过各种商品流通渠道向居民和社会集团供应的生活消费品来满足他们生活需要，是研究人民生活、社会消费品购买力、货币流通等问题的重要指标。社会消费品零售额包括：(1)售给城乡居民作为生活用的商品和修建房屋用的建筑材料；(2)售给机关、团体、学校、部队、企业、事业单位的职工食堂各种食品、燃料；(3)售给部队干部、战士生活用的粮食、副食品、衣着品、日用品、燃料；(4)售给来华的外国人、华侨、港澳台同胞的消费品；(5)售给社会集团的办公用品、纸张、帐册、文印用品、计算工具、书刊杂志和奖品；公共用品和纺织品、针织品；学校用的教学用具；文体用品；非专用的劳动保护用品，如工作服、套袖、围裙、手套、毛巾、肥皂等；日用百货和杂品，包括职工食堂用的餐具、炊具、设备和清洁卫生工具等；家具、设备、日用电器、电讯设备、电影器材和照相器材等；取暖用的设备和燃料、防暑、降温的饮料；非生产经营用的交通工具，如小轿车、面包车、工具车、卡车和油料；零星修理的各种零配件、材料、工具、建筑材料等；举办各种招待会、茶话会、宴会用的烟酒茶和各种食品及馈赠的礼品；从公费医疗经费中开支的中、西药品、中药材和医疗器材以及其他非生产性设备和用品。

限额以上批发零售贸易业 指批发贸易业年主营业务收入在2000万元及以上，零售贸易业年主营业务收入在500万元及以上的各种经济类型商贸企业。

商品销售总额 指对本企业(单位)以外的单位和个人出售(包括对国(境)外直接出口)的商品金额。这个指标反映批发零售贸易业在国内市场上销售商品以及出口商品的总量。商品销售总额包括：(1)售给城乡居民和社会集体团消费用的商品；(2)售给工业、农业、建筑业、运输邮电业、批发零售贸易业、餐饮业、服务业等作为生产、经营使用的商品；(3)售给批发零售贸易业作为转卖或加工后转卖的商品；(4)对国(境)外直接出口的商品，不包括：出售本企业(单位)自用的废旧包装用品，未通过买卖行为付出的商品，经本单位介绍，由买卖双方直接结算，本单位只收取手续费的业务，购货退出的商品以及商品损耗和损失等。

Explanatory Notes on Main Statistical Indicators

Total Retail Sales of Consumer Goods referring to the sum of retail sales of consumer goods sold by wholesale and retail, catering and lodging to urban and rural residents and social groups. This indicator is used to show the supply of consumer goods through various channels to households and institutions, and is very important for the study on people's livelihood, on the purchasing power of consumer goods and on the circulation of money. The retail sales of consumer goods include: (1) commodities sold to urban and rural residents for their daily use and building materials sold to them for the construction or repair of houses; (2) food and fuels sold to canteens of institutions, enterprises, schools and military units; (3) grains and non – staple food, clothing, daily articles and fuels sold to military personnel; (4) consumer goods sold to foreigners, overseas Chinese, and Chinese compatriots form Taiwan, Hong Kong and Macao during their stay in the mainland of China; (5) commodities sold to social groups. included under this heading are : office appliances, paper, account books, printing articles, calculaters, newspapers, magazines and prizes; public articles, textiles and knitgoods; realias for schools; cultural and sports articles; working articles for unspecial use i. e. working clothes, raglan sleeves, gloves, towels and soaps; commidities and miscellaneous goods for daily use i. e. dishwares, cookers and cleaning articles for canteens of institutions, enterprises, schools; furnishings, appliances, communications facilities , film and photograph equipments and materials; heating facilities, fuels and beverages; vehicles (exclude for business use) such as cars, microbuses, trucks and oils; parts , fittings, instruments and building materials, tobaccoes, alcohols, teas, foods for all kinds of reception meetings and banquets and prizes for presenting; Chinese and Western medicines, herbs and medical facilities expenditured by medical insurance fund and other non – production goods and equipments.

Wholesale And Retail Trade Above Designated Size wholesale trade, with year main business revenue over 20 million yuan of different status of registration; retail sale trade, with year main business revenue over 5 million yuan of different status of registration.

Total Sales of Commodities refer to selling of commodities by the establishments to other establishments and individuals (including direct export). This indictor is used to show the total value of sales of commodities at domestic markets and export. The total sales include: (1) commodities sold to urban and rural residents and social groups for their consumption; (2) commodities sold to establishments in industry, agriculture, construction, transportation, post and telecommunications, wholesale and retail trades, catering trade and public utility for their production and operation; (3) commodities sold to wholesale and retail establishment for re – selling, with or without further processing; and (4) commodities for direct export to other countries. Excluded are selling of waste packaging materials used by the establishments(units) themselves, commodities transferred without buying or selling procedures, commission income from brokerage in transactions whose settlement is directly handled by buyers and sellers, rejected commodities in the purchase, loss in commodities, etc.

九、对外经济、旅游

Ⅸ.FOREIGN ECONOMIC COOPERATION AND TOURISM

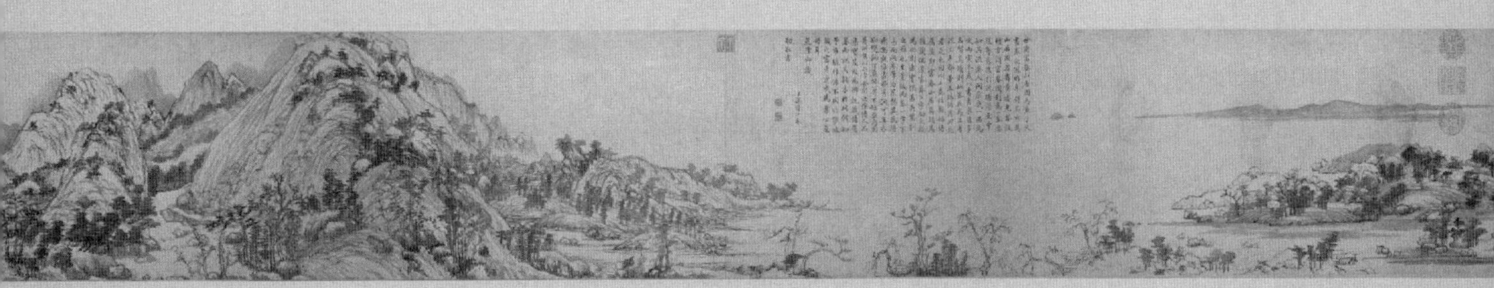

对外经济、旅游
Foreign Economic Cooperation and Tourism

主要统计指标
Major Statistical Indicators

协议利用外资金额	Total Contracted Foreign Investments	91.31	亿美元	(USD 100 million)
为上年	As Compared with the Preceding Year	110.5	%	(%)
实际利用外资金额	Foreign Investments Actually Utilized	52.76	亿美元	(USD 100 million)
为上年	As Compared with the Preceding Year	106.4	%	(%)
进出口总额	Total Imports and Exports	650.71	亿美元	(USD 100 million)
为上年	As Compared with the Preceding Year	105.5	%	(%)
# 出口总额	Total Exports	447.66	亿美元	(USD 100 million)
为上年	As Compared with the Preceding Year	108.5	%	(%)
接待境外旅游	Number of Oversea Visitor Arrivals	316.01	万人次	(10000 person-times)
为上年	As Compared with the Preceding Year	95.4	%	(%)
旅游外汇收入	Total Foreign Exchange Earnings from International Tourism	21.60	亿美元	(USD 100 million)
为上年	As Compared with the Preceding Year	98.1	%	(%)

9-01 外商直接投资情况(1978-2013)

Foreign Direct Investment(1978-2013)

单位:万美元 (USD 10000)

年 份 Year	项目个数(个) Number of Projects (unit)	协议总投资额 Total Investments of Agreements	协议利用外资金额 Contracted Foreign Investment	实际利用外资金额 Foreign Investments Actually Utilized
1978				
1979				
1980	3	153	128	
1981				
1982				
1983	2	356	100	
1984	9	6932	2697	
1985	21	6638	1731	907
1986	9	5722	2017	683
1987	10	2685	1256	1470
1988	23	6781	2734	696
1989	34	3897	1569	1860
1990	68	7817	3951	751
1991	121	11107	5551	2129
1992	583	125224	60915	9678
1993	1078	222325	121947	35713
1994	624	174406	110541	41098
1995	427	136662	90207	42659
1996	221	108150	70982	53651
1997	174	51682	27888	41187
1998	216	98219	51400	38425
1999	212	83416	56742	42025
2000	315	89781	64548	43093
2001	483	154447	103023	50324
2002	587	247888	96720	52186
2003	869	432660	200104	100850
2004	802	629727	307746	140982
2005	756	770941	400503	171274
2006	747	1080602	537986	225536
2007	574	854907	558059	280181
2008	483	862523	622788	331154
2009	554	948323	696486	401370
2010	545	1188055	770911	435627
2011	500	1291015	817108	472230
2012	510	1342616	826516	496061
2013	415	1419926	913144	527633

9-02 分行业外商直接投资情况(2013年)
Foreign Direct Investment by Sector(2013)

单位:万美元 (USD 10,000)

行业 Sector	项目数(个) Projects (unit)	占总数% Proportion (%)	合同外资 Total Contracted Foreign Investments	占总数% Proportion (%)	实际引资 Foreign Investments Actually Used	占总数(%) Proportion (%)
合 计 Total	**415**	**100**	**913144**	**100**	**527633**	**100**
第一产业 Primary Industry	**2**	**0.48**	**616**	**0.07**	**261**	**0.05**
农 业 Agriculture	2	0.48	616	0.07	261	0.05
第二产业 Secondary Industry	**87**	**20.96**	**213688**	**23.40**	**143492**	**27.20**
采矿业 Mining	-	-	7030	0.77	1240	0.24
制造业 Manufacturing	86	20.72	201742	22.09	136436	25.86
电力、燃气及水的生产和供应业 Production & Supply of Electricity, Gas & Water	1	0.24	5651	0.62	5311	1.01
建筑业 Construction	-	-	-735	-0.08	505	0.10
第三产业 Tertiary Industry	**326**	**78.55**	**698840**	**76.53**	**383880**	**72.76**
交通运输、仓储、邮政业 Transportation, Storage and Post	1	0.24	1305	0.14	23851	4.52
信息传输、计算机服务和软件业 Information Transmission, Computer Service and Software	41	9.88	64179	7.03	58556	11.10
批发和零售贸易、餐饮业 Whole sale and Retail Tvade. Catering Services	107	25.78	55804	6.11	31600	5.99
金融业 Banking and Insurance	13	3.13	29971	3.28	8875	1.68
房地产业 Real Estate	24	5.78	343706	37.64	192535	36.49
租赁及商务服务业 Renting and Business Service	47	11.33	88935	9.74	36850	6.98
科学研究和综合技术服务业 Scientific research and Integrated Technical Service	87	20.96	112426	12.31	30485	5.78
其他行业 Others	6	1.45	2514	0.28	1128	0.21

9－03 分国别(地区)外商直接投资情况(2013年)

Foreign Direct Investment by Region or Territory(2013)

单位:万美元 (USD 10000)

国 别(地区)	Country (territory)	历年累计 Accumulated			2013年 In Year 2013			
		项目(个) Projects (unit)	总投资额 Total Investments	协议外资金额 Total Contracted Foreign Investments	项目(个) Projects (unit)	总投资额 Total Investments	协议外资金额 Total Contracted Foreign Investments	实际引资 Foreign Investments Actually Utilized
合 计	**Total**	**12006**	**12372095**	**7531263**	**415**	**1419926**	**913144**	**527633**
#香港	#Hong Kong	5103	7310667	4600621	237	1146457	754280	417493
澳门	Macao	71	71611	40717	1	162	－102	576
台湾	Taiwan	1441	373084	204547	30	22339	16732	1960
日本	Japan	750	499526	242371	21	51433	16855	10863
美国	U. S. A	1555	933350	539795	35	30417	23256	7520
新加坡	Singapore	293	412712	246039	5	18777	25462	27870
澳大利亚	Australia	176	98568	63900	4	9292	9259	－
泰国	Thailand	38	12740	3424	2	－22	－22	36
意大利	Italy	204	149741	65958	6	20811	5295	2915
荷兰	Netherlands	83	101234	18909	3	35950	－5455	5
西班牙	Spain	67	59624	23965	1	50	－317	340
马来西亚	Malaysia	75	41361	22672	－	－	－	18
韩国	Republic of Korea	300	94237	56548	8	－1761	－3648	847
法国	France	120	70348	40166	5	997	1573	1000
玻利维亚	Bolivia	12	1770	1262	－	－	－	－
加拿大	Canada	199	99720	65117	9	14594	14342	213
英国	Britain	192	186392	106607	11	4616	1308	1788
奥地利	Austria	23	25123	13841	1	6000	3000	2050
波兰	Poland	4	240	147	－	－	－	－
洪都拉斯	Honduras	6	1118	563	－	－	－	－
德国	Germany	197	101807	52817	6	2185	1367	373
英属维尔京群岛	The British Virgin Islands	545	1090003	602180	10	42748	15146	16993

9－04 分地区外商直接投资情况
Foreign Direct Investment by Region

单位:万美元 (USD 10000)

区 域 Region	批准项目数(个) Number of Projects(unit)		协议利用外资金额 Total Contracted Foreign Investments		实际利用外资金额 Foreign Investments Actually Utilized	
	2013 年 In Year 2013	历年累计 Accumulated Until the End of 2013	2013 年 In Year 2013	历年累计 Accumulated Until the End of 2013	2013 年 In Year 2013	历年累计 Accumulated Until the End of 2013
全 市 Total	**415**	**12006**	**913144**	**7531263**	**527633**	**4041694**
市 区 Urban District	365	10027	775874	6475393	456432	3525184
#上 城 Shangcheng	27	632	44594	399911	17800	184410
下 城 Xiacheng	24	698	48155	401663	24500	197100
江 干 Jianggan	20	639	45533	420391	25100	180540
拱 墅 Gongshu	44	889	48840	454406	24500	265227
西 湖 Xihu	43	926	78273	493593	43300	274489
高新(滨江)区 Hi－Tech(Binjiang)	34	970	100725	813261	59300	501761
萧 山 Xiaoshan	81	1505	143395	837745	91168	472007
余 杭 Yuhang	47	1410	123106	704514	103077	397209
桐 庐 Tonglu	14	497	24130	194319	13642	97334
淳 安 Chun'an	10	185	20632	180714	10500	83427
建 德 Jiande	8	220	19490	115815	10963	41617
富 阳 Fuyang	15	681	48536	349492	21337	179615
临 安 Lin'an	3	396	24482	215530	14759	114517

9-05 分地区国内招商引资情况
Domestic Investment by Region

单位:亿元　　(100 million yuan)

区域 Region		批准项目数(个) Number of Projects(unit)		实际引进资金 Investments Actually Utilized	
		2013年 In Year 2013	2012年 In Year 2012	2013年 In Year 2013	2012年 In Year 2012
全市	**Total**	**1711**	**3034**	**860.60**	**778.69**
市区	Urban District	1332	2765	729.10	659.33
#上城	Shangcheng	89	175	79.10	75.57
下城	Xiacheng	149	454	107.60	99.56
江干	Jianggan	147	300	102.79	90.96
拱墅	Gongshu	343	594	106.06	100.62
西湖	Xihu	198	558	105.89	89.73
高新(滨江)区	Hi-Tech(Binjiang)	113	254	68.79	68.10
萧山	Xiaoshan	123	166	66.89	58.75
余杭	Yuhang	83	100	51.13	44.23
桐庐	Tonglu	96	108	26.34	23.91
淳安	Chun'an	92	66	25.94	24.13
建德	Jiande	61	34	26.03	23.07
富阳	Fuyang	67	34	27.06	24.22
临安	Lin'an	63	27	26.13	24.03

9-06 国家级开发区

The Construction of National -

项目	Item	合计 Total	杭州经济技术开发区 Hangzhou Economic and Technological Development Zone
规划面积（平方公里）	Area of planning (sq. km)	587.41	60.00
已开发面积（平方公里）	Area of Development (sq. km)	197.61	45.94
有偿出让土地面积（平方公里）	Area of Being Sold (sq. km)	94.13	18.64
累计由开发区投入基础设施款（亿元）	Investments in Infrastructure (100 million yuan)	1451.62	331.11
年末批准进区企业（个）	Number of Enterprises Approved (unit)	26616	6035
其中:三资企业（个）	Foreign Investments Enter-prises (unit)	2320	735
累计协议利用外资（亿美元）	Foreign Investments of Agreements (USD 100 million)	327.05	117.19
累计实际利用外资（亿美元）	Foreign Investments Actually Used (USD 100 million)	196.40	65.70
年末投产企业个数（个）	Number of Enterprises in Production or Operation (unit)	18132	3307
当年销售收入（亿元）	Sales Revenue (100 million yuan)	9560.68	1969.02
当年工业总产值（现价）（亿元）	Gross Industrial Output Value (100 million yuan)	6574.10	1527.57
当年实现利税（亿元）	Fulfilled Profits and Tax (100 million yuan)	889.69	195.91
当年出口创汇（亿美元）	Foreign Exchange Earmings of Export (USD 100 million)	160.93	58.45
当年财政收入（亿元）	Financial Revenue (100 million yuan)	273.97	50.90

建设发展情况(2013 年末)
Class Development Zones(End of 2013)

杭州高新技术开发区 Hangzhou High - tech Development Zone	杭州之江国家旅游度假区 Hangzhou Zhijiang National Tourism and Holiday Resort	萧山经济技术开发区 Xiaoshan Economic and Technological Development Zone	富阳经济技术开发区 Fuyang Economic and Technological Development Zone	余杭经济技术开发区 Yuhang Economic and Technological Development Zone
12.64	156.00	181.00	93.85	83.92
12.64	12.97	57.60	58.66	9.80
10.30	9.97	21.80	9.06	24.36
219.55	165.30	140.20	248.77	346.69
10428	106	991	1364	7692
509	106	593	139	238
80.55	23.16	59.97	20.30	25.88
53.53	14.92	35.27	13.59	13.39
2129	8	4394	1186	7108
2798.70	4.90	1682.90	1652.86	1452.30
1610.40	54.17	943.70	1289.46	1148.80
406.60	3.20	87.08	80.93	115.97
36.72	-	27.88	8.88	29.00
75.40	7.70	54.00	18.47	67.50

9－07　省级产业集聚区建设发展情况（2013 年末）
Development Statistics on Provincial－level Industry Cluster Districts（At the end of 2013）

项　　目	Item	大江东产业集聚区 Dajiangdong Industry Cluster District	城西科创产业集聚区 Chengxi Technological and Creative Industry Cluster District
入区企业数（个）	Proposed Enterprises （unit）	1063	3298
投产企业数（个）	Operating Enterprises （unit）	145	430
已开发建设面积（平方公里）	Land Space under Construction （sq. km）	36.86	26.57
已建成投产面积（平方公里）	Land Space Completed （sq. km）	14.57	14.51
当年产业增加值（亿元）	Current year's Value－added （100 million yuan）	113.60	402.62
#工业增加值（亿元）	Value－added of Industry （100 million yuan）	89.76	89.20
#服务业增加值（亿元）	Value－added of the Tertiary Industry （100 million yuan）	1.09	301.78
当年实际引进内资（亿元）	Current Year's Amount of Domestic Investment （100 million yuan）	41.20	63.52
当年实际到位外资（亿美元）	Current Year's Amount of Foreign Investment Actually Utilized （100 million USD）	4.80	5.19
当年科技活动经费支出（亿元）	Current Year's S & T Expenditure （100 million yuan）	13.52	34.09
科技活动人员数（人）	S & T Personnel （person）	4040	11059
当年财政预算总收入（亿元）	Current Year's Total Financial Revenue （100 million yuan）	35.50	78.42
#公共预算收入（亿元）	Public Financial Budgetary Revenue （100 million yuan）	16.44	43.14
当年固定资产投资完成额（亿元）	Current Year's Investment in Fixed Asset's （100 million yuan）	189.15	130.29
当年工业总产值（亿元）	Current Year's Gross Industrial Output Value （100 million yuan）	590.83	507.81
当年服务业营业收入（亿元）	Current Year's Operating Revenue of the Tertiary Industry （100 million yuan）	50.06	696.55
当年出口交货值（亿元）	Current Year's Export Delivery Value （100 million yuan）	46.34	75.48
当年利税总额（亿元）	Current Year's Total Taxes and Profits （100 million yuan）	30.68	340.02
#利润总额（亿元）	Total Profits （100 million yuan）	16.42	312.39

注：统计口径为重点规划区“四上”单位。

a）The Data of this table includes the Units above designated size in the key planning areas of the districts.

9-08 进出口情况(1978-2013)
Imports and Exports (1978-2013)

单位:亿美元 (USD 100 million)

年份 Year	进出口 Exports And Imports		出口 Exports		进口 Imports	
	总值 Total Value	为上年% As Compared with the Preceding Year(%)	总值 Total Value	为上年% As Compared with the Preceding Year(%)	总值 Total Value	为上年% As Compared with the Preceding Year(%)
1978						
1979						
1980						
1981						
1982						
1983						
1984						
1985						
1986						
1987						
1988						
1989	0.84		0.50		0.34	
1990	1.45	172.6	0.99	198.0	0.46	135.3
1991	2.18	150.3	1.48	149.5	0.70	152.2
1992	3.42	156.9	2.16	146.0	1.26	180.0
1993	8.73	255.3	4.92	227.8	3.81	302.4
1994	34.96	400.5	26.11	530.7	8.85	232.3
1995	45.18	129.2	33.18	127.1	12.00	135.6
1996	43.52	96.3	31.11	93.8	12.41	103.4
1997	48.83	112.2	37.43	120.3	11.40	91.8
1998	59.73	122.3	44.16	118.0	15.57	136.6
1999	73.40	122.9	50.79	115.0	22.61	145.3
2000	104.76	142.7	69.65	137.1	35.11	155.3
2001	112.98	107.9	72.84	104.6	40.14	114.3
2002	131.07	116.0	84.81	116.4	46.26	115.3
2003	182.38	139.2	109.55	129.2	72.83	157.4
2004	244.96	134.3	151.75	138.6	93.21	128.0
2005	298.70	121.9	198.04	130.5	100.66	108.0
2006	389.09	130.3	262.28	132.4	126.81	126.0
2007	434.26	111.7	299.66	114.3	134.60	106.2
2008	480.65	110.7	336.14	112.2	144.51	107.4
2009	404.20	84.1	271.80	80.9	132.40	91.6
2010	523.55	129.5	353.37	130.0	170.18	128.6
2011	639.72	122.2	415.21	117.5	224.50	131.9
2012	616.83	96.4	412.62	99.4	204.22	91.0
2013	650.71	105.5	447.66	108.5	203.05	99.5

9-09 分经济类型进出口情况

Imports and Exports by Status of Registration

单位:亿美元 (USD 100 million)

项　目	Item	2013 年 In Year 2013	2012 年 In Year 2012	为上年(%) As Compared with year 2012 (%)
全市进出口总值(海关口径)	Total Exports And Imports	650.71	616.83	105.5
一、出口总额	Exports	447.66	412.62	108.5
1.国有企业	State-owned Enterprises	78.03	75.93	102.8
2.三资企业	Foreign Investment Enterprises	131.50	133.43	98.6
(1)中外合作企业	Cooperation Enterprises	0.69	1.02	67.8
(2)中外合资企业	Joint-Venture Enterprises	63.71	65.17	97.8
(3)外商独资企业	Enterprises With Sole Foreign Investment	67.10	67.25	99.8
3.集体企业	Collective-owned Enterprises	19.20	17.74	108.2
4.私营企业	Private Enterprises	217.61	184.41	118.0
二、进口总额	Imports	203.05	204.22	99.5

9－10 分地区外贸进出口情况(2013 年)
Imports and Exports by Region(2013)

单位:万美元 (USD 10000)

区 域	Region	出口总值 Exports of This Year	为上年(%) As Compared with the Preceding Year(%)	进口总值 Imports of This Year	为上年(%) As Compared with the Preceding Year(%)
全市合计	**Total**	**4476570**	**108.5**	**2030532**	**99.5**
#不含省属	#Non－provincial	3841615	110.4	1808083	100.1
上 城	Shangcheng	135990	113.8	126637	96.0
下 城	Xiacheng	183944	112.1	162438	115.2
江 干	Jianggan	169254	105.1	24690	117.9
拱 墅	Gongshu	122606	118.7	63771	84.8
西 湖	Xihu	215783	112.2	80245	135.6
高新(滨江)区	Hi－Tech(Binjiang)	367219	115.8	109907	119.9
萧 山	Xiaoshan	946293	107.3	462637	95.3
余 杭	Yuhang	511946	108.7	43694	104.6
桐 庐	Tonglu	111626	115.7	7913	115.9
淳 安	Chun′an	17448	106.2	2244	40.0
建 德	Jiande	77733	102.4	9290	84.9
富 阳	Fuyang	120628	110.8	145159	125.9
临 安	Lin′an	133975	114.9	31120	107.8

9-11 自营出口企业前20位排名(2013年)

The List of Top Twenty Export Enterprises(2013)

单位:万美元 (USD 10000)

企业名称	Name of Enterprises	位次 Ranks	出口额 Export Value
东芝信息机器(杭州)有限公司	Toshiba Information Equipment (Hangzhou) Co., Ltd.	1	105569
中策橡胶集团有限公司	Zhongce Rubber Group Co. Ltd.	2	97706
杭州华三通信技术有限公司	H3C	3	69884
杭州巨星科技有限公司	Hangzhou Greatstar Indnserial Co., Ltd.	4	41106
杭州海康威视数字技术股份有限公司	Hangzhou Hikvision Digital Technology Co., Ltd.	5	32452
杭州市轻工工艺纺织品进出口有限公司	Hangzhou Hardicrafts and Textiles Import and Export Corporation	6	30674
浙江正泰太阳能科技有限公司	Zhejiang Astronergy Solar energy Technology Co., Ltd.	7	28390
博世电动工具(中国)有限公司	Bosch Power Tools(China) Co., Ltd	8	25976
杭州矢崎配件有限公司	HZ YAZAKI	9	25371
杭州余杭国际贸易有限公司	Hangzhou Yuhang International Trade Co., Ltd.	10	23792
杭州坤昂进出口贸易有限公司	Hangzhou Kunang Import & Enport Trade Co., Ltd.	11	23381
松下电化住宅设备机器(杭州)有限公司	Hangzhou Panasonic Home Appliances Washing Machine Co., Ltd.	12	21612
浙江恒逸石化有限公司	Zhejiang Hengyi Petrochemical Co., Ltd.	13	21388
杭州热联进出口股份有限公司	Hangzhou CIEC Group Co., Ltd.	14	21069
杭州鼎胜进出口有限公司	Hangzhou Dingsheng Import&export Co., Ltd.	15	20797
西子奥的斯电梯有限公司	XiZi Otis Elevator Co., Ltd.	16	20739
汇孚集团有限公司	Wellfull Group Co., Ltd.	17	20725
杭州松下家用电器有限公司	Hangzhou Panasonic Home Appliances Co., Ltd.	18	20517
浙江杭叉进出口有限公司	Zhejiang HC forklift Import&export Co., Ltd.	19	19759
杭州佩臻进出口有限公司	Hangzhou Peizhen Import & export Co., Ltd.	20	19419

9-12 外贸出口分国别(地区)情况

Export of Foreign Trade by Main Countries or Regions

单位:万美元 (USD 10000)

国别(地区)	Country (territory)	2013年 In Year 2013	2012年 In Year 2012	为上年(%) As Compared with the Preceding Year(%)
合　计	**Total**	**4476570**	**4126156**	**108.5**
#香港	#Hong Kong	84139	80476	104.6
台湾	Taiwan	46298	42366	109.3
德国	Germany	213213	211211	100.9
日本	Japan	366201	372995	98.2
美国	U.S.A	854871	798173	107.1
新加坡	Singapore	52873	47177	112.2
澳大利亚	Australia	97931	96145	101.9
泰国	Thailand	67169	59432	113.1
意大利	Italy	101203	104447	96.9
荷兰	Netherlands	143314	137129	104.5
西班牙	Spain	69644	61382	113.5
马来西亚	Malaysia	53966	42154	128.0
韩国	Republic of Korea	102385	93944	109.0
法国	France	90918	90771	100.2
比利时	Belgium	50202	49415	101.6
加拿大	Canada	82336	78791	104.5
英国	Britain	154802	145609	106.3
印度尼西亚	Indonesia	84586	78901	107.2
丹麦	Denmark	29605	27591	107.3
俄罗斯	Russia	120372	109118	110.3

9-13 旅游事业发展情况(1978-2013)
Development of Tourism(1978-2013)

年份 Year	旅游总收入(亿元) Total Tourism Revenue (100 million yuan)	国内旅游收入(亿元) Domestic Earnings (100 million yuan)	旅游外汇收入(亿美元) Foreign Exchange Earnings from International Tourism (USD 100 million)	旅游总人数(万人次) Total Tourists (10000 person-times)	国内游客人数(万人次) Domestic Tourists (10000 person-times)
1978			0.07		
1979			0.10		
1980			0.11		
1981			0.13		
1982			0.13		
1983			0.14		
1984			0.15		
1985			0.23		
1986			0.36		
1987			0.38		
1988			0.47		
1989			0.23		
1990			0.48		
1991			0.66		
1992			0.86		
1993			0.80		
1994			1.01		
1995	106.0	94.3	1.45	2148	2104
1996	136.5	122.6	1.67	2055	2009
1997	158.8	142.1	2.01	2150	2100
1998	163.4	146.0	2.10	2172	2121
1999	186.0	166.7	2.37	2266	2207
2000	214.3	190.0	2.92	2376	2305
2001	249.7	218.9	3.37	2592	2510
2002	294.4	254.8	4.77	2758	2652
2003	325.9	290.9	4.22	2862	2776
2004	410.1	361.2	5.97	3139	3016
2005	465.1	403.6	7.58	3417	3266
2006	543.7	471.2	9.09	3864	3682
2007	630.1	548.6	11.19	4320	4112
2008	707.2	617.2	12.96	4773	4552
2009	803.1	708.9	13.80	5324	5094
2010	1025.7	910.9	16.90	6581	6305
2011	1191.0	1063.8	19.60	7487	7181
2012	1392.3	1253.2	22.02	8568	8237
2013	1603.7	1469.9	21.60	9725	9409

9-14 境外旅游者人数(1978-2013)
Number of International Tourists (1978-2013)

单位:人次 (person-times)

年份 Year	合计 Total	外国人 Foreigners	华侨 Overseas Chinese	港澳台同胞 Compatriots from Hong Kong, Macao and Taiwan	平均逗留天数 Average days of Staying
1978	53475	728	728	26648	
1979	84914	44714	1069	39131	2.59
1980	124960	61710	1868	61382	2.70
1981	154745	87727	2004	65014	2.71
1982	152897	89100	2483	61314	2.49
1983	160564	97803	3136	59625	2.18
1984	179200	105771	2514	70915	2.12
1985	238385	156311	7011	75063	2.18
1986	266370	170960	8318	87092	2.38
1987	300603	183477	17048	100078	2.38
1988	349246	149512	39989	159745	2.08
1989	248502	66094	18819	163589	2.08
1990	388345	86621	33593	268131	2.09
1991	390197	136809	23698	229690	2.00
1992	489578	183781	38541	267256	2.03
1993	459620	199796	25184	234640	2.06
1994	337362	201692	11324	124346	2.10
1995	441262	249418	14608	177236	2.06
1996	462313	273477	9991	178845	2.07
1997	504276	288949	10060	205267	2.20
1998	507243	261353	14281	231609	2.20
1999	591853	324625	9250	257978	2.09
2000	707148	400906	-	306242	2.15
2001	819438	447689	-	371749	2.41
2002	1056266	631576	-	424690	2.50
2003	861163	482073	-	379090	2.72
2004	1234063	791616	-	442447	2.59
2005	1513585	1020840	-	492745	2.63
2006	1820171	1236792	-	583379	2.57
2007	2085997	1453650	-	632347	2.67
2008	2213329	1543665	-	669654	2.73
2009	2304045	1572838	-	731207	2.87
2010	2757147	1878528	-	878619	2.94
2011	3063140	2108263	-	954877	2.96
2012	3311225	2298763	-	1012462	2.95
2013	3160058	2198187	-	961871	2.93

注:从1995年起为全市数。

a) Data in this table has included the tourists of whole municipality since 1995.

9－15 接待境外游客及旅游外汇收入情况

Number of International Tourists and Foreign Exchange Earnings

项 目	Item	2013 年 In Year 2013	2012 年 In Year 2012	为上年(％) As Compared with the preceding year(％)
全年接待人数总计(人)	**Number of Foreign Tourists(person)**	**3160058**	**3311225**	**95.4**
#外国人	#Foreigners	2198187	2298763	95.6
港澳台同胞	Compatriots From Hong Kong, Macao and Taiwan	961871	1012462	95.0
全年接待人天数(人天)	**Total Person－days (person－days)**	**9263534**	**9764710**	**94.9**
#外国人	#Foreigners	6649138	6943834	95.8
港澳台同胞	Compatriots From Hong Kong, Macao and Taiwan	2614405	2820876	92.7
平均逗留天数(天)	**Average Days of Staying (days)**	**2.93**	**2.95**	**99.3**
#外国人	#Foreigners	3.02	3.02	100.0
港澳台同胞	Compatriots From Hong Kong, Macao and Taiwan	2.72	2.79	97.5
旅游外汇总收入(万美元)	**Total Foreign Exchange Earnings From International Tourism (USD 10000)**	**216048**	**220165**	**98.1**

9－16 接待境外游客分国别(地区)情况

Number of International Tourists by Country or Territory

单位:人次 (person－times)

国　别（地区）	Country（territory）	2013 年 In Year 2013	2012 年 In Year 2012	为上年(%) As Compared with the Preceding Year(%)
合　计	**Total**	**3160058**	**3311225**	**95.4**
#香港	#Hong Kong	361536	386462	93.6
澳门	Macao	49528	42511	116.5
台湾	Taiwan	550807	585309	94.1
日本	Japan	242954	309463	78.5
美国	U. S. A	210636	213726	98.6
新加坡	Singapore	85572	83452	102.5
澳大利亚	Australia	40397	42445	95.2
泰国	Thailand	80799	78535	102.9
意大利	Italy	26414	26730	98.8
荷兰	Netherlands	23278	24447	95.2
西班牙	Spain	21546	23584	91.4
马来西亚	Malaysia	102574	105283	97.4
韩国	Republic of Korea	538814	543052	99.2
法国	France	52263	51625	101.2
德国	Germany	68124	66284	102.8
加拿大	Canada	39941	40562	98.5
英国	Britain	53545	52522	101.9
印度尼西亚	Indonesia	29113	27347	106.5
印度	India	27353	28937	94.5
菲律宾	Filipine	11369	12013	94.6

主要统计指标解释

外商直接投资 是指外国企业和经济组织或个人(包括华侨、港澳台胞以及我国在境外注册的企业)按我国有关政策、法规,用现汇、实物、技术等在我国境内开办外商独资企业、与我国境内的企业或经济组织共同举办中外合资经营企业、合作经营企业或者合作开发资源的投资(包括外商投资收益的再投资)以及经政府有关部门批准的项目投资总额内,企业从境外借入的资金。

进出口总额 海关进出口总额指实际进出我国国境的货物总金额。包括对外贸易实际进出口货物,来料加工装配进出口货物,国家间、联合国及国际组织无偿援助物资和赠送品,华侨、港澳台同胞和外籍华人捐赠品,租赁期满归承租人所有的租赁货物,进料加工进出口货物,边境地方贸易及边境地区小额贸易进出口货物(边民互市贸易除外),中外合资经营企业、中外合作经营企业、外商独资经营企业进出口货物和公用物品,到、离岸价格在规定限额以上的进出口货样和广告品(无商业价值、无使用价值和免费提供出口的除外),从保税仓库提取在中国境内销售的进口货物,以及其他进出口货物。进出口总额以观察一个国家在对外贸易方面的总规模。我国规定出口货物按离岸价格统计,进口货物按到岸价格统计。

境外旅游人数 指来我国参观、访问、旅行、探亲、访友、休养、考察、参加会议和从事经济、科技、文化、教育、体育、宗教等活动的外国人、华侨、港澳和台湾同胞的人数。不包括外国在我国的常驻机构,如使领馆、通讯社、企业办事处的工作人员;来我国常住的外国专家、留学生以及在岸逗留不过夜人员。

境外旅游(外汇)收入 指入境旅游的外国人、华侨、港澳台同胞在中国大陆旅游过程中发生的一切旅游支出,对国家来说就是境外旅游(外汇)收入。

Explanatory Notes on Main Statistical Indicators

Direct Investment by Foreign Entrepreneurs refers to the investments inside China by foreign enterprises and economic organizations or individuals (including overseas Chinese, compatriots from Hong Kong, Macao and Taiwan, and Chinese enterprises registered abroad) , following the relevant policies and laws of China, for the establishment of ventures exclusively with foreign own investment, Sino – foreign joint ventures and cooperative enterprises or for co – operative exploration of resources with enterprises or economic organizations in China. It includes the re – investment of the foreign entrepreneurs with the profits gained from the investment and the funds that enterprises borrow from abroad in the total investment of projects which are approved by the relevant department of the government.

Total Imports and Exports at Customs refer to the value of commodities imported into and exported from the boundary of China. They include the actual imports and exports through foreign trade, imported and exported goods under the processing and assembling trades and materials, supplies and gifts as aid given gratis between governments and by the United Nations and other international organizations, and contributions donated by overseas Chinese, compatriots in Hong Kong, Macao and Chinese foreign citizenship, leasing commodities owned by tenant at the expiration of leasing period, the imported and exported commodities processed with imported materials, commodities trading in border areas (excluding mutual exchange goods) , the imported and exported commodities and articles for public use of the Sino – foreign joint ventures, cooperative enterprises and ventures exclusively with foreign own investment. Also included are import or export of samples and advertising goods for whose CIF or FOB value are beyond the permitted ceiling (excluding goods of no trading or use value and free commodities for export) , imported goods sold in China from bonded warehouses and other imported or exported goods. The indicator of the total imports and exports at customs can be used to observe the total size of external trade in a country. In accordance with the stipulation of Chinese government, imports are calculated at CIF, while exports are calculated at FOB.

International Tourists refer to foreigners, overseas Chinese compatriots from Hong Kong, Macao and Taiwan coming to China for sightseeing, visits, tours, family reunions, vacations, study tours, conferences and other activities of a business, scientific and technological, cultural, educational and religious nature. It does not include representatives and employees of resident institutions of foreign countries in China such as embassies, consulates, news agencies and offices of foreign companies and organizations, nor does it include long – term foreign experts or students residing in China, or persons in transition without spending a night in China.

Foreign Exchange Earnings from International Tourism refer to the total expenditures of foreigners, overseas Chinese, Chinese compatriots from Hong Kong, Macao and Taiwan during their stay in the mainland of China, which are earnings of foreign exchange form international tourism from the point of vies from China.

十、财政、金融、保险

X.FINANCE, BANKING AND INSURANCE

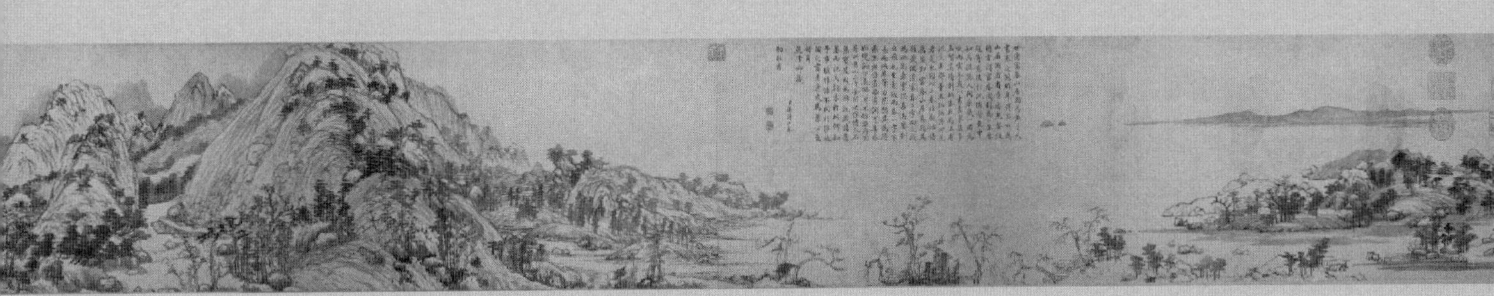

10 财政、金融、保险
Finance, Banking and Insurance

主要统计指标
Major Statistical Indicators

全市财政总收入	Total Financial Revenue	1734.98	亿元	(100 million yuan)
为上年	As Compared with the Preceding Year	106.6	%	(%)
地方公共财政预算收入	Public Financial Budgetary Revenue of Local Government	945.20	亿元	(100 million yuan)
为上年	As Compared with the Preceding Year	109.9	%	(%)
公共财政预算支出	Public Financial Budgetary Expenditure of Local Government	855.74	亿元	(100 million yuan)
为上年	As Compared with the Preceding Year	108.8	%	(%)
年末金融机构各项存款余额	Balance of Deposits of Financial Institutions at Year-end	22174.71	亿元	(100 million yuan)
为上年	As Compared with the Preceding Year	110.1	%	(%)
#城乡居民储蓄存款余额	Balance of Savings Deposits of Rural and Urban Residents at Year-end	6408.59	亿元	(100 million yuan)
为上年	As Compared with the Preceding Year	105.2	%	(%)
年末金融机构各项贷款余额	Balance of Loans of Financial Institutions at Year-end	19350.46	亿元	(100 million yuan)
为上年	As Compared with the Preceding Year	107.0	%	(%)

10-01 财政收入及支出(1978-2013)

Financial Revenue and Expenditure (1978-2013)

单位:万元 (10000 yuan)

年份 Year	财政总收入 Financial Revenue		地方公共财政预算收入 Public Financial Budgetary Revenue of Local Government		公共财政预算支出 Public Financial Budgetary Expenditure of Local Government	
	全市 Total	市区 Urban District	全市 Total	市区 Urban District	全市 Total	市区 Urban District
1978	94102	73396	-	-	16170	7779
1979	103259	81885	-	-	20334	11289
1980	118529	94015	-	-	21726	11867
1981	128564	100645	-	-	23964	13891
1982	140510	107298	-	-	24945	13687
1983	153941	116559	-	-	32765	17822
1984	172996	130757	-	-	46937	28710
1985	186472	131923	-	-	57710	35435
1986	205952	141943	-	-	73213	43959
1987	226262	152268	-	-	70717	41011
1988	246961	161208	-	-	95655	53031
1989	255003	156649	-	-	113571	61534
1990	252503	149904	-	-	118167	62587
1991	267597	158130	-	-	123134	62403
1992	286394	168341	-	-	132814	65984
1993	394946	233670	-	-	185168	90545
1994	484597	300014	197292	116733	215415	102430
1995	551262	339828	230431	135041	249050	120084
1996	635334	414557	268438	169987	302390	151016
1997	740725	485650	312797	196885	363834	197054
1998	869824	585615	368484	236269	424478	237221
1999	1026577	689394	449593	288002	563524	335243
2000	1428519	970937	691891	599910	734328	445698
2001	1884608	1612225	1042789	884738	1049330	849479
2002	2571408	2235021	1183153	1022964	1410199	1166298
2003	3297091	2861459	1503888	1290778	1635948	1340463
2004	3957516	3488744	1974523	1712813	1956282	1602303
2005	5207930	4584112	2504565	2172575	2383344	1957619
2006	6244906	5484645	3013888	2616084	2754809	2254347
2007	7884237	6929667	3916195	3421403	3357153	2747060
2008	9105489	7991043	4553531	3972842	4196674	3454599
2009	10194264	8965758	5207899	4535191	4903983	4000324
2010	12454323	10988265	6713413	5894414	6165836	4988197
2011	14889206	13009046	7851524	6822765	7475004	5971740
2012	16278879	14244888	8599875	7475989	7862800	6222930
2013	17349750	15157584	9452020	8207264	8557370	6662314

注:从2001年起市区数据包括萧山区和余杭区。

a) Data of urban district include Xiaoshan and Yuhang district since 2001.

10－02 分地区财政
Local Financial

单位:万元

指标	Item	全市 Total	市区 Urban District	#上城区 Shangcheng
财政总收入合计	**Total**	**17349750**	**15157584**	**905891**
一、地方公共财政预算收入	Public Financial Budgetary Revenue of Local Government	9452020	8207264	574322
(一)税收收入	Tax Revenue	9106690	7944744	558540
1. 国内增值税25%部分	25% of Domestic Value－added Tax	1122297	911972	34718
2. 改征增值税	Newly Changed Value－added Tax	593744	553604	26502
3. 营业税	Business Tax	2670660	2357668	261628
4. 企业所得税40%部分	40% of Corporate Income Tax	1518112	1366788	91526
5. 企业所得税退税	Corporate Income Tax Rebates	–	–	–
6. 个人所得税40%部分	40% of Individual Income Tax	573227	518965	58444
7. 城市维护建设税	City Construction and Maintenance Tax	658593	587543	31082
8. 耕地占用税	Tax on the Use of Arable Land	91622	58932	–
9. 契税	Contract Tax	674188	587742	–
10. 房产税	Real Estate Tax	323897	277891	31576
11. 其他税收	Others Tax	880350	723639	23064
(二)非税收入	Non－tax Revenue	345330	262520	15782
1. 专项收入	Special Revenue	267287	223547	11319
#教育费附加	Revenue from Extra－Charges for Education	249108	214589	11319
排污费	Revenue for Permitting Pollution	16385	8958	–
2. 行政事业性收费收入	Income from Administrative Fees	19738	9144	–
3. 罚没收入	Penalty and Confiscatory Income	148738	107687	4408
4. 国有资本经营收入	Seate－owned Assets Profits	－105699	－90499	–
#国有计划亏损补贴	Subsides to Loss－making of state－owned Enterprises	－105699	－90499	–
5. 国有资源(资产)有偿使用收入	Compensation for the Use of Seate－owned Assets Income	14314	11689	55
6. 其他收入	Others Revenue	952	952	–
二、上划中央二税小计	Subtotal Revenue of Central Government	4760717	4121686	106614
1. 消费税	Consumption Tax	1393824	1385769	2460
2. 国内增值税75%部分	75% of Domestic Value－added Tax	3366893	2735917	104154
三、中央所得税收入小计	Subtotal of Central Government Income Tax	3137013	2828634	224955
1. 企业所得税60%部分	60% of Corporate Income Tax	2277170	2050184	137289
2. 个人所得税60%部分	60% of Individual Income Tax	859843	778450	87666

总收入(2013 年)
Revenue by Region(2013)

(10000 yuan)

下城区 Xiacheng	江干区 Jianggan	拱墅区 Gongshu	西湖区 Xihu	滨江区 Hi－Tech (Binjiang)	萧山区 Xiaoshan	余杭区 Yuhang	桐庐县 Tonglu	淳安县 Chun'an	建德市 Jiande	富阳市 Fuyang	临安市 Lin'an
1247933	**964139**	**928274**	**1328715**	**1404962**	**2290096**	**2001035**	**374412**	**191999**	**307214**	**832116**	**486425**
774960	579681	554868	817772	753969	1265178	1261038	221378	125465	173139	463611	261163
755854	564457	537992	794327	731389	1210989	1219006	201235	115462	164910	430445	249894
64614	57515	74947	65051	83107	206958	121029	34797	11022	27703	82814	53989
54837	24203	32101	88887	101151	34262	173942	12662	3615	5121	14804	3938
282892	210250	201359	278018	143363	331463	360655	53608	48995	36344	103728	70317
114688	119704	74047	141564	151430	177847	172368	23557	14847	23212	60774	28934
–	–	–	–	–	–	–	–	–	–	–	–
67321	20802	24734	68411	116347	54870	75015	8797	4788	8720	18805	13152
43196	34152	39744	45703	58465	94207	80730	9602	5493	10308	25643	20004
–	–	–	–	–	42802	6007	7441	601	11274	10745	2629
–	–	–	–	–	79508	74409	12404	11300	13124	32003	17615
34890	24376	20195	39018	25474	52982	24188	8677	4403	6119	18385	8422
93416	73455	70865	67675	52052	136090	130663	29690	10398	22985	62744	30894
19106	15224	16876	23445	22580	54189	42032	20143	10003	8229	33166	11269
15726	12437	15098	16620	21287	38854	30145	6214	3609	6139	18590	9188
15726	12437	15098	16620	21287	35527	28463	5365	2997	4626	13388	8143
–	–	–	–	–	3327	1682	494	128	802	4958	1045
600	800	–	3447	–	–	–	1227	765	1224	4850	2528
2548	1742	1516	3191	1156	21003	17015	12531	5562	5394	11069	6495
–	–	–	–	–	－7099	－7000	–	–	－4700	－3000	－7500
–	–	–	–	–	－7099	－7000	–	–	－4700	－3000	－7500
232	245	262	187	137	1416	1872	171	67	172	1657	558
–	–	–	–	–	15	–	–	–	–	–	–
199959	173699	225234	195980	249327	675842	368922	104504	37081	86177	249136	162133
6117	1154	393	827	6	54967	5835	113	4014	3068	694	166
193842	172545	224841	195153	249321	620875	363087	104391	33067	83109	248442	161967
273014	210759	148172	314963	401666	349076	371075	48530	29453	47898	119369	63129
172032	179556	111071	212346	227145	266771	258552	35335	22271	34818	91161	43401
100982	31203	37101	102617	174521	82305	112523	13195	7182	13080	28208	19728

10－03 分地区公共

Local Public Financial Budgetary

单位:万元

指标	Item	全市 Total	市区 Urban District	#上城区 Shangcheng
公共财政预算支出	**Public Financial Budgetary Expenditure of Local Government**	**8557370**	**6662314**	**211909**
一、一般公共服务	Expenditure for General Public Services	915881	712903	22149
二、国防	Expenditure for National Defense	9313	7695	25
三、公共安全	Expenditure for Public Security	554377	455440	21078
四、教育	Expenditure for Education	1624445	1152076	53385
#教育费附加支出	Expenditure on Extra－Charges for Educations	213339	172784	8910
五、科学技术	Expenditure for Science and Technology	462600	385361	9516
六、文化体育与传媒	Expenditure for Culture, Sports and Media	223604	187085	1600
七、社会保障和就业	Expenditure for Social Safety Net and Employment Effort	946033	767454	39072
八、医疗卫生	Expenditure for Medical and Health Care	621518	459318	10913
九、节能环保	Expenditure for Energy Conservation Environmental Protection	197392	119226	4409
#排污费支出	Sewage Expenses	14180	9208	－
十、城乡社区事务	Expenditure for Urban and Rural Community Affairs	1064358	988104	30366
十一、农林水事务	Expenditure for Agriculture, Forestry and water Conservancy	506246	254213	80
十二、交通运输	Expenditure for Trarssportation	305919	173377	
十三、资源勘探电力信息等事务	Resources exploration eletricity information, etc	447523	404843	7300
十四、商业服务业等事务	Cornmercial and service business, etc	191742	167258	6273
十五、金融监管支出	Expenditure for Financial Supervision	16334	15674	735
十六、地震灾后恢复重建支出	Expenditure for Post－earthquake Recorery and Reconstruction	－	－	－
十七、援助其他地区支出	Expenditure for Aiding Other Territories	33881	29679	1114
十八、国土资源气象等事务	Land resources, meteorological services, etc	36340	25628	499
十九、住房保障支出	Expenditure on housing support	77290	47407	364
二十、粮油物资储备事务	Expenditure for Grrain and Ovl Reservation and other Materials Services	7924	4278	－
二十一、国债还本付息支出	Repayment and Interest payment of National Debt Expenditures	3700	1457	－
二十二、其他支出	Other Expenditure	310950	303838	3031

财政预算支出(2013 年)
Expenditure by Region(2013)

(10000 yuan)

下城区 Xiacheng	江干区 Jianggan	拱墅区 Gongshu	西湖区 Xihu	滨江区 Hi－Tech (Binjiang)	萧山区 Xiaoshan	余杭区 Yuhang	桐庐县 Tonglu	淳安县 Chun'an	建德市 Jiande	富阳市 Fuyang	临安市 Lin'an
227890	**345205**	**250037**	**407254**	**523109**	**1158080**	**1115000**	**299734**	**375928**	**274346**	**526852**	**418196**
25136	35713	38310	48623	24585	122877	132748	30911	45940	30350	51260	44517
445	–	102	778	23	2468	1696	379	151	500	33	555
19622	24876	23166	35940	13355	60021	55097	18268	16861	14040	28426	21342
50123	62943	49663	87056	62820	265950	234910	69480	74528	69668	158292	100401
9317	10027	10156	16240	21396	33401	29227	5480	3527	4315	18946	8287
11106	21667	9934	13599	50647	40595	54045	11625	7708	13513	23932	20461
6626	4901	3748	6851	12826	18594	21636	6636	5768	4854	11567	7694
32395	36058	29173	51116	49991	102878	113977	35559	28544	23381	53390	37705
12877	16857	13135	23206	15226	105643	82972	29271	36511	23316	37043	36059
1103	251	724	115	6780	39511	27773	9569	14631	11871	20738	21357
–	–	–	–	–	3323	1936	150	361	945	2696	820
40929	62217	60589	72756	158148	160645	137859	16387	8654	10992	24278	15943
24	7359	952	12009	10999	82100	75636	45080	44988	43938	69973	48054
–	27	100	63	50	44524	19929	13166	61430	12433	15212	30301
3378	2498	4310	11151	95314	73637	54569	1587	6394	3120	14344	17235
15623	3009	4662	10240	12745	12726	77837	3343	4396	3700	6502	6543
3018	3054	–	2776	1353	250	150	123	–	12	73	452
–	–	–	–	–	–	–	–	–	–	–	–
1379	1771	986	2105	2484	5385	4717	671	–	733	1825	973
387	219	684	2091	714	3789	5984	878	1242	2101	2921	3570
3719	762	2088	1872	4059	11429	3477	4693	11613	3533	6833	3211
–	–	–	–	–	–	163	1061	1515	240	210	620
–	–	–	–	–	–	1457	1032	24	–	–	1187
–	61023	7711	24907	990	5058	8368	15	5030	2051	–	16

10－04 全市金融机构存、贷款余额(1978－2013)
Balance of Deposits and Loans of Financial Institutions (1978－2013)

单位:万元 (10000 yuan)

年份 Year \ 项目 Item	各项存款 Deposits	#城乡储蓄存款 Savings Deposits Of Urban and Rural Residents	#城镇储蓄存款 Savings Deposits of Urban Residents	各项贷款 Loans
1978	86824	20714	17056	136759
1979	108998	28937	22640	135713
1980	180707	40447	30896	174153
1981	226949	51440	38889	236678
1982	262156	67192	50113	216040
1983	303130	86635	64736	236203
1984	388305	115766	85439	329195
1985	484999	159596	115592	580180
1986	635514	222110	153572	769841
1987	776105	302762	207505	967477
1988	839680	351943	241839	1145989
1989	1017087	501592	346318	1338984
1990	1646165	697515	479031	1803266
1991	2036334	904490	616308	2136903
1992	2652966	1144737	763309	2651983
1993	3469954	1563328	1048413	3415527
1994	5061345	2394370	1642498	4450932
1995	7079650	3423379	2448787	5672105
1996	9619291	4638458	3459439	7434243
1997	12251840	5583306	4229591	9388500
1998	14948225	6701158	5155548	11620537
1999	17886717	7425967	5760527	14937506
2000	20884723	7885579	6151084	16866431
2001	26215100	9418400	7396800	20877000
2002	33731500	11834000	9492300	27523800
2003	46527300	15899600	13079600	38187000
2004	57072000	18351700	15016100	48000400
2005	67487200	21916600	17960100	55453000
2006	78555500	25552400	20789600	66038600
2007	93109600	26348300	21154300	84306800
2008	113333500	34765900	27584600	100690500
2009	142842104	42869189	34027871	131133023
2010	170843548	49909744	39352353	150787269
2011	183965719	55474824	43464332	165737441
2012	201487672	60899841	46965391	180908011
2013	221747107	64085856	47733077	193504605

注:1989 年以前数据均为银行机构存贷款,1990 年及以后年份数据为调整后金融机构存贷款。2003 年起金融机构存贷款为本外币合并数据。

a) Data before 1989 belonged to banking system, data after 1990 adjusted for deposits and loans of financial institutions, data of 2003 included both RMB and foreign currency.

10-05 市区金融机构存、贷款余额(1978-2013)

Balance of Deposits and Loans of Financial Institutions of Urban District(1978-2013)

单位:万元 (10000 yuan)

年份 Year \ 项目 Item	各项存款 Deposits	#城乡储蓄存款 Savings Deposits of Urban and Rural Residents	#城镇储蓄存款 Savings Deposits of Urban Residents	各项贷款 Loans
1978	58372	13774	13246	101144
1979	73720	18055	17241	98792
1980	134275	24702	23282	121231
1981	172721	31358	29345	170539
1982	198350	39756	37047	142091
1983	226160	50439	46833	155297
1984	293145	66108	61934	194977
1985	359825	89114	82868	418214
1986	458142	115818	106703	557763
1987	565429	156704	142642	714313
1988	610601	180341	163466	846998
1989	737388	256238	229518	1000731
1990	1062574	354316	297390	1271779
1991	1309462	451756	397322	1469671
1992	1695011	572660	479248	1774158
1993	2263969	762234	662234	2298124
1994	3383877	1242379	1085363	3033010
1995	4851774	1853512	1639875	3907199
1996	6828786	2734904	2371657	5350499
1997	8831147	3287475	2873638	6772221
1998	10785066	3905602	3440607	8615412
1999	13051806	4336058	3835542	11462505
2000	15436286	4620235	4101716	13105849
2001	23765400	7976400	6460200	19237800
2002	30638400	10139800	8370100	25476700
2003	42522000	13834200	11693000	30297500
2004	52542100	16014700	13479900	44517600
2005	62249500	19231800	16208400	51455900
2006	72269600	22391800	18737800	61190700
2007	86197300	23124600	19132300	78456200
2008	104930100	30665200	24996500	93838100
2009	131800234	37837816	30801878	121473548
2010	156776515	43676938	35370599	138671334
2011	168052916	48263525	38996516	151756838
2012	183719227	52347969	41789531	156426086
2013	201596137	54488059	42142666	175670366

注:1989 年以前数据均为银行机构存贷款,1990 年及以后年份数据为调整后金融机构存贷款。2003 年起金融机构存贷款为本外币合并数据。

a) Data before 1989 belonged to banking system, data after 1990 adjusted for deposits and loans of financial institutions. data of 2003 included both RMB and foreign currency.

10－06 金融机构

Balance of Deposits and

单位:万元

指　标	Item	全市 Total 2013年末 At the End of Year 2013	全市 Total 为上年(%) As Compared with the Preceding Year(%)	市区 Urban District 2013年末 At the End of Year 2013	市区 Urban District 为上年(%) As Compared with the Preceding Year(%)
一、各项存款	**Deposits**	**221747107**	**110.1**	**201596137**	**109.7**
1.单位存款	Deposits of Enterprises	138848449	109.8	128982071	109.6
(1)活期存款	Current Deposits	37381774	102.2	33261134	101.8
(2)定期存款	Fixed Deposits	54783641	110.8	51592662	110.3
(3)通知存款	Deposits at Notice	4400073	92.0	4189604	91.9
(4)保证金存款	Margin Deposits	16204541	101.4	14966231	100.9
2.个人存款	Personal Deposits	68234173	108.8	58450564	108.0
(1)储蓄存款	Savings Deposits	64085856	105.2	54488059	104.1
活期储蓄	Current Deposits	24567812	103.3	20601621	102.5
定期储蓄	Fixed Deposits	39518043	106.5	33886437	105.1
(2)保证金存款	Margin Deposits	98670	99.4	96803	99.0
(2)结构性存款	Structured Deposits	4049648	232.7	3865703	233.4
3.财政性存款	Treasury Deposits	6193981	129.3	5895948	128.0
4.临时性存款	Temporary Deposits	613216	84.5	565490	80.4
5.委托存款	Entrusting Deposits	1289047	198.9	1249923	199.6
6.其他存款	Other Deposits	6568241	107.0	6452142	106.9
二、各项贷款	**Loans**	**193504605**	**107.0**	**175670366**	**106.4**
1.境内贷款	Domestic Loans	192134527	106.9	174300489	106.4
(1)短期贷款	Short－term Loans	90693502	103.7	79488032	102.5
(2)中长期贷款	Medium and Long term Loans	91459085	110.6	85247392	110.5
(3)融资租赁	Finance lease	4846187	116.3	4846187	116.3
(4)票据融资	Note Financing	4411464	98.2	4076447	96.2
(5)各项垫款	Advance Money	724289	88.4	642431	87.1
2.境外贷款	Foreign Loans	1370078	111.7	1369877	111.7

本外币存、贷款余额(2013 年)

Loans of Financial Institutions(2013)

(10000 yuan)

		桐庐县 Tonglu	淳安县 Chun'an	建德市 Jiande	富阳市 Fuyang	临安市 Lin'an
#萧山区 Xiaoshan	#余杭区 Yuhang					
30041865	**16875414**	**3151298**	**2359631**	**2703501**	**7924166**	**4012374**
17661382	8831099	1339817	1182987	971289	4442197	1930089
4820155	3377170	639070	520047	554377	1469214	937932
6849733	2887771	389057	511491	201203	1601996	487232
205732	156041	54588	4052	46348	53104	52378
3577884	1021092	98928	24815	64669	851365	198533
11461232	7429065	1628604	1156025	1670381	3318079	2010520
11185654	7242446	1596118	1134228	1640473	3252658	1974320
3536059	2343656	637353	493076	624782	1264525	946455
7649595	4898790	958765	641152	1015691	1988133	1027865
2747	3721	15	9	45	402	1395
272832	182897	32471	21788	29863	65018	34805
233250	410201	153868	13011	41436	57761	31958
51769	58961	27842	3201	2386	7490	6808
189319	70012	-3483	1	5000	37606	-
444913	76075	4652	4406	13009	61034	32999
26590949	**12183499**	**2593331**	**1763124**	**2258505**	**7870347**	**3348931**
26589513	12181275	2593217	1763124	2258432	7870347	3348918
20221034	6729248	1393278	765672	1229421	5725490	2091609
5899919	4936639	1184642	989522	928791	1866369	1242369
411986	496489	12958	7930	35284	267679	11166
56573	18899	2339	-	64936	10809	3774
1436	2224	114	-	74	-	13

10－07 金融机构人民币

Balance of RMB Deposits, RMB Loans

单位:万元

指 标	Item	全市 Total 2013 年	全市 Total 为上年(%) As Compared with the Preceding Year(%)	市区 Urban District 2013 年	市区 Urban District 为上年(%) As Compared with the Preceding Year(%)
一、各项存款	**Deposits**	**217490498**	**111.0**	**197477421**	**110.7**
1. 单位存款	Deposits of Enterprises	135526757	111.2	125771320	111.1
(1)活期存款	Current Deposits	35925637	103.6	31907092	103.2
(2)定期存款	Fixed Deposits	53840109	111.7	50649989	111.2
(3)通知存款	Deposits at Notice	4321244	91.1	4114433	91.1
(4)保证金存款	Margin Deposits	15452815	105.6	14218833	105.3
2. 个人存款	Personal Deposits	67503214	108.8	57745581	108.1
(1)储蓄存款	Savings Deposits	63397531	105.3	53825452	104.1
(2)保证金存款	Margin Deposits	95445	98.7	93597	98.4
(3)结构性存款	Structured Deposits	4010237	235.2	3826532	236.0
3. 财政性存款	Treasury Deposits	6193979	129.3	5895946	128.0
4. 临时性存款	Temporan Deposits	431730	70.4	384979	65.1
5. 委托存款	Entrusting Deposits	1285694	199.2	1246571	199.8
6. 其他存款	Other Deposits	6549123	107.4	6433024	107.3
二、各项贷款	**Loans**	**183995295**	**106.9**	**166365913**	**106.4**
1. 境内贷款	Domestic Loans	183927063	106.9	166297881	106.4
(1)短期贷款	Short－term Loans	85564212	103.9	74519863	102.8
(2)中长期贷款	Medium and Long term Loans	88496453	110.1	82304112	110.0
(3)融资租赁	Finance lease	4846187	116.3	4846187	116.3
(4)票据融资	Note Financing	4410751	98.2	4075734	96.2
(5)各项垫款	Advance Money	609460	91.5	551984	90.5
2. 境外贷款	Foreign Loans	68232	90.3	68031	90.3

存、贷款余额(2013 年)

of Financial Institutions(2013)

(10000 yuan)

#萧山区 Xiaoshan	#余杭区 Yuhang	桐庐县 Tonglu	淳安县 Chun'an	建德市 Jiande	富阳市 Fuyang	临安市 Lin'an
29596713	**16533811**	**3116523**	**2354026**	**2690276**	**7894145**	**3958106**
17262952	8545864	1310725	1180721	962758	4420628	1880605
4643302	3246715	610223	518640	545881	1448671	895129
6767418	2785940	389057	510631	201203	1601996	487232
191709	156041	54588	4052	46348	53104	48720
3452646	968265	98683	24815	64632	850339	195511
11420104	7413325	1623356	1152692	1665845	3309805	2005935
11146176	7226951	1590933	1130895	1635973	3244542	1969737
2602	3720	15	9	38	392	1393
271327	182654	32407	21788	29834	64871	34805
233250	410201	153868	13011	41436	57761	31958
46186	18334	27406	3195	2229	7311	6609
189309	70012	-3483	1	5000	37606	-
444913	76075	4652	4406	13009	61034	32999
25530709	**11913688**	**2586200**	**1762099**	**2217503**	**7782881**	**3280700**
25529273	11911464	2586086	1762099	2217430	7782881	3280687
19196844	6470279	1386146	764647	1216483	5653694	2023378
5865418	4925852	1184642	989522	925109	1850698	1242369
411986	496434	12958	7930	35284	267679	11166
55025	18899	2339	-	40554	10809	3774
1436	2224	114	-	74	-	13

10－08 城乡居民储蓄存款余额(2013 年)

Balance of Savings Deposits of Rural and Urban Residents(2013)

单位:万元 (10000 yuan)

地区 Region	总计 Total		城镇居民 Urban Residents		农村居民 Rural Residents	
	2013 年末 At the End of Year 2013	为上年(%) As Compared with the Preceding Year(%)	2013 年末 At the End of Year 2013	为上年(%) As Compared with the Preceding Year(%)	2013 年末 At the End of Year 2013	为上年(%) As Compared with the Preceding Year(%)
全 市 Total	**64085856**	**105.2**	**47733077**	**101.6**	**16352779**	**117.4**
市 区 Urban District	54488059	104.1	42142666	100.8	12345393	116.9
#萧山区 Xiaoshan	11185654	110.8	6404869	107.1	4780785	116.3
余杭区 Yuhang	7242446	115.6	3996540	109.2	3245907	124.7
桐庐县 Tonglu	1596118	115.1	940941	109.9	655176	123.4
淳安县 Chun'an	1134228	116.4	629163	112.8	505065	121.2
建德市 Jiande	1640473	110.7	1070307	104.9	570166	123.4
富阳市 Fuyang	3252658	111.9	1829873	110.5	1422785	113.7
临安市 Lin'an	1974320	109.7	1120126	103.2	854194	119.5

10－09　保险业务情况(2013 年)

Development of Insurance Business(2013)

单位:万元　　(10000 yuan)

指　标	Item	保险费收入 Premium	赔付金额 Indemnity Expenditure
全市总计	**Total**	**2792291**	**1023955**
为上年%	As Compared with the Preceding Year = 100(%)	112.6	119.9
一、财产保险	Property Insurance	1268727	778746
企业财产险	Enterprise Property Insurance	90526	58570
家庭财产险	Family Property Insurance	5172	829
机动车辆险	Transportation Equipment Insurance	969903	619381
工程险	Project Insurance	11551	2344
责任险	Responsibilihty Insurance	25969	13418
信用险	Export Credit Insurance	104133	52898
保证险	Guarantee Insurance	17809	5339
船舶险	Shipping Insurance	6638	3240
货运险	Cargo Insurance	18205	13836
特殊风险保险	Special Pisks Insurance	5053	1724
农业保险	Agriculture Insurance	12369	6571
其他险	Other	1400	595
二、人身险	Personal Insurance	1523563	245209
寿险	Life Insurance	1279158	181889
意外伤害险	Accidental Insurance	71238	13337
健康险	Health Insurance	173167	49983

主要统计指标解释

财政收入 包括:(1)各项税收。主要有增值税、营业税、土地增值税、城市维护建设税、资源税、城市土地使用税、印花税、个人所得税、企业所得税、关税和耕地占用税等。

(2)专项收入包括征收排污费、征收城市水资源费收入,教育费附加收入等。

存款 企业、机关、团体或居民根据可以收回的原则,把货币资金存入银行或其他信用机构保管并取得一定利息的一种信用活动形式。根据存款对象的不同可划分为企业存款、财政存款、机关团体存款、基本建设存款、城镇储蓄存款、农村存款等科目。它是银行信贷资金的主要来源。

贷款 银行或其他信用机构根据必须归还的原则,按一定利率,为企业、个人等提供资金的一种信用活动形式。我国银行贷款分为流动资金贷款、固定资产贷款、城乡个体工商户贷款城乡个体工商户贷款以及农业贷款等科目。

Explanatory Notes on Main Statistical Indicators

Financial Revenue It includes the following main items: (1) various tax revenues, including value added tax, business tax, land value added tax, tax on city maintenance and construction, resources tax, tax on use of urban land, stamp tax, personal income tax, enterprise income tax and tax on occupancy of cultivated land, etc. (2) Special revenues, including revenue collected from imposing fee on sewage treatment, revenue collected from imposing fee on urban water resources, and extra – charges for education, etc.

Deposit is a form of credit by which enterprises, institutions, organizations or households can put money into banks and other credit institutions for safekeeping and interest earning under the principle of free withdrawal. According to different depositors, deposits are divided into enterprise deposits, treasury deposits, deposits of government agencies and organizations, capital construction deposits, urban savings deposits, rural deposits and other deposits. Deposits are major sources of the credit funds of banks.

Loan is a form of credit by which banks and other credit institutions provide funds at certain interest rate to enterprises and individuals in the light of the principle of unconditional repayment. Loans from Chinese banks include circulating capital loans, fixed assets loans, loans to urban and rural individuals engaged in industrial and commercial business and agricultural loans.

十一、城市建设、环境保护

XI.URBAN CONSTRUCTION AND ENVIRONMENTAL PROTECTION

城市建设、环境保护
Urban Construction and Environmental Protection

主要统计指标
Major Statistical Indicators

市区建成区面积	Developed Area in Urban District	462.48	平方公里	(sq.km)
市区实有道路面积	Area of Roads in Urban District at Year-end	5426	万平方米	(10, 000 sq.m)
市区用电量	Electricity Consumption of Urban District	484.05	亿千瓦时	(100 million kw/h)
# 工业用电	Industrial Electricity Consumption	296.08	亿千瓦时	(100 million kw/h)
生活用电	Electricity Consumption for Residential Use	71.52	亿千瓦时	(100 million kw/h)
市区供水能力	Water-supply Capacity of Urban District	350	万吨/日	(10, 000 tons/day)
市区供水总量	Annual Volume of Tap Water Supplied in Urban District	60747	万吨	(10, 000 tons)
市区气化率	Percentage of Population with Access to Gas in Urban District	100	%	(%)
市区公共绿地面积	Public Green Area in Urban District	5820	公顷	(hectare)
市区空气质量达标(AQI < 100)天数	The Number of Days of Air Quality Reaching(AQI<100) the Standards	217	天	(day)

11－01 市区城市公共交通

Urban Public Transportation in Urban Districts

指　标	Item	2000	2005	2010	2011	2012	2013
一、轨道交通	Rail Transit						
年末运营线路总长度（公里）	Length of Operating Routes (year－end) (km)	－	－	－	－	47.97	47.97
客运总量（万人次）	Passenger Traffic (10,000 person－times)	－	－	－	－	561.40	9237.14
二、公共汽车	Bus						
年末运营线路条数（条）	Number of Operating Routes (year－end) (unit)	163	368	548	611	620	645
年末运营线路总长度（公里）	Length of Operating Routes (year－end) (km)	2016	4902	8594	11106	11351	12920
年末运营公共汽车（辆）	Number of Public Transportation Vehicles(year－end) (unit)	1781	3997	7209	7543	7450	8249
#无轨电车（辆）	Number of Operating Trolleys (unit)	223	189	65	54	51	101
客运总量（万人次）	Passenger Traffic (10,000 person－times)	57986	70653	127967	126999	131901	132221
全年票款收入（万元）	Income of Tickets (10,000 yuan)	43604	86448	150050	158373	159789	156292
三、出租汽车	Tax						
年末实有出租汽车数（辆）	Number of Taxis (year－end) (unit)	6300	8320	9362	10905	10344	10904
四、公共自行车	Bicycle						
年末免费公共自行车数（辆）	Number of free Public Bicycles (year－end) (unit)	－	－	60600	65000	68000	78000

注：运营线路和公共汽车数据2009年前不含萧山、余杭。

a) Data of Operating Routes and public transportation vehicles don´t include Xiaoshan and Yuhang district before 2009.

11－02 市区城市供电、供水

Urban Electricity and Water Supply in Urban Districts

指 标	Item	2000	2005	2010	2011	2012	2013
一、城市供电	**Urban Electricity Supply**						
全年用电总量（亿千瓦时）	Total Electricity Consumption (100 million kwh)	60.19	244.78	392.64	432.57	444.95	484.05
#工业（亿千瓦时）	Industrial Electricity Consumption (100 million kwh)	33.52	172.56	258.35	282.95	278.93	296.08
生活（亿千瓦时）	Electricity Consumption for Residential Use (100 million kwh)	9.86	27.98	50.74	55.49	63.62	71.52
二、城市供水（自来水）	**Urban Water Supply**						
总售水量（万吨）	Total Annual Volume of Tap Water Saled (10,000 tons)	27510	58332	45666	44335	49549	51709
平均日供水（万吨）	Per Capita Daily Consumption of Tap Water (10,000 tons)	92	201	147	144	159	166
供水能力（万吨/日）	Capacity of Water Supply (10,000 tons/day)	146	253	320	320	320	350
供水总量（万吨）	Total Annual Volume of Tap Water Supplied (10,000 tons)	33725	73331	53565	52660	58183	60747
#生产用水（万吨）	For Productive Use (10,000 tons)	8100	27327	11479	11884	12478	13005
生活用水（万吨）	For Residential Use (10,000 tons)	19410	35220	30978	22384	22861	23733
用水普及率（%）	Percentage of Population with Access to Tap Water (%)	100	100	100	100	100	100

注：从2001年起市区数据包括萧山区和余杭区。
a) Data of urban include Xiaoshan and Yuhang district since 2001.

11－03　市区市政建设

Public Utilities in Urban Districts

指　标	Item	2000	2005	2010	2011	2012	2013
一、市政建设	**Urban Infrastructure**						
建成区面积（平方公里）	Constructed Area (sq. m)	–	314.45	412.59	432.98	452.62	462.48
年末实有道路面积（万平方米）	Area of Roads (year－end) (10,000 sq. m)	1183	3175	4754	4900	5284	5426
年末实有道路长度（公里）	Length of Roads (year－end) (km)	1050	1782	2194	2255	2458	2479
年末实有桥梁数（座）	Number of Bridges (year－end) (unit)	291	991	1021	1059	1129	1165
排水管道长度（公里）	Length of Drainage Pipelines (km)	1431	2945	3904	4056	4280	4455
城市污水排放量（万立方米）	Volume of Sewage Drained (10,000 cu. m)	27010	55141	43746	44809	47330	48432
城市污水处理总量（万立方米）	the Total Volume of Urban Sewage Treatment (10,000 cu. m)	–	43352	41733	42781	45197	46251
二、城市液化气	**Urban Liquefied Petroleum Gas**						
供气总量（万吨）	Total Volume of Liquefied Petroleum Gas Supply (10,000 tons)	7.47	15.28	11.44	11.19	11.17	11.92
#家庭用气（万吨）	Supply for Residential Use (10,000 tons)	5.08	9.51	5.77	5.93	5.90	4.70
三、人工煤气及天然气	**Coal Gas and Natural Gas**						
家庭用气总量（万立方米）	Total Volume of Coal Gas Consumed (10,000 cu. m)	4367	3225	10053	11365	13397	13869
家庭用气户数（万户）	Residential Households with Access to Gas (10,000 households)	14.46	25.48	62.85	72.50	81.72	91.08
四、全社会气化率　%	**Percentage of Population with Access to Gas** (%)	**95.70**	**99.17**	**100**	**100**	**100**	**100**

注：从 2001 年起市区数据包括萧山区和余杭区。

a) Data of urban include Xiaoshan and Yuhang district since 2001.

11－04 市区园林绿化
Urban Forestation

指 标	Item	2000	2005	2010	2011	2012	2013
一、园林绿化	**Urban Forestation**						
建城区绿化覆盖面积（公顷）	The Green Areas Coveraged in Constructed Areas (hectare)	6083	11734	16483	17336	18135	18606
园林绿地面积（公顷）	Total Area of Parks, Gardens and Green Areas (hectare)	6035	10774	15118	15898	16647	17071
#公共绿地（公顷）	Public Green Area (hectare)	976	2564	5017	5287	5635	5820
建城区绿化覆盖率（%）	Rate of the Green Areas Coveraged in Constructed Areas (%)	34.33	37.31	39.95	40.00	40.07	40.23
公园景点个数（个）	Number of Parks and Scenic Resorts (unit)	70	184	176	181	185	190
公园景点面积（公顷）	Area of Parks and Scenic Resorts (hectare)	489	997	1906	2047	2065	2094
二、收费公园、风景点游人量（万人次）	**Number of Visitors to Parks and Scenic Resorts (10,000 persontimes)**	**1916**	**2396**	**5314**	**5478**	**5811**	**5610**

注：从2001年起市区数据包括萧山区和余杭区。

a) Data of urban include Xiaoshan and Yuhang district since 2001.

11－05 环境保护情况(2013 年)

Environmental Protection Situation (2013)

指标名称		Item		全 市 Whole City	市 区 Urban District
工业废水排放量	(万吨)	Industrial Wastewater Emissions	(10,000 tons)	39186	16930
工业废水中 COD 排放量	(吨)	COD Emissions in Industrial Wastewater	(tons)	31947	15728
工业废水中氨氮排放量	(吨)	Ammonia emissions in Industrial wastewater	(tons)	1373	680
工业二氧化硫产生量	(吨)	Industrial Sulfur Dioxide Produced	(tons)	171357	110962
工业二氧化硫排放量	(吨)	Industrial Emissions of Sulfur Dioxide	(tons)	82021	48539
工业氮氧化物排放量	(吨)	Industrial Nitrogen Oxide Emissions	(tons)	67283	36669
工业烟(粉)尘去除量	(吨)	Industrial Smoke, Powder and Dust Removal	(tons)	4172829	1320948
工业烟(粉)尘排放量	(吨)	Industrial Smoke, Powder and Dust Emissions	(tons)	40243	20499
一般工业固体废物综合利用率	(%)	Comprehensive Utilization Rate of General Industrial Solid Waste	(%)	94.0	94.0
城市污水集中处理率	(%)	Centralized Treatment Rate of Urban Sewage	(%)	93.9	95.5
城市生活垃圾无害化处理率	(%)	Harmless Treatment Rate of City's Living Garbage	(%)	100	100
空气质量达标(API < 100)天数	(天)	Number of Days of Air Quality Reach the Standards (API < 100)	(days)	–	217
集中式饮用水源地水质达标率	(%)	Compliance Rate of Centralized Sources of Drinking Water	(%)	100	100
COD 削减率	(%)	Reduction Rate of COD	(%)	4.12	–
SO_2 削减率	(%)	Reduction Rate of SO_2	(%)	4.80	–
氮氧化物削减率	(%)	Reduction Rate of Nitrogen Oxides	(%)	6.58	–

主要统计指标解释

自来水生产能力 指年底城建部门管理的自来水厂实际生产能力。

生活用水量 指居民日常生活与公共福利设施的用水量。包括居民、饮食店、旅馆、医院、理发店、浴池、洗衣店、游泳池、商店、学校、机关、部队等单位的用水量。

供气总量 指全年售给各类用户的全部煤气量。包括工业用量、家庭用量和其他用量。

年末实有道路长度 指除土路外,路面经过铺装宽度在3.5米以上的道路,包括高级、次高级道路和普通道路。

城市桥梁 指城市范围内,修建在河道上的桥梁和道路与道路立交、道路跨越铁路的立交桥,以及人行天桥。包括永久性桥和半永久性桥,不包括临时性桥、铁路桥、涵洞。

营运线路长度 指设置的固定营运线路的长度,包括郊区营运线路长度。不包括临时行驶的线路长度。

用水普及率 指城市用水的非农业人口数(不包括临时人口和流动人口)与城市非农业人口总数之比。计算公式为:

$$\text{用水普及率} = \frac{\text{城市用水非农业人口数}}{\text{城市非农业人口总数}} \times 100\%$$

城市园林绿地面积 指城市公共绿地、专用绿地、生产绿地、防护绿地、郊区风景名胜区的全部面积。

公共绿地面积 指供游览休息的各种公园、动物园、植物园、陵园以及花园、游园和供游览休息用的林荫道绿地、广场绿地。不包括一般栽植的行道树及林荫道的面积。

Explanatory Notes on Main Statistical Indicators

Production Capacity of Tap Water refers to the actual comprehensive production capacity of the waterworks administered by the urban construction department.

Consumption of water for Residential Use refers to the water consumption of households for daily life and the water consumption of public welfare facilities, including the consumption of restaurants, hotels, hospitals, barber shops, public bathhouses, laundries, swimming pools, shops, schools, institutions, army units and other units.

Volume of Gas Supply refers to the total volume of gas Sold to users in a year, including the volume for industrial use, residential use and other uses.

Length of Roads at the Year – end refers to the length of roads with a paved surface, and with a width of more than 3 – 5 meters, including high quality, medium quality and ordinary roads.

Urban Bridges refers to bridges over river courses, great separated junctions and overpasses in urban areas. Permanent bridges and semi – permanent bridges are included. Temporary bridges, railway bridges and culverts are excluded.

Length in Operation refers to the length of the roads in fixed operation, including the suburb one, but excluding the tomporary ones.

Percentage of Urban Population with Access to Tap Water refers to the ratio of the urban non – agricultural population(excluding temporary and mobile population) with access to tap water to the tolal urban non – agricultural population. The formula is:

$$\text{Percentage of Poputalion with Access to Tap Water} = \frac{\text{Urban Non – agricultural Population with Access to Tap Water}}{\text{Urban Non – agricultural Population}} \times 100\%$$

Area of Urban Gardens and Green Areas refers to the total area of urban public green land, special green land, production green land, protection green land and suburban scenic spots.

Public Green Area refers to green area of various parks, zoos, botanical gardens, cemeteries, amusement parks, tree – flanked boulevards Greenland squares for tourism and relaxing. Areas with trees planted along – side the streets and boulevards are excluded.

十二、科技、教育
文化、卫生、体育

Ⅻ.SCIENCE AND TECHNOLOGY, EDUCATION,CULTURE,PUBLIC HEALTH ANG SPORTS

科技、教育、文化、卫生、体育
Science and Technology, Education, Culture, Public Health and Sports

主要统计指标
Major Statistical Indicators

高等学校数	Number of Regular Institution of Higher Education	38	个	(unit)
高等学校在校学生数	Number of Students in Regular Institution of Higher Education	47.18	万人	(10, 000 person)
高中在校学生数	Number of Students in Senior High Schools	11.39	万人	(10, 000 person)
初中在校学生数	Number of Students in Junior High Schools	21.35	万人	(10, 000 person)
小学在校学生数	Number of Students in Primary Schools	48.35	万人	(10, 000 person)
医疗病床数	Number of Beds in Health Institutions	5.21	万张	(10, 000 bed)
#医院	Number of Beds in Hospitals	4.66	万张	(10, 000 bed)
卫生技术人员数	Number of Medical Technical Personnel	7.83	万人	(10, 000 person)
#执业(助理)医师	Number of Registered (Assistant) Doctors	2.97	万人	(10, 000 person)
公共图书馆	Public Library	15	个	(unit)

12-01 全市科技活动情况
The Situation of the City's Scientific and Technological Activities

指 标 Item	2013	2012
一、全社会科技活动 The Scientific and Technological Activities in whole Society		
研究与试验发展活动折合全时人员 (人年) Full-time Equivalent of R&D Personnel	81617	78275
研究与试验发展经费支出 (亿元) R&D Financial Expenditure (0.1 billion yuan)	248.73	228.00
研究与试验发展经费支出占 GDP 比重 (%) The Proportion of R&D Financial Expenditure in GDP (%)	2.98	2.92
二、规模以上工业科技活动 The Scientific and Technological Activities of Industrial Enterprises Above designated Size		
有研究与试验发展活动企业数 (个) The Number of Scientific and Technological Activities Enterprises (Unit)	1453	1229
企业有科技机构 (个) Scientific and Technological Institutions of Enterprises (Unit)	1273	1197
研究与试验发展人员 (万人) R&D Personnel (10,000)	6.88	6.12
每万名从业人员中研究与试验发展活动人员数 (人) The Number of R&D Activities Personnel per 10,000 Employees (Person)	578	501
企业技术开发费支出 (亿元) The Technological Development Expenses of Enterprises (0.1 billion yuan)	249.12	214.52
技术开发费占主营业务收入的比例 (%) The Proportion of Technological Development Expenses in Main Business Income (%)	2.06	1.71
研究与试验发展经费支出 (亿元) R&D Financial Expenditure (0.1 billion yuan)	160.21	143.47
研究与试验发展经费支出占主营业务收入的比例 (%) The Proportion of R&D Financial Expenditure in Main Business Income (%)	1.33	1.15

12－02 分地区含规上私营单位年末人才资源(2013 年)

Trained Personnel Resource Including Private Units above Designated Size by Region(2013)

单位:人 (person)

项目	Item	合计 Total	#非私营单位 Non－Private	#专业技术人员 Technical Personnel	#非私营单位 Non－Private	#技术工人 Technical Workers	#非私营单位 Non－Private
全市	**Whole City**	**2678023**	**1781697**	**899260**	**625000**	**1266588**	**781498**
市区	Urban District	2234180	1551762	750844	533187	1065207	701304
#上城区	Shangcheng	170129	146103	63771	54259	70818	61491
下城区	Xiacheng	179693	158721	80639	71264	56710	51453
江干区	Jianggan	195562	97138	51148	30512	113244	44074
拱墅区	Gongshu	218060	141601	63552	36951	123693	83846
西湖区	Xihu	349202	281136	115550	87919	153459	123081
高新(滨江)区	Hi－Tech(Binjiang)	175041	141296	97302	79030	48707	40471
萧山区	Xiaoshan	535397	307830	152411	85371	299286	169790
余杭区	Yuhang	271710	150847	87443	51510	128254	63589
桐庐县	Tonglu	66208	32420	22165	12362	30483	11412
淳安县	Chun'an	40651	24983	15817	11520	14936	5589
建德市	Jiande	57590	33666	19880	12565	24542	12208
富阳市	Fuyang	171083	76977	56030	31553	79158	26942
临安市	Lin'an	108311	61889	34524	23813	52262	24043

12－02 续表 continued

项 目	Item	合计 Total	#非私营单位 Non－Private	#专业技术人员 Technical Personnel	#非私营单位 Non－Private	#技术工人 Technical Workers	#非私营单位 Non－Private
按国民经济行业分组	**Total**						
农、林、牧、渔业	Farming, Forestry, Animal Husbandry and Fishery	1235	1200	498	474	293	293
采矿业	Mining	1754	633	385	118	1043	374
制造业	Manufacturing	747999	461102	172256	109046	450012	278150
电力、热力、燃气及水生产和供应业	Production & Supply of Electricity, Heat, Gas & Water	17818	16994	4601	4370	10845	10426
建筑业	Construction	921056	451563	230054	85224	597882	312191
批发和零售业	Wholesale & Retail Trades	120156	91828	31048	21655	51139	46948
交通运输、仓储和邮政业	Transportation, Storage and Posts	84370	74400	11465	9694	60949	55712
住宿和餐饮业	Hotels and Catering Services	28914	19889	6667	4028	10021	7635
信息传输、软件和信息技术服务业	Information Transmission, Software and Information Technology	86169	66675	65035	51486	7223	5441
金融业	Financial Intermediation	64013	63529	38333	38132	4199	4127
房地产业	Real Estate	57039	45187	20567	15474	16302	14870
租赁和商务服务业	Leasing and Business Services	59368	39106	25160	15403	15125	10373
科学研究、技术服务业	Scientific Research, Technical Services	95094	75364	71438	56965	7659	6582
水利、环境和公共设施管理业	Management of Water Conservancy, Environment and Public Facilities	24071	17127	7745	5151	10292	7428
居民服务、修理和其他服务业	Service to Honseholds, Repair and Other Services	6491	3327	1752	919	2282	865
教育	Education	143320	139037	114425	111918	9293	8330
卫生和社会工作	Health Care and Social Work	88070	84791	74858	72299	6425	6306
文化、体育和娱乐业	Culture, Sports and Entertainment	18875	17734	13014	12685	1617	1460
公共管理、社会保障和社会组织	Public Management, Social Security and Social Organizations	112211	112211	9959	9959	3987	3987

12－03 全市专利申请与授权情况(2013 年)

Patent Application and Authorization(2013)

单位:件 (item)

地　区	Region	专利申请合计 Patent Applications	专利申请发明 Inventions	专利申请实用新型 Utility Models	专利申请外观设计 Designs	专利授权合计 Patent Applications Granted	专利授权发明 Inventions	专利授权实用新型 Utility Models	专利授权外观设计 Designs
全市	**Whole City**	**58280**	**14031**	**25523**	**18726**	**41518**	**4903**	**23159**	**13456**
市区	Urban District	45399	13104	20866	11429	31561	4541	19251	7769
上城区	Shangcheng	2854	397	1014	1443	1703	104	820	779
下城区	Xiacheng	3890	1263	1541	1086	3036	473	1544	1019
江干区	Jianggan	8760	2630	4462	1670	5152	793	3228	1131
拱墅区	Gongshu	2544	416	1310	818	1838	96	1114	628
西湖区	Xihu	8118	4175	2722	1221	4989	1833	2364	792
高新(滨江)区	Hi－Tech(Binjiang)	5665	2335	2124	1206	3129	741	1628	760
萧山区	Xiaoshan	7466	1124	5123	1219	7155	243	6006	906
余杭区	Yuhang	6100	764	2570	2766	4559	258	2547	1754
桐庐县	Tonglu	1897	136	548	1213	1352	46	446	860
淳安县	Chun'an	908	60	536	312	745	49	267	429
建德市	Jiande	867	73	141	653	1151	56	142	953
富阳市	Fuyang	5525	301	2375	2849	3847	96	2082	1669
临安市	Lin'an	3684	357	1057	2270	2862	115	971	1776

12－04 文化事业单位数（2013 年末）
Number of Institutions for Culture（End of 2013）

单位：个 （unit）

指　标	Item	剧场 Theaters	剧团 Opera Troupes	文化馆 Cultural Centers	文化站 Cultural Stations	图书馆 Libraries	博物馆 Museums	展览馆 Exhibition Buildings
全市	**Total**	**11**	**21**	**15**	**189**	**15**	**65**	**1**
市区	Urban District	11	17	10	94	10	54	1
#萧山区	Xiaoshan	–	1	1	27	1	8	–
余杭区	Yuhang	2	1	1	19	1	4	–
桐庐县	Tonglu	–	1	1	14	1	2	–
淳安县	Chun'an	–	–	1	23	1	1	–
建德市	Jiande	–	1	1	16	1	4	–
富阳市	Fuyang	–	1	1	24	1	3	–
临安市	Lin'an	–	1	1	18	1	1	–

12－05 分县(市)艺术表演团体演出情况(2013 年)

Basic Statistics on Performance of Art Troupes by Region(2013)

指标	Item	艺术表演场所演出场次(场) Number of Performances in Artistic Performance Place (scene)	艺术表演场所演出收入(万元) Income of Performances in Artistic Performance Place (10000 yuan)	剧团演出场次(场) Number of Performances of Opera Troupes (scene)	#农村(场) #Rural Areas (scene)	剧团演出观众人数(万人次) Number of Spectators of Opera Troupes (10000 person－times)	剧团演出收入(万元) Income of Performances of Opera Troupes (10000 yuan)
全市	**Total**	**3863**	**2190**	**5868**	**2892**	**546**	**4591**
为上年(%)	As Compared with the Preceding Year (%)	88.9	119.0	87.4	97.3	96.6	65.5
市区	Urban District	3803	2180	5154	2259	424	4197
为上年(%)	As Compared with the Preceding Year (%)	88.3	119.3	89.3	106.3	103.2	65.5
#萧山区	Xiaoshan	－	－	73	50	11	22
余杭区	Yuhang	48	33	144	116	39	225
桐庐县	Tonglu	－	－	180	165	27	148
淳安县	Chun'an	－	－	－	－	－	－
建德市	Jiande	－	－	298	260	57	91
富阳市	Fuyang	－	－	109	98	33	129
临安市	Lin'an	60	10	127	110	5	26

12-06 市区历年文化事业单位数(1978-2013)
Cultural Institutions of Urban District (1978-2013)

单位:个 (unit)

年份 Year	电影院 Cinemas	剧团 Opera Troupes	剧场 Theaters	文化馆 Cultural Centers	文化站 Cultural Stations	图书馆 Libraries	博物馆 Museums
1978	7	13	6	5	-	2	1
1979	8	14	7	5	27	2	1
1980	8	15	7	5	37	2	1
1981	8	17	7	6	40	2	1
1982	9	17	7	6	45	3	1
1983	9	15	3	6	46	3	1
1984	9	15	4	6	49	3	1
1985	8	16	9	6	47	3	2
1986	8	15	8	6	48	3	2
1987	8	15	9	6	38	3	2
1988	7	14	9	6	50	3	2
1989	7	14	9	6	48	2	2
1990	9	14	9	5	48	3	2
1991	10	14	8	5	48	3	2
1992	11	14	8	5	48	3	6
1993	10	14	9	5	42	3	6
1994	11	13	9	5	48	3	6
1995	11	13	9	5	67	3	6
1996	10	13	8	5	55	3	6
1997	10	13	8	5	52	3	6
1998	9	13	8	6	55	3	7
1999	9	13	6	6	52	3	8
2000	8	12	6	6	52	3	9
2001	49	14	11	8	89	5	11
2002	-	14	10	8	90	4	11
2003	19	14	11	13	92	4	11
2004	18	14	14	8	93	5	12
2005	16	15	10	8	94	7	12
2006	16	15	10	8	94	8	12
2007	16	15	10	8	92	9	12
2008	18	15	11	8	92	9	13
2009	15	16	11	8	95	11	34
2010	25	17	11	8	96	11	54
2011	23	17	10	10	94	10	54
2012	31	17	10	10	96	10	54
2013	31	17	11	10	94	10	54

注:从2001年起市区数据包括萧山区和余杭区。

a) Data of urban include Xiaoshan and Yuhang district since 2001.

12－07　幼儿园基本情况(1978－2013)

Basic Statistics on Kindergartens(1978－2013)

单位:人　　　　(person)

年　份 Year	园　数(个) Kindergartens(unit)	在园幼儿数 Number of Children	教职员工数 Teachers and Staff	#教　师 Number of Full－time Teachers
1978	266	37597	2570	1439
1979	216	59245	3731	2201
1980	518	82182	4763	3398
1981	676	82808	5275	3691
1982	853	95733	6357	4269
1983	1034	95676	6271	4135
1984	1749	112095	7238	4900
1985	1743	115766	7360	5278
1986	1607	118792	7898	5659
1987	1678	133773	8622	6335
1988	1541	139883	9221	6608
1989	1397	132947	9595	6849
1990	1526	136277	9808	7167
1991	1422	150982	10472	7388
1992	1431	133773	9240	6487
1993	1328	171005	10779	7886
1994	1470	165860	10718	7891
1995	1493	149497	10102	7943
1996	1437	150587	10203	7625
1997	1504	146530	10480	7743
1998	1695	153035	10691	7956
1999	1787	156372	10719	8107
2000	2037	168414	11740	8770
2001	1249	174204	11447	7880
2002	1268	175891	11988	8086
2003	1285	176862	13702	9076
2004	1098	186472	14991	9544
2005	1188	188991	16161	10288
2006	1188	195552	17550	11053
2007	1071	212754	19330	12168
2008	1037	235867	21193	12917
2009	972	246336	22970	14211
2010	969	267352	25525	15203
2011	970	271128	27458	16023
2012	914	283421	29843	17811
2013	860	285406	32037	18945

12－08 小学基本情况(1978－2013)

Basic Statistics on Primary Schools(1978－2013)

单位:人 (person)

年 份 Year	学校数(个) Number of Schools(unit)	在校学生数 Number of Students	教职员工数 Number of Teachers and Staff	#专职教师数 Number of Full－time Teachers
1978	4959	605137	24103	22291
1979	4850	577811	25089	23220
1980	4781	560244	25388	22902
1981	4668	525503	22468	20832
1982	4528	479264	22213	20289
1983	4417	444301	20842	18945
1984	4345	427763	20496	18500
1985	4286	414839	20945	18415
1986	4250	413507	20796	18464
1987	4205	405856	21067	18751
1988	4137	426842	21658	19236
1989	4106	459162	22660	20177
1990	4077	460514	20542	18099
1991	3972	453055	20781	18369
1992	3654	450496	21452	19067
1993	3473	477026	22141	19775
1994	3352	504867	22751	20462
1995	3172	513988	23743	21380
1996	3006	525674	24553	22197
1997	2762	538390	25269	23022
1998	2395	532845	25718	23499
1999	1996	512874	26350	24120
2000	1659	485679	25938	23876
2001	1354	467982	25535	23179
2002	1197	456535	25425	23138
2003	1044	448969	25304	22955
2004	897	447971	25396	23066
2005	791	458942	25793	23541
2006	605	459529	26040	23848
2007	437	456152	26455	24251
2008	418	452143	26894	24743
2009	417	445132	27445	25424
2010	408	453897	27881	25709
2011	409	465289	27862	26395
2012	415	472613	25620	27777
2013	419	483489	30373	28949

12-09 初中基本情况(1978-2013)

Basic Statistics on Junior Middle Schools(1978-2013)

单位:人 (person)

年 份 Year	学校数(个) Number of Schools(unit)	在校学生数 Number of Students	专职教师数 Number of Full-time Teachers
1978	254	247209	11978
1979	363	208484	11020
1980	369	204073	10695
1981	359	194024	10015
1982	367	193135	10107
1983	370	190221	9948
1984	368	192971	9679
1985	361	196889	9799
1986	376	199638	9821
1987	385	195426	10264
1988	380	170079	10055
1989	376	151223	9825
1990	382	160111	9564
1991	387	185590	10020
1992	367	212022	10603
1993	365	203896	10876
1994	371	205388	11495
1995	373	216300	12058
1996	374	229466	12810
1997	368	227809	13370
1998	359	222191	13493
1999	339	239174	13723
2000	330	269484	14529
2001	314	285203	15685
2002	315	282951	15758
2003	316	268824	15836
2004	303	252291	16042
2005	289	241374	16205
2006	263	235527	16374
2007	262	238252	16591
2008	260	244464	16965
2009	252	241899	17317
2010	245	236014	17795
2011	246	223545	17652
2012	244	215701	17992
2013	241	213452	18260

12-10 高中基本情况(1978-2013)

Basic Statistics on Senior High Schools(1978-2013)

单位:人 (person)

年 份 Year	学校数(个) Number of Schools(unit)	在校学生数 Number of Students	专职教师数 Number of Full-time Teachers
1978	352	102815	5235
1979	182	58866	3471
1980	151	43661	3173
1981	118	34606	2825
1982	113	35136	2740
1983	111	38580	2740
1984	105	43167	2781
1985	104	47510	3016
1986	95	46379	2972
1987	92	44697	3006
1988	89	42196	2947
1989	88	39994	2898
1990	86	39829	2922
1991	82	37809	2896
1992	74	34620	2791
1993	72	32483	2641
1994	75	35720	2673
1995	72	40771	2880
1996	70	43692	3135
1997	69	47975	3388
1998	75	55688	3693
1999	82	64459	4172
2000	85	73049	4745
2001	88	79632	5262
2002	81	91635	6126
2003	77	108116	6879
2004	81	115303	7510
2005	80	120883	8041
2006	82	124177	8421
2007	80	122939	8542
2008	76	120294	8646
2009	75	118057	8751
2010	72	116983	8871
2011	71	117089	9061
2012	70	115652	9069
2013	70	113894	9125

12-11 中等专业学校基本情况(1978-2013)

Basic Statistics on Specialized Secondary Schools(1978-2013)

单位:人 (person)

年份 Year	学校数(个) Number of Schools(unit)	在校学生数 Number of Students	教职员工数 Teachers and Staff	#专职教师 Number of Full-time Teachers
1978	26	8711	3044	1080
1979	27	11093	2601	1124
1980	26	9453	2450	1101
1981	35	7309	3122	1276
1982	37	8284	3694	1529
1983	37	10516	3716	1604
1984	42	13419	4194	1758
1985	46	16527	5095	1959
1986	50	19114	5641	2336
1987	52	20929	6081	2623
1988	51	22117	6144	2741
1989	54	23302	6602	2888
1990	55	23564	6679	2948
1991	55	23331	6584	2770
1992	55	26373	6786	2825
1993	56	30336	6732	2780
1994	57	36079	6881	2840
1995	57	42784	6851	2888
1996	58	49593	6789	2904
1997	57	51752	6731	2896
1998	56	55796	6554	2746
1999	50	52272	5023	2272
2000	28	45238	2950	1421
2001	26	32763	2053	1051
2002	14	26255	1251	566
2003	13	21735	1058	457
2004	11	21262	869	416
2005	10	20344	893	443
2006	8	12540	410	184
2007	8	8927	414	194
2008	8	5514	345	152
2009	8	4016	233	65
2010	6	3999	348	151
2011	5	4071	369	154
2012	5	3909	376	150
2013	5	3656	390	158

12－12　高等学校基本情况(1978－2013)

Basic Statistics on Regular Institutions of Higher Education(1978－2013)

单位:人　　(person)

年　份 Year	学校数(个) Number of Schools(unit)	在校学生数 Number of Students	教职员工数 Teachers and Staff	#专职教师 Number of Full－time Teachers
1978	9	13319	8966	3946
1979	12	17518	10182	4458
1980	13	23545	12400	5278
1981	13	28936	13090	5359
1982	13	25821	14363	6067
1983	14	27443	15267	6172
1984	16	31384	15889	6387
1985	20	36996	17507	7247
1986	22	40051	18968	7845
1987	21	39922	18965	7876
1988	21	40787	19582	8133
1989	21	40330	19680	8107
1990	21	39866	19495	8075
1991	21	42192	19489	7737
1992	19	43787	19841	7561
1993	19	51063	19787	7561
1994	19	59109	19903	7703
1995	20	63124	19883	7799
1996	20	66023	19693	7824
1997	20	69391	19540	7793
1998	17	76546	19320	7723
1999	18	89109	20136	8135
2000	32	122386	23791	10477
2001	33	174894	25805	11866
2002	34	224048	27307	13605
2003	35	269798	34508	18141
2004	36	313599	33325	18445
2005	36	351918	34816	19583
2006	36	373563	36929	21375
2007	36	392770	38843	23197
2008	36	409559	39762	24017
2009	36	429774	40420	24765
2010	37	434811	41582	25003
2011	38	446721	42222	25735
2012	38	459181	43216	26689
2013	38	471820	43992	27544

注:在校学生数包括各高校研究生。

a) Number of students include graduate students in all schools.

12－13 小学、幼儿园及特殊

Basic Statistics on Primary Schools,

单位:人

指 标	Item	全 市 Total	市 区 Urban District	#萧山区 Xiaoshan
小 学	**Primary Schools**			
学校数(所)	Number of Schools(unit)	419	242	83
班数(班)	Number of Classes(unit)	12733	8944	2578
在校学生数	Number of Students	483489	349909	104957
本年招生数	Number of New Students Enrollment	88337	65458	17296
本年毕业生数	Number of Graduates	73682	50961	16217
专职教师数	Full－time Teachers	28949	20521	5843
2014 年预计毕业生数	Number of Students Will Graduate in 2014	73226	51516	16277
幼儿园	**Kindergartens**			
园数(个)	Number of Kindergartens(unit)	860	592	180
班数(班)	Number of Classes(unit)	9695	7057	1802
在园幼儿数	Number of Children	285406	212432	54098
教师数	Full－time Teachers	18945	14348	3476
盲聋哑学校	**Schools for the Blind,Deaf and Deaf－mute**			
学校数(个)	Number of Schools(unit)	2	1	－
在校学生数	Number of Students	495	257	－
本年招生数	Number of New Students Enrollment	54	10	－
本年毕业生数	Number of Graduates	78	34	－
专职教师数	Number of Full－time Teachers	150	88	－
弱智学校	**Schools for Weaken in Intelligence**			
学校数(个)	Number of Schools(unit)	12	7	1
在校学生数	Number of Students	1065	829	231
本年招生数	Number of New Students Enrollment	177	142	60
本年毕业生数	Number of Graduates	109	89	20
专职教师数	Number of Full－time Teachers	294	233	56
工读学校	**Reformatory Schools**			
学校数(个)	Number of Schools(unit)	1	1	－
在校学生数	Number of Students	281	281	－
本年招生数	Number of New Students Enrollment	216	216	－
本年毕业生数	Number of Graduates	60	60	－
专任教师数	Number of Full－time Teachers	47	47	－

教育基本情况(2013 年)

Kindergartens and Special Education(2013)

(person)

#余杭区 Yuhang	桐庐县 Tonglu	淳安县 Chun'an	建德市 Jiande	富阳市 Fuyang	临安市 Lin'an
45	26	37	28	46	40
1917	618	596	574	1214	787
78738	22638	17216	20988	44068	28670
14277	3894	2745	3634	7539	5067
11077	3675	3427	3990	6976	4653
4418	1289	1612	1350	2536	1641
11224	3571	3089	3587	6812	4651
84	51	35	35	75	72
1315	437	294	465	821	621
42098	11882	7231	12469	23928	17464
2863	733	467	710	1548	1139
–	–	–	–	1	–
–	–	–	–	238	–
–	–	–	–	44	–
–	–	–	–	44	–
–	–	–	–	62	–
1	1	1	1	1	1
79	58	33	28	47	70
10	20	–	2	6	7
–	–	2	–	8	10
16	12	6	6	19	18
–	–	–	–	–	–
–	–	–	–	–	–
–	–	–	–	–	–
–	–	–	–	–	–
–	–	–	–	–	–

12－14 普通中学、职业中学

Basic Statistics on Senior, Junior High

单位：人

指 标	Item	全 市 Total	市 区 Urban District	#萧山区 Xiaoshan
高 中	**Senior High Schools**			
学校数(所)	Number of Schools(unit)	70	47	9
在校学生数	Number of Students	113894	69083	22108
本年招生数	Number of New Students Enrollment	36897	22743	7031
本年毕业生数	Number of Graduates	37810	22253	7635
专职教师数	Full－time Teachers	9125	5807	1784
2014 年预计毕业生数	Number of Students Will Graduate in 2014	38860	23354	7870
初 中	**Junior High Schools**			
学校数(所)	Number of Schools(unit)	241	154	46
在校学生数	Number of Students	213452	144489	43994
本年招生数	Number of New Students Enrollment	72581	50233	15338
本年毕业生数	Number of Graduates	71006	45748	14416
专职教师数	Full－time Teachers	18260	12324	3525
2014 年预计毕业生数	Number of Students Will Graduate in 2014	68833	45276	13974
职业中学	**Vocational Schools**			
学校数(所)	Number of Schools(unit)	35	21	4
在校学生数	Number of Students	68891	45228	14797
本年招生数	Number of New Students Enrollment	22609	15182	4972
本年毕业生数	Number of Graduates	23298	14989	5010
专职教师数	Full－time Teachers	4408	2908	817
2014 年预计毕业生数	Number of Students Will Graduate in 2014	23699	15140	5063
技工学校	Technical Schools			
学校数(所)	Number of schools(unit)	17	13	1
在校学生数	Number of Students	27935	24520	1466
专职教师数	Full－time Teachers	1303	1119	106

和技工学校基本情况（2013 年）

Schools and Vacational, Technical Schools（2013）

（person）

#余杭区 Yuhang	桐庐县 Tonglu	淳安县 Chun'an	建德市 Jiande	富阳市 Fuyang	临安市 Lin'an
11	3	4	5	6	5
13181	6226	7246	9077	13537	8725
4467	1791	2193	3041	4388	2741
4212	2227	2514	3174	4492	3150
1018	503	515	625	997	678
4341	2296	2542	3039	4579	3050
35	14	17	21	16	19
29372	10611	11345	13237	20681	13089
10526	3515	3449	3968	6904	4512
9266	3825	4317	5204	7388	4524
2521	930	1069	1206	1635	1096
9142	3558	4041	4766	6989	4203
5	2	2	3	3	4
10822	3085	3942	2995	9197	4444
3646	992	1371	952	2775	1337
3433	952	1379	1077	3044	1857
703	195	200	173	549	383
3481	1081	1302	1097	3434	1645
1	–	1	1	1	1
1302	–		1885	618	912
74	–	13	73	41	57

12－15 高等学校

Basic Statistics on Regular

单位:人

单位名称	Item	在校学生数 Number of Students	
		2013	为上年(%) As Compared with the Preceding Year(%)
全　　市	**Total**	**425897**	**102.46**
#市　　区	**Urban District**	**405776**	**102.59**
浙江大学	Zhejiang University	23438	102.22
杭州电子科技大学	Hangzhou Dianzi University	16491	102.13
浙江工业大学	Zhejiang Univesity of Technology	21171	98.29
浙江理工大学	Zhejiang Sci－Tech University	17498	101.87
浙江农林大学	Zhejiang Forestry University	14013	101.45
浙江中医药大学	Zhejiang University of Traditional Chinese Medicine	5790	101.7
杭州师范大学	Hangzhou Normal University	15969	106.28
浙江工商大学	Zhejiang Gongshang University	15213	101.03
中国美术学院	China Academy of Art	8733	100.44
中国计量学院	China Institute of Metrology	14217	103.1
浙江科技学院	Hangzhou Application Engineering and Technology College	15618	100.74
浙江广播电视大学	Zhejiang Radio & TV University	11357	108.3
浙江水利水电专科学校	Zhejiang Water Conservancy and Hydroelectricity College	7933	102.2
浙江财经学院	Zhejiang Institute of Finance and Economics	13400	101.01
浙江警察学院	Zhejiang Police College	3639	123.31
浙江传媒学院	Zhejiang Institute of Media and Communications	12185	109.23
浙江树人大学	Zhejiang Shuren University	14725	101.9
浙江大学城市学院	Zhejiang University City College	13143	98.52

注:本表不含在校研究生。

基本情况(2013 年)
Institutions of Higher Education(2013)

(person)

本年招生数 Number of New Students Enrollment	本年毕业生数 Number of Graduates	教职员工数 Number of Teachers and Staff	
		合计 Total	其中:专职教师 Full - time Teachers
123046	**108688**	**43992**	**27544**
117831	**103722**	**41969**	**26144**
5854	5060	8045	3302
4228	3874	1688	1321
5086	5287	2867	1821
4366	4057	1789	1325
3648	3318	1586	1054
1408	1305	905	642
4102	3169	2494	1456
3843	3762	1696	1238
2322	2241	1032	655
3757	322	1371	932
3961	3517	1185	857
4477	3447	255	90
2958	2676	620	428
3498	3320	1325	953
1021	516	428	195
3537	2344	1161	669
4070	3550	804	578
3328	3216	995	711

a) Data in this table does not contain post - graduate students.

12－16 各级成人教育

Basic Statistics on

单位:人

指 标	Item	成人高等学历教育 Higher Education for Adults	成人高校 Adult Institutions of Higher Education	普通高校成人高等学历教育 Adult Higher Education in Ordinary Universities
全 市	**Total**			
学校数(所)	Number of Schools(unit)	4	4	–
在校学生数	Number of Students	122864	15398	107466
本年招生数	Number of New Students Enrollment	60698	5964	54734
本年毕业生数	Number of Graduates	49658	4041	45617
教职员工数	Number of Teachers and Staff	601	601	–
#专职教师	#Full－time Teachers	314	314	–
市 区	**Urban District**			
学校数(所)	Number of Schools(unit)	4	4	–
在校学生数	Number of Students	118354	15398	102956
本年招生数	Number of New Students Enrollment	58911	5964	52947
本年毕业生数	Number of Graduates	47993	4041	43952
教职员工数	Number of Teachers and Staff	601	601	–
#专职教师	#Full－time Teachers	314	314	–

基本情况(2013 年)

Various Adult Education(2013)

(person)

成人中等学历教育 Adult Secondary Education	成人中等专业 Adult Secondary Specialized	成人中学 Secondary Schools for Adults
225	8	217
408687	25560	383127
10877	10877	–
364251	9242	355009
3376	703	2673
1781	337	1444
124	8	116
338002	25560	312442
10877	10877	–
278209	9207	269002
2914	632	2282
1522	337	1185

12 - 17 医疗卫生机构数(1978 - 2013)

Number of Health Institutions(1978 - 2013)

单位:个 (unit)

年份 Year	全市合计 Total	#医院 Hospitals	市区合计 Urban District	#医院 Hospitals
1978	1361	421	689	45
1979	1390	426	696	50
1980	1381	425	675	51
1981	1476	424	749	51
1982	1540	432	798	56
1983	1540	435	800	58
1984	1574	437	807	54
1985	1582	404	787	47
1986	1636	407	826	53
1987	1693	420	865	55
1988	1710	438	878	55
1989	1721	443	882	57
1990	1738	440	890	58
1991	1789	441	889	58
1992	1767	436	885	58
1993	1730	403	882	68
1994	1717	416	882	72
1995	1712	414	883	72
1996	1712	416	893	83
1997	1711	411	891	81
1998	1491	419	757	89
1999	1530	400	789	85
2000	1599	396	853	85
2001	1496	391	1072	191
2002	1817	116	1277	88
2003	1901	99	1323	73
2004	1985	114	1396	87
2005	2196	127	1604	97
2006	2570	134	1886	107
2007	2607	138	1872	104
2008	2544	141	1813	108
2009	2687	144	1887	111
2010	2819	151	1906	113
2011	2958	167	1992	122
2012	3017	198	2004	146
2013	4139	208	2233	156

注:从2001年起市区数据包括萧山区和余杭区。2002年起医院数据不包括卫生院。

a) Data of urban include Xiaoshan and Yuhang district since 2001. From 2002, the figures of hospitals exclude health centers.

12 – 18 医疗病床数(1978 – 2013)
Number of Beds in Health Institutions(1978 – 2013)

单位:张 (bed)

年 份 Year	全 市 Total	#医 院 Hospitals	市 区 Urban District	#医 院 Hospitals
1978	14042	11704	6588	5789
1979	15124	12682	7335	6282
1980	16317	13478	8244	6940
1981	17408	13576	9646	7185
1982	17179	14350	9194	7580
1983	17338	14584	9411	7833
1984	17694	14691	9536	7867
1985	19637	15010	11095	7933
1986	20555	16035	11657	8448
1987	21465	16770	12203	8863
1988	23394	17954	13204	9651
1989	24111	18363	13581	9773
1990	24121	18879	13219	10041
1991	24966	19444	13968	10437
1992	25606	20243	14206	10821
1993	25653	20884	14058	10982
1994	25984	20870	14231	11045
1995	26684	21360	14731	11336
1996	28141	22217	15427	12132
1997	26616	22341	15076	12190
1998	27327	23110	15530	12766
1999	26713	22952	14988	12691
2000	27166	23303	15496	13068
2001	27063	23520	20523	17770
2002	27609	22797	21200	18667
2003	29144	22036	22641	18205
2004	31738	24444	25008	20338
2005	33251	25907	26732	21931
2006	33972	27186	27172	23184
2007	36928	29987	29884	25664
2008	38114	31416	30663	26882
2009	40226	33094	32412	28031
2010	42828	36148	34693	30639
2011	45291	39363	36633	33291
2012	49471	44019	40534	37383
2013	52056	46636	42506	39489

注:从 2001 年起市区数据包括萧山区和余杭区。
a) Data of urban include Xiaoshan and Yuhang district since 2001.

12－19 医疗卫生

Number of Health

单位:个

指 标	Item	全 市 Total	市区 Urban District
总 计	**Total**	**4139**	**2233**
一、医院	Number of Hospitals	208	156
1. 综合医院	General Hospitals	109	88
2. 中医医院	Hospitals of Chinese Medicine	29	14
3. 中西医结合医院	Chinese Therapeutics with Western	4	3
4. 专科医院	Specialized Hospitals	63	48
口腔医院	Hospitals for Mouth	10	8
眼科医院	Hospitals for Eye	2	2
肿瘤医院	Tumor Hospitals	3	2
妇产(科)医院	Hospitals for Pregnant Woman	8	7
儿童医院	Children Hospitals	2	2
精神病医院	Mental Hospitals	4	2
传染病医院	Hospitals for Infectious Diseases	1	1
皮肤病医院	Dermatology Hospital	1	1
骨科医院	Orthopaedics Hospitals	8	4
康复医院	Healing Hospitals	8	7
整型外科医院	Plastic Hospitals	1	1
美容医院	Beauty Hospitals	8	7
其他专科医院	Other Special Hospitals	7	4
5. 护理院	Nursing Centers	3	3
二、基层医疗卫生机构	Community Medical Institutions	3832	2018
1. 社区卫生服务中心(站)	Health Service Centers for Community	1266	844
社区卫生服务中心	Health Service Centers	127	95
社区卫生服务站	Health Service Stations	1139	749
2. 卫生院	Health Service Centers	93	-
街道卫生院	Rural Township Hospitals in Subdistrict	3	-
乡镇卫生院	Rural Township Hospitals in Country	90	-
村卫生室	Health Offices in Village	1016	151
3. 门诊部	Clinics	305	263
诊所、卫生所、医务室、护理站	Other Health Care Institutions	1152	760
三、专业公共卫生机构	Professional Public Health Institutions	63	33
疾病预防控制中心	Centers for Disease Prevention and Control	15	10
专科疾病防治所(所、站)	Specialized Centers for Disease Prevention and Control(stations)	6	1
健康教育所(站、中心)	Education Center for Health(stations)	2	1
妇幼保健院(所、站)	Maternity and Child Care Centers(stations)	9	4
急救中心(站)	First－aid Centers(stations)	10	4
采供血机构	Blood Supplying Agencies	3	2
卫生监督所	Institutions of Public Health Inspection	16	11
计划生育服务机构	Family Planning Service Institutions	2	-
四、其他卫生机构	Other Health Care Institutions	36	26
疗养院	Sanatoriums	9	4
医学科学研究机构	Research Institutions of Medical Science	1	1
医学在职培训机构	Medical Training Organization for Incumbent	7	4
临床检验中心(所、站)	Clinical Laboratory Center	2	2
统计信息中心	Statistical Information Centers	1	1
其他	Other	16	14

机构数(2013 年末)

Institutions(End of 2013)

(unit)

#萧山区 Xiaoshan	#余杭区 Yuhang	桐庐县 Tonglu	淳安县 Chun'an	建德市 Jiande	富阳市 Fuyang	临安市 Lin'an
727	**345**	**305**	**310**	**375**	**457**	**459**
47	10	9	6	8	8	21
40	6	5	4	3	2	7
4	1	1	2	1	3	8
–	–	–	–	1	–	–
3	2	3	–	3	3	6
1	–	–	–	–	1	1
–	–	–	–	–	–	–
–	–	–	–	–	1	–
–	–	–	–	–	–	1
–	–	–	–	–	–	–
–	1	1	–	1	–	–
–	–	–	–	–	–	–
1	–	–	–	–	–	–
–	1	1	–	1	–	2
1	–	–	–	1	–	–
–	–	–	–	–		–
–	–	–	–	–	–	1
–	–	1	–	–	1	1
–	1	–	–	–	–	–
671	330	293	296	358	437	430
320	184	106	49	36	159	72
29	20	3	2	1	25	1
291	164	103	47	35	134	71
–	–	10	21	22	9	31
–	–	–	–	–	–	3
–	–	10	21	22	9	28
151	–	122	172	213	183	175
35	45	7	0	13	8	14
165	101	48	54	74	78	138
6	4	3	7	7	7	6
1	1	1	1	1	1	1
–	–	–	1	1	2	1
1	–	–	–	–	–	1
–	1	1	1	1	1	1
2	1	–	3	1	1	1
1	–	–	–	1	–	–
1	1	1	1	1	1	1
–	–	–	–	1	1	–
3	1	–	1	2	5	2
1	–	–	–	–	5	–
–	–	–	–	–	–	–
1	1	–	1	1	–	1
–	–	–	–	–	–	–
–	–	–	–	–	–	–
1	–	–	–	1	–	1

12－20　医疗病床
Number of Beds in

单位:张

指　　标	Item	全　　市 Total	市区 Urban District
总　　计	**Total**	**52056**	**42506**
一、医院	Number of Hospitals	46636	39489
1. 综合医院	General Hospitals	29173	24681
2. 中医医院	Hospitals of Chinese Medicine	7435	5710
3. 中西医结合医院	Chinese Therapeutics with Western	1175	1049
4. 专科医院	Specialized Hospitals	8667	7863
口腔医院	Hospitals for Mouth	143	108
眼科医院	Hospitals for Eye	98	98
肿瘤医院	Tumor Hospitals	2407	2387
妇产(科)医院	Hospitals for Pregnant Woman	1211	1191
儿童医院	Children Hospitals	1046	1046
精神病医院	Mental Hospitals	1640	1370
传染病医院	Hospitals for Infectious Diseases	580	580
皮肤病医院	Dermatology Hospital	40	40
骨科医院	Orthopaedics Hospitals	461	213
康复医院	Healing Hospitals	563	477
整型外科医院	Plastic Hospitals	136	136
美容医院	Beauty Hospitals	163	143
其他专科医院	Other Special Hospitals	179	74
5. 护理院	Nursing Centers	186	186
二、基层医疗卫生机构	Community Medical Institutions	3415	2404
1. 社区卫生服务中心(站)	Health Service Centers for Community	2656	2369
社区卫生服务中心	Health Service Centers	2636	2369
社区卫生服务站	Health Service Stations	20	–
2. 卫生院	Health Service Centers	714	–
#街道卫生院	Rural Township Hospitals in Subdistrict	83	–
乡镇卫生院	Rural Township Hospitals in Country	631	–
3. 门诊部	Clinics	45	35
三、专业公共卫生机构	Professional Public Health Institutions	1193	250
专科疾病防治所(所、站)	Specialized Centers for Disease Prevention and Control(stations)	517	–
妇幼保健院(所、站)	Maternity and Child Care Centers(stations)	657	250
急救中心(站)	First－aid Centers(stations)	19	–
四、其他卫生机构	Other Health Care Institutions	812	363
#疗养院	Sanatoriums	812	363

数(2013 年末)

Health Institutions(End of 2013)

(bed)

#萧山区 Xiaoshan	#余杭区 Yuhang	桐庐县 Tonglu	淳安县 Chun'an	建德市 Jiande	富阳市 Fuyang	临安市 Lin'an
6806	**3260**	**1592**	**1328**	**2114**	**2617**	**1899**
6335	2355	1310	1137	1502	1538	1660
5269	1370	1067	777	750	850	1048
879	300	200	360	200	573	392
–	–	–	–	126	–	–
187	625	43	–	426	115	220
15	–	–	–	–	15	20
–	–	–	–	–	–	–
–	–	–	–	–	20	–
–	–	–	–	–	–	20
–	–	–	–	–	–	–
–	520	–	–	270	–	–
–	–	–	–	–	–	–
40	–	–	–	–	–	–
–	105	38	–	70	–	140
132	–	–	–	86	–	–
–	–	–	–	–	–	–
–	–	–	–	–	–	20
–	–	5	–	–	80	20
–	60	–	–	–	–	0
411	655	202	113	278	255	163
401	655	42	–	28	217	–
401	655	42	–	8	217	–
–	–	–	–	20	–	–
–	–	160	113	250	38	153
–	–	–	–	–	–	83
–	–	160	113	250	38	70
10	–	–	–	–	–	10
–	250	80	78	334	375	76
–	–	–	–	300	150	67
–	250	80	78	24	225	–
–	–	–	–	10	–	9
60	–	–	–	–	449	–
60	–	–	–		449	

12－21　卫生事业
Number of Medical

单位：人

指　　标	Item	全　市 Total	市　区 Urban District
总　　计	**Total**	**95600**	**77240**
一、卫生技术人员	Number of Medical Technical Personnel	78340	63359
1. 执业（助理）医师	Registered（Assistant）Doctor	29686	23886
#执业医师	Registered Doctor	27314	22438
2. 注册护士	Registered Nurse	30996	25808
3. 药剂师	Druggist	5467	4240
4. 技师人员	Checking Member	4492	3674
#检验师	Docimaster	3260	2656
5. 其他	Others	7699	5751
二、其他技术人员	Other Medical Technical Personnel	4221	3518
三、管理人员	Managerial Personnel	3814	3174
四、工勤人员	Logistics Worker	8332	7021

人员数(2013 年末)

Technical Personnel(End of 2013)

(person)

#萧山区 Xiaoshan	余杭区 Yuhang	桐庐县 Tonglu	淳安县 Chun'an	建德市 Jiande	富阳市 Fuyang	临安市 Lin'an
12136	**7726**	**3429**	**2206**	**3639**	**5490**	**3596**
9907	6508	2887	1830	2906	4347	3011
3654	2282	1002	743	1045	1687	1323
3125	1961	809	628	892	1438	1109
3863	2408	974	593	1145	1474	1002
708	482	259	178	265	270	255
487	372	168	116	179	193	162
350	277	135	80	138	139	112
1195	964	484	200	272	723	269
522	202	82	56	44	326	195
425	234	169	49	160	174	88
1114	782	272	103	321	458	157

12－22　卫生技术人员(1978－2013)

Number of Medical Technical Personnel(1978－2013)

单位:人　　(person)

年　份 Year	全　市 Total	#执业(助理)医师 Number of Registered (Assistant) Doctors	注册护士 Registered Nurses	市　区 Urban District	#执业(助理)医师 Number of Registered (Assistant) Doctors	注册护士 Registered Nurses
1978	19059	7375	3483	10867	4346	2510
1979	20060	7539	3536	11779	4733	2632
1980	21110	8311	3885	12376	5179	2804
1981	22737	9284	4139	13697	5946	3032
1982	23558	9883	4369	14221	6204	3193
1983	24914	10833	4562	15213	6990	3352
1984	25648	11291	4817	15807	7393	3487
1985	25593	11503	5071	15840	7644	3705
1986	26489	12623	5391	16543	8239	3940
1987	27663	12369	5805	17361	8329	4156
1988	28676	13674	6938	18022	8710	4801
1989	29791	14177	7348	18619	9146	5085
1990	30990	14483	7822	19231	9374	5397
1991	32169	14858	8153	19630	9494	5610
1992	32628	14842	8417	19690	9373	5736
1993	33172	15181	8643	19708	9499	5797
1994	33964	15465	8979	19907	9472	5940
1995	34245	16465	9531	19943	9607	6249
1996	34946	16789	9794	20695	9889	6508
1997	35423	17112	10019	20728	9902	6571
1998	35857	16022	10577	21035	9452	6788
1999	35256	16668	10587	20519	9610	6856
2000	35487	16317	11186	20344	9050	7300
2001	36643	16994	11576	28293	12968	9343
2002	37193	16092	11922	28818	12332	9653
2003	39019	16614	12460	30299	12731	10161
2004	39816	16770	13248	30886	12894	10840
2005	42353	17833	14514	33206	13802	12034
2006	45375	18831	15557	35904	14689	12986
2007	49780	20701	17455	39860	16290	14601
2008	52379	21223	18702	42015	16747	15556
2009	56270	22753	20997	45219	17996	17530
2010	61117	24345	23418	49232	19414	19481
2011	65869	25773	25231	53008	20566	20949
2012	71618	27369	28382	57971	22004	23760
2013	78340	29686	30996	63359	23886	25808

注:从 2001 年起市区数据包括萧山区和余杭区。

a) Data of urban include Xiaoshan and Yuhang district since 2001.

12－23 体育运动情况

Basic Statistics on Sports Activities

单位:人 (person)

指　　标	Item	2013 年	2012 年
一、年末体委工作人员数	**Workers in Sports Commissions at Year－end**	**923**	**985**
#教练员	#Full－time Coaches	140	75
二、等级裁判员发展人数	**Number of Referees in Grades**	**417**	**341**
#女	#Female	140	103
一级裁判员	First Grade Referees	89	42
二级裁判员	Second Grade Referees	328	299
三级裁判员	Third Grade Referees	－	－
三、等级运动员发展人数	**Number of Athletes in Grades**	**385**	**426**
#女	#Female	149	151
一级运动员	First Grade Athlete	47	96
二级运动员	Second Grade Athlete	338	330
三级运动员	Third Grade Athlete	－	－

主要统计指标解释

文化事业机构　指从事专业文化工作和为专业文化工作服务的独立建制的单独核算的单位。不包括这些单位另外举办独立核算的其他机构和各部门的业余文化组织。

艺术表演团体　指从事戏曲、音乐、舞蹈、杂技等专业艺术表演,有独立帐户,实行单独核算的团体。不包括半工半艺、半农半艺和民间职业剧团。

普通高等学校　指按照国家规定的设置标准和审批程序批准举办,通过国家统一招生考试,招收高中毕业生为主要培养对象,实施高等教育的全日制大学、独立设置的学院和高等专科学校、短期职业大学。

成人高等学校　指按照国家有关规定审批,招收通过全国成人高教统一招生考试的具有高中毕业或同等学历的在职从业人员利用脱产、半脱产、业余或函授等多种形式对其实施高等学历教育,培养高等教育专科或本科毕业水平的专门人才,修业年限、课程设置和总学时数均按高等学历教育要求付诸实施的学校。包括广播电视大学、职工高等学校、农民高等学校、管理干部学院、教育学院、独立设置的函授学院等。

小学学龄儿童入学率　指调查范围内已入小学学习的学龄儿童占校内外学龄儿童总数(包括弱智儿童在内,但不包括盲聋哑儿童)的比重。计算公式:

$$\text{小学学龄儿童入学率}=\frac{\text{已入学的小学学龄儿童数}}{\text{校内外小学学龄儿童总数}}*100\%$$

等级运动员人数　指经考核正式批准授予等级运动员称号的人数。运动员等级分为国际级运动健将、运动健将、一级运动员、二级运动员、三级运动员、少年级运动员。

等级裁判员人数　指经考核正式批准授予等级裁判员称号的人数。裁判员等级分为国际裁判、国家级裁判、一级裁判、二级裁判、三级裁判。

卫生机构　卫生机构是指从卫生行政部门取得《医疗机构执业许可证》,或从民政、工商行政、机构编制管理部门取得法人单位登记证书,为社会提供医疗保健、疾病控制、卫生监督等服务或从事医学科研、医学教育等卫生单位和卫生社会团体。不包括卫生行政机构、香港和澳门特别行政区以及台湾所属卫生机构。

卫生技术人员　卫生技术人员包括执业(助理)医师、注册护士、药剂人员、检验和影像技师(士、员)等卫生专业人员。

执业(助理)医师、执业(中)药师和注册护士　执业(助理)医师、执业(中)药师和注册护士是指领取医师、药师执业证书和注册护士证书的人员。不包括从事管理工作的医师、药师和护士。

Explanatory Notes on Main Statistical Indicators

Cultural Institutions refer to units which have their own organizational system and independent accounting system and specialize in or serve cultural development. They exclude other establishments run by these cultural institutions and amateur cultural groups established by various departments.

Art Troupe refers to the troupe which is engaged in drama, opera, music, dance, acrobatics or other art performance, opens independent accounts with banks and has self – supporting accounting system; excluding the troupes which are engaged partly in industrial or agricultural activities, partly in art performance and the professional troupes organized by the people.

Regular Institutions of Higher Learning refer to educational establishments set up according to the government evaluation and approval procedures, enrolling graduates from senior secondary schools and providing higher education courses and training for senior professionals, They include full – time universities, colleges, high professional schools and short – term professional universities.

Institutions of Higher Learning for Adults refer to educational establishments, set up in line with relevant rules approved by the government, enrolling staff and workers with senior secondary school or equivalent education, and providing higher education courses in many forms of full – time, part – time, space – time, or correspondence for adults. Professionals thus trained receive a qualification equivalent to graduates studying regular courses at regular universities, colleges and professional colleges. Institutions of higher learning for adults include Radio and TV universities, schools of high education for staff and workers and peasants, colleges for management cadres, pedagogical colleges, independent correspondence colleges.

Enrollment Rate of Primary School – age Children refer to the proportion of school – age children enrolled at schools to the total number of school – age children both in and outside schools (including retarded children, but excluding blind, deaf and mute children). The formula is:

$$\text{Enrollment Rate of Primary School – age Children} = \frac{\text{Total primary School – age Children at Schools}}{\text{Total Primary School – age Children Both at and Outside Schools}}$$

Number of Athletes in Grades refers to the number of athletes who have been given titles through examination. The titles of athletes include international masters of sports, masters of sports, first – grade, second – grade and third – grade sportsmen and young athletes.

Number of Referees in Grades refers to the number of referees who have been given titles after examination. They are classified as international referees, national referees and referees of the first, second and third grades.

Health Institutions refers to the Institutions and Society organization that get the registered license of health and medical institution from the health adiministration department, or get the registered license of units from civil administration department, industry and business administration and organization management department, and offers medical treatment, controlling of disease, supervision of sanitation. Health institution excludes health administration department and Institutions of Hong Kong, Macao, and Taiwan.

Medical Technical Personnel include registered (Assistant) doctor, registered nurse, druggist, checking members and photo artificer.

Registered (Assistant) Doctor, Registered Druggist and Registered Nurse refers to the personnel who get the licence of doctor, druggist and nurse, the management staff excluded.

十三、人民生活、物价、民政

XIII.PEOPLE'S LIVELIHOOD, PRICE INDICES AND CIVIL ADMINISTRATION

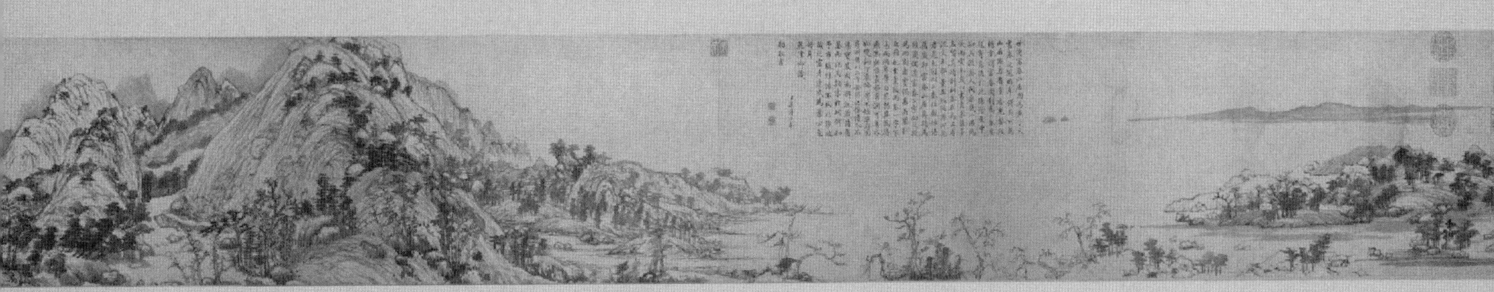

13 人民生活、物价、民政
People's Livelihood, Price Indices and Civil Administration

主要统计指标
Major Statistical Indicators

非私营单位就业人员工资总额	Total Wages of Employed Persons of Non-private Units	1758.23	亿元	(100 million yuan)
非私营单位就业人员平均工资	Annual Average Wages of Employed Persons of Non-private Units	63664	元	(yuan)
城镇居民人均年可支配收入	Per Capita Annual Disposable Income of Urban Households	39310	元	(yuan)
为上年	As Compared with the Preceding Year	110.1	%	(%)
农民人均年纯收入	Per Capita Annual Net Income of Rural Households	18923	元	(yuan)
为上年	As Compared with the Preceding Year	111.2	%	(%)
市区居民消费价格指数	Consume Price Index of Urban District	102.5	上年=100	(Preceding Year=100)
市区商品零售价格指数	Commodity Retail Price Index of Urban District	101.5	上年=100	(Preceding Year=100)
工业品出厂价格指数	Ex-factory Price Index of Industrial Products	98.5	上年=100	(Preceding Year=100)

13－01　城镇住户调查情况(1978－2013)

Basic Conditions of Urban Households (1978－2013)

年　份 Year	调查户数(户) Number of Households Surveyed (household)	平均每户人口(人) Average Household Size (person)	平均每户就业人数(人) Average Number of Employed Persons Per Household(person)	年人均可支配收入(元) Per Capita Annual Disposable Income (yuan)	年人均消费性支出(元) Per Capita Annual Living Expenditure (yuan)	人均住房使用面积(平方米) Per Capita Living Space in City Areas (sq. m)
1978	28	4.20	2.89	338	301	–
1979	28	4.19	2.77	396	365	–
1980	28	4.18	2.79	521	491	–
1981	100	3.97	2.37	540	513	–
1982	100	3.90	2.35	532	532	–
1983	100	3.90	2.42	578	535	8.8
1984	100	3.90	2.36	729	679	9.3
1985	150	3.53	2.26	1026	908	9.7
1986	150	3.49	2.27	1169	1072	9.9
1987	150	3.42	2.25	1260	1118	10.6
1988	200	3.41	2.16	1565	1515	10.6
1989	200	3.40	2.15	1764	1615	10.6
1990	200	3.37	2.15	1985	1685	10.9
1991	200	3.40	2.20	2128	1894	10.8
1992	200	3.28	2.14	2580	2296	11.1
1993	200	3.21	2.10	3525	3183	11.2
1994	200	3.31	2.10	5249	4559	11.9
1995	200	3.20	2.05	6301	5559	11.7
1996	200	3.20	2.00	7206	6095	11.9
1997	200	3.14	1.99	7896	6766	12.4
1998	300	3.12	1.93	8465	7235	14.1
1999	300	3.11	1.92	9085	7424	14.6
2000	300	3.10	1.83	9668	7790	14.9
2001	440	2.98	1.72	10896	8968	15.5
2002	500	2.93	1.53	11778	9215	16.3
2003	500	2.92	1.51	12898	9950	17.2
2004	500	2.92	1.48	14565	11213	17.8
2005	600	2.84	1.42	16601	13438	20.7
2006	600	2.81	1.44	19027	14472	21.0
2007	600	2.72	1.45	21689	14896	21.6
2008	600	2.75	1.29	24104	16719	22.4
2009	600	2.68	1.25	26864	18595	23.1
2010	600	2.70	1.25	30035	20219	23.2
2011	600	2.71	1.32	34065	22642	25.3
2012	600	2.69	1.31	37511	22800	25.8
2013	1360	2.67	1.45	39310	24833	25.3

注:2000 年及以前为主城区数据;2001－2012 年为包括萧山区和余杭区在内的市区数据;2013 年是包括五县市在内的全市数据。

a) The data on the table includes the main urban districts before 2000; The data includes Xiaoshan districts and Yuhang district in 2001－2012; The date in cludes all districts and counties since 2013.

13－02 主要年份城镇居民家庭人均收入支出

Per Capita Annual Cash Income and Expenditure of Urban Residents in Main Years

单位:元 (yuan)

项目 Item	1995	2000	2005	2010	2011	2012	2013
家庭总收入 Total Income	**9121**	**9709**	**18762**	**33810**	**38276**	**41842**	**43868**
#可支配收入 Disposable Income	9085	9668	16601	30035	34065	37511	39310
一、工薪收入 Income from Wages	6776	7075	12961	21075	23760	25436	28132
1. 工资及补贴收入 Bonus and Subsidy	6447	6703	12235	20713	23040	24886	27531
2. 其他劳动收入 Other Income of Staff & Workers From Their Working Units	330	372	726	362	721	549	601
二、经营净收入 Income of Staff & workers in Other－owned Units	277	236	1041	1651	1607	1648	2750
三、财产性收入 Property Income	132	117	586	2189	2587	2210	2136
四、转移性收入 Transfer Income	1935	2282	4173	8896	10321	12550	10850
#养老金或离退休金 Annuities & Retirement Pension	1705	1751	3385	7689	8698	10855	8184
#赡养收入 Supporting Income	15	24	48	277	271	255	639
#捐赠收入 Income from Donation	119	231	354	377	528	446	919
借贷收入 Credit Income	**1680**	**2157**	**4289**	**23065**	**24312**	**22080**	**－**
#提取储蓄存款 Money Drawn from Bank	1465	1870	3779	21893	23586	20915	－
#借入款 Money Borrowed	85	62	119	18	120	91	－
家庭总支出 Total Expenditure	**6532**	**9169**	**17260**	**29956**	**33510**	**32719**	**－**
消费性支出 Living Expenditure	5559	7790	13438	20219	22642	22800	24833
#服务性消费支出 Service Living Expenditure	－	－	3833	5427	6230	6340	－
非消费性支出 Other Non－Living Expenditure	973	1380	3822	9737	10868	9919	－
1. 购买商品住宅及建房支出 Expenditure for House－purchasing	732	752	435	1852	2741	1347	－
2. 赡养支出 Supporting Expenditure	55	109	345	1695	1647	1282	－
3. 捐赠支出 Living Expenditure	124	456	920	1851	1707	2579	－
4. 各种非储蓄性保险支出 Expenditure for Non－saving Insurance	5	29	43	242	381	179	－
5. 社会保障支出 Expenditure for Social Security	－	－	1740	2963	3476	3693	3643
#个人交纳的养老基金 Annuities	－	－	618	1088	1278	1426	1484
#个人交纳的住房公积金 Accumulated Expenditure for House－purchasing	－	－	873	1405	1539	1578	1469
#个人交纳的医疗基金 Expenditure for Medical Treatment	－	－	199	376	560	579	537
借贷支出 Expenditure for Credit	**1319**	**2155**	**4548**	**27961**	**29976**	**31604**	**－**
#存入储蓄款 Saving in Bank	1008	1659	3298	25551	27019	30100	－
#借出款 Money Lent	55	42	28	0	1	18	－
#储蓄性保险支出 Expenditure for Saving Insurance	26	110	191	233	386	144	－
期末手存现金 Per Capita Cash in Hand at Year－end	**513**	**1375**	**2256**	**783**	**1044**	**673**	**－**

注:2000 年及以前为主城区数据;2001－2012 年为包括萧山区和余杭区在内的市区数据;2013 年是包括五县市在内的全市数据。

a) The data on the table includes the main urban districts before 2000; The data includes Xiaoshan districts and Yuhang district in 2001－2012; The date in cludes all districts and counties since 2013.

13－03 主要年份城镇居民家庭人均消费性支出

Per Capita Annual Living Expenditure of Urban Residents in Main Years

单位:元 (yuan)

项目 Item	1995	2000	2005	2010	2011	2012	2013
消费性支出 Total Living Expenditure	**5559**	**7790**	**13438**	**20219**	**22642**	**22800**	**24833**
食品类 Food	2774	3303	4682	7790	8355	8470	8528
#粮食 Grain	235	207	250	394	474	509	473
油脂类 Oil and Fats	49	57	73	150	174	158	155
肉禽及制品 Meat, Poultry and Related Products	555	515	574	984	1197	1301	1126
蛋类 Eggs	57	44	55	100	123	122	99
水产品类 Aquatic Products	395	514	466	809	852	963	767
菜类 Vegetables	267	303	365	664	724	818	682
酒和饮料 Liquor and Beverage	147	192	298	485	497	352	468
干鲜瓜果类 Dried and Fresh Melons and Fruits	212	214	335	610	701	743	373
在外用餐 Out－dining	369	531	1233	2033	2015	1982	2322
衣着类 Clothing	665	645	1299	2061	2261	1991	2421
家庭设备用品及服务 Facilities, Articles and Service	491	627	674	956	1052	1255	1580
医疗保健 Medicine and Medical Service	145	444	983	994	1027	1159	1265
交通和通信 Transportation and Communication	280	548	2234	3910	4678	4299	4725
教育文化娱乐服务 Education, Cultural and Recreation Service	433	1079	1970	2089	2614	2976	2998
居住 Residence	488	701	1151	1853	1945	1749	2305
杂项商品和服务 Miscellaneous Commodities and Service	282	443	445	566	710	902	1011

注:2000 年及以前为主城区数据;2001－2012 年为包括萧山区和余杭区在内的市区数据;2013 年是包括五县市在内的全市数据。

a) The data on the table includes the main urban districts before 2000; The data includes Xiaoshan districts and Yuhang district in 2001－2012; The date in cludes all districts and counties since 2013.

13－04 主要年份城镇居民家庭平均每百户耐用消费品拥有量
Number of Major Durable Consumer Goods Owned Per 100 Urban Households in Main Years

项目 Item		1995	2000	2005	2010	2011	2012	2013
摩托车 Motorcycle	(辆) (unit)	1.5	3.6	11.0	4.5	4.1	4.0	3.5
助力电动车 Electric－bicycle	(辆) (unit)			28.7	42.4	46.0	48.2	50.9
家用汽车 Family Car	(辆) (unit)		0.7	12.8	22.8	31.2	34.3	42.1
微波炉 Micro－wave Oven	(个) (unit)		39.0	68.2	78.8	73.5	74.1	64.1
普通电话 Telephone	(部) (set)		95.0	99.8	89.6	84.7	83.6	54.0
移动电话 Mobile Phone	(部) (set)		19.0	178.7	193.6	211.0	213.1	212.3
淋浴热水器 Water Heater	(台) (unit)	43.5	81.3	92.3	99.4	103.4	105.4	93.9
洗衣机 Washing Machine	(台) (unit)	93.5	96.3	94.2	96.2	96.3	96.6	85.9
电冰箱 Refrigerator	(台) (unit)	103.5	101.7	100.0	102.3	102.5	102.5	89.5
家用电脑 Personal Computer	(台) (unit)		23.0	74.5	99.0	109.7	112.2	112.0
彩色电视机 Color TV Set	(台) (unit)	102.3	146.7	182.7	179.2	176.9	178.4	161.9
组合音响 Music Center	(套) (set)	12.0	28.7	37.8	30.0	25.5	25.9	15.2
摄像机 Video Recorder	(架) (unit)		3.3	7.5	11.1	11.6	12.4	12.0
照相机 Camera	(架) (unit)	54.0	64.7	59.0	54.8	62.1	63.5	57.7
空调器 Air Conditioner	(台) (unit)	43.0	104.0	183.3	214.6	212.0	214.7	195.8

注:2000 年及以前为主城区数据;2001－2012 年为包括萧山区和余杭区在内的市区数据;2013 年是包括五县市在内的全市数据。
a) The data on the table includes the main urban districts before 2000; The data includes Xiaoshan districts and Yuhang district in 2001－2012; The date in cludes all districts and counties since 2013.

13－05 全市农村住户调查情况(1978－2013)

Basic Conditions of Whole Municipality Rural Households(1978－2013)

年　份 Year	调查户数(户) Number of Households Surveyed (household)	平均每户人口(人) Average Number of Residents per Household (person)	平均每户劳动力(人) Average Number of Laborers Per Household(person)	农民人均年纯收入(元) Per Capita Annual Net Income of Rural Households (yuan)	人均生活费支出(元) Per Capita Annual Living Expenditure (yuan)	人均居住面积(平方米) Per Capita Floor Space (sq. m)
1978	–	–	–	162	–	–
1979	–	–	–	204	–	–
1980	60	4.72	2.93	250	287	23.3
1981	60	4.60	2.70	333	294	25.2
1982	60	4.43	2.73	405	328	26.3
1983	170	4.55	2.85	395	355	29.9
1984	170	4.44	2.81	510	416	31.7
1985	420	4.40	2.88	624	542	29.9
1986	620	4.39	2.88	675	601	31.3
1987	620	4.34	2.86	820	714	33.1
1988	620	4.26	2.87	996	925	35.5
1989	620	4.17	2.85	1117	1011	36.8
1990	620	4.16	2.89	1171	923	39.6
1991	620	4.03	2.81	1308	1018	38.0
1992	620	4.01	2.81	1493	1129	37.5
1993	540	3.91	2.76	1748	1276	37.1
1994	630	3.85	2.35	2267	1884	37.8
1995	630	3.87	2.30	3012	2373	40.5
1996	630	3.81	2.77	3482	2772	42.2
1997	630	3.87	2.86	3785	2762	42.0
1998	630	3.87	2.88	4006	2858	46.2
1999	630	3.80	2.80	4209	2851	48.0
2000	630	3.61	2.59	4894	3393	49.0
2001	630	3.57	2.53	5330	3909	52.0
2002	630	3.53	2.53	5708	4444	52.7
2003	670	3.48	2.53	6250	5142	54.7
2004	670	3.48	2.54	6950	5608	58.9
2005	1100	3.34	2.34	7655	6004	66.0
2006	1100	3.63	2.52	8515	6901	66.5
2007	1100	3.60	2.61	9549	7568	68.0
2008	1100	3.56	2.58	10692	8446	69.7
2009	1100	3.57	2.59	11822	9065	70.7
2010	1100	3.58	2.59	13186	10267	71.2
2011	1100	3.46	2.49	15245	12125	72.5
2012	1100	3.45	2.50	17017	13612	71.0
2013	1520	3.47	2.40	18923	14600	70.4

13－06　主要年份农村居民家庭人均纯收入

Per Capita Annual Gross and Net Income of Whole Municipality Rural Households in Main Years

单位:元　　(yuan)

项　目 Item	1995	2000	2005	2010	2011	2012	2013
全年纯收入 Net Income	**3012**	**4894**	**7655**	**13186**	**15245**	**17017**	**18923**
1. 劳动者的工资性收入 Laborers´Remuneration	896	2045	3347	7777	9079	10054	11550
2. 家庭经营收入 Income from Household Business Operation	1960	2363	3358	4049	4478	4935	4928
#农业收入 Income from Farming	578	1016	1858	1005	1159	1230	1082
林业收入 Income from Forestry	142	71	311	365	445	477	429
牧业收入 Income from Animal Husbandry	397	382	310	223	271	315	184
渔业收入 Income from Fishery	24	31	185	73	45	55	5
工业收入 Income from Industry	112	262	392	473	469	484	641
建筑业收入 Income from Construction	77	102	228	345	430	476	434
交通、运输、仓储及邮电业收入 Transportation, Posts, Storage and Telecommunication	136	163	483	517	532	614	417
批发和零售贸易、餐饮业收入 Income from Retail Wholesale & Trade and Catering Services	118	150	391	699	742	845	1418
社会服务业收入 Social Serve Trade	59	73	127	210	205	279	200
3. 转移性收入 Transfer Income	83	312	481	719	945	1168	1400
#在外人口寄回或带回 Income of Going out to Work	5	21	93	101	133	166	－
农村外部亲友赠送 Present from Rural Friends and Relatives	9	7	133	23	58	56	－
4. 财产性收入 Property Income	73	174	469	641	743	859	1045
#土地征用补偿收入 Compensation for Confiscating Land	6	100	243	190	206	236	－

13－07　主要年份农村居民家庭人均支出

Per Capita Gross Expenditure of Whole City's Rural Households in Main Years

单位:元　　　　(yuan)

项　　目 Item	1995	2000	2005	2010	2011	2012	2013
全年总支出 Gross Expenditure	**3457**	**3789**	**8043**	**13439**	**15941**	**18257**	**－**
生活消费支出 Living Expenditure	**2373**	**3393**	**6004**	**10227**	**12125**	**13612**	**14600**
1. 食品 Food	1213	1392	2145	3333	4076	4455	4820
#在外饮食 #Out－dining	43	83	221	487	570	626	874
食品加工费 Food－processing	13	15	11	12	8	10	－
2. 衣着 Clothing	169	169	381	609	819	969	1115
3. 居住 Residence	396	694	1143	2603	2845	2876	2640
#住房 #Housing	284	509	724	1855	2144	2005	－
电费 Electricity	22	56	110	255	282	349	468
燃料 Fuel	53	38	77	126	155	162	196
4. 家庭设备、用品及服务 Household Facilities, Articles and Services	155	163	307	512	645	749	853
5. 医疗保健 Medicines and Medical Services	99	329	474	623	753	854	1124
#医药卫生保健用品 #Medicines	39	99	189	252	226	266	287
医疗保健服务费 Medicines Services	58	64	256	371	528	589	837
6. 交通和通讯 Transportation and Communications	102	204	680	1451	1865	2303	2573
#交通工具 #Vehicles	67	123	158	784	857	1098	1135
交通费 Traffic	18	36	83	90	94	111	145
邮电费 Postage	4	62	219	264	242	252	571
7. 文教娱乐用品及服务 Cultural, Educational and Recreational Articles and Services	156	318	735	934	861	1007	1060
文化教育娱乐用品 Cultural, Educational and Recreational Articles	43	70	114	227	268	309	276
文化教育娱乐服务 Culrural, Educational and Recreational Services	113	248	621	707	593	698	784

单位:元　　13－07　续表　continued　　(yuan)

项目 Item	1995	2000	2005	2010	2011	2012	2013
#学杂费 #Tuition and Incidental Expenses	94	210	430	344	175	301	–
技术培训费 Technical Training Expenses	5	5	32	31	48	73	–
文娱费 Recreational and Cultural Expenses	11	9	22	53	45	46	–
8.其他商品和服务 Other Commodities and Services	84	124	139	202	261	330	415
家庭经营费用支出 Expenditure of Household Business Operation	**681**	**427**	**1157**	**1285**	**1831**	**1725**	**–**
种植业生产支出 Expenditure of Farming	199	183	245	279	404	385	–
林业生产支出 Expenditure of Forestry	3	10	71	87	143	260	–
牧业生产支出 Expenditure of Animal Husbandry	267	121	168	184	377	232	–
渔业生产支出 Expenditure of Fishery	4	10	116	48	11	61	–
工业生产支出 Expenditure of Industry	62	61	276	449	313	264	–
建筑业生产支出 Expenditure of Construction	3	3	35	74	149	176	–
运输业生产支出 Expenditure of Transportation	64	29	141	175	128	154	–
批发和零售贸易、餐饮业支出 Expenditure of Wholesale and Retail Trade & Catering Services	53	6	84	53	129	110	–
服务业支出 Expenditure of Services Trade	5	1	9	8	52	43	–
其他经营支出 Others	22	3	12	6	16	39	–
购置生产用固定资产支出 Expenditure of Purchasing Fixed Assets	**135**	**86**	**202**	**121**	**178**	**138**	**–**
税费支出 Expenditure of Taxes	**23**	**50**	**31**	**10**	**10**	**7**	**–**
其他非借贷性支出 Others Expenditure not for Loans	**235**	**206**	**649**	**1079**	**1477**	**2211**	**–**
#寄给和带给在外人口 Posting and Giving to People Outside	6	23	396	260	168	190	–
赠送农村外部亲友 Present to Rural Friends and Relatives	7	8	7	7	8	10	–
附:生产用固定资产累计折旧 Depreciation of Fixed Assets for Production	**63**	**79**	**218**	**–**	**–**	**–**	**–**

13-08 主要年份农村居民家庭平均每百户耐用消费品拥有量

Number of Major Durable Consumer Goods Owned Per 100 Rural Households in Main Years

项　　目	Item	1995	2000	2005	2010	2011	2012	2013
洗衣机（台）	Washing Machine (Unit)	14.0	34.0	62.0	85.1	78.2	87.8	87.0
电冰箱（台）	Refrigerator (Unit)	23.0	46.0	72.0	98.1	93.3	101.8	99.7
空调机（台）	Air Conditioner (Unit)	1.0	8.0	12.0	111.2	120.3	143.3	151.3
抽油烟机（台）	Somoke Exhauster (Unit)	4.0	17.0	39.0	61.6	56.6	65.8	64.6
吸尘器（台）	Dust Collector (Unit)	2.0	3.0	5.0	10.0	8.6	11.3	-
微波炉（个）	Micro - wave Oven (Unit)				28.8	34.3	41.4	39.0
热水器（台）	Water Heater (Unit)				84.5	80.7	90.9	87.7
摩托车（辆）	Motorcycle (Unit)	13.0	38.0	73.0	66.2	40.8	42.6	31.9
汽车(生活用)（辆）	Family Car (Unit)			4.0	15.7	21.6	27.5	36.7
移动电话（部）	Mobile Phone (Set)		17.0	125.0	212.9	230.4	253.1	245.4
彩色电视机（台）	Color TV Set (Unit)	34.0	86.0	141.0	186.3	192.5	210.6	203.0
摄像机（架）	Video Recorder (Unit)				2.0	1.3	1.8	2.6
照相机（架）	Camera (Unit)	4.0	7.0	14.0	22.6	21.7	26.5	24.6
家用计算机（台）	Personal Computer (Unit)		1.0	12.0	44.2	51.3	60.4	67.4

13-09 全市就业人员工资总额(1978-2013)

Total Wages of Employed Persons(1978-2013)

单位:万元 (10000 yuan)

年份 Year	全市(含规上私营) Total (includes private units above designated size)	#非私营单位 Non-private	市区(含规上私营) Urban District (includes private units above designated size)	#非私营单位 Non-private
1978		43775		28256
1979		52127		34318
1980		67918		45574
1981		72896		48809
1982		75584		50959
1983		78336		52909
1984		102223		69135
1985		130114		87774
1986		157471		105995
1987		180077		121003
1988		230868		152859
1989		253956		167055
1990		277910		182985
1991		313906		209052
1992		377614		253653
1993		534537		359041
1994		772236		521669
1995		890488		615450
1996		973592		683244
1997		1073862		762957
1998		1112718		803264
1999		1180947		864418
2000		1267524		949872
2001		1481659		1279749
2002		1614676		1398222
2003		1867776		1617504
2004	2844691	2188159	2313930	1859164
2005	3711915	2970200	3112937	2584779
2006	4526841	3811735	3830043	3338568
2007	6233799	4954813	5256791	4317965
2008	8592198	6416424	7338932	5679543
2009	9909330	7549145	8475547	6665279
2010	12305726	9330552	10531483	8238017
2011	15012179	11222834	12934215	9954506
2012	19540005	14839012	17115217	13217453
2013	23604682	17582336	20762852	15820468

注:口径范围,1997年及以前为全市全部职工,1998-2012为在岗职工,2013年为就业人员。2004年起包含规模以上私营单位。

a) Data on this table refer to wages of all employees before 1997, that refer to all staff and workers in 1998-2012, and refer to employed persons in 2013. Data on this bill includes Private units above designated size since 2004.

13－10　全市就业人员年平均工资(1978－2013)

Average Annual Wages of Employed Persons(1978－2013)

单位:元　　(yuan)

年　份 Year	全市(含规上私营) Total (includes private units above designated size)	#非私营单位 Non－private	市区(含规上私营) Urban District (includes private units above designated size)	#非私营单位 Non－private	附:市区全社会 a) The Whole City in Urban districts
1978		597		642	
1979		643		692	
1980		777		814	
1981		783		810	
1982		791		809	
1983		813		835	
1984		1036		1071	
1985		1266		1316	
1986		1469		1536	
1987		1616		1690	
1988		1986		2073	
1989		2173		2261	
1990		2382		2486	
1991		2586		2706	
1992		3071		3233	
1993		4220		4561	
1994		6118		6597	
1995		7156		7786	
1996		7966		7851	
1997		9108		10048	
1998		10555		11512	
1999		12187		13225	
2000		14257		15454	
2001		18319		18962	18205
2002		21418		22091	19749
2003		24668		25535	20113
2004	21879	28891	24204	30719	22235
2005	24685	31069	26366	32166	22645
2006	27620	32791	29397	33967	23581
2007	29864	36496	31625	37991	25489
2008	32513	40193	34107	41501	27863
2009	35638	43947	37270	45149	30480
2010	39772	48772	41303	49938	34330
2011	45775	54408	47695	55958	38837
2012	51077	56417	52610	57548	42493
2013	55124	63664	56857	64941	46831

注:非私营单位1997年及以前为全市全部职工,1998－2012为在岗职工,2013年为就业人员。含规模以上私营单位从2004年统计。全社会包括独立核算的机关、事业单位,非私营企业和私营企业,但不包含个体工商户。

a) The data of Non－private refer to all employees before 1997, refer to staff and workers in 1998－2012, and refer to employed persons in 2013. Since 2004, refers to independent accounting units of government organizations and institutions, non－private and private enterprises, but excluding individual business.

13-11 全市含规上私营单位就业人员工资总额(2013年)

Total Wages of Employed Persons Including Private Units Above Designated Size(2013)

单位:万元 (10000 yuan)

项目 Item		年末单位人员就业人员工资总额 Total Wages of Employed Persons at Year-end	#非私营 Non-private	在岗职工工资总额 Total Wages of Fully Employed Staff and Workers	#非私营 Non-private	其他就业人员工资总额 Total Wages of Other Employed Persons	#非私营 Non-private
全市总计	**Whole city Total**	**23604682**	**17582336**	**22439498**	**16824084**	**1165184**	**758252**
市区总计	Urban District	20762852	15820468	19708660	15110063	1054192	710405
#上城区	Shangcheng	1964764	1764121	1780311	1585476	184453	178645
下城区	Xiacheng	2042166	1880892	1972803	1820606	69363	60286
江干区	Jianggan	1803818	1140615	1560354	1075688	243463	64927
拱墅区	Gongshu	1797129	1073642	1704876	1005481	92253	68161
西湖区	Xihu	3062337	2632485	2920212	2537387	142126	95098
高新(滨江)区	Hi-Tech(Binjiang)	2220064	1895202	2170790	1852489	49274	42713
萧山区	Xiaoshan	4235558	2673209	4115690	2597453	119868	75757
余杭区	Yuhang	2271481	1486547	2209818	1447929	61663	38618
桐庐县	Tonglu	434141	244874	411234	233269	22907	11605
淳安县	Chun'an	298298	210343	281227	203533	17072	6810
建德市	Jiande	368136	251501	351650	243683	16486	7818
富阳市	Fuyang	1045909	589701	1005282	577660	40627	12041
临安市	Lin'an	695345	465449	681445	455876	13901	9573

单位:万元　　13－11　续表　continued　　(10000 yuan)

项　目 Item	年末单位人员就业人员工资总额 Total Wages of Employed Persons at Year－end	#非私营 Non－private	在岗职工工资总额 Total Wages of Fully Employed Staff and Workers	#非私营 Non－private	其他就业人员工资总额 Total Wages of Other Employed Persons	#非私营 Non－private
按国民经济行业分组 **Grouped by Sector**						
农、林、牧、渔业 Farming, Forestry, Animal Husbandry & Fishery	8040	7869	7849	7681	191	188
采矿业 Mining	14265	6533	14071	6441	194	92
制造业 Manufacturing	5884116	3991639	5779721	3911499	104395	80140
电力、热力、燃气及水生产和供应业 Production & Supply of Electricity, Heat, Gas & Water	194311	189588	192358	187635	1953	1953
建筑业 Construction	6091567	3156142	5407883	2816088	683685	340054
批发和零售业 Wholesale & Retail Trades	1357718	1072622	1318396	1039176	39322	33446
交通运输、仓储和邮政业 Transportation, Storage and Post	830560	768175	821567	759925	8993	8250
住宿和餐饮业 Hotels and Catering Services	370449	256956	352375	241517	18074	15439
信息传输、软件和信息技术服务业 Information Transmission, Software and Information Technology	1374023	1180940	1366669	1175743	7354	5197
金融业 Financial Intermediation	1412541	1406473	1375556	1369822	36985	36651
房地产业 Real Estate	612960	497895	591239	481788	21721	16107
租赁和商务服务业 Leasing and Business Services	713413	553077	683802	529307	29612	23770
科学研究、技术服务业 Scientific Research, Technical Services	840134	735119	797589	702129	42546	32990
水利、环境和公共设施管理业 Management of Water Conservancy, Environment and Public Facilities	231250	173128	217348	161425	13903	11704
居民服务、修理和其他服务业 Service to Honseholds, Repair and Other Services	71452	39621	67846	37910	3606	1711
教育 Education	1319888	1301518	1274656	1256652	45232	44866
卫生和社会工作 Health Care and Social Work	917289	896690	855852	836511	61437	60179
文化、体育和娱乐业 Culture, Sports and Entertainment	206068	193717	198611	186726	7457	6992
公共管理、社会保障和社会组织 Public Management, Social Security and Social Organizations	1154637	1154637	1116111	1116111	38525	38525

13－12　全市含规上私营单位就业人员平均工资(2013 年)

Average Annual Wages of Employed Persons Including Units Above Designated Size(2013)

单位:元　　　　(yuan)

项　　目	Item	全市 Total	#非私营单位 Non－private
全市	**Total**	**55124**	**63664**
市区	Urban District	56857	64941
#上城区	Shangcheng	75474	84671
下城区	Xiacheng	76328	83674
江干区	Jianggan	50886	58281
拱墅区	Gongshu	49901	60166
西湖区	Xihu	53801	56562
高新(滨江)区	Hi－Tech(Binjiang)	81313	89948
萧山区	Xiaoshan	46818	52630
余杭区	Yuhang	53085	64248
桐庐县	Tonglu	44918	55008
淳安县	Chun'an	50551	57053
建德市	Jiande	45509	52721
富阳市	Fuyang	43980	55084
临安市	Lin'an	44585	52022
按国民经济行业分组	**Grouped by Sector**		
农、林、牧、渔业	Farming, Forestry, Animal Husbandry & Fishery	46046	46424
采矿业	Mining	43946	44866
制造业	Manufacturing	48538	54578
电力、热力、燃气及水生产和供应业	Production & Supply of Electricity, Heat, Gas & Water	90251	92468
建筑业	Construction	40929	43528
批发和零售业	Wholesale & Retail Trades	55022	60886
交通运输、仓储和邮政业	Transportation, Storage and Post	65029	69623
住宿和餐饮业	Hotels and Catering Services	33694	35053
信息传输、软件和信息技术服务业	Information Transmission, Software and Information Technology	110252	122290
金融业	Financial Intermediation	154460	155704
房地产业	Real Estate	54071	57439
租赁和商务服务业	Leasing and Business Services	54071	54845
科学研究、技术服务业	Scientific Research, Technical Services	77181	87074
水利、环境和公共设施管理业	Management of Water Conservancy, Environment and Public Facilities	48422	50432
居民服务、修理和其他服务业	Service to Honseholds, Repair and Other Services	37128	45567
教育	Education	75050	76306
卫生和社会工业	Health Care and Social Work	92852	95267
文化、体育和娱乐业	Culture, Sports and Entertainment	75571	81006
公共管理、社会保障和社会组织	Public Management, Social Security and Social Organizations	87893	87893

13－13　市区消费价格指数(1978－2013)
Consumer Price Indices in Urban District(1978－2013)

(上年＝100)　　(Preceding Year＝100)

年份 Year	居民消费价格指数 General Consumer Price Index	商品零售价格指数 General Retail Price Index
1978	100.1	100.1
1979	100.4	100.9
1980	100.8	109.3
1981	102.0	102.0
1982	102.0	102.3
1983	102.1	102.3
1984	103.1	103.1
1985	117.2	117.5
1986	106.0	106.1
1987	110.5	111.3
1988	121.9	123.4
1989	117.8	118.2
1990	104.6	104.4
1991	107.5	106.9
1992	110.4	110.2
1993	121.4	117.3
1994	121.5	118.8
1995	116.5	113.3
1996	110.5	107.2
1997	106.7	102.4
1998	101.8	99.8
1999	100.4	98.2
2000	100.8	98.3
2001	99.5	95.3
2002	98.8	97.9
2003	99.5	98.1
2004	102.5	101.6
2005	101.7	100.3
2006	101.2	100.2
2007	103.5	103.1
2008	104.9	106.0
2009	98.6	98.6
2010	103.9	103.7
2011	104.8	104.4
2012	102.5	101.9
2013	102.5	101.5

13－14　市区居民消费价格分类指数(2013年)

Consumer Price Indices by Category in Urban District(2013)

(上年＝100)　　(Preceding Year＝100)

项　目	Item	指数 Indices
居民消费价格总指数	**Consumer Price Indices**	**102.5**
一、食品	**Food**	**104.2**
1. 粮食	Grain	103.5
2. 淀粉及制品	Starches and Tubers	104.2
3. 干豆类及豆制品	Bean and Its Products	100.8
4. 油脂	Oil and Fat	97.2
5. 肉禽及其制品	Meal Poultry and Their Products	103.9
6. 蛋	Eggs	99.5
7. 水产品	Aquatic Products	106.8
8. 菜	Vegetables	108.3
9. 调味品	Flavoring	99.9
10. 糖	Sugar	100.2
11. 茶及饮料	Tea and Beverages	101.4
12. 干鲜瓜果	Dried and Fresh Melons and Fruits	103.6
13. 糕点饼干面包	Cake、Biscuit and Bread	102.3
14. 液体乳及乳制品	Milk and Its Products	107.1
15. 在外用膳食品	Outward Dinner	102.9
16. 其他食品	Other Food	100.6
二、烟酒及用品	**Tobacco、Liquor and Articles**	**99.5**
1. 烟草	Tobacco	100.0
2. 酒	Liquor	97.9
三、衣着	**Clothing**	**101.3**
1. 服装	Garments	100.9
2. 衣着材料	Clothing Material	100.8

项目	Item	指数 Indices
3.鞋袜帽	Shoes, Socks and Hats	102.6
4.衣着加工服务费	Clothing Processing Service	106.5
四、家庭设备用品及维修服务	**Household Facilities, Articles and Repair Service**	**103.3**
1.耐用消费品	Durable Consumer Goods	100.0
2.室内装饰品	Interior Decorations	102.1
3.床上用品	Bed Articles	109.2
4.家庭日用杂品	Daily Use Household Articles	100.8
5.家庭服务及加工维修服务	Household and Repair Service	114.0
五、医疗保健和个人用品	**Medical Articles and Personal Articles**	**101.1**
1.医疗保健	Medical Care	101.5
2.个人用品及服务	Personel Articles and Service	99.6
六、交通和通信	**Transportation and Communication**	**99.5**
1.交通	Transportation	99.0
2.通信	Communication	100.8
七、娱乐教育文化用品及服务	**Recreation, Education and Culture Articles**	**103.9**
1.文娱用耐用消费品及服务	Durable Consumer Goods and Recreation Service	96.9
2.教育	Education	104.9
3.文化娱乐类	Cultural and Recreational Articles	99.7
4.旅游	Tourism and Outgoing	106.8
八、居住	**Residence**	**102.1**
1.建房及装修材料	Construction and Upholstery Materials	101.3
2.住房租金	House Renting	102.8
3.自有住房	Private Owned Houses	102.6
4.水、电、燃料	Water, Electricity and Fuels	101.2

13－15 市区零售价格分类指数(2013 年)

Retail Price Indices by Category in Urban District(2013)

(上年＝100)　　(Preceding Year＝100)

项　目	Item	指数 Indices
商品零售价格总指数	**Retail Price Indices**	**101.5**
一、食品	**Food**	**104.2**
1.粮食	Grain	103.6
2.淀粉及制品	Starches and Tubers	104.2
3.干豆类及豆制品	Bean and Its Products	101.0
4.油脂	Oil and Fat	97.2
5.肉禽及其制品	Meal Poultry and Their Products	103.5
6.蛋	Eggs	99.5
7.水产品	Aquatic Products	106.8
8.菜	Vegetables	108.3
9.调味品	Flavoring	99.9
10.糖	Carbohydrate	100.1
11.干鲜瓜果	Dried and Fresh Melons and Fruits	103.7
12.糕点饼干面包	Cake、Biscuit and Bread	102.4
13.液体乳及乳制品	Milk and Its Products	106.4
14.在外用膳食品	Outward Dinner	103.1
15.其他食品	Other Food	100.6
二、饮料、烟酒	**Beverages,Tobacco and Liquor**	**99.5**
1.茶及饮料	Tea and Beverages	101.2
2.烟草	Tobacco	100.0
3.酒	Liquor	97.6
三、服装、鞋帽	**Garments,Shoes and Hats**	**101.3**
1.服装	Garments	100.9
2.鞋袜帽	Shoes,Socks and Hats	102.5
3.其他	Other	106.1
四、纺织品	**Textiles**	**104.5**
1.衣着材料	Clothing Material	100.8
2.床上用品	Bed Articles	107.2
五、家用电器及音像器材	**Household Electric Appliances,Audio and Video Equipment**	**99.5**
1.家庭设备	Household Equipment	100.3
2.文娱用耐用消费品	Durable Consumer Goods for Entertainment	96.6

(上年=100) 13-15 续表 continued (Preceding Year=100)

项目	Item	指数 Indices
3. 专业音像器材	Audio and Video Equipment	101.6
六、文化办公用品	**Stationery and Office Supplies**	**98.8**
七、日用品	**Commodities**	**100.6**
1. 日用百货	General Merchandise for Daily Use	99.9
2. 日用杂品	Sundries for Daily Use	101.2
3. 洗涤用品	Washing Articles	100.1
4. 其他日用品	Other Commodity	101.8
八、体育娱乐用品	**Sports and Entertainment Goods**	**100.4**
1. 体育用品	Sports Goods	102.1
2. 娱乐用品	Entertainment Goods	99.8
九、交通、通信用品	**Transportation and Communications Articles**	**98.9**
1. 交通运输机械	Transportation Vehicles	99.4
2. 通讯器材	Equipment of Communication	94.8
十、家具	**Funishings**	**99.0**
十一、化妆品	**Cosmetics**	**104.1**
十二、金银珠宝	**Jewellery**	**98.5**
十三、中西药品及医疗保健用品	**Chinese and Western Medicine, Health Care Articles**	**101.5**
1. 医疗器具及用品	Medical Instruments and Articles	100.0
2. 中药材及中成药	Chinese Medicinal Materials and Chinese Traditional Medicine	101.8
3. 西药	Western Medicine	99.9
4. 保健器具及用品	Articles for Health Care	105.1
十四、书报杂志及电子出版物	**Books, Newspapers, Magazines and Electron Publications**	**100.0**
1. 教材及参考书	Teaching Materials and Reference Books	100.0
2. 书报杂志	Books, Newspapers and Magazines	100.0
3. 电子音像制品	Electronic Music and Film Products	100.0
十五、燃料	**Fuels**	**101.3**
1. 煤炭及制品	Coal and Coal Products	105.6
2. 石油及制品	Oil and Oil Products	100.6
十六、建筑材料及五金电料	**Construction Materials and Hardware**	**99.1**
1. 建筑装潢材料	Construction and Upholstery Materials	98.3
2. 五金电料	Hardware and Electric Materials	101.1

13－16 主要年份工业生产者出厂价格分类指数

Producer Price Indices for Industrial Products by Category in Main Years

(上年＝100) (Preceding Year＝100)

项目 Item	1999	2000	2005	2010	2011	2012	2013
工业生产者出厂价格总指数 Total Producer Price Indices for Industrial Products	**96.9**	**100.3**	**103.5**	**104.9**	**104.7**	**97.2**	**98.5**
一、按轻重工业分 Grouped by Industries							
轻工业 Light Industry	**95.8**	**99.3**	**101.8**	**105.0**	**105.5**	**98.1**	**99.9**
以农产品为原料 Made from Agricultural Products	96.9	99.9	102.0	103.9	104.6	99.4	100.8
以非农产品为原料 Made from Non－agricultural Products	95.3	98.0	101.7	106.0	106.8	96.1	98.4
重工业 Heavy Industry	**98.0**	**101.1**	**105.6**	**104.7**	**104.2**	**96.5**	**97.5**
采掘 Mining & Quarrying Industry	－	99.5	103.0	114.0	116.6	101.3	101.0
原料 Raw Materials Industry	99.0	104.4	107.7	110.7	108.7	96.9	97.5
加工 Manufacturing Industry	97.6	98.9	104.3	102.5	102.8	96.4	97.5
二、按二大部类分 Grouped by Means of Producting and Consumer Goods							
生产资料 Means of Production	**97.9**	**101.9**	**104.8**	**106.2**	**105.1**	**95.5**	**97.8**
采掘 Mining	－	99.6	103.0	114.0	116.6	101.3	101.0
原料 Raw Materials	98.4	103.8	110.7	114.5	110.6	92.6	96.5
加工 Manufacture	97.7	100.3	101.6	103.9	103.3	96.4	98.2
生活资料 Consumer Goods	**95.7**	**97.5**	**101.2**	**101.0**	**103.7**	**102.6**	**100.6**
食品 Foods	98.8	96.4	101.6	100.1	104.3	101.8	101.0
衣着 Clothing	95.2	101.1	101.4	102.4	104.5	104.6	102.0
一般日用品 Articles for Daily Use	94.9	97.8	101.7	100.8	103.9	102.3	99.8
耐用消费品 Durable Consumer Goods	94.8	94.5	99.5	100.9	101.5	102.0	99.6

(上年＝100)　　13－16　续表　continued　　(Preceding Year＝100)

项目 Item	1999	2000	2005	2010	2011	2012	2013
三、按工业部门分 Grouped by Industrial Sector							
冶金工业 Metallurgical Industry	95.6	104.0	104.8	108.0	107.1	93.3	95.4
电力工业 Power Industry	99.8	96.0	106.2	105.2	102.0	101.7	99.1
煤炭及炼焦工业 Coal and Coking Industry	99.8	107.9	102.1		–		
石油工业 Petroleum Industry	108.1	131.6	124.7	117.0	110.4	103.0	100.5
化学工业 Chemical Industry	97.2	101.1	106.0	111.9	109.3	93.8	97.3
机械工业 Machine Building Industry	94.9	96.7	102.9	100.8	101.3	97.6	98.1
建材材料工业 Building Materials Industry	103.1	103.0	91.7	109.3	109.8	94.0	97.3
森林工业 Timber Industry	96.6	96.9	101.4	101.6	102.0	100.7	101.0
食品工业 Food Industry	98.0	95.8	100.6	100.1	105.1	102.0	101.2
纺织工业 Textile Industry	97.3	107.3	103.4	107.5	105.1	95.5	101.1
缝纫工业 Tailoring Industry	96.3	100.5	101.5	102.2	105.6	104.6	102.6
皮革工业 Leather Industry	91.6	98.0	101.4	102.9	101.9	103.4	101.1
造纸工业 Paper Industry	96.2	102.9	100.3	104.6	102.0	96.7	96.3
文教艺术用品工业 Cultural, Educational & Handicrafts Articles	90.4	98.7	99.7	97.3	100.9	100.1	100.0
其它工业 Others	101.1	103.6	102.2	104.7	109.0	103.9	101.3

13－17 主要年份工业生产者购进价格分类指数

Purchasing Price Indices for Industrial Producers in Main Years

（上年＝100）　　　　（Preceding Year＝100）

项　　目 Item	1999	2000	2005	2010	2011	2012	2013
工业生产者购进价格指数 Purchasing Price Index for Industrial Producers	**97.2**	**107.4**	**106.9**	**112.1**	**110.8**	**94.6**	**97.3**
燃料动力类 Fuel and Power	103.0	108.0	116.4	111.3	110.6	98.2	96.9
黑色金属材料类 Ferrous and Metals	96.3	102.7	105.2	108.6	107.0	88.7	95.0
1. 钢材 Rolled －steel	94.9	103.2	104.9	108.2	106.6	88.5	95.4
2. 其他 Other	98.2	101.0	105.7	113.0	113.1	91.2	90.1
有色金属材料及电线类 Non－ferrous Metals and Electric Wire	97.6	108.0	111.2	129.3	113.4	93.1	93.7
化工原料类 Chemical Raw Materials	97.6	111.0	110.1	113.3	114.3	94.2	97.0
木材及纸浆类 Wood and Paper Pulps	95.5	104.5	101.0	106.4	104.0	97.7	98.8
建筑材料及非金属类 Building Materials	98.2	100.6	102.3	108.8	116.8	99.5	99.4
其他工业原材料及半成品类 Other Industrial Raw Materials and Semi－products	97.2	111.0	103.6	109.8	107.2	99.1	97.8
农副产品类 Farm and Sideline Products	95.0	104.0	103.9	114.1	112.8	97.2	98.4
纺织原料类 Textile Raw Materials	89.4	104.7	99.9	110.4	110.5	96.3	101.9

13－18 住宅销售价格指数(2013 年)
Sales Price Indices of Houses(2013)

月份 Month	新建住宅 New Residential Building		#新建商品住宅 New Residential Commodities Building		二手住宅 The Second－hand House	
	上月＝100	上年同期＝100 Preceding Year＝100	上月＝100	上年同期＝100 Preceding Year＝100	上月＝100	上年同期＝100 Preceding Year＝100
全年 Annual Total	**－**	**105.7**	**－**	**105.9**	**－**	**102.0**
一月 January	100.9	93.6	100.9	93.4	99.5	99.1
二月 February	100.9	94.7	100.9	94.5	101.4	101.1
三月 March	101.2	100.3	101.2	100.3	100.2	101.6
四月 April	101.4	105.2	101.4	105.4	100.2	102.5
五月 May	100.8	106.7	100.8	107.0	100.1	102.7
六月 June	101.0	107.1	101.0	107.4	100.3	103.0
七月 July	100.7	107.5	100.8	107.9	99.9	102.0
八月 August	101.1	108.3	101.1	108.7	100.2	101.8
九月 September	101.2	109.4	101.3	109.8	100.6	102.8
十月 October	100.8	110.5	100.8	111.0	100.0	102.8
十一月 November	100.5	111.2	100.6	111.7	100.3	103.0
十二月 December	100.1	111.0	100.1	111.5	100.2	102.9

注:按国家统计局每月公布的城市房价数据整理。

Note:The data was organized by the urban housing prices which were pubushed monthly by National Bureall of Statistics of China.

13－19 优抚对象

Number of Persons Enjoying

单位:人

指　　标 Item	全　市 Total	市　区 Urban District	#萧山区 Xiaoshan
享受定期抚恤金人数 Number of Persons Receiving Periodical Commiseration	608	186	90
烈属 Number of Martyr Kinsfolk	280	74	32
牺牲军人家属 Number of the Sacrifice Soldiers	108	30	12
病故军人家属 Number of Kinsfolks of the Illness－died Soldiers	220	82	46
享受定期补助人数 Number of Persons Enjoying Regular Subsidies	32736	11677	7217
#红军失散人员 Number of Persons be Scattered of the Red Army	－	－	－
在乡复员军人 Rural Demobilized Soldier	2926	981	432
抗日 The War of Resistance Against Japan	24	15	2
优待优抚对象带病回乡退伍军人 Number of Rural Veterans with Illness Receiving Subsiders	5346	810	559
优待优抚对象户数 Number of Households Receiving Subsiders	28117	14852	6110
优待军属户数 Number of Households Sacrifice Soldiers	6617	3476	1171

人员情况(2013 年)
Public Subsidies(2013)

(person)

#余杭区 Yuhang	桐庐县 Tonglu	淳安县 Chun'an	建德市 Jiande	富阳市 Fuyang	临安市 Lin'an
49	89	88	77	110	58
19	37	55	47	37	30
10	19	6	11	33	9
20	33	27	19	40	19
3418	4478	2954	3898	5015	4714
–	–	–	–	–	–
394	474	297	295	390	489
1	3	–	–	–	6
206	714	919	1248	628	1027
3853	615	498	5101	4174	2877
822	615	498	639	782	607

13－20 市、县级社会

Basic Statistics on Institutions and

单位:个

指标 Item		全市 Total	市区 Urban District	#萧山区 Xiaoshan
合计	**Total**	**2550**	**1707**	**241**
按活动区域分	**Grouped by Region**			
地级社团	City－level Societies	681	681	–
县级社团	County－level Societies	1869	1026	241
按性质分	**Grouped by Category**			
科技与研究	Technology and Research	81	53	–
生态环境	Ecological Envirenment	68	12	4
教育	Education	96	40	3
卫生	Health	92	53	10
社会服务	Social Services	254	128	16
文化	Culture	245	154	35
体育	Sport	194	133	14
法律	Law	27	22	–
工商业服务	Industry and Business Services	388	289	25
宗教	Religion	32	15	5
农业及农村发展	Agricure and Rural Development	180	74	26
职业及从业组织	Vocational and Business Organizations	191	129	2
国际及涉外组织	International and Foreign Organizations	20	18	–
其他	Other	682	587	101

团体机构情况(2013 年)

Organizations at County Level(2013)

(unit)

#余杭区 Yuhang	桐庐县 Tonglu	淳安县 Chun'an	建德市 Jiande	富阳市 Fuyang	临安市 Lin'an
245	**146**	**110**	**189**	**210**	**188**
–	–	–	–	–	–
245	146	110	189	210	188
1	1	4	7	13	3
7	46	2	5	2	1
3	38	4	6	2	6
19	11	6	8	6	8
6	41	31	30	22	2
21	9	7	22	35	18
23	–	4	25	15	17
3	–	1	2	2	–
75	–	9	18	48	24
5	–	3	6	4	4
17	–	29	21	31	25
64	–	10	24	19	9
–	–	–	–	2	–
1	–	–	15	9	71

13－21　社会办福利院情况(2013 年末)

Basic Statistics on Welfare Homes(End of 2013)

指标
Item
	单　位
	(个)
	Homes
	(unit)
		职工人数(人)
		Staff and Workers
		(person)
			床位数(张)
			Beds
			(bed)
				在院人数
				(人)
				Persons Housed
				(person)
					#老　人(人)
					Seniors(person)

全　市 Total	**284**	**4001**	**42869**	**17072**	**15805**
市　区 Urban District	170	3182	30656	11886	10901
#萧山区 Xiaoshan	38	904	7990	2235	2148
余杭区 Yuhang	37	242	4705	1423	1374
桐庐县 Tonglu	15	129	1543	953	949
淳安县 Chun'an	25	95	1992	766	751
建德市 Jiande	26	183	3109	1575	1438
富阳市 Fuyang	23	263	2760	825	758
临安市 Lin'an	25	149	2809	1067	1008

13－22 近年来社会保障情况
Social Security in Recent Years

单位:万人 (10000 persons)

指标 Item	2000	2005	2010	2011	2012	2013
城镇登记失业人员 Number of the Registered Unemployed Persons in Urban	5.60	6.09	4.85	4.40	3.97	4.60
城镇登记失业率(%) The Registered Rate of Unemployment in Urban (%)	3.48	3.71	2.19	1.86	1.63	1.85
失业人员再就业 The Re－employed Persons of Unemployment	14.69	13.09	15.54	13.17	13.29	13.13
职工基本养老保险参保人数 Number of Persons in the Basic Pension Program in Urban	123.69	227.58	383.97	428.12	492.62	530.70
失业保险参保人数 Number of Persons in the Unemployment Insurance Program	96.66	118.36	243.98	277.53	299.78	316.36
职工基本医疗保险参保人数 Number of Persons in the Basic Medical Insurance Program		187.71	345.24	386.33	425.82	448.35
工伤保险参保人数 Number of Persons in the Work－injure Insurance Program	47.86	111.03	314.95	355.28	382.21	394.82
生育保险参保人数 Number of Persons in the Bear Insurance Program	63.99	96.41	228.53	254.38	277.11	292.01
城乡居民养老保险(障)人数 Number of Persons in the Urban and Rural old－age Security			106.30	112.35	112.98	106.40
城乡居民参加医疗保险人数 Number of urban and rural residents participated in medical insurance		350.60	408.32	392.69	378.99	373.93

注:城乡居民参加医疗保险人数:2009 年前为参加新型农村合作医疗的人数。

a) Number of urban and rural residents participated in medical insurance:before 2009, it was the number of people who participated in new rural cooperative medical insurance.

13－23 分地区社会保障情况(2013年末)

Social Security by Region(End of 2013)

单位:人 (persons)

指标 Item	职工基本养老保险参保人数 Number of Employed Persons in the Basic Pension Program	职工基本医疗保险参保人数 Number of Persons in the Basic Medical Insurance Program	工伤保险参保人数 Number of Persons in the Work－injure Insurance Program	生育保险参保人数 Number of Persons in the Bear Insurance Program	失业保险参保人数 Number of Persons in the Unemployment Insurance Program
全 市 Total	**5307029**	**4483529**	**3948165**	**2920119**	**3163604**
市 区 Urban District	4356500	3773780	3251964	2493923	2731968
#萧山区 Xiaoshan	1182137	676092	710465	501912	506141
余杭区 Yuhang	705342	590519	492432	350520	364759
桐庐县 Tonglu	139485	109703	102186	63598	54721
淳安县 Chun'an	91104	87749	83933	42346	41517
建德市 Jiande	173861	119212	90780	70513	72402
富阳市 Fuyang	341019	234235	267405	160631	179750
临安市 Lin'an	205060	158850	151897	89108	83246

主要统计指标解释

从业人员劳动报酬 指各单位在一定时期内直接支付给本单位全部从业人员的劳动报酬总额。

在岗职工工资总额 指各单位在一定时期内直接支付给本单位全部在岗职工的劳动报酬总额。

工资总额的计算原则应以直接支付给职工的全部劳动报酬为根据。各单位支付给本单位全部职工的劳动报酬,不论是计入成本的还是不计入成本的,不论是以货币形式支付还是以实物形式支付的,不论是单位自筹的资金还是上级(或政府财政部门)下拨的资金,不论是厂级单位筹集的资金还是下属车间(科室)及附属经营单位筹集的资金,均应列入工资总额计算的范围。

在岗职工平均工资 指各单位的在岗职工在一定时期内平均每人所得的货币工资额。它表明一定时期内在岗职工工资收入的高低程度,是反映在岗职工工资水平的主要指标。计算公式为:

$$在岗职工平均工资=\frac{报告期实际支付的全部在岗职工工资总额}{报告期全部在岗职工平均人数}$$

全社会单位 包括独立核算的机关、事业单位,非私营企业和私营企业,但不含个体工商户。

城镇居民家庭总收入 指被调查的城镇居民家庭全部收入。包括经常或固定得到的收入和一次性收入,不包括周转性收入。如:提取银行存款、向亲友借入款、收回借出款以及其他各种暂收款。

城镇居民家庭可支配收入 指被调查的城镇居民家庭在支付个人所得税、个人交纳的社会保障支出之后,所余下的实际收入。

计算公式为:可支配收入=总收入-个人所得税-个人交纳的社会保障支出

城镇居民家庭消费性支出 指被调查的城镇居民家庭用于日常生活的全部支出,包括购买商品支出和文化生活、服务等非商品性支出。不包括罚没、丢失款和缴纳的各种税款(如个人所得税、牌照税、房产税等),也不包括个体劳动者生产经营过程中发生的各项费用。

农村居民家庭纯收入 指农村常住居民家庭总收入中,扣除从事生产和非生产经营费用支出、缴纳税款和上交承包集体任务金额以后剩余的,可直接用于进行生产性、非生产性建设投资、生活消费和积蓄的那一部分收入。它是反映农民家庭实际收入水平的综合性的主要指标。农民家庭纯收入,既包括从事生产性和非生产性的经营收入,又包括取自在外人口寄回带回和国家财政救济、各种补贴等非经营性收入;既包括货币收入,又包括自产自用的实物收入。但不包括向银行、信用社和向亲友贷款等属于借贷性的收入。

计算公式为:

纯收入=总收入-家庭经营费用支出-生产用固定资产折旧-税收-上交集体承包任务

离休、退休、退职人员 指正式办理了离休、退休、退职手续,并享受相应的离休、退休、退职待遇的人员。

保险福利费用 指企业、事业、机关单位在工资以外实际支付给职工和离休、退休、退职人员个人以及用于集体的劳动保险和福利费用。

社会福利事业单位 指集中收养社会孤、老、残、幼的机构。包括由民政部门管理的社会福利院、儿童福利院、精神病人福利院和城镇集体办的福利院,以及农村集体举办的敬老院。

社会福利事业单位收养人数 包括民政部门管理和城镇及农村集体举办的社会福利事业单位中收养的老人,少年儿童,缺乏生活自理能力的残疾人员和精神病人。

商品零售价格指数 是反映城乡商品零售价格变动趋势的一种经济指数。零售物价的调整变动直接影响到城乡居民的生活支出和国家的财政收入,影响居民购买力和市场供需平衡,影响消费与积累的比例。因此,计算零售价格指数,可以从一个侧面对上述经济活动进行观察和分析。

居民消费价格指数 是反映一定时期内城乡居民所购买的生活消费品价格和服务项目价格变动趋势和程度的相对数。是综合了城市居民消费价格指数和农民消费价格指数计算取得。利用居民消费价格指数,可以观察和分析消费品的零售价格和服务价格变动对城乡居民实际生活支出的影响程度。

工业生产者出厂价格指数 是反映全部工业产品出厂价格总水平的变动趋势和程度的相对数。其中除包括工业企业售给商业、外贸、物资部门的产品外,还包括售给工业和其他部门的生产资料以及直接售给居民的生活消费品。通过工业生产价格指数能观察出厂价格变动对工业总产值的影响。

Explanatory Notes on Main Statistical Indicators

Labour Remuneration refers to total payment by various units to their employees during a certain period of time, including total wage bill of permanent workers and staff and remuneration payment to other employees.

Total Wages of Fully Employed Staff and Workers refer to the total remuneration payment to fully employed staff and workers in various units during a certain period of time. The calculation of total wages is based on the total remuneration payment to the staff and workers. Therefore, all the wages and salaries and other payments to staff and workers are included in the total wages regardless of their sources, category, and forms (in kind or cash). (Total wages of staff and workers in this yearbook include only total wages of fully employed staff and workers, excluding the living allowances distributed to those who have left their working units while keeping their labour contract/employment relation unchanged).

Average Wage of Fully Employed Staff and Workers refers to the average wage in money terms per person during a certain period of time for fully employed staff and workers in enterprises, institutions, and government agencies, which reflects the general level of wage income during a certain period of time and is calculated as follows:

$$\text{Average Wage of Fully Employed Staff and Workers} = \frac{\text{Total wages of Fully employed staff and workers in Reference Period}}{\text{Average Number of Fully employed Staff and workers in Reference period}}$$

Units of Whole Society refers to independent accounting units of government organizations and institutions, non – private and private enterprises, but excluding individual business.

Total Income of Urban Households refers to the total actual income of the sample households, including regular or fixed income and occasional income. The income of a circulating nature such as withdrawal from bank deposit, loans borrowed from relatives or friends, repayment of loans received and various temporary collection of many is excluded.

Disposable Income of Urban Households refers to total income minus income tax, personal contribution to social security and subsidy for keeping diaries in being a sample household. The following formula is used:

Disposable Income = total households income – income tax – personal contribution to social security

Expenditure for Consumption of Urban Households refers to total expenditure of the sample households for consumption in daily life, including expenditure for various commodities and expenses for non – commodity items such as culture and service, etc., but excluding fines and confiscation, loss, tax payments (such as income tax, license tax, real estates tax, etc.) and various expenses by individual laborers for business purposes.

Net Income of Rural Households refers to the total income of the permanent residents of the rural households during a year after the deduction of the expenses for productive and non – productive business operation, the payment for taxes and productive constriction, for consumption in daily life and for savings deposit. It is a comprehensive indicator to show the actual level of the income of the peasants' household. The net income of the rural households includes not only the income from the productive and non – productive business operation, but also the income from the non – business operation, such as the money remitted or brought back by the members of the household who are in other places, the government relief payment and various subsidies. It includes not only the money income, but also the income in kind. But the income from borrowing from banks, friends and relatives is excluded.

Retired and Resigned Person refers to the persons who have form ally gone through the formalities for their retirement or quitting work and enjoy the corresponding treatments.

Insurance and welfare Funds refers to labour insurance and welf are funds paid by enterprises, organizations and institutions to their staff and workers as well as retired and resigned persons in addition to their wages and salaries.

Social Welfare Institutions refer to institutions taking care of old people without children, handicapped people and orphans. They include social welfare institutions run by civil affairs departments, children welfare institutions, social welfare institutions for mental patients, and collective – owned old people's home in rural areas.

Number of People Taken in by social welfare Institutions refers to the number of old people, children, totally dependent handicapped people and mental patients taken in by social welfare institutions run by civil affairs departments and those run by collective units in urban and rural areas.

Retail price Index reflects the general change in retail prices of commodities. The change and adjustment in retail prices directly affect the living expenditure of urban and rural residents, government revenue, purchasing power of residents and the equilibrium of market supply and demand, and the ratio of consumption to accumulation. Therefore, the calculation of retail price index is useful to analyze the changes of the above economic activities.

Consumer Price Index reflects the trend and degree of changes in prices of consumer goods and services purchased by urban and rural residents, and is a composite index derived from the urban consumer price index and the rural consumer price index. Consumer price index can be used to analyze the impact of consumer price change on actual expenditure for living cost of urban and rural residents.

Ex – factory price index of Industrial Products reflects the trend and degree of changes in general ex – factory prices of all industrial products, including sales of industrial products by and industrial enterprise to all units outside the enterprise, as well as sales of consumer goods to residents. It can be used to analyze the impact of ex – factory prices on gross industrial output value.

中国统计出版社最新图书简目

（仅供参考，以最后出书为准）

统计资料

综合类：中国统计年鉴　中国统计摘要　中国发展报告

国际资料类：国际统计年鉴　金砖国家联合统计手册　世界能源资源年鉴

区域资料类：中国区域经济统计年鉴　中国县域统计年鉴　中国城市统计年鉴　中国农村统计年鉴　中国地区经济监测报告

经贸与投资类：中国贸易外经统计年鉴　中国对外直接投资统计公报　中国商品交易市场统计年鉴　大中型批发零售和住宿餐饮企业统计年鉴　中国零售和餐饮连锁企业统计年鉴

住户与物价类：中国住户调查年鉴　中国价格统计年鉴　中国农产品价格调查年鉴　全国农产品成本收益资料汇编

资源与环境类：中国环境统计年鉴　中国能源统计年鉴

产业类：中国工业统计年鉴　中国建筑业统计年鉴　中国房地产统计年鉴　中国第三产业统计年鉴　中国证券期货统计年鉴

科技类：中国科技统计年鉴　中国高技术产业统计年鉴　工业企业科技活动资料

人口与就业类：中国劳动统计年鉴　中国人口和就业统计年鉴　中国人才资源统计报告

社会与文化类：中国社会统计年鉴　中国文化及相关产业统计年鉴

公共管理类：中国民政统计年鉴　中国民族统计年鉴　中国乡镇街道行政区域简册

省级综合统计年鉴系列

北京 天津 河北 山西 内蒙古 辽宁 吉林 黑龙江 上海 江苏 浙江 安徽 福建 江西 山东 河南 湖北 湖南 广东 广西 海南 重庆 四川 贵州 云南 西藏 陕西 甘肃 青海 宁夏 新疆 新疆生产建设兵团

市（县）级综合统计年鉴系列

天津滨海新区 石家庄 唐山 邯郸 太原 大同 阳泉 长治 晋城 朔州 晋中 运城 忻州 临汾 呼和浩特 鄂尔多斯 包头 沈阳 大连 长春 吉林市 四平 哈尔滨 黑龙江垦区 上海浦东新区 南京 无锡 徐州 常州 苏州 南通 连云港 淮安 盐城 扬州 镇江 泰州 宿迁 江阴 丹阳 杭州 宁波 温州 嘉兴 绍兴 金华 衢州 舟山 台州 丽水 合肥 福州 厦门 宁德 福州经济技术开发区 南昌 济南 青岛 郑州 洛阳 平顶山 三门峡 南阳 武汉 十堰 荆州 宜昌 荆门 咸宁 长沙 广州 深圳 惠州 东莞 南宁 柳州 桂林 来宾 海口 三亚 成都 贵阳 昆明 西安 兰州 庆阳 银川 乌鲁木齐 兵团一师 兵团十师

调查年鉴系列

山西 内蒙古 吉林 辽宁 上海 福建 湖北 广西 重庆 四川 云南 甘肃 宁夏 新疆 南宁 桂林

“十二五”规划教材

统计学（经济管理类专业本科适用，单薇 等）　抽样调查理论与方法（冯士雍 等）

贝叶斯统计（茆诗松 等）　统计学（黄良文 等）　试验设计（茆诗松 等）

统计学：从数据到结论（吴喜之）　医学统计学（于浩）　统计学（经济、管理类专业基础教材，张小斐）

概率论与数理统计三十三讲（魏振军）　概率论与数理统计三十三：学习指导与习题解答（魏振军）

非参数统计（吴喜之 等）　统计学：经济与管理中的数据分析（李慧云 等）

卫生管理统计学（新编医学院校基础课教材，尚磊）　医院统计学（新编医学院校基础课教材，徐天和 等）

社会统计学（蒋萍 等）　现代金融投资统计分析（李腊生 等）

国民经济核算初级教程（经济类、统计类、管理类专业适用，蒋萍 等）

重点图书

新中国65年　新编英汉汉英统计大词典　中华医学统计百科全书

挑大学选专业2014—考研择校指南　挑大学选专业2014—高考志愿填报指南